MOTHER JONES

MOTHER JONES

The Most Dangerous Woman

in America

★

ELLIOTT J. GORN

〰 **Hill and Wang**

A division of Farrar, Straus and Giroux

New York

Hill and Wang
A division of Farrar, Straus and Giroux
19 Union Square West, New York 10003

Copyright © 2001 by Elliott J. Gorn
All rights reserved
Distributed in Canada by Douglas & McIntyre Ltd.
Printed in the United States of America
First edition, 2001

Second Printing, 2001

Library of Congress Cataloging-in-Publication Data
Gorn, Elliott J., 1951–
    Mother Jones : the most dangerous woman in America / Elliott J.
Gorn.
        p.   cm.
    Includes index.
    ISBN 0-8090-7093-6 (alk. paper)
    1. Jones, Mother, 1843?–1930.   2. Women labor union
members—United States—Biography.   3. Working class women—
United States—Biography.   4. Women labor leaders—United States—
Biography.   5. Women in the labor movement—United States—
Biography.   I. Title.

HD8073.J6 G67 2000
331.88'092—dc21
    [B]   00-044997

Designed by Jonathan D. Lippincott

For

Annette Gorn

Jade Yee-Gorn

and

Lisa Vollendorf

Contents

List of Illustrations

Acknowledgments

I bought my first books, a dictionary and a pocket atlas, when I was about eleven years old, using a coupon I had clipped from the newsletter of the Amalgamated Clothing Workers of America. My father was a member of that organization, so the ACWA newsletter came to our home each month. A retail clothing salesman, he was an ardent supporter of the union, and from him I learned about textile mills and sweatshops, about boycotts and strikes. A straight line runs from that early awareness of the labor movement to my writing about Mother Jones. Although they are gone now, both my father and my mother are present in this book.

I could not have finished this project without taking time from my university duties. The largest chunk of research was done during a fellowship year funded by the National Endowment for the Humanities in 1993–1994 at Chicago's Newberry Library. A grant from the Irish American Cultural Institute allowed me to explore Mother Jones's Irish beginnings. The manuscript was largely written under a fellowship from the John Simon Guggenheim Memorial Foundation in 1997–1998. Finally, a semester away from teaching provided by Purdue University's Center for Humanistic Studies in spring 2000 allowed me to finish. To these agencies and their staffs this book owes its existence.

Five friends generously took the time to read the entire manuscript—Lynn Dumenil, Alice Kessler-Harris, Nancy Hewitt, Tim Gilfoyle, and Kate Rousmaniere. All made wonderful suggestions on both style and substance. Their ideas greatly improved my writing and sharpened my thinking; I thank them all for their help and their friendship.

Since 1993, the Newberry Library has served as my intellectual home. The library is a national treasure, not just for its collections but also for its devotion to scholarly work. Several Newberry fellows and staff members read parts of this manuscript; I wish to thank Al Young, Helen Tanner, Richard Brown, Fred Hoxie, Jim Grossman, Terry Bouton, Amy Froide, Ann Little, Laura Edwards, Wayne Boddle, Sid Harring, Tim Spears, Young-soo Bae, and Kirsten Fischer for their ideas and support. The Newberry staff has been remarkably helpful, but let me single out John Aubrey and the late David Thackery for their unfailing assistance.

I would also like to thank the following institutions, where I did archival research, and their staffs: Catholic University of America, Archives Department, Washington, D.C.; Shelby County Public Library, Memphis, Tennessee; the Irish National Archives, Dublin, Ireland; Provincial Archives of Ontario, Toronto, Canada; the Archives of the Roman Catholic Archdiocese of Toronto; the State Historical Society of Wisconsin, Madison; West Virginia University Library, the West Virginia and Regional History Collection, Morgantown; University of Colorado Library, Archives and Special Collections, Boulder; Denver Public Library, Western History Collection, Denver, Colorado; Colorado Historical Society Archives, Denver; Colorado State Archives, Denver; Walter P. Reuther Library of Labor and Urban Affairs, Wayne State University, Detroit, Michigan (special thanks to Michael Smith); Library of Congress, Manuscripts Division, Washington, D.C.; National Archives and Records Administration, Washington, D.C.; the Chicago Historical Society (special thanks to Archie Motley); the Huntington Library, San Marino, California.

During most of the time that I worked on this book, I was employed by Miami University in Oxford, Ohio. Miami is remarkably supportive of scholarship, and special thanks are due to the Dean's Office of the College of Arts and Sciences and to the Office of Research and Sponsored Programs. I would also like to thank my old friends in history and American studies Allan Winkler, Jack Kirby, Mary Cayton, Drew Cayton, Peter Williams, Dan Nathan, Sheldon Anderson, Mary Frederickson, and Art Casciato for their friendship and intellectual aid. In the short time I've been at Purdue, my new colleagues have been equally supportive.

Others offered good counsel and helpful suggestions: Lou Erenberg, Sue Hirsch, Ellen Skerrett, Lawrence McCaffrey, Carl Smith, Edward Steel, Lois McLean, Paul Buhle, Patrick Miller, Archie Green, Timothy Lynch, and Keith Gallagher. Gerry McCauley helped find a good home for this work; Arthur Wang, who originally agreed to publish the book, offered fine advice early on; Lauren Osborne and Catherine Newman have been wonderful editors; and Ingrid Sterner did a fine job copyediting the manuscript. My brother, Michael, also a professional historian, has been a source of quiet inspiration for his grace during very difficult times. And other friends—Larry Malley, Fred Hobson, Michael Khodarkovsky, Larry Levine, Harvey Kaye, Tony Cardoza, Bruce Levine—have been unfailing suppliers of ideas and humor.

This book is dedicated to three women, each in her own way a daughter of Mother Jones. My sister-in-law, Annette Gorn, an Irish immigrant herself, passed away last year; she was gracious and goodhearted, a person who always thought of others before herself. Jade, my daughter, has survived her childhood and grown up to be a good person, and an independent one. Finally, Lisa Vollendorf read and improved every page of this work. More, she lived it with me.

Elliott J. Gorn
Chicago, Illinois

MOTHER JONES

Introduction

The life of Mother Jones is a faded memory, a half-forgotten story. A black-and-white image of an old woman or perhaps the words "Pray for the dead, and fight like hell for the living" are all that most people know of her. Yet during the early twentieth century, Mother Jones was one of the most famous women in America. Passionate speeches and dramatic street theater kept this fiery agitator in the news. For over a quarter century she held center stage, exposing disturbing truths about child labor, the poverty of working families, and the destruction of American freedoms. Her admirers called her labor's Joan of Arc and the miners' angel; enemies labeled her a dangerous radical—indeed, the most dangerous woman in America.

Picture her, grandmotherly, sweet-faced, white-haired, swaying throngs of working-class people with her resonant oratory. Legend tells how she faced down gun-toting thugs and how she endured frequent imprisonment without fear. She cherished her image as a fighter. When introduced to a crowd as a great humanitarian once, she snapped, "Get it straight, I'm not a humanitarian, I'm a hell-raiser." She articulated for working men and women the belief that they had created the world with their own hands and that by right it belonged to them. She was a militant matriarch uniting the family of labor through her words and her raw physical courage.

Although Mother Jones was most vividly associated with bitter mine wars, she also worked with railroad, trolley-car, textile, brewery, garment, and steel workers. In an age of outrageous exploitation, her fight was wherever people organized for humane hours and decent pay. She was the Johnny Appleseed of American activists, giving speeches and organizing across the continent, sleeping in workers' cabins, boardinghouses, or the homes of friends. Asked to state her residence to a congressional committee, she declared, "I live in the United States, but I do not know exactly in what place, because I am always in the fight against oppression, and wherever a fight is going on I have to jump there . . . so that really I have no particular residence." She added, "My address is like my shoes; it travels with me wherever I go."

Her contemporaries marveled at her. "She is a wonder," the poet Carl Sandburg wrote of Mother Jones during World War I. "Close to 88 years old and her voice a singing voice; nobody else could give me a thrill just by saying in that slow, solemn, orotund way, 'The kaisers of this country are next, I tell ye.' " Clarence Darrow, America's greatest trial lawyer of the early twentieth century, wrote that "her deep convictions and fearless soul always drew her to seek the spot where the fight was hottest and the danger greatest." The feminist author Meridel Le Sueur was only fourteen years old when she first heard Mother Jones speak, but she never forgot it: "I felt engendered by the true mother, not the private mother of one family, but the emboldened and blazing defender of all her sons and daughters."

At first glance, Mother Jones was not a likely candidate for such renown. An Irish immigrant who had survived famine, fire, plague, hard labor, and unspeakable loss, she was nearly as dispossessed as an American could be. She had ambition and talent, certainly, but those were no guarantee of success. How did she come to prominence?

Her fame began when, toward the end of the nineteenth century, she transformed herself from Mary Jones into Mother Jones. Her new persona was a complex one, infused with overtones of Christian martyrdom and with the suffering of Mother Mary. Perhaps it is best to think of Mother Jones as a character performed by Mary Jones. She exaggerated her age, wore old-fashioned black dresses, and alluded often

1. Mother Jones arranged countless street demonstrations like this one in Trinidad, Colorado, in 1913 (Courtesy Newberry Library)

to her impending demise. By 1900, she had stopped referring to herself as Mary altogether and signed all of her letters "Mother." Soon laborers, union officials, even Presidents of the United States addressed her that way, and they became her "boys."

The persona of *Mother* Jones freed Mary Jones. Most American women in the early twentieth century were expected to lead quiet, homebound lives for their families; few women found their way onto the public stage. Ironically, by making herself into the symbolic mother of the downtrodden, Mary Jones was able to go where she pleased and speak out on any issue that moved her. She defied social conventions and shattered the limits that confined her by embracing the very role that restricted most women.

Her fame did not last. Eugene Debs, labor leader and Socialist Party candidate for President, recalled of his old friend, "She has won her way into the hearts of the nation's toilers, and her name is revered at the altars of their humble firesides and will be lovingly remembered by their children and their children's children forever." Debs was wrong;

few grandchildren ever heard of her exploits. Mother Jones fell victim to what the English historian E. P. Thompson has called "the enormous condescension of posterity."

My purpose in writing this book is to resist such amnesia. The early decades of the twentieth century were filled with dissent and conflict; radicals helped foster a creative dialogue in American society. During the years of her greatest visibility, from the turn of the century through the early 1920s, Mother Jones had one of the most unique and powerful voices in that dialogue.

One hundred years after she first appeared in the news, almost a fifth of America's children live in poverty. They are the children of Mother Jones. Working families struggling for decent lives are her heirs, too. Indeed, all who raise their voices against social injustice and resist the easy complacency of our times are the sons and daughters of Mother Jones.

★ 1 ★

Mary Harris

"I was born in the city of Cork, Ireland, in 1830" begins *The Autobiography of Mother Jones.* "My people were poor. For generations they had fought for Ireland's freedom. Many of my folks have died in that struggle. My father, Richard Harris, came to America in 1835, and as soon as he had become an American citizen, he sent for his family." Mother Jones thus describes her entire childhood in five sentences. What was her mother's name, did Mary have siblings, did she go to school, did she speak Irish, did her family attend church, how did they make their living? All questions unasked and unanswered. In a book almost 250 pages long, there are only six pages on the first half of her life.[1]

The early twentieth century was not an age of personal revelation, but Mother Jones carried reticence to an extreme. The *Autobiography* was published in 1925, when, by her own reckoning, she was ninety-five (actually, she was eighty-eight). Perhaps her memory was deteriorating. More likely, she did not consider her youth terribly important. The book was written to inspire action, to teach the power of political commitment, to keep alive the history of labor organizing, and to promote radical change. Her autobiography continued the work she had begun decades before as a labor organizer and orator. Most of all, the book sought to perpetuate the memory of Mother Jones, not Mary Jones.[2]

Biography is a literary genre. A good life history unfolds like a novel; the writer plots the story, develops character, cuts from scene to scene, employs metaphor and allusion. Biography, however, must cleave to known facts. So how does one write a biography of someone who preferred not to reveal her past? There are two answers, for we are dealing with two people, a person and a persona, and the relationship between the two. We will never know *Mary* Jones (née Mary Harris) well. She came from an obscure background, and she was not the sort of person to leave behind a diary or a cache of letters. But *Mother* Jones left dozens of speeches and scores of letters (all written after 1900); journalists interviewed her and wrote hundreds of articles about her. The single greatest clue about the life of *Mary* Jones was her desire to become someone else.[3]

The difficulty of knowing Mary Jones can be attributed in part to the Victorian era, when men and women were relegated to separate spheres. Journalists, reformers, and religious writers insisted that men dominate the public realm—work, business, and politics—while women control the private domain of home, family, and worship. By refusing to say much about her private life, Mother Jones revealed her radical intentions: even as she took for her name the most sacred role of the private sphere, she ignored family life and lived entirely in the public realm. More precisely, if motherhood was at the center of the family circle, Mother Jones widened that circle to embrace the entire family of labor.[4]

Even the most basic facts about Mary Jones are difficult to pin down. For example, her birthday was not May 1, 1830, as she declared in countless speeches, as her autobiography repeated, as journalists reaffirmed. When Mother Jones first came to public attention around the beginning of the twentieth century, newspapers reported that she was born sometime in the late 1830s or early 1840s; only after she became quite famous did she insist on 1830. Only then too did she declare that May Day—the international workers' holiday that began in 1886 when laborers demanded the eight-hour day—was her birthday. So reconstructing her early life means combining a few reliable facts with informed speculation, then placing it all in historical context.[5]

County Cork

On February 9, 1834, Richard Harris and Ellen Cotter were married in Inchigeelagh, County Cork, Ireland. Ellen was about twenty years old and her husband roughly a decade older. It was customary for weddings to take place in the bride's home parish, so Ellen Cotter was almost certainly born in Inchigeelagh, which one visitor described as "a poor, small, and irregular village" (the entire town consisted of about a dozen buildings). Although Richard had kin in the parish, he was from the city of Cork, about thirty miles to the east.[6]

Richard and Ellen baptized their second-born child, Mary, at St. Mary's Cathedral in Cork on August 1, 1837. Mary's older brother, Richard (born in 1835), was baptized in Inchigeelagh, but her younger siblings all began life in the city—Catherine in 1840, Ellen in 1845, and William in 1846.[7]

So for more than a generation, the Harrises and the Cotters moved between town and country, between Cork and Inchigeelagh. It is impossible to know exactly how they lived their lives. Clearly, their roots ran deep in rural soil, but by the time Mary was born in 1837, the family had moved to the city. It is likely, though, that the Harris children knew firsthand both urban streets and country ways, especially since the river Lee and a good carriage road connected Cork to Inchigeelagh.[8]

One chronicler described the landscape of Inchigeelagh Parish as "a country gradually assuming wilder and more imposing features; everywhere it is broken up by rocky hills, partially clothed with purple heath and furze. . . . Slight patches of cultivation diversify the succession of crag and heath, snatched as it would seem from the surrounding barrenness, by the hand of industry." Six thousand people, almost all of them Roman Catholic, lived in this remote, six-by-nine-mile parish. Folk memory recalled great families like the O'Learys, who in better times built imposing castles. But ownership of most of the land had long since passed into English and Protestant hands. Those Cotters and Harrises of Inchigeelagh who retained enough land to be assessed held modest, mostly rented plots.[9]

So how did Mary Harris's ancestors make their living? They might have been farmers with a score of acres to their name, or maybe they tended one or two dozen cows for the thriving dairy trade. Much more likely, they were small cottiers, rural laborers who subsisted mainly on potatoes grown in tiny rented plots.[10]

Well into the eighteenth and even the nineteenth century, small un-fenced patches of land were distributed to Irish peasants for tilling or grazing cattle. Since the plots varied considerably in quality, they were redistributed periodically by communal agreement. This system began to break down as ambitious farmers sought to benefit from Ireland's expanding rural economy. Exports and imports increased, seaport towns like Dublin, Cork, and Belfast prospered with trade, and by the beginning of the nineteenth century, even the most remote Irish villages had become part of the commercial economy.[11]

Economic growth brought rising prices, but the spread of potato culture supplied a source of food that was easily cultivated. Landlords now subdivided land into plots as small as a quarter acre and charged exorbitant rents. Economic expansion was paralleled by a population boom. The census of 1841 conservatively estimated eight million people (a fourfold increase in a century), making Ireland one of the most densely populated nations in Europe.[12]

There was, of course, no such thing as a "typical" Irish parish. Although Ireland was rapidly modernizing due to the strength of its economy, Inchigeelagh was a bit backward; it had a higher rate of illiteracy, lower land values, more stable population, and more Irish speakers than other rural parishes. But even such remote places were affected by the commercialization of Ireland's economy and the Anglicization of Irish culture. The development of commerce certainly allowed many to prosper, but it also subjected the vast majority to chronic uncertainty, poverty, and even forced emigration.[13]

The writer William Cobbett described the homes of the rural poor he found in county Cork early in the nineteenth century:

> I went to a sort of hamlet near to the town of Midleton. It contained about 40 or 50 hovels. I went into several of them. . . . They all consisted of mud-walls, with a covering of rafters and straw. . . . I took a particular account of the

first that I went into. It was 21 feet long and 9 feet wide. The floor, the bare ground . . . No table, no chair. . . . Some stones for seats. No goods but *a pot*, and a shallow tub, for the pig and the family both to eat out of. . . . Some dirty straw and a bundle of rags were all the bedding. . . . *Five small children*; the mother, about thirty, naturally handsome, but worn into half-ugliness by hunger and filth. . . . The man BUILT THIS PLACE HIMSELF, and yet he has to pay a *pound a year* for it with perhaps a rod of ground! . . . *All built their own hovels*, and yet have to pay this rent.[14]

So here was the paradox: Ireland was growing, changing, expanding. But the commercialization of the economy, combined with English colonial policies, brought wealth for a few, poverty for the masses. The trend was unmistakable—the majority of Irish people faced poverty in their own country or emigration.[15]

Mary Harris's kin were not only poor, they were also Catholic. Pre-famine Ireland did contain some prosperous and influential Catholics, but about ten thousand Protestant families virtually owned the country, and of those, a few hundred possessed the bulk of the land. Typically, the landowner (if he was not an absentee landlord) lived in a large home, employed several servants and estate workers, and perhaps owned the local grain mill. Magistrates, bailiffs, sheriffs, and estate agents were generally Protestants; the Protestant Church of Ireland was supported by a tithe paid by Protestant and Catholic alike; Protestants dominated politics and commerce.[16]

But English Protestants could not destroy traditional Irish culture entirely. Travelers commented on Ireland's distinctive brand of folk Catholicism, which incorporated old pagan idols into the cult of the saints. The sacraments and rituals of Rome stretched thin over alternative traditions: belief in an animate world filled with dangerous beings, wakes for propitiating the dead, patterns of worship designed more to secure kinship and communal identity than to attain personal grace. In Inchigeelagh Parish, for example, pilgrims came each summer to bathe in the sacred waters of Gougane Barra and walk in the path of

Saint Finbar. Rural life retained many of the old country ways that helped pass the time but that the English took as signs of laziness— races, fights, dances, storytelling, bouts of drinking.[17]

Above all, there were words, Irish words and English words inflected with Irish, words with their own rhythms, molded into stories and songs. A traveler in Connemara noticed a youth wearing a tally stick (which was hung around children's necks and notched every time they were caught speaking Irish). The traveler asked the boy's father if he did not love the Irish language:

> "I do," said he, his eyes kindling with enthusiasm; "sure it is the talk of the ould country, and the ould times, the language of my father and all that's gone before me—the speech of these mountains, and lakes, and these glens, where I was bred and born; but you know," he continued, "the children must have larnin', and as they tache no Irish in the National School, we must have recourse to this to instigate them to talk English."[18]

The man might well have spoken the same words in Inchigeelagh Parish, where the Irish language held on with unusual tenacity.

But the Harris children, after all, grew up in the city; the lanes and alleys of Cork, more than the fields of Inchigeelagh, were their home. Yet city and countryside were inextricably tied in pre-famine Ireland. Many city people were recent migrants from the country who left the land in search of work. Families like the Harrises brought parish ways with them.[19]

St. Mary's Cathedral, where the Harris children were baptized, was located in a densely populated part of North Cork. The sight of the poor wandering the streets, of the hospitals and asylums, provided daily evidence of the harshness and fragility of life. Even the smells of Cork were vivid. The feces of countless animals choked the pathways with filth, while the lime works and the local tannery gave the air its characteristic stench. Until she was thirteen or fourteen years old, Mary Harris lived within blocks of the bustling Cork Butter Market, with its stream of butter-bearing pack animals coming in from the country, with its brokers buying the goods and its laborers hauling barrels down to the river Lee. Mornings, she awakened to the famous Bells of Shandon ringing from nearby St. Anne's (Protestant) Church. Perhaps the family lived in one of the tiny houses that still survive in the twisted alleyways of the neighborhood. Mary walked and played in those lanes, she went to Mass at the newly rebuilt St. Mary's Cathedral. Maybe she learned to read and write at the North Presentation Convent, where the nuns gave free education to hundreds of poor girls.[20]

The same market forces transforming the rural economy marked the city. The growing merchant class thrived on the trade in foodstuffs brought in from the hinterlands. Most Irish butter, beef, and pork bound for North America were shipped out of Cork Harbor; trade was the single most important part of the urban economy. By the early nineteenth century, prosperous new elites began to move out of the old disease- and crime-ridden medieval city center into new homes on the outskirts of town. Nearly three-quarters of those who remained in the city dwelled in slums. Cork's population stood at about eighty thousand in the 1840s. The wages of working-class people had been stagnant for decades, and the poverty of the rural parishes ensured a steady flow of migrants to the city in search of work, alms, or passage out of Ireland. Although Cork was only a midsized town, lacking the satanic mills we associate with manufacturing centers like Manchester, its dense slums—nearly forty people per acre—and tenacious poverty made it a frightful place to live.[21]

Such conditions led to some very unsettled politics, but Cork's working class never became a well-organized, radical force. The powerful English workers' movement of the 1830s and 1840s known as Chartism failed to catch hold in Ireland, even though it was founded by Feargus O'Connor, who was raised near Cork. Nonetheless, these were turbulent times. Workers generally sought not the remaking of society but the reestablishment of old patterns that free markets and the beginnings of industrialization had upset. Journeymen artisans—weavers, carpenters, printers—organized themselves into unions that opposed the vagaries of the marketplace with the precapitalist notion of the just price, the idea that wages must conform to what tradition dictated as fair, not to the cruel forces of supply and demand. Cork journeymen used petitions, strikes, and even riots in an attempt to secure living wages, to shorten the workday, and to limit the loss of jobs to machines. Common laborers, too, organized themselves to protect what they described as their traditional rights as workers.[22]

The crosscutting divisions of class, religion, and nationalism, however, ensured that no one political movement became singularly powerful in Cork. Not only was the working class split—artisans feared that the unskilled would take their jobs, while the masses resented the artisans' prerogatives—but the issues of home rule for Ireland and Catholic political equality also divided the city. The Act of Union, which at the turn of the century abolished the Irish Parliament and gave the country a handful of representatives in London, united diverse Irishmen who sought repeal of this loathsome law. But nationalist unity could blunt class solidarity, with merchants and manufacturers in leadership roles and labor marching behind. Moreover, religious conflict among working people often grew bitter. Mary Harris was baptized in the new St. Mary's Cathedral because the old one had been gutted by fire a few years earlier, a fire allegedly started by congregants from St. Anne's. Only the intervention of priests from St. Mary's prevented Catholics from burning the Shandon Church in revenge. Such conflicts—dramatized by the monster rallies held by the great patriot Daniel O'Connell for repeal of the Act of Union—were woven into the fabric of daily life in Cork. It was not, however, a city gripped by revolution, not a place, as Mother Jones later claimed, where rebels were hanged from scaffolds.[23]

Indeed, the countryside often was more militant than the city. From the late eighteenth century until the famine, secret societies were an important part of rural life, especially in the southwest. These groups—with names like the Whiteboys, Rightboys, Rockites, and Molly Maguires—sought to preserve traditional ideals of justice. Mostly they attempted to rectify particular violations of people's rights, such as evictions, farm consolidations, or rent hikes. Except in their most utopian moments, they did not attempt to raise up the indigent and overthrow the wealthy. They targeted not the rich absentee landowners but middlemen—estate agents, substantial farmers, mill owners, and shopkeepers. Intimidation was the method of choice: a cow killed, a house burned, a farmer beaten. Men who took the societies' oaths of secrecy and committed such "outrages," as officials called them, sought only to defend their right to rent a bit of land under customary terms.[24]

Local constabularies organized against the rural secret societies, and the government passed a series of insurrection acts. Officials feared that in places like county Cork, where rural outrages occurred with some frequency, guerrilla action might turn into genuine revolt. Their fears were not unfounded in the sense that the secret societies sometimes transcended custom-bound ways of viewing the world. The radical dreams of the 1790s—spawned by the French Revolution, by Thomas Paine's *Rights of Man,* by the nationalist United Irishmen—all suggested possibilities for radical social change. Even books of religious prophecy now predicted the ouster of the hated Protestants. The secret societies were part of a growing Irish restiveness.[25]

Despite Mother Jones's claims to a radical lineage, there is no hard evidence linking her kin to secret-society activities around Inchigeelagh. Cotters showed up with some frequency in police records for crimes like petty theft and mayhem—hardly the stuff of political rebellion. Still, there are hints of something more. A song called "The Battle of Keimaneigh"—which can still be heard in Inchigeelagh—commemorates a series of events that took place in 1822. Keimaneigh is located at the west end of the parish. Hundred-foot cliffs rise up over the road connecting Bantry with Cork in this rugged country. The winter of 1821–1822 was particularly grim, and fear of famine drove the poor to new acts of desperation. By January, hundreds, some said as many as five thousand, had encamped in the hills. All over West Cork, and in neighboring counties, the followers of a mysterious "Captain Rock" organized, and local officials responded by raising ever greater numbers of troops.[26]

On January 7, five hundred Rockites raided the homes of several Bantry gentlemen, looking for weapons. As they retreated east to Keimaneigh, they were pursued by fifty troops. The gentry tried to kill and capture as many of the insurgents as possible, while the Rockites took up positions in the cliffs. During the next several days, Protestant troops shot anyone who got in their way, broke up wakes and dances with bayonets, and captured many of the rebels near Inchigeelagh. The insurgents had their revenge, ambushing soldiers and allegedly raping Protestant women. The Rockites held their position until early February, then dispersed.[27]

Lord Lieutenant Richard Wellesley, the English magistrate of Cork city, wrote of the uprising, "The prevalent distress combined with the Character and habits of the people of Ireland furnishes the most apt materials for the work of Sedition, and it requires no great Skill to inflame a nation in such a Condition." A special commission tried dozens of rebels, sentenced thirty-six of them to the gallows, and immediately hanged five. The countryside soon settled down, the executions ended, and most of the remaining prisoners were shipped to the penal colony in New South Wales.[28]

There are tantalizing connections between the uprising of 1822 and Mary Harris's people. On January 17, magistrates arrested two young men, Garrett Cotter and John Leary, and charged them with "Whiteboyism." They were tried, found guilty, and sentenced to hang, though the court eventually commuted their sentences and shipped them to Australia. Cotter was only twenty years old, however, so he could not have been the grandfather who Mary Harris claimed died for Ireland's freedom. In another intriguing story, a magistrate who pursued several rebels on January 31 described their leader: "A fellow by the name of Cotter commanded on friday last that Banditti of Assassins Over Three hundred in number armed with Guns, blunderbusses, Pistols, Swords, Sythes, etc." Perhaps neither of these mysterious Cotters was related to Mary Harris. But the shared name in such a small parish could mean something. Even if they were not ancestors at all, perhaps Ellen Cotter's people transformed such dashing and legendary figures into fictive kin, embracing them as part of their family history.[29]

Mary Harris's father was about seventeen years old during the Battle of Keimaneigh, but absolutely no surviving evidence links him to that incident. It is possible that he was involved in outrages, but his name does not turn up in any official records. Mother Jones once described his escape on an American fishing vessel; soldiers searched the Harris home and troops marched the streets with Irish men's heads mounted on bayonets. But these stories ring false. There were no beheadings in Cork at this time, only a few arrests of middle-class revolutionaries.[30]

Irish immigrants often told stories of rebellious kin who resisted the English until forced to flee. But reality was not so romantic for most of the exiles. There is a simpler, albeit less thrilling, explanation for why the Harrises and hundreds of thousands of others left Ireland, an explanation of which Mother Jones never spoke.

Late in the summer of 1845, farmers found the fungus *Phytopthora infestans* in gardens around Cork. Potato blights had been common in Irish history, but this new disease, which originated in North America, was particularly virulent, and by the fall, the damage was extensive. Hopes were high for a good harvest in 1846, but the scale of the impending disaster now became clear. An unbearable stench rose from field after field throughout Ireland, signaling nearly total destruction of the country's staple food. In the next five years, over one million people—about 12 percent of the population—perished from hunger and disease. And in the decade following the first signs of blight, nearly two million Irish fled their homeland.[31]

Landlords, backed by the government, simply pushed poor tenants off their estates. Those who did not quickly die of starvation took to the roads in search of relief. Many went to the local poor-law unions, institutions that had been set up to dispense charity. Founded under the strictures of English laissez-faire capitalism, the poor-law unions assumed that poverty was a sign of laziness, of bad character, and so dispensed charity with wary parsimoniousness. The flood of victims quickly overwhelmed the unions. The English government stepped up emergency grain shipments, employed thousands on road-building crews, and encouraged private charity. But these efforts were mere palliatives. Political conservatives, evangelical Protestants in particular, had long viewed the periodic shortfalls of the potato crop as a divine judgment against Irish sloth; the famine merely offered more evidence of Ireland's fecklessness. English politicians denied the existence of the crisis and used euphemisms like "distress" and "scarcity" to describe the situation, thereby justifying heartless policies: they evicted those who could not pay their landlords, denied relief to any peasant renting even a quarter acre of land, and sanctioned the demolition of homes across the country to consolidate farms. There is truth in the Irish saying "God created the potato blight, but the English made the famine."[32]

Mass hunger could not have been wholly prevented, especially given the small size of public bureaucracies in the mid-nineteenth century. And surely it is too strong to say, as some have, that England caused this holocaust. But rigid belief in laissez-faire ideology, in the justice of markets, the laziness of the poor, and the virtue of the rich, prevented relief measures that would have saved countless lives. For decades after it was over, Irish exiles told bitter legends of neighbors losing their tiny farms to the wealthy, of magistrates forcing starving people off the land, of courts enforcing the laws of property with draconian punishments for anyone caught so much as stealing a turnip.[33]

Apparitions of death were everywhere. At the town of Skull in county Cork, an English midshipman came ashore and watched a crowd of five hundred half-naked people waiting for soup. A local doctor told him that not one would be alive in three weeks. The sailor described the situation:

> 20 bodies were buried this morning, and they were fortunate in getting buried at all. The people build themselves up in their cabins, so that they may die together with their children and not be seen by passers-by. Fever, dysentery, and starvation stare you in the face everywhere—children of 10 and 9 years old I have mistaken for decrepit old women . . . Babes are found lifeless, lying on their mothers' bosoms . . . Dogs feed on the half-buried dead, and rats are commonly known to tear people to pieces.

Visions of the dying "will never wholly leave the eyes that beheld them," declared one shocked traveler; "their demonic yells are still ringing in my ears," said another.[34]

Irish cities were no havens from the rural catastrophe. Dublin and Belfast were not so hard hit, but cities in the south were devastated. As impoverished migrants poured in from the countryside, the streets became breeding grounds for the diseases that accompanied famine, especially typhus, scurvy, "relapsing" fever, and dysentery. By late 1846, little food was left in Cork, and prices had risen so dramatically that even workers who still had jobs could scarcely feed their families.[35]

Emigration seemed the only way out. Before the Great Hunger, English officials had advocated and even assisted emigration to England, Australia, and North America. Though tens of thousands departed, most resisted leaving home and kin. But now the floodgates opened. Between 1847 and 1853, an average of 200,000 people per year emigrated. The town of Cobh on Cork Harbor became a spigot into the Atlantic for the masses streaming from the devastation.[36]

And what of the Harris family? Ellen and Richard managed to keep their family alive, but their means were surely meager. They must have been horrified by the sight of tens of thousands of refugees straggling into town. Many of the dispossessed first entered the city near their home, and young Mary surely witnessed the destitute coming for aid, coming to die. Here, no one could avoid seeing the living corpses, the feverish children, the dysentery- and cholera- and bloody-flux-racked bodies.[37]

When Mary was about ten, Richard Harris and his twelve-year-old son, Richard junior, left for the New World. Perhaps friends gave them an American wake, a mock funeral for those who would never return, filled with songs of longing for home and family, of mourning for those already gone, of anger at Ireland's enemies. For the next few years, Ellen Harris waited in Cork city, somehow keeping the family together, even as misery, disease, and death surrounded them.[38]

Ireland in the end was a blasted land for the Harris family. If Mary's people did not literally go out fighting for the country's freedom, as she later claimed, they did go with an awareness of themselves as "the poor," with stories of the martyrs who fought the oppressors, and with deep resentment against the greedy ones who pillaged the land and drove them out. When she finally left at age fourteen or fifteen, Mary brought a stony silence about the terror and sadness of those formative years.[39]

Toronto

Mother Jones's autobiography gives short shrift to her family's coming to North America: "[My father's] work as a laborer with railway construction crews took him to Toronto, Canada. Here I was brought up but always as the child of an American citizen. Of that citizenship I have ever been proud." She goes on to describe briefly how she attended Toronto's common schools and the normal school (for teacher education), then took her first teaching job at a convent in Monroe, Michigan. Meanwhile, she learned the skills of dressmaking and soon moved to Chicago. In a mere page, Mother Jones covers her passage from birth to adulthood. Most striking, once again, are the inaccuracy of many of the details and how much she chose not to discuss.[40]

Except for occasional markings in official registers—census records, tax rolls, city directories—little evidence of the Harris family's first several years in North America survives. So how do we place the Harrises among those two million refugees who left Ireland in the decade after the famine began? Once again, we must chase down contradictory leads from incomplete documents, then place the fragments into the larger themes of mid-nineteenth-century history.[41]

The Harrises first appear in the U.S. census of 1850. That year, Richard Harris and his son Richard junior were living in Burlington, Vermont. They were listed as propertyless, illiterate Irish laborers, boarding with a local family. The Harris men no doubt worked hard at poorly paid jobs, perhaps in construction like so many of their countrymen, and sent money home regularly.[42]

Knowing that Richard Harris was in Burlington in 1850, and would soon move to Toronto, gives us an important clue about his migration to North America. Burlington is close to Canada and far from ports of entry in the United States. Many Irish immigrants entered North America via the St. Lawrence River and passed south from Quebec to northern New England. But only in one year, 1847, did Canada rival the United States as a destination for the Irish. In that year, fares to Canada were considerably cheaper, and American immigration restrictions higher. The Harris men most likely followed this path.[43]

Immigration is always filled with sadness and longing, but the passage to Canada was a wager with death, for "Black '47" was one of the grimmest episodes of the Great Hunger. Many of the 200,000 refugees took their chances on a dangerous winter crossing. These were among the poorest, the least skilled, the most desperate of all the famine immigrants. They booked passage aboard any vessel that might hold them; timber, grain, and cotton ships were the most common carriers. On average, the voyage took five weeks. One in twenty of those who sailed in 1847 did not reach North America alive; for those who embarked from Cork Harbor, the mortality rate was over one in ten.[44]

There were lucky ones, of course, for whom the weather smiled and disease never struck. The crossing might have been pleasant for them, as stories, songs, and dances of the old country rang out over the Atlantic. More common was the experience of a passenger who sailed in steerage in April 1847:

> Hundreds of poor people, men, women and children of all ages, from the drivelling idiot to the babe just born, huddled together without light, without air, wallowing in filth and breathing a fetid atmosphere, sick in body, dispirited in heart.

2. Hundreds of thousands of Irish refugees, the Harris family among them, fled the Great Hunger for England, Australia, and especially North America in the mid-nineteenth century. From the *Illustrated London News*, July 6, 1850 (Courtesy Newberry Library)

The greed and incompetence of boat owners and ship captains, he added, all too often exacerbated the wretched conditions of the immigrants.[45]

The horror did not end when the ships entered port. Grosse Isle near Quebec City was the main point of disembarkation in Canada. Eighteen forty-six had strained its capacities, but authorities managed in a rough sort of way to detain the sick and move the rest on into the country. Eighteen forty-seven was another matter. By May, ship after ship had approached flying the flag that foretold illness aboard. At the end of the month, forty ships lay at anchor, stretching a mile back into the St. Lawrence, their holds filled with the dead, the dying, and all the rest who had been exposed. Keeping the passengers on board was a death sentence; allowing them ashore spread the epidemic. Workmen labored to expand the island's facilities, while doctors, nurses, and orderlies, dozens of whom perished themselves, worked to save as many lives as possible.[46]

As more and more ships arrived, it became impossible to prevent illness from spreading. Immigrants entered the cities or fanned out along the rivers and the Great Lakes. Disease and hunger raged in Montreal and Quebec City, while residents of towns like Toronto and Kingston fled to the countryside. Roughly 30 percent of those who survived the passage to Canada were dead before the end of 1847. Some survivors were lucky enough to find shelter with kin. The Canadian government made modest efforts to feed and house the sufferers, and farmers or businessmen not overcome with fear sometimes offered work to the able-bodied. But thousands of refugees simply wandered between "Irishtowns" and "Corktowns" at the edges of Canadian cities. A third of the immigrants, probably including the Harris men, made their way into the United States.[47]

It is unlikely that Richard senior and junior stayed long in Burlington; they must have followed the work gangs in search of labor, like thousands of other Irish men. By the early 1850s, they had saved enough for Ellen and the children to set sail for North America. The family was soon established in Toronto, with Richard Harris, approaching fifty, working on the rapidly growing Canadian railroads.[48]

Two themes that emerge for the Harris children in their early years in Canada are education and religion. Mother Jones reported in her autobiography that she attended the public schools, though Catholic children usually enrolled in parochial "separate" schools. Indeed, her sisters went to St. Mary's, and her younger brother, William, attended seminary at St. Michael's in Toronto, where he studied for the priesthood. There was, then, a distinct connection to Catholicism in the Harris family. Mary's familiarity with the religion must have been strong—her local parish priest recommended her for admission to the teachers' college, and her first job was in a convent school. The emphasis on literacy among the Harris children is also striking, not only because neither Richard nor Ellen could read or write but also because the children of working-class Irish Catholic families tended to spend less time in school than those of native-born Canadians or even other immigrants.[49]

Sources like local tax rolls and the 1861 census reveal more. Sometime in the middle 1850s, when Mary was well into her teens, the Harrises moved into a house at 210 Bathurst Street, on the far west side of town, and they resided there until Richard senior died in 1869. The family rented the six-hundred-square-foot, single-story frame house for one dollar per week. Richard junior, though in his mid-twenties by 1861, remained unmarried and still lived with the family, so the household had at least two incomes, which helps explain how they afforded so much schooling for the children. The family also had two other residents, Mary and Isabella Dunlop, aged five and two. These Dunlop children might have belonged to unfortunate friends who could not care for them; or maybe there was some financial arrangement that brought extra income into the Harris household in exchange for child care. So many people in a house so small must have afforded absolutely no privacy. For better or worse, the Harrises lived intensely in each other's midst.[50]

If the house was small, the lot, at 40 by 135 feet, was big enough for the family's cow and two pigs. Indeed, in Toronto's 1869 tax assessment, Richard Harris was listed no longer as a laborer but as a "milkman" who owned five cows. Here, no doubt, was a bridge back to Inchigeelagh. Probably the Harrises churned butter at home for local sale, just as families had done in county Cork. Like other working-class people in North American cities, they no doubt kept chickens on their lot and vegetables growing in the spring and summer.[51]

During the time the Harrises lived on Bathurst Street, Toronto was growing on the strength of trade and the beginnings of industrial production. Income and ethnic background sorted people into neighborhoods, though not as rigidly as later in the nineteenth century. The central business district of Toronto had the most exclusive housing. Outlying areas, like the far west side of town where the Harrises lived, tended to be cheaper. Most of the heads of households on the Harrises' block were laborers, along with an occasional blacksmith or mason. The block south of their house was a bit more exclusive; St. Mary's Church anchored a street of skilled tradesmen—machinists, carpenters, marble workers, even an attorney. The Harrises' neighborhood had a large share of Irish families, but Irish people were certainly not the only ones who lived along Bathurst Street.[52]

To call the Harris family "typical" would be inaccurate, but in many respects, they and the neighborhood in which they lived replicated larger patterns among the Toronto Irish. Unskilled, Irish Catholics worked hard to live in decent and respectable circumstances. Nearly half of all families owned or rented small houses, and often they took in boarders to help cover their costs. Below these solidly working-class families, a substantial minority lived in shanties down by the docks on Lake Ontario. If the Harrises escaped the poverty and urban disorder that victimized many of their countrymen, still they knew that a downturn of the business cycle or a crippling on-the-job injury could send them hurtling into penury.[53]

The Harris family saga was one small story arising from a seismic shift in the world's history, a shift that sent tidal waves of immigrants across the oceans over the next several decades. Throughout Europe, individuals and families, most of whom were no longer serfs or peasants, were squeezed off the land as farm consolidation and new agricultural techniques resulted in more crops being produced with less labor. Simultaneously, the capitalist market was extending its reach throughout the world, and flows of commodities (including labor) grew heavier with each passing decade. As work on the land grew scarce, wages for building railroads, digging canals, tending looms, or molding iron became available. Between 1801 and 1935, over thirty-eight million immigrants arrived in the United States; from the 1820s to the 1920s, four and a half million people went to Canada, five million to Africa, another five million to Brazil, and seven and a half million to Argentina.[54]

The railroad, on which Richard Harris labored, was emblematic of the changing world. Railroads depended on technological inventions like steam power, innovations in banking, insurance, and finance, the rise of great cities, and perhaps most important, state intervention in the economy. In 1850, a little before the family arrived in Toronto, there were seventy-two miles of track in Canada; by 1865, two thousand miles had been laid. Railroads gave Montreal and Toronto new power over their hinterlands, as goods and people moved across the landscape. Great fortunes were built by those who captured the government's largesse. The railroads were where politicians and entrepreneurs came together in a nexus of vision and greed. Men like Richard Harris worked for wages determined by capitalists who themselves bent to the vagaries, the booms and busts, of the marketplace.[55]

The 1850s in Toronto were mixed times for laboring families. Despite severe downturns in the business cycle, the dominant trend was toward strong demand for goods and labor. But rising prices were a constant source of discontent. Workers in a number of trades organized unions to keep from losing ground, and the Irish press in North America often supported their efforts. Occasional acts of violence and intimidation were accompanied by escalating rhetoric that revealed a growing sense of class consciousness. Toronto stonecutters asked, "Are [we] to be trampled under the feet of despotic, dollar hunting railway contractors? Are canals . . . to be built on the skulls and marrow of men? Freedom says no! Common sense and public opinion echo no!" Many workers believed that the new marketplace calculus was morally wrong. They had faith in an older ideal: that a man's skill and effort earned him the right to provide for his family, to make enough so that his wife would not have to work outside the home, and to train and educate his children up to respectability. Whether or not strikes and lockouts directly touched the Harris family in the 1850s is unclear, but as working-class Irish immigrants, they must have been aware of the labor conflicts around them.[56]

Moreover, the Canadian Irish entered a world that was overwhelmingly British and Protestant in outlook. Toronto at mid-century was one-third Irish, but only one-quarter Catholic, so when the Harrises left Cork, they did not leave behind ethnic and sectarian conflicts. Toronto was often called the Belfast of North America, because of its large number of pre-famine Protestant immigrants from northern Ireland, many of whom were Orangemen (the Orange Order was a fraternal society that was loyal to the British crown). Allied with Conservative politicians, who controlled municipal licensing of taverns, public works, and the police force, the Orange Order impinged directly on the daily lives of Irish Catholics.[57]

The Canadian press abetted discrimination, even violence, against Irish Catholics. The Toronto *Globe* declared the "monstrous delusion of Catholicism" to be the "enemy of the human race." Rome's mission was "the subversion of the civil and religious liberty of the masses." The sloth, filth, and drunkenness of the Irish, concluded the *Globe*, made them as great a plague to Canada West as the locusts had been to Egypt. The Irish responded to bigoted deeds and words by organizing groups much like the old secret societies back home. A series of battles in Toronto between Orange and Green (Catholic) gangs beginning in 1856 led to the Saint Patrick's Day riot of 1858, and then to the founding of the Hibernian Benevolent Society for the protection of the Irish Catholic community. The Hibernians soon became associated with the militant Fenian movement, an organization devoted to Irish nationalism.[58]

Most Irish did not become radical nationalists, but prejudice encouraged them to continue thinking of themselves as exiles. As the historian Kerby Miller describes it, the need of the Irish to see themselves not as immigrants but as expatriates created a fundamental contradiction. In pre-famine Ireland, parish, family, and kin mattered most; individual ambition was a threat to this way of life. Yet very few immigrants returned when the famine ended; they chose to stay overseas to enjoy relative prosperity and opportunity. How could they do this while still denying that they had betrayed their fellows and their homeland? It was easier, Miller argues, for most of them to disavow their ambitions for a better future, even as they acted on them. We are not immigrants, we are exiles; the British and the Protestants have forced us out of our homeland. The idea of exile allowed the famine generation to have it both ways, to stay in North America and still to yearn for Ireland.[59]

Perhaps on summer evenings, Richard Harris and his elder son raised a glass in a local pub and sang "My Inchigeelagh Lass," a ballad of deep longing about an Irish patriot exiled to Boston, pining for his lover back home in the village. Or maybe they joined in a rousing chorus of "Remember Skibbereen," an anthem of revenge for the ravages wrought by the English:

> *Oh, father dear, the day may come*
> *when in answer to the call,*
> *Each Irishman, with feeling stern,*
> *will rally one and all,*
> *I'll be the man to lead the van beneath*
> *the flag of green,*
> *When loud and high we'll raise the cry—*
> *"Remember Skibbereen."*

The Harris men might have been active in the Irish nationalist movement that emerged in Canada and America during these years. Possibly Mary Harris's memories of her family fighting for Ireland's freedom included her father or elder brother joining the Fenian movement. Certainly Irish nationalism was in the air as Mary Harris grew to adulthood.[60]

The Catholic Church was an even greater source of community than the rebel groups—especially for women. According to the historian Emmet Larkin, pre-famine Ireland was not a land of single-minded piety and devotion. The Irish were rather dilatory in their observance of Mass, and the number of priests, nuns, and churches per capita was low. It was only after the famine, Larkin argues, in the New World and the Old, that Irish Catholicism gained its reputation for piety. This "devotional revolution" caused the Church to become a powerful center of Irish identity and an institution for combating prejudice. In the 1850s, increasing numbers of Irish entered the Catholic hierarchy in North America, and they made a concerted effort to bolster the faith of immigrants, guard against attacks on the Church, and counteract Protestant evangelizing.[61]

Just as the Harrises arrived in Toronto, an assertive new bishop, Armand de Charbonnel, helped build several churches, orphanages, refuges, and schools, spurred a broad-based temperance crusade—patterned on that of Father Theobald Mathew back in Ireland—and transformed St. Patrick's Day into a major religious festival, linking Catholicism to Irish nationalism. The activism of the episcopacy was part of an international movement within Catholicism known as ultramontanism, which, in order to bring more of the laity into the pews, sought to centralize the authority of the bishops. For anti-Catholics, all of this confirmed the old charge that the Church was a despotic institution. But the new activism, especially in places like Toronto, brought members into the fold rapidly, gave them a cradle-to-grave culture quite distinct from that of their Protestant neighbors, and enhanced the sense of Irish Catholic separateness.[62]

The figure of Mother Mary became pivotal to the countless women now swept up by Catholic revitalization. Two large women's lay organizations—the Sodality of the Blessed Virgin Mary and the Children of Mary—were among the most powerful in the Toronto diocese. The recitation of the rosary invoked the purity and maternal solicitude of the Virgin Mother and transformed the devotional lives of Irish Catholic women in Toronto. Mary provided a model of maternal piety; she represented feminine virtues raised to spiritual heights. And even as they taught meekness and obedience, women's devotional societies offered important opportunities for activism and leadership.[63]

Moreover, the women most likely to become involved came from precisely the sort of background as the Harrises—from the working class, those for whom respectability was both important and elusive. These were people whose best efforts in the world still might leave them in need of aid, Catholics for whom close association with the Church was an insurance policy against hard times.[64]

There is every reason to assume that Mary Harris participated actively in the Church as a youth. As we shall see, the persona that she created many years after leaving Canada resonated with images of Mother Mary—perhaps not meekness or humility, but purity, devotion, nurturance, and self-sacrifice for the faithful. Indeed, the very title "Mother" echoed that of women in the convents whom she came to know, and the plain black dresses that would become her signature apparel even looked a bit like the garb of the Sisters.[65]

What more can we say about the world in which Mary Harris grew up? Before she reached adulthood, it is difficult to imagine her apart from her kin. The labor of working-class mothers and children was essential for family survival, and as the eldest daughter, she must have shouldered many of the responsibilities of the household—cleaning and cooking, caring for the younger children, tending the garden and the livestock, shopping for food, sewing and mending, washing clothes, hauling water, and chopping wood.[66]

The first hints of an independent life for Mary emerge from the sources just as she was becoming an adult. Growing numbers of Irish women and their daughters sought employment outside the home, especially in domestic work and the needle trades. Mary learned the skills of dressmaking, but she was intent on another career. Late in 1857, at age twenty, she obtained a certificate from the priest at St. Michael's Cathedral attesting to her good moral character. With this credential, she took the examinations for admission to the Toronto Normal School, passed, and enrolled in November 1857. She never graduated, but she attended classes through the spring of 1858, getting more than enough training to secure a teaching position.[67]

Teaching was one of the few careers open to women. Opportunities were numerous, for the Harris family came to Toronto during a great change in the educational structure of Upper Canada. Reformers had long argued for universal education, and the arrival of the famine Irish provided impetus for a state-controlled, universal free school system. Schools, reformers believed, countered the immigrants' tendencies toward crime, disorder, and broken homes. Indeed, rich and poor, native- and foreign-born, Protestant and Catholic, all needed instruction in Canadian nationalism, British constitutional government, and nonsectarian Christianity. Schools taught hard work and steady habits, reinforced respect for private property, molded citizens for a growing, competitive society.[68]

Despite their high rate of illiteracy, the famine Irish accepted the importance of education for their children. Their experience with National Schools of Ireland, which denigrated their culture and dismissed Catholicism, however, had made them wary. Canada's Common School Act of 1850 was no sooner in place than the Catholic community began petitioning for funds to build their own separate schools. The Protestant middle class, which controlled the school board, saw its goals as universal, but for Catholics, common schools indoctrinated students into an alien culture. In the early 1850s, the local and provincial governments gave in and helped fund the separate schools. By 1854, seven parish schools had opened their doors in Toronto.[69]

The expansion of both kinds of schools was facilitated by women's move into the teaching profession. Three out of ten teachers in Upper Canada were women when Mary Harris enrolled in the normal school, and within a few years, they became a majority. But the profession remained distinctly hierarchical. Men took jobs teaching upper-level students, or serving as headmasters and superintendents, and confined women to teaching younger children. Women, men argued, could not handle more than the simplest intellectual or disciplinary tasks. Moreover, schools paid women half of what they paid men.[70]

The Toronto Normal School, the crown jewel of pedagogy in Canada West, was opened in 1847. Here Mary Harris's ambitions found an outlet. Not only was tuition free, but books were supplied to all students, and a small stipend of one dollar per week was given to those who completed each semester. Beyond training teachers, the normal school provided a rigorous, broadly based education that was otherwise unavailable to most of its students.[71]

It was a remarkable opportunity for any poor person. Mary's admittance tells us that she had a good basic education. However, she never finished the normal school, never received her certificate. Perhaps she was not fully prepared for such a difficult curriculum. Maybe she chafed under the strict rules—men and women, for example, were forbidden to speak to each other in class, and they were kept rigidly segregated at all times. The normal school was deeply patriarchal; teachers and administrators were all men. Certainly Mary felt culturally isolated—the roster of students included few Irish names, and in the nineteenth session, when she entered, she was the only Catholic woman, one of only two Catholics in total. Indeed, given the institution's mission of spreading British bourgeois culture throughout Canada, someone with Mary Harris's background probably found the normal school deeply alienating.[72]

Early in 1860, little more than a year after leaving the normal school, Mary Harris departed Toronto for a teaching job in Monroe, Michigan. There is no hint anywhere why she left her home and family. Perhaps she was driven by a rift with her parents, or maybe wanderlust born of exile, or a desire to practice her profession, or some unnamed crisis, or all of these together. It was not uncommon for young Irish women to leave home before marriage to secure an income and see a bit of the world. But Irish families tended to be quite close, and although Mary must have had contact with her kin in coming years, she barely ever mentioned them. In any event, she was ambitious and eager for new experiences. The stability that the Harris family worked so hard to achieve after the horrors of the famine failed to hold her.[73]

So once again, Mary was on the road, and once again the baggage she carried consisted less of material goods than of ideas, feelings, memories. Her family's saga was part of a larger story of poor people in Europe and America tempest-tossed by the marketplace. In Ireland, she witnessed misery and death firsthand, and she inherited a way of thinking about oppression, of personalizing its origins and glorifying the martyrs who fought it. In Toronto, she was exposed to labor's early response to the vagaries of working-class life, to the heady rhetoric of freeing Ireland from its English oppressors, and to the cult of womanly renunciation in the name of Mother Mary. All of this she brought to the United States at the age of twenty-three.[74]

★ 2 ★

Mary Jones

The years 1860 through 1890 were dramatic ones in American history, and in the life of Mary Jones. Yet she introduces that era in her autobiography with a bland description of her young adulthood: "My first position was teaching in a convent in Monroe, Michigan. Later, I came to Chicago and opened a dress-making establishment. I preferred sewing to bossing little children. . . . However, I went back to teaching again, this time in Memphis, Tennessee. Here I was married in 1861. My husband was an iron molder, and a staunch member of the Iron Molders' Union."[1] How did she feel about being a wife and mother? Did her husband have family in Memphis? Was he Irish Catholic? What kind of community did they live in? There is little evidence with which to answer these questions.

Mary probably landed the Michigan job through a contact in her Toronto parish. Mother Mary Joseph, who was in charge of the order in Monroe, sought a secular teacher to aid her small staff of eight Sisters and three novitiates. She hired Mary Harris on August 31, 1859, and paid her eight dollars per month. The school was an austere and depressing place, especially since dwindling enrollments constantly threatened its existence. Then too, the academy's self-described mission might have felt onerous to young Mary: "The morals and general deportment of the pupils are assiduously watched by the sisters, who,

while forming their hearts to virtue and their minds to the usages of re-
fined society, give every attention to their advancement in the different
sciences, and their comforts and personal habits receive the same attention as if they were in the bosom of their own families." Early in
1860, Mary collected $36.43 in back pay and headed for Chicago.[2]
There, she became a dressmaker, but she did not settle down for
long. Before the year was out, her wanderlust took her south to Memphis, Tennessee, where she began teaching again. Within a few short
months, she met and married George Jones.[3]

Memphis

Memphis might seem an unusual destination for someone from the
North in late 1860. Perhaps Canada insulated Mary from the sectional
crisis that was about to explode in the United States. Nevertheless, she
was one of thousands of migrants to Memphis shortly before the Civil
War. Crises of the Union were regular events in the nineteenth century, so many believed that this one would blow over like the others.
Besides, with its brisk river trade, growing industries, and commercial
ties to border cities like St. Louis and Cincinnati, Memphis had strong
Unionist sympathies until just before the Confederacy was formed.[4]

Memphis was a lively Mississippi River port, the sixth-largest city in
the South, growing rapidly on the strength of German and especially
Irish immigration. It was not quite an ethnic stronghold on the level of
St. Louis (50 percent immigrant), New Orleans (40 percent), or even
Louisville (33 percent). Still, Memphis's population more than doubled between 1850 and 1860, and the Irish population grew sixfold, to
over four thousand people. The city had become one of the most important points in the country for collecting, grading, and shipping cotton. Slaves in the hinterlands planted, cultivated, and harvested the
crop, and the railroads brought both cotton and prosperity to Memphis. In 1860, four lines—built partly with slave, partly with Irish
labor—terminated in the Bluff City, and two more were under construction. Measured by population, trade, or wealth, Memphis was the
fastest-growing city in the South.[5]

For Irish men, Memphis offered jobs building docks and levees, laying rails, grading roads, and hauling goods to market; according to the 1860 census, three-quarters of them worked as unskilled laborers. For Irish women, Memphis had the same sorts of jobs as other North American cities—domestic service, housecleaning, laundry work, and sewing. Before the late 1840s, much unskilled labor was performed by slaves or free blacks, and only the presence of a very low-cost alternative workforce, such as the famine Irish, could compete with them. Ireland's refugees settled predominantly in the First Ward, the poorest in the city, in a neighborhood known as "Pinch," short for "Pinch Gut," because of the leanness of its denizens. Before the famine, blacks had been the predominant ethnic presence in Pinch. African Americans and Irish, then, competed for space in the most unhealthy and overcrowded part of town and for positions on the lowest rungs of the economic ladder.[6]

Among native-born Memphians, anti-black racism had its analogue in anti-Irish nativism. Memphis developed a local version of America's Know-Nothing movement of the 1850s. Nativism gained support from people across the (white) social spectrum, but it had special appeal to the business class—cotton merchants, professionals, and owners of stores and factories.[7]

The sectional crisis, however, made allies of immigrants and businessmen. Urban laborers tended to oppose secession, and commercial ties to the North caused many businessmen to be less than enthusiastic about the Confederacy. In the end, Tennessee secessionists outnumbered Unionists, and when the time came, Memphians supported the Confederacy. As it turned out, the war did relatively little damage. Less than a year after the conflict began, Grant's troops advanced along the Tennessee, the Cumberland, and the Mississippi Rivers, surrounding the city. By March 1862, martial law had been declared, trade cut off, and town officials began to leave for safer places. Finally, after a brief naval battle witnessed by citizens from the bluffs along the Mississippi, Memphis fell to Union forces. Although life did not exactly return to the *status quo ante*, at least trade was restored, much of it smuggling to the Confederacy.[8]

New problems sprouted from the ashes of the Civil War. Freed from bondage, cut adrift in the devastation that Union armies brought to the countryside, black men and women began to migrate across the South. Their movement was an exercise of newly won freedom, but even more, they were searching for work and a better life. Many went to the cities, and Memphis's free black population grew exponentially. Southern journalists and politicians sketched terrifying images of freedmen out of control. But the unspoken fear was that African Americans would compete successfully with whites for work and status. For the Irish, still working at low-paying, unskilled jobs, worries of economic and social competition with blacks ran especially deep. They had learned to fear blacks' stigma and crave whites' status.[9]

Tensions boiled over in the spring of 1866. Black soldiers, newly mustered out of the Union army, went looking for jobs along the river docks and train depots. Beginning on May 1, and lasting for three days, one of the ugliest race riots in American history occurred. Irish police and firemen led the way in terrorizing African Americans. White rioters killed forty-six blacks, shot or beat two hundred more, and raped five women. The mob burned eighty-nine homes, four churches, and twelve schoolhouses; only the arrival of Union troops restored order. The riot was a prelude to the campaign of violent intimidation that the Ku Klux Klan, founded by the Memphian Nathan Bedford Forrest, began against the freedmen in 1867.[10]

Large social events provide a context for lives that are lived in sheer dailiness. War, emancipation, federal occupation, and race riots were the backdrop for the young Jones family. George and Mary were not among the proletariat, nor were they of the business class. As a teacher, Mary had reached the top of the occupational ladder for Irish women; indeed, it was usually not until the second generation that Irish Americans attained her level of accomplishment. Still, the pay was low, and because most schools in this era would not employ mothers, Mary quickly ceded the role of breadwinner to George. As an iron molder, George Jones was part of the aristocracy of labor. Foundry work was a highly skilled trade, one that preserved some of the old training and hierarchy of traditional crafts. Molders had their economic difficulties, but George Jones possessed skills that ensured considerable security for a man and his family.[11]

What had changed for iron molders was the transformation of

shops into factories. Jones worked for the Union Iron Works and Machine Shop, a large company that specialized in building and repairing steam engines, freight cars, sawmills, and gristmills. Spurred in part by wartime demand, foundries that manufactured capital goods had become an important part of Memphis's economy. With the consolidation of small shops into highly capitalized ones, a man like Jones, though possessing great knowledge of his craft, would rarely have owned his own shop and tools. Jones might be a highly skilled employee, but he was an employee nonetheless.[12]

Not only did Jones work in a factory, he was a member of the International Iron Molders Union. The nascent trade organizations of the early nineteenth century had blossomed into several unions by the Civil War era. Coopers, blacksmiths, machinists, shoemakers, and workers in other trades had their own organizations, but the iron molders union was the most powerful. "Labor has no protection," declared William Sylvis, the man responsible for organizing the North American molders union: "the weak are devoured by the strong. All wealth and all power centers in the hands of the few and the many are their victims and their bondsmen." Sylvis never questioned the right of shop owners to their property. He advocated self-help, temperance, and Christian free agency as sources of both religious salvation and upward social mobility. But he was adamant that more of the money produced by workers end up in their hands. Sylvis insisted that labor not allow capital to take a disproportionate share of wealth, that the producing classes not be reduced to poverty.[13]

As Sylvis organized tirelessly, his union grew from a few locals with dozens of members to two hundred locals and upwards of nine thousand men. By the end of the Civil War, the International Iron Molders Union had attained substantial control of the trade. Three-quarters or more of America's journeyman iron molders were union members, and closed shops were the rule in many of the largest foundry towns. High demand for foundry goods during the war meant steady hours and good pay. Men at the top of the trade made up to fifteen hundred dollars per year, roughly four times the wages of unskilled workers. Moreover, the union advocated the end of the piecework system, uniform pay scales, and a ten-hour workday.[14]

Every month the *Iron Molders' International Journal*—with the words

"Equal and exact justice to all Men, of whatever state or persuasion" emblazoned across the masthead—came into the Jones household. Reading the *Journal* was probably Mary Jones's first direct exposure to the American labor movement. George's early commitment to the union and his relatively high income must have made the family steadfastly pro-union. And Sylvis's message of the dignity of labor no doubt resonated deeply for Mary, given the hard circumstances of her parents' lives.[15]

As the molders union reached the height of its power with the war's end, Sylvis and other labor leaders began planning a new organization, the National Labor Union, which would unite various trades in one large umbrella organization. Sylvis shared in the racism of his day, yet he insisted that freed blacks, as well as women and immigrants, be allowed to join, because labor could not afford to exclude anyone who might end up competing for jobs. Although the National Labor Union eventually foundered in the economic turbulence of the Reconstruction era, Sylvis's ideas circulated widely. His faith in unions, his charisma as an organizer, and his belief that "it is not what is done for people, but what people do for themselves, that acts upon their character and condition" fed the ideals of Mother Jones decades later.[16]

For now, Mary and George had established a solid household in America. They had four children—Catherine in 1862, Elizabeth in 1863, Terence in 1865, and baby Mary in 1867—and as a new mother, Mary was constantly busy with the same tasks she had performed in Toronto, cooking and cleaning, sewing and mending. They lived in the newly established St. Mary's Parish, and even though the church was not yet built and services were held in an old schoolhouse, they affiliated themselves with the new congregation.[17]

The family home was on tiny Winchester Street, one of a few blocks of freestanding houses in the neighborhood. Unfortunately, Pinch lay between the two forks of the Bayou Gayoso, an open cesspool that became stagnant in the summer and flooded in the rainy season. The swampy landscape was a breeding ground for disease, and the city's lack of sanitation services made matters worse. Still, the neighborhood had its compensations—voices with an Irish lilt, an immigrant-dominated church, and strength in numbers against the larger, sometimes hostile, population.[18]

The life George and Mary built for their family did not last. When the war ended, a sluggish economy cut into the molders' business, and owners of the largest shops used slack demand to counterattack the union. Businesses merged, locked out workers, and rolled back wages. During the second half of 1867, with hard times continuing, many foundries shut down. At the end of the year, Sylvis estimated that three-quarters of union molders were unemployed. Membership fell, debt rose, and internal disputes threatened to tear apart the organization.[19]

But all of this pales beside the horror that now struck the Jones family. Yellow fever came west from Africa with the spread of the slave trade. It was most virulent in tropical climates, so while American cities as far north as Philadelphia and Boston experienced horrible outbreaks over the years, it hit hardest in the South. By the 1830s, epidemics of yellow fever, often accompanied by deadly cholera, had swept into cities like New Orleans and Memphis, leaving hundreds or even thousands dead in their wake. Yellow fever's unpredictability and its mysterious origins added to the terror. Not until 1905 did medical science discover that it was passed from person to person by the female *Aedes aegypti* mosquito. Ironically, the very symbols of industrial progress, steamboats and railroads, became vehicles for transporting the disease-bearing insects in their water supplies.[20]

All of the necessary elements—the long rainy season, the dense population, the large numbers of people without previous exposure to the illness—were in place in Memphis in 1867. The disease spread like a wave: "The Yellow fever has assumed an epidemic form in Galveston, Indianola, and other Texan gulf ports, while at New Orleans it is raging beyond precedent," warned the *Memphis Daily Appeal* on September 7. From late September through the end of November, yellow fever had its way with Memphis, and those who could afford to fled for their lives. No organized board of health kept accurate statistics, but around twenty-five hundred people contracted the disease in 1867, and another six hundred developed cholera. The epidemic struck hardest at those who lived near the Bayou Gayoso. Southerners called yellow fever "strangers' disease" because immigrants and Northerners, having developed no immunity, suffered the highest casualties. Indeed, the illness was often blamed on outsiders and on the laboring poor, who could not afford to leave town when epidemics swept in.[21]

Yellow fever was horrifying to behold. Flu-like symptoms—headache, chills, aching joints—lasted a day or two, then, in mild cases, disappeared. Those less lucky might be bedridden for a week, first with migraine or lower-back pains, followed by nausea, stomach cramps, and rising fever. As the disease progressed, mucous membranes hemorrhaged, so patients bled from the nose, gums, and tongue, as well as from the uterus and urethra. Soon hemorrhages filled the stomach and intestines. Victims vomited black blood (whence comes the Spanish term for the disease, *vómito negro*), and delirium set in. Finally came jaundice, liver failure, and death.[22]

Memphians tried anything to halt yellow fever's spread. They set barrels of tar on fire in the streets and spread lime, carbolic acid, and other disinfectants. Citizens held sponges to their noses to avoid inhaling noxious vapors, and they burned the bedclothes of the disease's victims. Newspapers, fearing panic and bad publicity, alternated detailed (and often contradictory) advice on how to treat the afflicted with stories downplaying the severity of the outbreak. All in vain. A doctor writing during a later epidemic in 1878 left the following account of his patient: September 11: "Mouth dry; thirst great; gums ragged and inclined to bleed, lips scarlet; nasal passages dry; urine scanty . . ." September 12: "He was bleeding from the nose, gums, and lips; dejections from the bowels black, watery, and frequent; thirst intense; he said he was 'burning up inside' . . ." September 13: "Slept in snatches; vomited several times mucus and water containing dark flocculi . . . Delirium had set in; he was unmanageable, except by force. The extremities were getting cold. He died early next morning."[23]

Mary Jones recalled her experience of the epidemic almost sixty years later, and for the first time, the matter-of-fact tone of her autobiography breaks with emotion:

> In 1867, a yellow fever epidemic swept Memphis. . . . Across the street from me, ten persons lay dead from the plague. The dead surrounded us. They were buried at night quickly and without ceremony. All about my house I could hear weeping and the cries of delirium. One by one, my four little children sickened and died. I washed

their little bodies and got them ready for burial. My husband caught the fever and died. I sat alone through nights of grief. No one came to me. No one could. Other homes were as stricken as mine. All day long, all night long, I heard the grating of the wheels of the death cart.[24]

How can we even imagine Mary Jones's helplessness, her emptiness? She must have felt cursed—first the death carts' grating wheels in Cork, then resurrection from those horrors, now that sound again, death carts real or imagined, bearing away her family. She no doubt struggled against the disease, fought for her husband's and children's lives. Did she blame herself for the agony her babies underwent? Being alive had to fill her with anguish for surviving those she loved, especially since she could only watch helplessly as they died. But feeling accursed because she had outlived her family only brought more guilt for thinking of herself. How did she bury them? Did the rituals of the Church ease her pain? How did she bear the loneliness? Better to forget, to seal out memories of the family and its deathwatch. Yet forgetting only fed remorse: George deserved to be remembered for his hard work and devotion, prayers must be said and candles lit for the children. As if forgetting was possible anyway. What nightmares haunted her? Did she dream of baby Mary, her namesake, whimpering with pain, vomiting black blood, then dying?[25]

Local 66, the Memphis chapter of the International Iron Molders Union, held a special meeting in honor of George Jones and adopted resolutions to "the memory of our departed brother." The men draped their charter in mourning, sent condolences to the widow, and published an obituary for their "earnest and energetic brother." Mary Jones soon left Memphis a thirty-year-old widow, as bereft as any human being could be. It would be decades before she got over her personal tragedy, if people ever get over such things. But she came away from Memphis with images and feelings that would emerge again in her life. It was in Memphis that Mary witnessed how greed caused some men to reduce others to slavery, in Memphis too that she saw armies come to liberate the slaves from bondage. Here she witnessed the explosive mix of racial hatred and class. In Memphis also she first became familiar with the American labor movement and thought about what solidarity meant for people like herself. And, in Memphis, she was called Mother, a title she would not hear again for thirty years.[26]

Chicago

Even decades later, Mary Jones rarely mentioned her bereavement, and the *Autobiography* says little about her loss: "After the union had buried my husband, I got a permit to nurse the sufferers. This I did until the plague was stamped out. . . . I returned to Chicago and went again into the dressmaking business with a partner." Mary Jones carried to her grave these days of sorrow.[27]

After recounting the death of her family in the *Autobiography*, she describes her new life in Chicago. The quiet grief of the yellow fever passage gives way to indignation over the greed of the rich and the plight of the poor. The suppressed rage over her own tragedy emerges when she describes the lives of the needy, those whom she eventually came to think of as her people. She does not so much forget her own pain as displace it:

> We worked for the aristocrats of Chicago, and I had ample opportunity to observe the luxury and extravagance of their lives. Often while sewing for the lords and barons who lived in magnificent houses on the Lake Shore Drive, I would look out of the plate glass windows and see the poor, shivering wretches, jobless and hungry, walking along the frozen lake front. The contrast of their condition with that of the tropical comfort of the people for whom I sewed was painful to me. My employers seemed neither to notice nor to care.

Mother Jones positions herself as an observer of the separation between the two classes, seeing through the glass a rigidly divided world that denied the existence of its own divisions.[28]

She saw even the summer heat through the lens of social class:

"From the windows of the rich, I used to watch the mothers come from the west side slums, lugging babies and little children, hoping for a breath of cool, fresh air from the lake." Chicago's elite donated a few dollars to the charity ice fund, then headed out of town to the seaside or the mountains. Despite the outrage Mary Jones expresses in her autobiography, she was probably too numb from her personal tragedy to dwell for long on class divisions. Her time was absorbed by the day-to-day realities of a working woman's life.[29]

The details of Mary Jones's existence in Chicago are few, but the social context of those details is important. She returned to dressmaking; maybe she found it too painful to spend her time with children. Her shop was located on Washington Street, downtown near Lake Michigan. The 1871 Chicago City Directory gives her address as 174 Jackson Street, within easy walking distance of work. She and her unidentified partner seem to have done custom work, so although Mary must have been quite skilled, she was constantly reminded of her status as a worker by her frequent contact with wealthy patrons.[30]

When Mary Jones returned to Chicago, it was the greatest boomtown in America. Chicago had prospered with wartime demand and entered the last third of the nineteenth century trumpeting its position as the capital of the West and the fastest-growing city in America. A third of a million people lived there in 1870, though the city had been incorporated only thirty-three years before. The railroads, rivers, and canals that fanned out from Lake Michigan were the key. Raw goods poured into Chicago, where they were milled, processed, and packaged, then shipped east along trunk lines or by boat on the Great Lakes. The city was new and full of energy, an economic dynamo. It was a place where people came to work and to restart their lives. There was opportunity for the likes of Mary Jones, but opportunity was, of course, limited by prejudice against the Irish and women.[31]

Chicago was a divided city, and these divisions grew deeper as large-scale capitalist enterprises became entrenched. Wealth displayed itself shamelessly alongside shocking scenes of poverty. Immigrants crowded into neighborhoods once filled with native-born rural folk. Ethnicity coincided roughly with social and economic status. Simply put, the wealthiest fifth of Chicago's population—mostly native-born Protestants—held 90 percent of the city's total assets, while the poorest half (which included most of the Irish) possessed less than 1 percent.[32]

The stability Mary Jones created for herself stitching garments did not last. Four years after the horror of Memphis, disaster stalked her again. On the night of October 8, 1871, around the fourth anniversary of her family's death, an unusually strong and steady southerly wind began to howl through the city. Recent fires, caused by an unprecedented drought, had exhausted Chicago's firemen, and when another one started southwest of downtown in a barn owned by the O'Leary family, it quickly got out of control. Within hours, the fire spread north and east, advancing along a broad front. By early morning it had turned into a firestorm—the updraft of heated air generated winds so strong that they sucked fuel into the flames, fanned the fire to over two thousand degrees, and tossed burning timbers into the dark. From Harrison to Fullerton and from the Chicago River east to Lake Michigan—three and a half square miles—Chicago burned to the ground. Miraculously, only three hundred people died, but seventeen thousand structures vaporized, nearly $200 million worth of property vanished, and a hundred thousand people were left homeless.[33]

The fire took all of Mary Jones's belongings. Like thousands of others, she raced east to the lake to stay ahead of the flames, remained all night and the next day by the shore, stranded without food, forced by the heat to retreat into the water. People stood with the few goods they managed to save as falling embers threatened to set their clothes ablaze and flames from the still-burning city blistered their skin. Later Mary Jones huddled in Old St. Mary's Church on Wabash Street until she found other accommodations.[34]

The rebuilding of Chicago became part of the city's mythology. Everyone pulled together, it was said, and within a few years, Chicago rose from the ashes. Chicagoans felt a sense of civic pride in resurrecting their town. But the social divisions that preceded the fire remained and, if anything, grew deeper in coming years. Some newspapers attributed the fire to a radical plot and printed alleged confessions by European terrorists. Even as the flames died, rumors spread that incendiaries conspired to torch the city again. The unfounded legend of Mrs. O'Leary's cow knocking over a gas lamp that ignited the barn, then the whole city, also grew out of widespread stereotypes of the poor and the Irish as the "dangerous classes." *The Chicago Times*, the city's largest-circulation newspaper, ran a story claiming that before the fire, O'Leary had fraudulently collected relief. When a Cook County agent cut her off, she swore revenge.[35]

As architects planned and workers rebuilt with unprecedented speed, the construction boom only seemed to feed the suspicions that capital and labor held for each other. Before the panic and depression of 1873 ended the building spree, both sides articulated their positions as never before. Business and civic leaders insisted on a vision of the new city based on individual workers selling their labor in free markets. But local building trade unions and the National Labor Union argued that individualism was a formula for disaster. They rejected the alien doctrine of laissez-faire capitalism, insisting that only workers' solidarity gave them protection from the ravages of the marketplace.[36]

The great Chicago fire struck when Mary Jones was thirty-four years old. She gave it only a few sentences in her autobiography, after having described her entire life up to that point in just three pages. From then on, however, she turned her narrative wholly into an account of her involvement in the labor movement. Amid the still-smoldering ruins of the Chicago fire, she tells us, she began to attend lectures of the Knights of Labor, America's largest union of the late nineteenth century. Those stirring lectures, she declared, made her appreciate more than ever the struggles of the working class, and so she joined the organization.[37]

The problem with her story is that the Knights did not organize in Chicago until years after the fire, and they did not admit women until 1880. Yet there probably is a core of truth here. The *Autobiography* must be treated less literally than metaphorically; its specific details are often incorrect, but the book is best thought of as akin to religious testimony, to bearing witness, to a pilgrim's story. Mary Jones underwent a sort of conversion, probably in the 1870s. Her ideas matured as she immersed herself in the labor movement in the 1880s. She must have joined the Knights of Labor around the height of its power in the mid-1880s, and before the decade was over, she began her lifelong friendship with fellow Irish Catholic Terence Powderly, the head of the organization.[38]

"Those were the days of sacrifice for the cause of labor," she wrote of the late nineteenth century. "Those were the days when we had no halls, when there were no high salaried officers, no feasting with the enemies of labor. Those were the days of the martyrs and the saints." The legacy she wished to impart from those early years was the purity of the cause, purity uncorrupted by institutions. Here was labor's springtime, to which subsequent generations must rededicate themselves. Her rhetoric was a labor version of the American jeremiad, that pattern of thought and speech which comes down to us from the Puritans, where we confess our sins and return to the old ways, to the memory of those who sacrificed themselves for the true religion. The next ten pages of the *Autobiography* describe the great railroad strike of 1877 and the Haymarket affair of 1886. She was no more than a bit player in these events (she implies a much larger role for herself), but just living in Chicago was enough to make a lasting impression.[39]

In September 1873, a financial panic, fueled by rampant speculation, closed the bank of Jay Gould, and America slid into the deepest depression it had ever experienced. For five years, faith in the beneficence of capitalism was challenged by the specters of unemployment, poverty, and homelessness. In 1874, a million workers were without jobs, and some cities had unemployment rates approaching 25 percent. Railroad employees saw their workdays grow longer and their pay drop. With so many men desperate for work, the labor organizing of previous years began to unravel. William Sylvis's National Labor Union crumbled; so did two-thirds of the nation's trade unions, as the number of union members shrank from 300,000 to 50,000 during the crisis. Business leaders and their supporters in editorial offices and pulpits declared that nothing could be done to ease the suffering, that relief efforts would ruin worker incentives to look for jobs, that economic contractions were as natural as the seasons, that the task of entrepreneurs was to run their companies as efficiently as possible. "The necessities of the great railroad companies demanded that there should be a reduction of wages," the prominent minister Henry Ward Beecher told his rich Brooklyn congregation. "Was not a dollar a day enough to buy bread! Water costs nothing. . . . The man who cannot live on bread and water is not fit to live."[40]

With so many unemployed laborers willing to work for less than those who still had jobs, strikes were doomed to failure. But that did not stop the beginnings of militant organizing. In Chicago, mass meetings, hunger marches, armies of tramps—whom the *Tribune* suggested be handled like farm rodents, with strychnine and arsenic—appeared. The police, acting at the behest of city fathers, responded with intimidation and violence. Despite the repression, the Working-Men's Party was born in 1876. Here, unionists and political radicals joined together in an uneasy but militant alliance.[41]

The patience of many American workers finally broke in July 1877. The heads of four railroads—the Erie, the New York Central, the Baltimore and Ohio, and the Pennsylvania—cut employee wages by 10 percent (the second such cut within a year) though stockholder dividends had continued through the depression. Employees of the Baltimore and Ohio in Martinsburg, West Virginia, reacted first; they walked off the job. President Rutherford B. Hayes sent in federal troops to put down the "insurrection," but the strike spread. The single most dramatic episode occurred in Pittsburgh. America's largest corporation, the Pennsylvania Railroad, which employed over thirty thousand people, was already very unpopular in that city. Small businessmen and workers blamed the company for unfair freight rates and corrosive competition. On July 19, railroad workers, iron molders, and other tradesmen shut down the train yards. Local militia, filled with working-class men, refused to enforce laws against their compatriots, but troops sent from across the state in Philadelphia were not so sympathetic. Bayonets were met with rocks, rocks with bullets. Twenty protesters were killed, including several women and children. As workers poured toward the train yards, the strike turned into a riot. The crowd routed the soldiers, surrounded the roundhouse, tore up miles of track, and set fire to countless trains and cars.[42]

Mary Jones claims in her autobiography that she was in Pittsburgh for this bloody denouement, that the workers sent for her to come help them. This is almost certainly untrue. There is no evidence that she had yet achieved any prominence in the labor movement, and given the spontaneity of the strike, it makes little sense that anyone had called for her help. Moreover, her narrative gives no feeling of familiarity with specific people or places; it reads like a description cribbed from published sources, not like an eyewitness account. But mere facts were not the point. Placing herself in Pittsburgh for this first great national strike was a way of projecting her activism backward in time, validating her claim to being the founding mother of the labor movement. Writing in 1925 that the boys "sent for me to come help them" meant that she had been at the center of the storm for half a century. Above all, she claimed that 1877 revealed new truths to her: "Then and there I learned in the early part of my career that labor must bear the cross for others' sins, must be the vicarious sufferer for the wrongs that others do." Organizing workers required Christlike sacrifice, even as false prophets blamed the just for others' sins.[43]

Even if Mary Jones was not in Pittsburgh, the great strike must have left a deep impression on her. In Chicago, news of events from Pennsylvania touched off a citywide general strike that had the flavor of open class warfare. Strikers—men and some women from all ethnic groups—roamed through industrial sections of town, calling other workers to join them, as bands in the streets played the "Marseillaise." Workers took control of factories, foundries, and loading docks; they fought strikebreakers, police, and local militia. The upheaval lasted three days, and only the troops' firing grapeshot into crowds—killing thirty and wounding two hundred—ended the troubles. Meanwhile, headlines screamed that "Howling Mobs of Thieves and Cut-Throats" had taken over the city. Local businessmen organized their clerks and managers into militia units and contributed to special police funds; after the crisis was over, they began to collect money to build armories.[44]

Nationwide, a hundred thousand workers participated in the strike, at least one hundred died, and hundreds more were wounded. The strikers were not well organized and did not have a clear ideology. They responded viscerally to their own immiseration, to the growing arrogance of corporations, and to the erosion of their rights to secure economic well-being for themselves, their families, and their communities. The great strike lasted only two weeks, but it spread from coast to coast, and for the first time, the federal government intervened decisively for capital and against labor.[45]

America changed in 1877, and the events of that year caused forty-year-old Mary Jones to think more deeply about the place of labor in America. The strikers included not just railroad workers but farmers, miners, and mill hands. Despite its failure to restore laborers' pay, the strike signaled the beginnings of a broadly based working-class movement, more powerful than anything seen before. For a few days, all of the trappings of a ruling class fighting for its survival were on display. Chicago's civic elite, including men like George Pullman and Marshall Field, believed that revolution was imminent. And labor activists for the first time found their ideas had resonance with masses of workers.[46]

Prosperity returned during the late 1870s and early 1880s, only to be punctured by another long depression beginning in 1883. Trade unions revived, and the Knights of Labor grew rapidly. The Knights had a strong strain of worker radicalism, of defiant republican mistrust of the growing power of business. They hoped to form a bulwark against new corporations by organizing workers of all trades. Meanwhile, the old Working-Men's Party, now known as the Socialist Labor Party, elected a few people to office around the country and was especially popular among German immigrants. Perhaps most important, various anarchist organizations called for the overthrow of capitalism in America, by violence if necessary. Anarchists held radical ideals of equality, but they were suspicious of efforts to harness state power because centralization was the problem, not the solution. Anarchists valued the creativity of labor and the freedom of individuals; they wanted not only a living but a way of life, including a broad sense of participation in human affairs. Strains of anarchist ideas came from France, Russia, Germany, and from within America, so that by the mid-1880s, the movement was dynamic and growing. With the economic downturn that began in 1883, mass rallies led by articulate orators became commonplace. Chicago's enormous immigrant population, gifted leaders, and active press (five newspapers in three languages promulgated anarchist ideas) made it the center of the movement.[47]

By 1885, anarchists had taken leadership positions in the Central Labor Union, Chicago's largest worker organization. The Alabama-born former Confederate Albert Parsons told several thousand members in September 1885, "We are revolutionists. We fight for the destruction of the system of wage-slavery. . . . The claim of capital to profit, interest or rent is a robber claim, enforced by piratical methods. Let robbers and pirates meet the fate they deserve! . . . Proletarians of the world unite! We have nothing to lose but our chains, we have a world to win!" A wave of strikes broke, mostly for restoration of wages. The reaction was swift and violent, making the logic of anarchist ideas even more compelling. Police repression was met by an escalation in the anarchists' rhetoric; their talk was generally more violent than their acts, but the threat of rebellion was real.[48]

Trade unionists, too, grew restive, and they demanded the eight-hour day for all workers. Anarchists at first opposed the eight-hour movement as a mere cosmetic gesture, but it caught the imagination of masses of workers willing to fight to gain control of their time. So while the original impetus came from the Federation of Organized Trades and Labor Unions (forerunner to the American Federation of Labor), anarchist leaders became closely associated with the eight-hour movement. Three hundred thousand American workers left their jobs on May 1, 1886, forty thousand of them in Chicago, the center of the strike. *The Chicago Mail* said of the anarchist leaders Albert Parsons and August Spies, "They are looking for riot and plunder. They haven't got one honest aim nor one honorable end in view. . . . Hold them personally responsible for any trouble that occurs." Radicals hoped a revolution was about to begin; businessmen felt now was the time to smash radicalism for good.[49]

May Day itself was tense yet peaceful. The walkout for the eight-hour day continued, however, and it became entwined with the ongoing strike at the enormous McCormick harvester plant. McCormick was attempting to roll back wages by replacing its entire force of iron molders. Police, commanded by the notorious John Bonfield, attacked workers—first with clubs, then with guns—who had rallied in front of the plant on May 3. Two workers were killed and many wounded. The next night, May 4, the anarchists called an open meeting in Haymarket Square. The crowd was disappointingly small, perhaps three thousand people, and was on the verge of breaking up when the police appeared, obviously ready to begin a new assault. As they charged, a bomb hurtled toward them, landed in their midst, and exploded. Windows shattered for blocks around, police began to fire their revolvers indiscriminately as the crowd fled in panic, and before it was over, seven officers lay dead (mostly from "friendly fire"), along with an undetermined number of civilians.[50]

Fear and indignation gripped the public. The connection between the violent rhetoric of the anarchists and the blood flowing in the streets seemed inescapable. All the talk about dynamite, all the words about revolution now were thrown back at the radicals—indeed, at anyone who had advocated the cause of labor. The press whipped up an intense anti-red hysteria. Wild rumors circulated that the Haymarket bomb was a signal for a full-scale uprising. Mainstream labor unions began to distance themselves from the radicals. The Chicago newsletter of the Knights of Labor disavowed any connection with the anarchists, called them "a band of cowardly murderers, cut-throats and robbers," and urged that they be treated as such. Not a shred of evidence was ever produced to prove who threw the bomb, but that did not stop authorities from rounding up Chicago's leading radicals. For two months, civil liberties were suspended and newspapers shut down as police questioned, detained, and beat hundreds of activists and laborites, especially those of foreign birth. Sensational stories in the newspapers convinced the public that a gigantic conspiracy existed, which justified extreme police measures to root out the troublemakers.[51]

Eight anarchist leaders were arrested and tried for conspiracy to commit murder. Their militant rhetoric was enough to convict them. Four, including Parsons and Spies, were hanged in November 1887, three were given life sentences, then pardoned a few years later, and the last man, Louis Lingg, committed suicide just before his scheduled execution. Tasting blood, businessmen and editors widened their assault on labor and the left. Unprecedented numbers of workers were locked out of their jobs as a wave of union busting began. The Knights of Labor had about one million members just before the bomb exploded in Haymarket. A year later, that number was cut in half, and in 1890, only a tenth of the members remained. Repression caused many workers to turn to much more narrow organizing along craft lines. The Knights' bold vision of labor engaged in a moral struggle for autonomy suffered a major setback, and the business unionism of Samuel Gompers's American Federation of Labor—defining issues narrowly in

3. The press often depicted the police under siege and the demonstrators as rabble during the Haymarket affair. Here a patrol wagon is "attacked by a mob of 12,000 rioters." Mother Jones described Haymarket as a formative moment in her life. From *Frank Leslie's Illustrated Newspaper*, May 15, 1886 (Courtesy Newberry Library)

terms of wages and hours, not ownership or control of the workplace—seemed the prudent strategy to many unionists.[52]

Forty years later, Mary Jones remembered the 1880s as a time when the working class everywhere was in rebellion. Foreign agitators, she recalled, gave men vision and hope; the police gave them clubs. Haymarket was a turning point in her life: "Although I never endorsed the philosophy of anarchism, I often attended the meetings on the lake shore, listening to what these teachers of the new order had to say to the workers." The radicals alienated many would-be supporters with their extreme rhetoric, but they died heroes, as their funeral attested: "Thousands of workers marched behind the black hearses, not because they were anarchists but they felt that these men, whatever their theories, were martyrs to the workers' struggle."[53]

The Haymarket affair was a watershed. The ideological passions of 1886 and the resulting clash of power continued to perturb all who struggled with the meaning of massive social and economic changes.

Mary Jones remained obscure for several more years, but the great issues of her day already consumed her. She paid deference to the Haymarket martyrs, those "teachers of the new order," in her own way. After the turn of the century, as May Day increasingly became recognized as a labor holiday, Mary Jones began declaring May 1 to be her birthday. And in a symbolic sense, it was the day she was born into the labor movement.[54]

Survivor

Early in the twentieth century, journalists reported that one or another epiphany led Mary Jones to militant activism. Some had her traveling abroad during the 1870s or 1880s, where she discovered that the American working class was even worse off than the European. Others claimed that in the late 1870s she was converted on the sandlots of San Francisco, where she developed her oratorical skills declaiming for the Working-Men's Party against the perils of Chinese immigration. Certainly such travels, if she made them at all, fit the footloose pattern of her later life. But these stories, even if true, fail to tell us much about how Mary Jones became Mother Jones.[55]

Above all, there is silence. How did she become a radical? The *Autobiography* implies that her political ideas were only logical, natural. Any heir of true American ideals who witnessed things like poverty and child labor would become a socialist and a militant laborite. But most people became no such things. The Irish had even less tendency than other groups to join anarchists or militants. The Catholic Church discouraged class-conscious politics, Irish nationalism focused energies overseas, and Irish American politicians were dependent on the entrenched party structure.[56]

Being unencumbered by a family may have freed her to explore radical ideas that helped make sense of her past and of the life she saw around her. She left no hints of intimacy. Assuming that her personal life before the turn of the century resembled that after 1900 (when we start to have records), her connections to people were cordial but not particularly deep. A middle-aged, working-class Irish widow, she had every reason to feel that her life was more than half over and that her best days were behind her. But Mary Jones had no intention of accepting whatever fate had in store for her.[57]

Although there is much we do not know about Mary Harris and Mary Jones, one thing we do know: long before she conceived the persona of Mother Jones, she witnessed repeated, unspeakable tragedies. Literally unspeakable—later in life, she never mentioned the Great Hunger, the passage to North America, the fever sheds of Canada, the American Civil War, or the Memphis riots. She gave the barest descriptions of George Jones and the deaths of her children, never said a word about her mother, mentioned her successful brother William a few times to reporters around 1900 then dropped the subject, named none of her siblings or children in her autobiography, and failed to note events such as the deaths of her parents. Mother Jones had a history; Mary Harris and Mary Jones did not.[58]

Mary Jones remained on the fringes for a while longer. But if there was a crucible of her faith, it was Chicago. Chicago in the late nineteenth century was the most radical city in America, a hotbed of ideological ferment. There, a constant upsurge of ideas—foreign and domestic versions of trade and industrial unionism, anarchism, socialism, populism—was part of daily working life. The radical ideas, the mix of peoples from so many lands, the city's mythology of rebuilding itself out of the ashes, all made it remarkable. But much more than that, Chicago was where people came to transform themselves. With a population that doubled then doubled again every ten years, it truly was a city of strangers. Here, amid a culture whose hallmark was the manipulation of images, changes of identity were not only possible but desirable. What brought so many to Chicago was ambition, and the mutability of cityscape and self fed their desires. The reinvention of identity in a city that constantly re-created itself was all part of the protean quality that Americans had identified with urban life at least since the early nineteenth century, but never before on the scale of Chicago.[59]

The city was one big flow of commodities—timber, grain, coal, steel, clothing, cattle, people—all floating on a river of capital. When we think of Mary Harris and Mary Jones before she became Mother Jones, there is a profound sense of her life being tossed in the floods of social and economic change. If she was prey to natural forces and naturalized ones like the marketplace, becoming Mother Jones, as we shall see, was a way of rejecting the victim's role. Rather than give in to the epic changes that reshaped the world in the nineteenth century and buffeted working-class lives like the Harrises' and the Joneses', *Mother Jones refused to accept her fate passively.*[60]

The first half of Mary Jones's life prepared her for the task of becoming Mother Jones. She was, above all, a survivor—she passed through horrific times and transcended them. That is how the twentieth century came to know her. Every time the frail old woman in her outdated black dress was arrested, issued proclamations from jail, then emerged to lead a parade of strikers, the image of her as a survivor was reinforced.

But Mary Harris Jones was a survivor in a darker way too. Famine, war, and plague took those around her. Why she remained alive while others fell must have been a mystery to her. Beyond grief and shock and loneliness at the loss of loved ones comes a sense of culpability. How could it be otherwise? This is not to reduce Mary Jones's words and deeds to mere psychologizing. Her life as Mother Jones was a story of astonishing courage, of fighting the good fight. While others of her generation shrank from the issues of the day, Mother Jones was consumed with them. But who she became was inseparable from who she had been. Tragedy freed her for a life of commitment.

Looked at another way, though, Mary Jones was never truly free. The ghosts of her past haunted her so deeply that she could not even speak about them. Probably she achieved a small exorcism when she set out on the road sometime late in the nineteenth century, when she gave up possessions, home, self and became Mother Jones. Her witness against the horrors visited on the poor by the rich was energized, in part, by a need to expiate her own survival. Poor and homeless, she reenacted her parents' exile; a tireless union organizer, she continued her husband's commitments; mother to the poor, she nurtured a family again. Chicago gave her an arena to develop her political ideas, while profound loss enabled her to find commitments outside a woman's normal sphere. It was the tragedies of her early days, then, that energized the life of Mother Jones.

★ 3 ★

Mother Jones

On June 15, 1897, several hundred people gathered in Chicago for the convention of the American Railway Union. Their goal was to fold the ARU into a larger organization known as Social Democracy for America. Eugene Debs, the charismatic president of the ARU, was there, along with Edward Bellamy, the author of the enormously popular socialist-utopian novel *Looking Backward*. Their plan was to start a "cooperative commonwealth," a socialist community. The governor of Washington even invited them to build their colony in his state. Debs gave a ringing speech in support of the new plan. "When he finished," the *Chicago Evening Journal* reported, "white-haired 'Mother' Jones, who occupied a prominent position, proposed three cheers for the governor of Washington for inviting the organization to make its experiment in that state."[1]

The reference to " 'Mother' Jones" is one of the first times the name was used publicly for Mary Jones. One journalist claimed that the men of Debs's ARU conferred the title on her. Even in 1897, however, her moniker was not universally acknowledged, since that same year the *National Labor Tribune* referred to her simply as Mrs. Mary Jones of Chicago. Although the cooperative commonwealth never got off the ground, by 1901, Social Democracy for America had evolved into a political party, the Socialist Party of America. And Mary Jones, now over sixty years old, had become Mother Jones.[2]

In fact, by the turn of the century, she had disappeared into her new persona. The articles she wrote bore the name Mother Jones; she was introduced that way at the podium; letters to her began "Dear Mother"; and she always signed her missives "Mother Jones," or simply "Mother." Everyone from miners to Presidents called her Mother. But she was not the first Mother Jones.[3]

The First Mother Jones

In February 1887, Mrs. Henry B. Jones, the wife of a coal miner, became the editor of the Ladies Department of the *Railroad Brakemen's Journal*. A few years before, she wrote for the *Locomotive Firemen's Magazine*, edited by Eugene Debs, then a rising young leader in the railroad brotherhoods. Jones even penned a few lines for Debs in honor of his marriage:

> *Ever alert to the laboring man's right,*
> *Upright in all he e'er tries to do,*
> *God ever keep him by day and by night!*
> *Ever to him may his lady prove true . . .*

Working man's rights, moral rectitude, divine protection, a faithful marriage—these four lines express the sensibility of labor's first Mother Jones.[4]

Jones was born in England in 1843, migrated to America with her husband in 1870, moved first to Wilkes-Barre, Pennsylvania, then to Washington, Indiana. The *Brakemen's Journal* said of her when she became Ladies Department editor: "Mrs. Jones takes a deep interest in railway matters and is always ready to champion the cause of railway employees. . . ." She soon started signing herself "Mother" and "Mother Jones," and the women who wrote to the magazine also began to address her that way.[5]

But her world was very different from that of our Mother Jones. The *Brakemen's Journal* billed itself as the "Official Organ of the Brotherhood of Railroad Brakemen." The various brotherhoods—of locomotive firemen, engineers, conductors, and so forth—were all late-nineteenth-century craft unions, organizing men according to their specialties.

Compared with unskilled or semiskilled workers, the men of such brother-hoods were the aristocracy of labor, and they were very protective of their autonomy and their moral authority as productive citizens.[6]

Mrs. Henry Jones (her own first name was never published) opened the Ladies Department to the wives and sweethearts of the brakemen. These columns expressed an ideal of domestic harmony, of strong men doing their jobs with dignity, of devoted women taking care of their homes. Mrs. Jones's columns were always written with an eye to Victorian proprieties.[7]

Poetry was a staple of the Ladies Department, most of it echoing the sentimental conventions of the late nineteenth century. Louise Gaffney, of New Haven, for example, dedicated "The Brakeman's Mother" to her local lodge. The poem described a mother's reaction to her son's death:

> *His poor old mother heard the story,*
>   *And with a sob laid down her head;*
> *When her friends strove to comfort her,*
>   *They found that her soul had fled.*
> *In the quiet country churchyard,*
>   *Side by side lie this loving pair.*
> *But the gates of Heaven have opened,*
>   *Two blessed souls have entered there.*

Devotion, sacrifice, even death—this was the stuff of mother love.[8]

Alongside domestic verse, the *Brakemen's Journal* printed labor song poems. These staples of the labor movement were sung or spoken at meetings and celebrations. Mrs. Henry Jones herself was well known for her song poems, which commemorated the heroism and devotion of the brakemen. For example, in "A Dream," Jones described herself transported to heaven, where she stood before God as an army of railroad workers looked on:

> *I said: "O Judge, that army there that's*
>   *reaching o'er the vale*
> *Are the boys whose lives were sacrificed upon*
>   *the treacherous rail. . . . "*

Song poems were emblematic of labor movement culture in the late nineteenth century. Recitations accompanied speeches and band music on festive occasions, strengthening the bonds of brotherhood and building esteem within the movement.[9]

At the end of 1889, just six years after it began, the *Brakemen's Journal* was absorbed into a larger publication, the *Railroad Trainmen's Journal.* Mrs. Henry Jones—Mother Jones—disappeared from print. Equally important, song poems became more rare in the labor movement, because the movement itself was changing. The elite brotherhoods became less effective as American businesses consolidated into enormous corporations. The old producer ideology that had animated the brotherhoods—all who worked with their hands to create wealth were united in a virtuous endeavor—bore less and less relationship to the social landscape. The ideals of duty, virtue, and uplift grew out of Victorian conventions that might be appropriate for old-style artisans who identified with their social betters but were jarringly out of place in an increasingly class-conscious labor movement.[10]

By the 1890s, local, state, and federal governments intervened consistently on behalf of management, often with military force. Violent repression of organized labor during the Homestead steel strike of 1892 and the Pullman railroad strike of 1894 helped dispel illusions of mutual interest between sturdy tradesmen and paternalistic owners. Moreover, businessmen mechanized their plants, wresting skill away from workers and placing it in the hands of managers. Many laborers now had lost control over the production process, and they were easily replaced by immigrant, unskilled, and less well educated workers.[11]

These changes brought new challenges to organized labor. Some union leaders like Samuel Gompers, president of the American Federation of Labor (1886), made their peace with capitalism. The AFL's "business unionism" assumed that ownership of productive property would remain in private hands but that workers—organized according to their trades—would use their collective power to garner the highest possible wages. Moreover, the AFL chose to organize mainly skilled workers into unions based on craft—cigar makers in one organization, carpenters in another—each with a loose affiliation to the larger Federation. Such an organizational structure was designed to make incremental gains, not to promote class-wide solidarity.[12]

At the same time, industrial unions appeared. For example, the United Mine Workers of America, founded in 1890, sought to organize all who worked in coal mines, regardless of their skills. Even more militant in the mining country were the Western Federation of Miners (1893) and eventually the Industrial Workers of the World (1905). Similarly, Eugene Debs, who lost his faith in the brotherhoods and in American capitalism, founded the American Railway Union along industrial lines in 1893. Such organizations reflected a growing class consciousness among many American laborers. As corporations grew larger and more hierarchical, the image of workers and owners united as fellow producers seemed ludicrous. Indeed, many laborers now saw themselves in opposition to business. Debs abandoned the railroad brotherhoods because they included only a quarter of all railroad workers; if relations between capital and labor were in fact antagonistic, not paternalistic, then organizing all workers along industrial lines made sense.[13]

The first Mother Jones spoke a republican language that came straight out of the early labor movement. The dignity of honest toil, workers' freedom to better themselves, their pride in helping the nation progress, their sense that work conferred rights, the importance of honorable family life, all resonated for the labor movement into the twentieth century. Mary Jones imbibed this ideology and invoked its republican themes throughout her life. But unlike the first Mother Jones, she eschewed sentimentality and mawkishness. And like early laborites going back to the mid-nineteenth century, she enlisted republicanism in the cause of radical social transformation.[14]

Becoming Mother Jones

The exact date Mother Mary Jones first appeared remains a mystery. Her autobiography says 1877; sometimes she implied an even earlier date. Venerability was a key part of her legend, a legend she masterfully polished over the years. Of course she never mentioned the first

Mother Jones; to do so would muddy her claim to a history stretching deep into the nineteenth century. Mary Jones's role in any labor struggle before the 1890s could not have been a central one, but this very obscurity allowed her to create the legend of Mother Jones and enhance the drama of her appearance on the public stage.[15]

The first newspaper notice of Mary Jones came from her involvement with Coxey's Army in 1894. The depression that began in 1893 lasted four long years. Those workers who managed to keep their jobs saw their pay cut drastically. Beggars and the homeless were everywhere. Businessmen, academics, and journalists urged self-reliance, arguing that laws of laissez-faire economics and the Darwinian struggle for survival dictated that the crisis be allowed to run its course. Pundits insisted that charity be given sparingly to protect the poor's ambition.[16]

Even before the depression, Edward Bellamy's *Looking Backward* dared to imagine an America without private corporations, where productive property had been taken over and run by the state. Bellamy became an instant celebrity, his novel a best-seller, and Bellamite clubs sprang up across the country. Other books, like Henry George's *Progress and Poverty* and Henry Demarest Lloyd's *Wealth against Commonwealth,* questioned the concentration of capital. And in politics, the People's Party began to mount a serious challenge to the Democrats and Republicans.[17]

In the spring of 1894, as the depression deepened, Jacob Coxey, a small-business owner from Massillon, Ohio, organized a remarkable movement. He wanted the government to create jobs for the unemployed. Coxey and his followers were dismissed as "cranks"—crazy, wild, and dangerous. Yet thousands of the unemployed took up Coxey's idea, and leaders emerged who organized a march to Washington, D.C. Columns of poor men on the road frightened many local townsfolk. But others empathized with Coxey's "Army," as the newspapers called it, and they supplied the food and transportation that kept the men heading east.[18]

Mary Jones was one of the volunteers who aided the men. She traveled with two hundred of them down the Missouri Valley toward Kansas City. The depression struck hard in the West, and despite the words of politicians invoking "frontier" initiative and self-reliance, many found themselves desperate for work. For such men, Mary Jones, the "mother of the commonwealers," as *The Kansas City Star* called her, gave speeches, raised money, and helped bolster morale. She told a story a few years later about those hungry men: "You see that camp below," she said to a group of them as they looked down from the bluffs to an outpost of the federal army. "Well, the food that is there you men helped to produce, and as you are boys of Uncle Sam's as well as those uniformed fellows you are entitled to it; go and get it." The hungry Coxeyites swooped down and had their fill.[19]

Coxey's march, however, was only partly successful. Most of the marchers never made it to Washington. As Mary Jones's group camped in Kansas City, their leader, "General" Henry Bennett, absconded with the treasury of $108, which had been raised from the local Populist convention to purchase boats for the trip downriver. Nonetheless, a core of men vowed to continue, so Mary Jones kept a day or two ahead of them, raising money and provisions all the way to St. Louis. It is impossible to know if her group made it all the way, but their hardships were not unusual. Only a few hundred marched in Washington on May Day, 1894, though thousands of citizens, many of them sympathetic, looked on. The marchers' request for a jobs program was ignored, they were quickly disbanded by the police, and their leaders arrested. Coxey's men headed home as best they could. Still, they had captured the nation's attention. And Mary Jones was now on the road, where she would stay for thirty years.[20]

Almost simultaneous with Coxey's march, the new United Mine Workers began a nationwide coal strike in April 1894. To everyone's surprise, 125,000 miners walked off the job. The strike grew especially militant in Alabama, largely over the issue of convict labor. The *Chicago Tribune* reported on April 24 a "monster parade" in Birmingham, five thousand strong: "For the first time in this district, no distinction as to color was made. Negroes marched in companies sandwiched between the white men. A negro and a white miner carried a banner to which was inscribed, 'The Convicts Must Go.' "[21]

By June, the coal strike had started to lose momentum, but just then, Eugene Debs's ARU began a massive railroad strike, precipitated by the Pullman Palace Car Company. Injunctions were quickly issued,

Debs imprisoned, the ARU broken, and federal troops forced the men back to work—but not before the two strikes, against coal and trains, briefly merged into one impressive show of solidarity.[22]

Mary Jones observed these events from Alabama: "There was a long drawn out fight," she recalls in her autobiography. "I was forbidden to leave town without a permit, forbidden to hold meetings. Nevertheless, I slipped through the ranks of the soldiers without their knowing who I was—just an old woman going to a missionary meeting to knit mittens for the heathens of Africa." Although the state militia had stopped the coal strike in Alabama by July, she had witnessed firsthand the power of industrial unions and the promise of solidarity across racial lines.[23]

When Debs was finally released from prison in 1896, Mary Jones orchestrated a show of support for him by thousands of Birmingham workers: "The train pulled in and Debs got off. . . . Those miners did not wait for the gates to open but jumped over the railing. They put him on their shoulders and marched out of the station . . . through the street, past the railway office, the mayors office, the office of the chief of police. 'Debs is here! Debs is here!' they shouted." That night, "the crowd heard a real sermon by a preacher whose message was one of human brotherhood." Debs, too, recalled the incident years after it occurred, but in his telling, it was Mother Jones who carried the day:

> I was informed that the meeting I was to address had been forbidden by the authorities; that the opera house which had been engaged was closed by order of the police board. Mother Jones, hearing of those orders, hurriedly marshaled her forces and notified the authorities that the meeting would be held as advertised and that if the doors were not open they would be opened. . . . The authorities hastily convened in special session, reconsidered their action, ordered the doors opened and instructed the police force to see that there was no interference with the meeting.

This was Debs's first encounter with Mother Jones, whom he called a "modern Joan of Arc."[24]

It was a fortuitous meeting. Debs had returned to Birmingham to preach the socialist gospel to which he had been converted in prison. He and Mother Jones were groping their way toward a new vision of the world. Neither was given to ideological abstractions; both were inclined to organize workers, not write treatises; both sought emotionally satisfying ways of reimagining politics and revitalizing American liberties.[25]

Socialism gained much of its energy from American populism, a movement Mary Jones also followed. Originating in the Farmers' Alliances of the 1870s and 1880s, the Populist (or People's) Party encompassed a wide range of political ideas, but all shared disaffection from mainstream Democrats and Republicans. Strongest in the South and Midwest, the Party included small farmers and laborers who suffered most in the depression of the early 1890s. Populists were fiercely anti-monopoly. Some sought to restore pre-corporate, rural, and small-town America. But the People's Party also had committed socialists like Thomas Morgan and Henry Demarest Lloyd of Chicago, who supported government ownership of basic industries. The movement emphasized mass participation in organizing and decision making. This must have appealed to Mary Jones, for at the core of her work for the next thirty years was her belief that workers must engage in debate, education, cooperation, that only together, democratically, could they create a just world.[26]

We know very little about Mary Jones's involvement with the Populists; we have no evidence beyond her brief mention of attending the disastrous 1896 People's Party Convention in St. Louis. "I remember it so well," she wrote in a 1913 letter to Caroline Lloyd, Henry Demarest Lloyd's sister. As was her habit, Mary Jones placed herself at the center of the action. "Mother," Lloyd allegedly said on the floor of the convention, "this is the last of the Populist movement, this is its funeral." The struggle for the soul of the People's Party in 1896 was won by the conservatives, including office seekers and AFL-style unionists, who were willing to merge with the Democratic Party and to nominate William Jennings Bryan under the reformist policy of "free coinage of silver," a cheap monetary fix rather than a fundamental economic change. With Bryan's defeat in November, populism was all but dead.[27]

But perhaps the greatest influence on Mary Jones as she transformed herself into Mother Jones was Julius Wayland. One historian has called him the Tom Paine of the 1890s. Wayland was born dirt-poor in Versailles, Indiana. Despite only two years of formal education, he prospered as a printer, started his own newspaper, moved to Pueblo, Colorado, speculated in real estate, and by age thirty-six in 1890, had amassed a small fortune. His politics were pro-business, conservative, Republican.[28]

A rags-to-riches businessman, Wayland was an apostle of the old producer ideal, for it promised the ultimate goal, autonomy. But autonomy was deeply threatened in Pueblo, Colorado, late in the nineteenth century. A mining boom caused that city's population to grow tenfold in a few years, and the presence of enormous companies, controlling the local economy and bringing in thousands of poor laborers to live in company towns, made a mockery of the republican faith of men like Wayland. Under these conditions, populism got an early and fierce start in Colorado. If not scientific socialism, with its intellectual sophistication (and ideological hairsplitting), homegrown antimonopolism grew strong in the Rocky Mountains. As Wayland told it, a Pueblo shoemaker gave him a handful of pamphlets, including Lawrence Grunland's *Cooperative Commonwealth*. He read these and saw the light.[29]

Wayland returned to Indiana, and in 1893, he launched a newspaper, *The Coming Nation*, to convert people to socialism. He had begun a heartland crusade, not always ideologically consistent, sometimes pragmatic to a fault, but committed to curing Americans of their political myopia. Wayland was a propagandist; he wrote in short, clipped paragraphs, and his epigrammatic style was designed for people who felt betrayed by railroads and other large corporations, but had neither the time nor the patience for Karl Marx. This was guerrilla journalism, coruscating with outrage. Its emotional power came from a sense of loss for the small-town individualism, the Protestant morality, and the free-labor economics that corporate rapaciousness destroyed.[30]

The Coming Nation was an instant success, and in 1894, Wayland announced that he would plow his profits into a communal living experiment. Three years before the ill-fated Social Democracy for America idea, Wayland acquired land in central Tennessee, named his colony

Ruskin for the English social critic John Ruskin, and brought in set-tlers. Utopian colonies had a long history in America, and like most of the dozens that had been founded in the nineteenth century, Ruskin soon foundered on clashes of personality, differences over ideology, and ultimately lack of money. Mary Jones visited Ruskin; probably that was where she met Wayland. She decided not to join. Personal and ideological differences soon caused Wayland himself to withdraw from his experiment and leave *The Coming Nation* in the hands of the colonists.[31]

Wayland launched another newspaper, the *Appeal to Reason*, in 1896. His ideas captured Mary Jones's imagination, and she offered to help him. In her telling of the story thirty years later, she played the pivotal role in making the *Appeal* a success:

> "We have no subscribers," said Wayland.
>
> "I'll get them," said I. "Get out your first edition and I'll see that it has subscribers enough to pay for it."
>
> He got out a limited first edition and with it as a sam-ple I went to the Federal Barracks at Omaha and secured a subscription from almost every lad there. Soldiers are the sons of working people and need to know it. I went down to the City Hall and got a lot of subscriptions. In a short time I had gathered several hundred subscriptions and the paper was launched.

It was a vintage depiction of herself—while others fumbled, she took practical action, got out among the people, made converts.[32]

It would be hard to overestimate the importance of the *Appeal to Reason* over the next two decades for the American left and for Mother Jones. Produced in Girard, Kansas, the *Appeal* had become the nation's leading radical publication by 1900 and perhaps America's most widely disseminated political weekly. Circulation peaked at three-quarter mil-lion subscribers in 1913 (particular issues hit one million), a figure that has never been equaled among leftist American periodicals. Debs, who became a contributing editor, declared, "Wherever the *Appeal* is at work, and that seems everywhere, socialism has at least a nucleus and the light is spreading." The *Appeal to Reason,* Debs concluded, "literally was honey-combing capitalism." Others agreed. Early on, Wayland began addressing his columns "Dear Comrade" and signing them "Yours for the Revolution." The habit caught on with his readers. The novelist Jack London, himself a Socialist, observed in 1905 that nearly a million Americans began their letters "Dear Comrade" and ended them "Yours for the Revolution."[33]

Mother Jones became one of the *Appeal*'s main subjects in coming years. Stories about her work in the coal wars of West Virginia and Colorado were among the newspaper's biggest stories. Friendship and politics converged. Wayland wrote that he "learned to love her great heart and grey hairs" back when she stayed with his family in Girard during the winter and spring of 1898–1899, and Mother Jones reminisced in a letter to Wayland's son Walter twenty years later how she and Julius would stay up late into the night, discussing Voltaire, Victor Hugo, and Thomas Paine. From those early days with the *Appeal,* she went out to the coalfields and the textile mills, then returned to Girard for brief stays until Julius's passing in 1912.[34]

Mary Jones, then, created her new persona during a particular moment of radical ferment. Mother Jones, the United Mine Workers, and the Socialist Party all emerged at roughly the same time. Individuals like Debs, Wayland, and Mary Jones invented a new American radicalism, one as comfortable in Kansas and Indiana as in New York and Chicago. Homegrown American radicals were not steeped in the writings of Marx and his commentators; their ideas were shaped by popular authors with a socialist or unionist bent, writers who sought economic transformation while preserving, paradoxically, American freedom, democracy, and individualism. Mary Jones felt right at home in this heartland radicalism.[35]

So there is no easy answer to how or when Mary Jones became Mother Jones. All we have really are hints of her early associations: the Knights of Labor, Coxey's Army, the Populist Party, the American Railway Union, the United Mine Workers, and the *Appeal to Reason.* We can say with certainty that by the end of the 1890s, she had *become* Mother Jones, had embraced the name and embellished the persona. Once she did that—constructed her appearance, her speech, her public demeanor, learned to tailor that persona to the needs and expectations of her audiences—her real career was launched.

Coal

Coal powered America's industrial revolution. It ran steam engines and supplied the concentrated heat for fabricating iron and steel— iron for carriages, rails, boilers; steel for structural I beams, engines, automobiles. In 1840, 7,000 men mined coal in America; in 1870, there were 186,000 miners; in 1900, that number multiplied nearly fourfold to 677,000. The coal they dug grew from less than 2 million tons in 1840, to 37 million tons in 1870, to 350 million tons in 1900.[36]

Coal powered technological changes that altered American culture forever. It enabled locomotives to smash ancient conceptions of time and skyscrapers to change forever our ideas about space. It facilitated the transformation of America from a land of small businesses and farms to one where corporations dominated the economy. Coal enabled change, and the coal industry provides an excellent example of these transformations.[37]

Coal mining in the years after the Civil War was skilled but dangerous work. Until late in the nineteenth century, most of America's coal miners were immigrants from Ireland, Scotland, Wales, and England. Deep underground by the light of flames, they practiced the old techniques for undercutting, scoring, and blasting a coal seam.[38]

Ownership of coal mines was never as concentrated as ownership in the oil industry, where John D. Rockefeller's Standard Oil Company controlled 90 percent of the market. But by the beginning of the twentieth century, mining had consolidated. In Colorado, for example, the Victor Coal Company and the Colorado Fuel and Iron Company (which Rockefeller controlled) mined most of the coal. In 1900, no firm owned more than 3 percent of the total national market; but out of America's one hundred largest corporations, a dozen were mining companies. Most important, since coal was heavy, bulky, and difficult to ship, a handful of companies could control a regional market and become an oligopoly.[39]

Because the demand for coal increased so rapidly, operators needed ways of getting it out quickly and dependably. The key was to make each miner more easily replaceable. For example, the difficult task of scoring coal by hand was obviated by cutting machines. Whereas nineteenth-century miners exercised considerable control over their time, deciding when to take a few hours or even a day off, by 1900 operators had tightened discipline. Each man was paid according to how much coal he loaded, but most miners were expected to enter and leave the mine at prescribed times, sometimes for ten- or even twelve-hour shifts.[40]

The growing demand for coal and the simplification of mining also helped change the ethnic makeup of the miners. Many of the southern and eastern Europeans who began migrating to America in the 1880s ended up in the mine country, alongside the descendants of the old British miners. Hungarians, Italians, Slavs, and their descendants poured into the coalfields of western Pennsylvania, Ohio, Indiana, Illinois, West Virginia, and Colorado in search of work. In 1905, nearly half of America's coal miners were "new immigrants."[41]

The American-born population in the mines changed, too. In West Virginia, the same international processes of market expansion and industrialization that cast European peasants adrift sent many Appalachian mountaineers to the mines. In addition, thousands of African Americans left the old plantation lands seeking employment. At the turn of the century, half of the coal miners in Alabama were black, a quarter of those in West Virginia, and almost one out of ten nationwide.[42]

Such changes had enormous implications. Many of the old Scottish, English, and Irish hands of the 1870s and 1880s became mine superintendents, inspectors, operators, even union officials. Moreover, ethnic diversity made it doubly difficult for unions to organize the miners. And the surplus of new workers imposed labor discipline, because men easily replaced were less inclined to make demands on management.[43]

Mining was an extraordinarily dangerous occupation. Fifty thousand coal miners died in industrial accidents between 1870 and 1914. The most common killers were collapsed roofs and cave-ins; more men were crushed by coal cars moving freight in and out of the mines.

Blasting mishaps as well as methane or coal-dust explosions accounted for still more dead. In the worst accidents, bodies were counted by the score. Less dramatic but no less devastating were black lung, rheumatism, and emphysema. If mining coal was inherently dangerous, it was doubly so in the United States. In the first decades of the twentieth century, over 3.3 miners per thousand died annually, a figure triple that of western European countries.[44]

Women rarely worked in the mines in America—superstitions proscribed their entry. They ran the domestic economy and often sought employment outside the home to maintain a decent family wage. Children were part of the family economy as well, working at home tasks like cleaning, cooking, and child care. But more and more of them had entered the cash economy by the end of the century. Textile and sewing mills often opened near the mines to take advantage of the large pool of unmarried daughters. Boys worked with their fathers, sometimes before the age of ten. Parents would lie about their children's ages because the small incomes of trap boys (who opened and closed the doors for mules carrying their cargoes out of the mines), breaker boys (who worked above ground sorting the coal from slate), and mill girls could be the difference between starving and surviving. In many mining towns, child labor became a way of life.[45]

The mining towns themselves were a unique feature of coal culture. Most coal mines were isolated, so companies built housing and opened their own stores. Necessity proved advantageous to the operators; company stores became sources of enormous profit because isolation made it impossible for people to shop elsewhere and because company rules forbade rival stores. Local farmers or itinerant peddlers who tried to sell to miners were thrown off company property. Many mines even paid their employees in scrip, slips of paper declaring that the bearer was owed so much worth of goods at the company store.[46]

Miners resisted these conditions. In 1868, even before they formed a union, Pennsylvania miners laid down their tools until the owners agreed to abide by an eight-hour law that was pending before the state legislature. The strike resulted in a compromise, not a limited workday but a pay increase of 10 percent. This successful action spurred thousands to join the Workingmen's Benevolent Association in the 1870s.

But Franklin Gowen, president of the Reading Railroad—which not only owned the coal lands but also controlled transportation in and out of the mine country of eastern Pennsylvania—was determined to break the union. In 1876, with the help of a Pinkerton agent named James McParlan, Gowen—who was also prosecuting attorney for Schuylkill County—brought charges against twenty Workingmen's Benevolent Association members, claiming that they were part of a secret Irish terrorist gang, the Molly Maguires, and that they had murdered a mine owner and several foremen. With sensational testimony from McParlan, most of it probably false, Gowen not only secured the conviction and execution of the accused but also linked the Mollys to the Workingmen's Benevolent Association. By connecting labor organizing with terrorism, Gowen sent the union reeling, and the deep depression of the 1870s dealt it a death blow.[47]

The Knights of Labor took their turn in the mine country during the 1880s. Seeking to restore a society of small-scale, autonomous farms and shops, the Knights embraced all "producers." Their inclusiveness even extended to women and blacks. Bringing farmers, small businessmen, merchants, artisans, and laborers into a single organization was unwieldy at best. And the Knights' official policy against striking—they favored boards of arbitration and conciliation—was a little genteel for the brutal business of mining.[48]

In 1885, the Knights created National Trades Assembly 135, an affiliate just for miners, and that same year, a new organization, the National Federation of Miners and Mine Laborers, was also formed. The two unions were quite similar. Both called for production quotas to prop up the market, the eight-hour day, abolition of company stores, and immigration restrictions. But their insistence on arbitration evaded the confrontational nature of the industry. Worse, two miners unions were not better than one; they spent more time battling each other than fighting the coal companies.[49]

In January 1890, the United Mine Workers of America emerged. UMW members could affiliate with either of the nation's two largest unions, the Knights of Labor or the American Federation of Labor. The Knights were already in decline, and within a few years, the UMW became nominally part of the AFL, though it retained considerable autonomy, and was the only industrial union in the Federation. The new organization sidestepped many divisive issues to concentrate on those that united the miners. For the first few years, the UMW hedged its position on strikes versus arbitration, then in 1894, in the midst of the depression, plunged into a disastrous nationwide strike that almost destroyed it (the same strike that found Mary Jones in Birmingham, Alabama). The union survived its first decade, though sometimes with under ten thousand members. It quickly disavowed the Knights' old dream of a producers' commonwealth, confronted operators directly for improvement in working conditions, and struck when necessary. Despite plenty of racism and immigrant bashing, the UMW was generally more open to all workers in the industry than other unions.[50]

From its rocky start, the UMW quickly became the largest, most powerful, and most embattled union in the country, a status it would hold for decades. One of the keys to success was fielding organizers who could explain the union's mission to mine families. In Mother Jones, the UMW found someone with remarkable energy, eloquence, and unquenchable passion.[51]

John Brophy, a young miner from Pennsylvania who later became a UMW official, remembered seeing Mother Jones for the first time in the late 1890s:

> She came into the mine one day and talked to us in our workplace in the vernacular of the mines. How she got in I don't know; probably just walked in and defied anyone to stop her. When I first knew her, she was in her late middle age, a woman of medium height, very sturdily built but not fat. She dressed conventionally, and was not at all unusual in appearance.

It would have been hard for the miners to ignore her:

> She would take a drink with the boys and spoke their idiom, including some pretty rough language when she was talking about the bosses. This might have been considered a little fast in ordinary women, but the miners knew

and respected her. They might think her a little queer, perhaps—it *was* an odd kind of work for a woman in those days—but they knew she was a good soul and a friend of those who most lacked friends.

A labor organizer's goal was simple enough—persuading workers to join the union. In part it was a job of educating families and small groups. Organizers usually got to know the workers in their gathering places, spoke to them personally, gave them literature to read. All this sounds ordinary enough, until we picture our organizer, neither male nor a former miner, but an old woman, drinking with the boys, telling off-color stories, and "talking union."[52]

Oratory was an important tool, especially when it came time to establish a union local. Brophy recalled Mother Jones's style:

> When she started to speak, she could carry an audience of miners with her every time. Her voice was low and pleasant, with great carrying power. She didn't become shrill when she got excited; instead her voice dropped in pitch and the intensity of it became something you could almost feel physically.

Good organizers appealed not just to the head with rational arguments; they moved men and women emotionally, motivated them to take risks. Mother Jones succeeded not only because she was a great orator in a golden age of oratory. Equally important was her commitment. Again, John Brophy:

> She had a complete disregard for danger or hardship and would go in wherever she thought she was needed. And she cared no more about approval from union leaders than operators; wherever people were in trouble, she showed up to lead the fight with tireless devotion. With all this, she was no fanatic. She had a lively sense of humor— she could tell wonderful stories, usually at the expense of some boss, for she couldn't resist the temptation to agi-

tate, even in a joke—and she exuded a warm friendliness
and human sympathy.

And always, always she was with her people.[53]

Mother Jones and the United Mine Workers found each other at
just the right moment. She had drifted from one cause to another for
several years now. From the late 1890s until the early 1920s, she spent
more time as a "walking delegate"—an organizer—with the coal miners than with the workers of any other trade. Mother Jones tramping
the dusty back roads, heading to yet another rally, was one of the most
vivid collective memories of the mine country.[54]

Exactly how she became involved with the UMW remains obscure.
Some newspapers reported, erroneously, that her husband was a miner
who had been killed on the job. Perhaps she was attracted to coal mining because the industry had such great promise in the labor movement. In any given year after 1890, from half a million to a million men
mined coal, and many of them were eager to join the union. More
than any other field, such as steel or petroleum, coal seemed ripe for
aggressive organizing along industrial lines. Harsh conditions made
the mine country a place for militants and gave coal mining a rough
poetry. Crude exploitation heightened the drama of men burrowing
into the earth to bring out the rocks that burn. There was a romance to
coal that appealed to Mother Jones. And she probably felt comfortable
with many UMW officials because they were Irish.[55]

At the turn of the century, the union staged two spectacular organizing drives. When they ended, the Mine Workers had over 300,000
members, making it the largest and most progressive union in America.

The Great Anthracite Strikes

On July 4, 1897, just three weeks after the first Social Democracy for
America meeting in Chicago, the United Mine Workers called a nationwide strike of bituminous (soft coal) workers. The UMW was down
to only nine thousand members when coal operators asked the miners

to take a 20 percent cut in pay. But tens of thousands of men laid down their tools, and coal production was cut to a trickle. In the Pittsburgh area alone, twenty thousand miners who worked ten to twelve hours a day for about fifty cents a ton walked off the job.[56]

The problem for such a small, weak union was how to feed and house families and keep the strike going. Mother Jones brought to western Pennsylvania the same talent for impromptu organizing that she had used with Coxey's Army. She visited farmers and asked them to donate food, then she helped escort their wagons to "Camp Determination," the strike headquarters near Turtle Creek. She invited the wives of workers and farmers to "pound parties," where the price of admission was a pound of food or other supplies. And, of course, she gave speeches and staged rallies to buoy the miners' spirits. She had a gift for pageantry, for dramatic gestures—she staged parades of children, for example, in which one was crowned queen of the strikers. Perhaps most important, she brought women into the strike. She gave expression to a particular ideal of womanhood, of militant, working-class mothers fighting for their families. The *National Labor Tribune* concluded, "She has done more missionary work for miners of the Pittsburgh district than any two of the [UMW] officials and done it better. . . . To her, more than anyone else, the miners owe much of their success in this unpleasantness."[57]

Mother Jones's efforts around Pittsburgh contributed to a much larger victory. The strike that ended in January 1898 overturned the pay cut that the operators had tried to impose; instead, the miners got a small raise. More important, the strike made the old bituminous Central Competitive Field (western Pennsylvania, Ohio, Indiana, and Illinois) a single unit for bargaining between the UMW and the operators. This worked to the operators' advantage as well as the miners'. No enormous companies dominated this field, and owners needed a way of stopping cutthroat competition and wildcat strikes. Recognizing the union stabilized the market and allowed the operators to act as a cartel. One estimate claimed that wages nearly doubled between 1897 and 1903 in the Central Competitive Field, from an average of $270 per year to $522. Miners won the eight-hour day, the checkoff of union dues, and most important, a revivified UMW, now with over a hundred thousand members. The bargain excluded the anthracite (hard coal) miners of eastern Pennsylvania and the new fields of West Virginia, whose cheap, plentiful bituminous coal constantly threatened the Central Competitive Field. But the 1898 Interstate Joint Agreement created stable markets for Midwestern miners and operators until the 1920s.[58]

With the Central Competitive Field organized, the UMW turned its attention to anthracite country. Anthracite is solid carbon, pure and hard. It burns hot for smelting iron and smoke-free for heating homes. Industrialization meant rapidly increased demand for anthracite, and production quadrupled between 1870 and the new century.[59]

Anthracite country had witnessed bursts of labor militancy for decades, but the operators remained firmly in control until the end of the century. Then, just as the bituminous miners of the Midwest attained unprecedented solidarity, a wildcat strike near Hazleton ignited eastern Pennsylvania. On September 10, 1897, three hundred men marched peacefully toward the mines of Lattimer. Armed deputies blocked the road, strikers refused to turn back, and the guards shot and killed nineteen workers. The "Lattimer Massacre" galvanized the miners, and the UMW organized aggressively for the next three years. The union called a strike in the fall of 1900, and 120,000 miners walked out for six weeks. Then in May 1902, almost 150,000 men struck for nearly half a year.[60]

The anthracite fields, like the bituminous ones, had witnessed an ethnic succession from British to eastern and southern European laborers. In 1900, half the mine families were immigrants (Poles, Lithuanians, and over a dozen other nationalities) or the children of immigrants. Companies recruited them because they demanded little; magazine articles routinely commented on how slothful, dirty, and unintelligent these new "races" were.[61]

In fact, immigrants were well attuned to labor-management issues and understood that the companies exploited them. The UMW hired Slavic organizers, and the *United Mine Workers Journal* began publishing stories in languages other than English. Leaders like "Big Mary" Septek, who led marches against strikebreakers, emerged. With the Lattimer Massacre, labor militancy increased among the rank and file, and workers often pushed the union leadership toward greater activism. When the great anthracite strikes of 1900 and 1902 finally began, it was militant miners who led the way, while the union leadership raced to catch up.[62]

UMW officials were cautious because they feared that the odds against a successful strike were immense. Only a tiny fraction of anthracite miners had joined the union. Moreover, the men were divided by skill levels, pay scales, local loyalties, and ethnicity. Unionism's history of failure also divided the men, with older miners recounting how golden ideals of solidarity in the past had turned to defeat and humiliation. In addition, union leaders were painfully aware that the depres-

4. Coal miners near Scranton, Pennsylvania. The anthracite strikes were among the great early victories of the United Mine Workers, and Mother Jones's organizing efforts led the way (Courtesy State Historical Society of Wisconsin)

sion of the 1890s left an oversupply of both labor and coal. Finally, the operators' cartel looked ominously united, for after a series of buyouts, the entire region was under the financial control of J. P. Morgan.[63]

The UMW's young president, John Mitchell, was temperamentally and ideologically inclined toward negotiation, toward making agreements with businessmen. He opposed socialism, accepted capitalists' ownership of property. "I am a strict trade-unionist," he declared. "I believe in progress slowly—by evolution rather than revolution. I believe a better day is in store for the American workingman, but it has to come through no radical change in the organization of human society. It must come one step at a time, and through a slow upward movement, by his own efforts." Recognizing Mother Jones's effectiveness, he agreed to make her an "international organizer," a title she held for most of the next twenty years. Yet the two were very different, for she represented the left wing of the UMW. Still, there was genuine affection and respect between Jones and Mitchell. The metaphor of mother and son pervaded their letters, and in the early years, a creative tension resulted from their ideological and temperamental differences.[64]

The leadership's conservatism notwithstanding, a series of wildcat strikes pushed the UMW toward a full-scale walkout. One of these began in August 1899 in Arnot, Pennsylvania, but within a month the men were ready to give up. Mother Jones arrived in town, held a meeting, then went to her room for the night. A coal company owned the boardinghouse and, discovering her presence, turned her out. A local mining family took her in and, for their pains, were evicted from their company-owned cabin the following morning. Mother Jones brought them to her next rally, talked about their plight, and later declared that it was the sight of this homeless family, with all their furniture and children and holy pictures loaded onto a wagon, that turned the tide.[65]

When companies brought in strikebreakers, Mother Jones organized the miners' wives into "mop and broom" brigades, which shamed and intimidated scabs out of the mines. She remembered those women a quarter century later: "The women kept continual watch of the mines to see that the company did not bring in scabs. Every day women with brooms or mops in one hand and babies in the other arm wrapped in little blankets, went to the mines and watched that no one went in.

And all night long they kept watch. They were heroic women. In the long years to come the nation will pay them high tribute for they were fighting for the advancement of a great country." The operators saw it differently. They considered it grossly unjust that "outsiders," "foreigners," like Mother Jones had such influence with their workers. *The New York Times* agreed, condemning agitators who aroused the miners' passions and persuaded them to quit work.[66]

The companies urged local farmers not to help the strikers, so Mother Jones went out in an old wagon with "a union mule that had gone on strike" and a miner's son for a driver and held meetings in the country. She would return to the coal camps, her wagon bearing the produce of sympathetic farmers. "Sometimes it was twelve or one o'clock in the morning when I would get home," she recalled, "the little boy asleep on my arm and I driving the mule. Sometimes it was several degrees below zero. The winds whistled down the mountains and drove the snow and sleet in our faces." Even with the kindness of strangers, these were difficult times: "We were all living on dry bread and black coffee. I slept in a room that never had a fire in it, and I often woke up in the morning to find snow covering the outside covers of the bed." Still, the strikers held on. Farmers kept feeding the hungry, and residents of nearby towns put up families evicted from company housing.[67]

William Wilson, president of UMW District 2 in eastern Pennsylvania, was a former anthracite miner, and later, America's first Secretary of Labor. Mother Jones told how representatives of the operators came to Wilson's home and offered him thousands of dollars to sell out his men. She quoted Wilson's reply: "Gentlemen, if you come to visit my family, the hospitality of the whole house is yours. But if you come to bribe me with dollars to betray my manhood and my brothers who trust me, I want you to leave this door and never come here again." As the strike went on, Wilson opened his home to evicted miners, shared everything he had with their families. If the mop-and-broom brigades represented Mother Jones's ideal of working-class womanhood, Wilson here embodied her laborite model of manhood: loyalty to one's brothers, to one's class, and to collective betterment.[68]

The strike, which seemed doomed when Mother Jones arrived, ended with modest gains for the union early in 1900. Hundreds of mining families came to Blossburg on a bitter snowy night to pay tribute to her. "It was one night of real joy and a great celebration," she recalled. "I bade them all good bye. A little boy called out, 'Don't leave us, Mother. Don't leave us!' The dear little children kissed my hands." She moved on to the mines at Elkton, Frostburg, and Lonaconing in Maryland.[69]

By 1900, the UMW had a handful of seasoned organizers who moved in and out of the districts as needed. They each drew a regular salary, approved by the union's executive board. Mother Jones made five hundred dollars in 1900, though sometimes she had to use her own money to rent halls and pay the bills for local rallies. She earned her pay. In the five days between September 13 and September 17, 1900, for example, she held meetings across the Pennsylvania anthracite country, in Girardville, Ashland, Mahonoy City, Forestville, Locust Gap, Shamokin, and Pottsville. She was everywhere, exhorting, shaming, pleading with the miners.[70]

Mother Jones was developing her distinct speaking style, and her signature technique was telling stories about herself. Always there was some hapless foil against whom she set herself:

> Not far from Shamokin, in a little mountain town, the priest was holding a meeting when I went in. He was speaking in the church. I spoke in an open field. The priest told the men to go back and obey their masters and their reward would be in Heaven. He denounced the strikers as children of darkness. The miners left the church in a body and marched over to my meeting.
>
> "Boys," I said, "this strike is called in order that you and your wives and your little ones may get a bit of Heaven before you die."
>
> We organized the entire camp.

She scoffed at "sky pilots" (priests and ministers) and made the union itself into an object of faith. "Labor must be its own religion," she declared.[71]

Humor helped dispel the fears that workers faced: eviction, unemployment, hunger, defeat. Here, speaking in her slight brogue, she told an Irish joke in the popular idiom of the day:

> An old Irish woman had two sons who were scabs. The women threw one of them over the fence to his mother. He lay there still. His mother thought he was dead and she ran into the house for a bottle of holy water and shook it over Mike.
>
> "Oh for God's sake, come back to life," she hollered. "Come back and join the union."
>
> He opened his eyes and saw our women standing around him.
>
> "Shure, I'll go to hell before I'll scab again," says he.

Scabs and hell, holy water and union.[72]

She inserted dialogue into her stories, and she was especially fond of conversations between herself and more prominent or powerful figures. While John Mitchell slept in Hazleton, she and her women organized the men of Coaldale. Told that Mother Jones was "raising hell up in the mountains with a bunch of wild women," Mitchell spoke to her:

> "My God, Mother, did you get home safe? What did you do?"
>
> "I got five thousand men out and organized them. We had time left over so we organized the street car men and they will not haul any scabs into camp."
>
> "Did you get hurt, Mother?"
>
> "No, we did the hurting."

She polished and honed these stories, for they were her tools to teach and motivate. There were no defeats, only victories. An organizer could not persuade workers to join the union or support a strike by exuding anything but optimism for the future. Mother Jones's task was to tell a vivid story about a brighter future and convince her listeners that the story would come true.[73]

Reality proved messier. Mine owners were not always pusillanimous, local sheriffs did not all cave in. Nor was Mother Jones always so saintly. In her zeal, she often made very negative comments about other organizers, and her attitude toward mine families on occasion could be patronizing: "Send any request to me," she wrote Mitchell. "I am ever ready to help our poor helpless people. Just Say the word and I am off. Suffering Humanity needs our best efforts and we Should not Spare ourselves particularly the Slaves of the Caves need to be Saved."[74]

Still, few would have denied Mother Jones's success in the anthracite region. She marched fifteen miles from McAdoo to Coaldale, Pennsylvania, with a corps of women wearing aprons, brandishing brooms, clanging pans. The sheriff stopped them on the road, foresaw no trouble, and let them pass. But as Mother Jones put it, "an army of strong mining women makes a wonderfully spectacular picture"; they shamed the men of Coaldale out of the mines. In Lattimer, a mop-and-broom brigade created a diversion, while the men slipped in to meet the strikebreakers; local officials were forced to close the mines. Such tactics were controversial. Mitchell allowed Mother Jones to organize the women but disavowed all knowledge of it. Finally, he asked her to stop the practice, fearing that violence committed by or against women was publicity the union could ill afford.[75]

The strike was working, and as winter approached, fears of insufficient fuel to heat eastern homes grew. With the presidential election of 1900 just days away, Mark Hanna, President William McKinley's closest adviser, persuaded the coal companies to settle the strike rather than risk the election of Democrat William Jennings Bryan, no radical but still a man whom businessmen found threatening. The companies agreed and offered a 10 percent raise but withheld union recognition. The UMW accepted, and the agreement lasted for a year and a half. If not completely victorious, the union demonstrated its ability to mobilize miners and to bring real benefits to them.[76]

Mother Jones did not slow down. She helped organize miners' daughters who worked in the silk-weaving mills of Scranton, Pennsylvania, as well as coal miners in Virginia, West Virginia, and Maryland, and she began writing a series of articles about her experiences for the *International Socialist Review*. But soon she was back in anthracite country. As the old agreement expired between the hard-coal miners and the operators, District 2 sanctioned a new strike in May 1902. The men demanded union recognition, and they asked Mitchell to call a national convention authorizing a general strike throughout the entire coal industry, including the Central Competitive Field, whose agreement remained in force for another year. Mitchell opposed violating contracts, resisted calling the convention for as long as he could, then lobbied hard (using money supplied by Hanna) against a general coal strike.[77]

Mother Jones respected Mitchell and owed much to him. She took a conciliatory tone in her speech at the UMW convention in mid-July but also revealed clearly that her sympathies were with the militants. She praised Mitchell and professed her loyalty to him; she endorsed the convention's decision to exercise all peaceful, conservative methods "before you rise and enter the final protest." But she made it clear that her preference would have been for an immediate nationwide coal strike, to show that the miners could halt *all* of American industry. "These fights," she said, "against the oppressor and the capitalists, the ruling classes, must be won if it takes us all to do it." She then proceeded to speak fervently about West Virginia, not Pennsylvania. Clearly she believed that now was the time for the union to consolidate its power over the entire coal industry. She closed by pleading, "Be true to your manhood, be true to your country, be true to children yet unborn"—in other words, be true to the union. After the convention, she returned to Parkersburg, West Virginia, to face trial for violating a court injunction against organizing.[78]

Mitchell won the day; the soft-coal miners of the Central Competitive Field did not go out. Nonetheless, in one of the great strikes in American labor history, over a hundred thousand anthracite workers shut down the hard-coal mines. Mother Jones returned to Pennsylvania and helped rally families to the cause. Harking back to Coxey's Army, she considered organizing a march of the miners' wives to Washington. As the cold weather closed in and fears of a coal shortage rose, the companies indicated their willingness to settle—but only on their own terms. Public opinion had taken a decided turn for the miners, especially after a widely publicized statement by Reading Railroad president George F. Baer: "The rights and interests of the laboring man will be protected and cared for—not by the labor agitators, but by the Christian men to whom God in His infinite wisdom has given the control of the property interests of the country, and upon the successful management of which so much depends." Next to such paternalistic arrogance, Mitchell's pleas for impartial arbitration seemed a model of accommodation.[79]

President Theodore Roosevelt did not like labor unions, but he liked businessmen challenging his authority even less. He wanted a settlement, and the intransigence of the operators led him to insist on arbitration. For the first time, the federal government treated unions not as pariahs but as responsible institutions with which to negotiate. Secretary of War Elihu Root persuaded J. P. Morgan to sidestep the likes of Baer and accept President Roosevelt's plan for an anthracite commission to work out a settlement. Morgan's nonnegotiable demand was that the operators not recognize the union. The commission compromised on wages and hours, set up arbitration boards, and, true to the wishes of management, did not press the issue of union recognition.[80]

The UMW accepted the commission's plan, and the settlement pleased most miners, who were happy to return to work. The national press hailed Mitchell, now head of America's most powerful union, as a hero, a labor statesman. But the settlement infuriated the more radical unionists, and among these, Mother Jones was most vocal. She argued that with winter approaching and anthracite depleted, the operators could have been forced to recognize the UMW as the sole bargaining agent for the hard-coal miners and to accept a working agreement like that operating in the Central Competitive Field. Mitchell, she felt, squandered a golden opportunity.[81]

Years after the settlement, Mother Jones charged that the flattery of Roosevelt and Morgan won over Mitchell. Although they continued to work together, the tension between them deepened, their differences over fundamental philosophy grew sharper. Mitchell argued that the ideal forum for settling disputes was the National Civic Federation, a business-led group created by the former coal operator Mark Hanna, now a U.S. senator and presidential kingmaker. Mother Jones, on the other hand, increasingly felt that workers must depend on no one but themselves. Only by organizing and demonstrating their strength—withholding their labor if necessary and creating shortages—would they receive fair treatment. Unlike Mitchell, she questioned the very legitimacy of a system that allowed a few individuals to own and control the world's wealth.[82]

Mitchell and Mother Jones each read recent history differently. The UMW's great victory in the Central Competitive Field strengthened Mitchell's belief that class conflict was not inevitable, for after the strike, the union and the operators worked out an agreement that brought order to a chaotic market. But for Mother Jones, the lesson of 1897 was that only worker power moved capitalists. She was pleased when the miners won concessions, but her ultimate goal was worker control in industry, the very thing that Mitchell disavowed.[83] Still, the worst of their troubles were in the future. For now, they were two of the most successful labor leaders in America.

★ 4 ★

"There Comes
the Star of Hope"

Coal miners, UMW president John Mitchell declared, "have had no more staunch supporter, no more able defender than the one we all love to call Mother." Mitchell exaggerated—but only a little—when he added, "I don't believe there is a Mine Worker from one end of the country to the other who does not know her name." Mother Jones's star was rising. The newly appointed "International Organizer" addressed the UMW convention in 1901 and laid out her ideas about the future of the United Mine Workers and about the responsibilities of women and men in the coming labor struggles.[1]

It was unjust to deny prerogatives like voting and higher education to American women, Mother Jones declared; their labors earned them the right to participate in public affairs. She asked whether it was appropriate for a woman to be discussing miners' affairs. "Why shouldn't she?" Mother Jones lectured the men in her audience. "Who has a better right? Has she not given you birth? Has she not raised you and cared for you? Has she not struggled along for you? Does she not today, when you come home covered with corporation soot, have hot water and soap and towels ready for you? Does she not have your supper ready for you, and your clean clothes ready for you?"[2]

Women's special gift to civilization was love. Love made their work sacred, and it was the source of their hidden power. She invoked the story of Jesus: "When the Galilean was here did he appeal to men for sympathy, for love? No. When all the world looked dark around him, when men said 'Hang him' Mary and the others stood by him and said 'We love you.' Woman's mission here below is that of love, not that of war, and when the whole world turns you out, you come home to your loving wife, or mother, or sister, and they take you in." But love did not mean passivity. It was women's love for humankind, Mother Jones predicted, that would bring many more like herself into the labor movement.[3]

So mother-love bound families together, and what was the union but an extended family? Unions were not just about men making a little more money; good wages were necessary to raise decent families, to nurture children, to make life fulfilling. Unions taught devotion, selflessness, sacrifice; solidarity meant caring for each other. It was only a short step, of course, to thinking of Mother Jones herself as the matriarch of the family of labor. Her devotion to her children in the movement offered an example of the love they must have for each other, as well as the passion with which they must fight their battles.[4]

If love brought women into the cause, manhood required loyalty to each other and to the union. Any man who betrayed his own organization was "the demon incarnate." Traitors to the union sold their children into industrial slavery and therefore "had not a particle of manhood" in them. Above all, manhood meant resisting oppression. Mother Jones invoked the memory of Patrick Henry, insisted that union men must fight for the American creed, and told them "no battle was ever won for civilization that the jails and the scaffolds did not hold the salt of the earth." And she offered herself as a model of such devotion. She declared that she was going back to organize in West Virginia and hinted that she might confront her own martyrdom on that bloodstained ground: "Before you meet here again it may be that I shall have gone home; that I may be at rest in my grave. I may never again meet you in convention; but I plead with you to be true, to be men, not cringing serfs, and above all, not traitors to your organization."[5]

So women must love, and men must be loyal—rather conventional ideas about gender, but Mother Jones put them in the service of militant labor organizing. The union, she concluded, was far more than a mere economic institution. "It is the school, the college, it is where you learn to know and to love each other and learn to work with each other and bear each other's burdens, each other's sorrows and each other's joys." Again, the union was family, a family under siege by corporations bent on impoverishing the many to enrich the few. More, the union movement, her union movement, was a culture, a way of life. Its founding charter was holy Scripture, its history a chapter in the chronicles of American patriotism.[6]

These were the themes Mother Jones developed in the coming labor struggles, and they helped make her one of the most effective organizers in the country. She would need all of her rhetorical skill for the impending drives in West Virginia and Colorado, where the mine workers faced their greatest challenge yet.

West Virginia

Even as the miners fought in the anthracite country, Mother Jones's heart was in West Virginia. "The man or woman who would witness such scenes as I have witnessed in West Virginia would betray God Almighty if he betrayed those people," she told a UMW convention. "Ah, my brothers, I shall consider it an honor if, when you write my epitaph upon my tombstone, you say 'Died fighting their battles in West Virginia.' " Part of her growing frustration with John Mitchell was his slighting of that state. To concentrate its efforts in eastern Pennsylvania, the UMW pulled resources from West Virginia, which Mother Jones believed was the more important battleground. Although there were three times more miners in the former than the latter, the bituminous mines of West Virginia were vital because they competed directly with the Central Competitive Field. Cheap labor and well-exposed seams allowed West Virginia coal to drive the higher-priced union product from the market. In Mother Jones's view, West Virginia coal was a dagger at the heart of the UMW.[7]

There was a crude, rapacious quality to the state's recent history. Once railroads penetrated the Appalachians, the rush for coal was on.

Judges, amenable to bribes, allowed companies to buy old land grants that the federal government issued to Revolutionary War pensioners a century before. Local constables evicted people who had logged, hunted, and farmed the land for generations, and corporations and syndicates consolidated tens of thousands of acres. Coal production skyrocketed—miners extracted half a million tons in 1867; five million in 1887; ninety million in 1917. Because absentee landowners held over 90 percent of Mingo, Wayne, and Logan Counties by 1900, New York, Boston, and London had become influential in West Virginia's affairs. As the owners of property changed, so did the workforce. In 1880, there were no black miners in West Virginia; twenty years later, there were five thousand; and in 1910, there were twelve thousand, almost all concentrated downstate. Fewer than a thousand European immigrant miners in 1880 had become more than twenty-five thousand by 1910.[8]

The difficult conditions found in other coal regions were most extreme in West Virginia. Between 1890 and 1912, the death rate in West Virginia's coalfields surpassed that in all other mining states; indeed, it exceeded that in the worst European countries fivefold. West Virginia spent less on mine safety per ton of coal extracted than any other state. Moreover, 94 percent of mining families lived in company towns (as high as 98 percent downstate), compared with 53 percent in Illinois. For their pains, miners were rewarded with the lowest pay in the industry, roughly $275 per year. Because companies usually paid in scrip rather than dollars, mine families were forced to spend exorbitant amounts for rent, food, clothes, and supplies.[9]

Equally appalling were politics in West Virginia. Because company towns were not incorporated, they often lacked democratic governments. Where town offices did exist, mine supervisors controlled the mayor and city council, the school superintendent, the local judiciary. Mine guards—armed security agents employed by private detective agencies like the notorious Baldwin-Felts Company—often acted as poll watchers for the operators; sometimes they even pre-marked the miners' ballots. Many West Virginia governors had served as coal company officials, and the operators put their henchmen in key legislative positions. Indeed, the state's chief mine inspector was president and general manager of several companies. Worse, the state failed to enforce its own laws. West Virginia forbade payment in scrip, required a checkweighman on every tipple (a structure at each mine's opening where coal was sorted and weighed), and outlawed the labor of children under fourteen years of age. But any miner who demanded his pay in dollars, or asked that his coal be weighed by a neutral party, or objected to underage breaker boys, found himself unemployed.[10]

By controlling the land around the mines, coal firms restricted freedom of speech and assembly. They routinely confiscated critical newspapers, silenced those who spoke out for unions, and outlawed dissident political parties. Local sheriffs harassed union organizers and forced them out of town, and when the constabulary proved inadequate, private armed guards moved in. Company dollars paid the doctors who delivered miners' babies, the teachers who educated their children, the preachers who ministered to mine families, and the undertakers who buried their dead.[11]

Mother Jones first came to the Mountain State in 1897 as part of the Mine Workers' drive to organize the Central Competitive Field. On July 27, just a few weeks after the bituminous strike began, she participated in a "monster rally" in Charleston, the state capital, joined by AFL president Samuel Gompers, Grand Master Workman James Sovereign of the Knights of Labor, Eugene Debs, and representatives of printers, tailors, railroad trainmen, and workers in other trades. Seventeen thousand people heard them pledge to organize the state's coal mines. She went on to hold large meetings in such towns as Monongah and Flemington in the Fairmont field. West Virginia operators responded with armed guards, strikebreakers, and court injunctions.[12]

Efforts to bring West Virginia into the Central Competitive Field agreements failed in 1897, and the UMW had fewer than four thousand miners in the state when the strike ended. At the turn of the century, a third of the nation's bituminous coal came from West Virginia, but less than 2 percent of UMW members resided there. The United Mine Workers stepped up its efforts once again at the end of 1900, and Mother Jones headed the drive in the southern field. Organizers worked the area slowly over months, quietly talking to the men and their families, and when the time was ripe, Mother Jones came in and held grand rallies. Sometimes she swept whole mining camps into the fold; other times she failed completely.[13]

She pursued her work with boundless energy. The organizer George Scott reported to the *United Mine Workers Journal*, "Often I have murmured and whined and thought the battle not worth the candle. But with a tenacity worthy of emulation she moves on step by step without a complaint. . . . No mountain seems too high, or path too rugged as long as she can find a receptive audience." Mother Jones described in a letter to John Mitchell how she and some of the others were walking down a goat path in the mountains after midnight, heading to their next rally: "I had to slide down most of it. . . . My bones are all sore today." Mitchell cautioned her to take care of herself, even as he reminded her that failure to organize West Virginia this time could spell defeat for Midwestern miners in their next contract.[14]

Fred Mooney, a fellow organizer who traveled with Mother Jones in West Virginia, declared that she "could arouse more fight in men than any speaker I have ever seen behind a rostrum." According to Mooney, she had a special gift for organizing foreign-born miners, with whom she communicated through a combination of broken English, gestures, and "French Classics" (swearing). To set a festive mood and attract attention, she traveled with a band—"Mother Jones' Band" she called it—and later she acquired a phonograph. Sometimes she read from the Declaration of Independence; other times she held up miners' contracts, read passages aloud, told the men that the czar of Russia would be dethroned if he attempted to enforce such tyranny on his subjects. She wrote to John Mitchell that at Kelly's Creek in the Kanawha field, the men called themselves "Mother Jones' Boys." When the mine superintendent expelled them from their jobs, they told him they were free men, exercising the rights that their Revolutionary ancestors died for; then they hooted him down and cheered for Mother Jones. Such incidents energized her, and she predicted to Mitchell early in 1902 that with more money and good assistants, she could organize West Virginia inside a year.[15]

She knew it would not be that simple. Conflicts arose among the organizers. She accused William Warner of corruption, declared that she would leave the field if Thomas Burke interfered with her, and called an organizer named Tinchure "no Gods Earth good." In a letter to Mitchell, she accused a union man named Boskill of being in the hands of the enemy—"I thought that good motherly council might keep him on the right track but some *natures are rotton* to the core." She advised he be fired immediately. Always there was her own virtue and others' perfidy. "I will fight for right even if those traitors stab me to the heart," she wrote UMW secretary William Wilson without further elaboration. Her self-righteousness must have gotten tiresome even to the patient Wilson. Less melodramatically, she confided to him regarding some of her union brothers, "I have come to the conclusion that those fellows don't want a woman in the field." Which fellows? What did they do or say? Unfortunately, she did not provide details.[16]

But Mother Jones loved her work, had found her true calling. She was full of fight, and so were her metaphors. If she administered a tongue-lashing to a mine superintendent, she said she made him "come to time" and then "laid him out." Military phrases also peppered her letters. She "made a raid on Kelly's Creek," for example, where "our people are responding like braves." She added that "after I capture three or four more Strong holds I can move to the Norfolk and Western." She especially enjoyed supervising the union efforts in the southern field. "My boys are doing good work," she reported to Mitchell. "We meet every Monday morning and hold a council—outline our work for the week so that each worker will know where to go and all know where the others are. . . . Every night if we are near each other we gather in the General Managers Room (That's me) and [discuss?] things in general." She grew very fond of many of the organizers, almost all of whom were former miners themselves.[17]

To "Comrade" William Wilson, she wrote that three hundred miners greeted her aboard her train: "All rushed to get my hand and the cry of Mother you are going to stay with us went up from young and old . . . black and white. . . . For all my weary tramps in the dead of night counting the rails on the R R track . . . I would not exchange that meeting for all the palaces or millions earth has." Or again, even as she wrote to Mitchell that she did not feel well, her spirits rallied when she thought of the larger cause: "It has been frightful weather Mud up to my knees hard Tromping but it has been done with good grace Who

5. Mary Jones as she appeared shortly after becoming Mother Jones (Courtesy Library of Congress)

would not Tramp for the young boys and break their chains. My heart goes out to these boys We are doing good work."[18]

Mother Jones's organizing in West Virginia was marked by broad inclusiveness. One historian has described the UMW of this era as perhaps the most integrated organization in the United States. This assessment is too rosy; racism always threatened to divide the workers, and the union hierarchy remained overwhelmingly white. Mother Jones herself never recanted her stance against Chinese immigration, long the standard UMW position. A few racist remarks appeared in her personal letters over the years. Still, she had nothing but praise for African American miners, and she declared that they were among the staunchest unionists in West Virginia: "One of the best fellows we have is the black man. He knows what liberty is; he knows that in days gone by the bloodhounds went after his father over the mountains and tore him to pieces, and he knows that his own Mammy wept and prayed for liberty. For these reasons he prizes his liberty and is ready to fight for it." This unity, this solidarity, this manhood, most delighted her. She described how she and fellow organizer John Walker called a meeting one dark night: "When we got to the top of the mountain, besides the stars in the sky we saw other little stars, the miners' lamps, coming from all sides of the mountains." She told Walker, "There comes the star of hope, the star of the future . . . the star that is lighting up the ages yet to come; there is the star of the true miner laying the foundation for a higher civilization, and that star will shine when all other stars grow dim."[19]

But even as her organizing efforts progressed in West Virginia's southern field, trouble broke out in the north. There, the Fairmont Coal Company had bought up mines, incorporated itself, and consolidated its hold on the region. Fairmont ran classic company towns and, of course, refused to discuss grievances. The UMW sent a band of 140 organizers from the southern field north.[20]

John Mitchell specifically asked Mother Jones to take on this assignment. He noted that many of the union men were frightened, and with good reason, given the violence directed against them. "I dislike to ask you always to take the dangerous fields," Mitchell wrote her, "but I know that you are willing." District 17, the West Virginia chapter of the UMW, called a strike on June 7, 1902. Just two days after the strike started, sheriffs began arresting UMW officials, and circuit courts issued injunctions against organizing as fast as the operators petitioned for them. Meanwhile, mine guards stepped up their violence. Returning from a meeting one night, Mother Jones and several organizers crossed a covered bridge in a particularly dark and isolated spot. Mine guards ambushed one of the organizers, Joe Poggiani, and beat him senseless with brass knuckles. Mother Jones recalled years later tearing strips from her petticoat to wrap his wounds and stop the bleeding. Only after weeks of convalescence could Poggiani get up from his hospital bed.[21]

The Fairmont Coal Company next persuaded federal circuit court judge John J. Jackson, who had been appointed by Abraham Lincoln, to issue a new and sweeping injunction, on the grounds that the union threatened out-of-state investors' money. Organizing for a strike, the judge ruled, constituted conspiracy to injure the complainant, a Baltimore financier. This new injunction did not stop at county lines like those issued by district courts, and it included a ban on all demonstrations within sight of the mines, even on property leased by the union. Acting under the injunction, a federal marshal arrested Mother Jones on June 20 as she spoke to a crowd near Clarksburg. She insisted on finishing her talk, in which she excoriated the mine owners and Judge

Jackson, condemned the courts for not taking action against mine-guard violence, and called all miners who failed to join the union cowards. She was taken into custody along with several other organizers and brought to Parkersburg, some eighty miles away. She refused the offer of a hotel room instead of prison and asked to be incarcerated with her "boys" in the Parkersburg jail. The jailer and his wife refused her a cell, insisting that she stay with them in their apartment. Three weeks after the strike began, virtually all of the UMW organizers were under arrest. So pervasive had the court's intervention become that Mother Jones commented, "I have been served with injunctions in quantities sufficient to form a shroud for me when I am cold in death."[22]

The organizers were released on bond, and Mother Jones went to the UMW convention in Indianapolis, where she spoke passionately of the struggle in West Virginia. On her way back to Parkersburg, she stopped off in Cincinnati to address that city's Central Labor Council. She talked for an hour and a half, hitting hard at many of her favorite themes—child labor, the czarist conditions in West Virginia, the horrendous lives of the mine families. "Thirty-nine years ago the black slaves were freed," she thundered. "Today we are the white slaves to a corrupt judiciary." She vilified politicians, said they were bought and paid for by the rich, then castigated workers who voted against their own interests: "Why is it they cannot stand together at the ballot box? No bayonet, no injunction can interfere there. You pay Senators, Governors, Legislators, and then beg on your knees for them to pass a bill in labor's protection." The solution, she said, was a "class conscious proletariat party"—the Socialist Party. And the way of attaining that led her back to a theme she had hammered home in Pennsylvania—the need for women's activism and women's votes. She told the Arnot story, how she organized the women and they rejuvenated the strike. "Women are fighters," she concluded. "You will never solve the problem until you let in the women. No nation is greater than its women."[23]

Mother Jones returned to face charges in Judge Jackson's court on July 24, 1902. U.S. district attorney Reese Blizzard, during the course of his arguments, allegedly pointed to Mother Jones and called her "the most dangerous woman in America," because on her word alone, thousands of contented men laid down their tools. In handing down his opinion, Judge Jackson argued that the organizers created a climate of fear and intimidation, making it impossible for miners to work. He described UMW leaders as outside agitators, "vampires that live and fatten on the honest labor of coal miners of the country." Judge Jackson added that the right to work deserved at least as much protection as freedom of speech. Abuse of free expression had led to the recent assassination of President McKinley (by the anarchist Leon Czolgosz), and it was time to exclude seditious statements from legal protection. Turning to Mother Jones, he declared that she spoke the language of communists and anarchists, that such words "should not emanate from a citizen of this country who believes in its institutions." The judge concluded that she must not be allowed to hide behind the Declaration of Independence and the First Amendment.[24]

Jackson found all of the defendants guilty of contempt and gave them sixty-day jail sentences. But the judge suspended Mother Jones's sentence. He said that he would not make her a martyr, and he lectured her from the bench:

> I cannot forbear to express my great surprise that a woman of the apparent intelligence of Mrs. Jones should permit herself to be used as an instrument by designing and reckless agitators, who seem to have no regard for the rights of others, in accomplishing an object which is entirely unworthy of a good woman. It seems to me that it would have been better far for her to follow the lines and paths which the Allwise Being intended her sex should pursue. There are many charities . . . that she could engage in of a lawful character that would be more in keeping with what we have been taught and what experience has shown to be the true sphere of womanhood.[25]

Mother Jones thanked him for his advice, said she was no martyr but had a duty to perform. She predicted that she would be arrested again, and added that if she violated the law, she deserved the same punishment as the others. Mother Jones noted that both she and Jackson were quite old, hoped that they could be friends and that they would meet in heaven. The courtroom burst into applause. Later she called him a scab. She also called the operators robbers and Jackson their hireling, and she declared that the reason the court backed the owners was that robbers liked each other. But Judge Jackson's decision stood; it was sustained on appeal, and another federal judge issued a similar injunction for the southern field. Labor leaders as well as many newspapers and magazines were appalled, but to no avail. Mother Jones said goodbye to the other organizers who were still behind bars and returned to the anthracite country for the 1902 strike.[26]

The failure in the northern field reveals the obstacles facing the Mine Workers union. Simply put, business and government worked hand in glove. The attorney Aretas Brooks Fleming had orchestrated the legal battle against the UMW. He was the son-in-law of James Otis Watson, the founder of the Fairmont Coal Company, brother-in-law to the three Watson sons who ran the company. Fleming served as chief counsel for Fairmont. He was friends with Judge Jackson and a close associate of Reese Blizzard; he even knew the federal marshals who served papers on the organizers. Fleming moved comfortably among local bankers, businessmen, politicians, and judges. For such a consummate insider, people like Mother Jones truly were outside agitators who threatened to upset a comfortable situation. Given the resources at his disposal, Fleming's victory was all but inevitable.[27]

But the crisis did not end there, and the situation grew increasingly bitter before the union finally called off the strike in the southern field in mid-1903. Mother Jones returned to West Virginia several times as the violence escalated. During one of her meetings, someone opened fire with a gun, and a miner carried her on his back across a stream and out of harm's way. On December 2, she was forced to flee from her hotel room when a fire started suspiciously in the unoccupied room next door. She wrote an open letter to Julius Wayland and the *Appeal to Reason* about the worsening conditions:

> The wind blows cold this morning, but these cruel coal
> barons do not feel the winter blast; their babes, nay even

their poodle dogs are warm and have a comfortable breakfast, while these slaves of the caves, who in the past have moved the commerce of the world, are out on the highways without clothes or shelter. Nearly 3,000 families have been thrown out of the corporation shacks to face the cold blasts of winter weather.[28]

Amid the deepening crisis came new incidents of terrorism. In February, Federal Marshal Dan Cunningham attempted to serve an injunction on a group of strikers in the town of Stanaford. Cunningham retreated when the union men brandished weapons. He returned early the next morning with the county sheriff and a contingent of Baldwin-Felts detectives. They shot up the town, killing seven people while sustaining no casualties of their own. A few days later, the courts in nearby Beckley responded by indicting two hundred unionists for violating a court injunction. The strike finally was crushed by this combination of violence and legal coercion. For the next ten years, the UMW barely existed in West Virginia.[29]

When Mother Jones wrote for the socialist press, or went on the road to speak in subsequent years, the horrors of West Virginia took a central place. Referring to Judge Jackson's lecture to her, she wrote to Henry Demarest Lloyd in April of her desire to tear down every charitable institution in the country and build on its ruins a temple of justice. She concluded her letter: "After two years of hard work, the Miners have won a victory . . . little by little we are getting the poor slaves awakened." This was absurd: West Virginia was a crushing defeat for the UMW, and she knew it.[30]

At least her sense of humor remained intact. At the Fourteenth Annual United Mine Workers Convention (1903), one order of business was to nominate sites for the next year's meeting. Indianapolis, Chicago, Pittsburgh, Washington, and other cities received support. Mother Jones suggested Parkersburg, West Virginia, because, she said, "she would like to have the convention held under Judge Jackson's eyes."[31]

Setbacks in West Virginia notwithstanding, the legend of Mother Jones grew. A poem memorialized her in the pages of the *United Mine*

Workers Journal just after Judge Jackson issued his injunction. Not prison, not even death, could silence her:

> For the soul and the spirit of old Mother Jones
> Will march up and down
> Like the soul of John Brown,
> Till justice shall vanquish our burdens and groans
> And kill all injunctions on old Mother Jones.

The comparison to John Brown must have been especially gratifying. During her time in West Virginia, indeed, during her whole career, Mother Jones made frequent references to the abolitionist crusade against slavery. It was said that she carried a worn volume of Wendell Phillips's antislavery speeches everywhere. But John Brown, the great martyr to the cause, was her favorite. Brown had been vilified for his radical egalitarianism and his willingness to use violence. But once Lincoln made the Civil War a struggle to preserve the Union *and* end slavery, Brown became a hero, a martyr to Southern perfidy. In coming years, when Mother Jones faced the issue of violence in the labor movement, she invoked Brown's name to show how visionaries sometimes were reviled as fanatics then vindicated as heroes.[32]

Indeed, she was especially proud when journalists compared her to the likes of Brown and Phillips, and beginning in West Virginia, she made labor's old analogy between chattel slavery and wage slavery explicit. The comparison could be dismissive of the horrific exploitation of African Americans, implying that their suffering had been little different from that of modern-day white workers. Yet black miners appreciated Mother Jones's references to the slaves' plight. They "lustily cheered" her and called out, "Hit 'em again, Mother Jones!" and "Tell it to 'em again." The war against slavery was a theme to which she returned over and over. Martyrs died once before to stop the strong from oppressing the weak. In living memory, a few dedicated reformers turned public indifference into outrage, helped good defeat evil.[33]

Colorado

More coal lay half a continent away from West Virginia in the Rocky Mountain states, especially Colorado. The industry developed late in the West, but by the turn of the century, coal, iron, and steel production boomed. The two largest firms merged in 1892 to form the Colorado Fuel and Iron Company, which by the turn of the century had become one of America's hundred largest corporations, dominating coal production in the state. Although the industry in the West had its unique patterns, it should not be seen as distinct from the rest of the country. Mining families moved from the Midwest to Colorado and back, responding to market conditions; management relied heavily on eastern expertise and capital; and western mining grew ever more racially and ethnically diverse, as owners imported blacks, Mexicans, Italians, Slavs, and Chinese. The patterns of labor-management conflict also prevailed, as the Rocky Mountain states witnessed several regional strikes in the years before 1903.[34]

Grievances were similar to those in West Virginia. Mine inspectors served the companies' interests more than the miners'; company stores and company housing gouged families; local governments were dominated by the operators. There were pay issues too: compensation was determined by tonnage, but the miners said a ton meant two thousand pounds, whereas the operators insisted on twenty-four hundred pounds, and miners trusted neither the scales nor the men who weighed their coal. The operators claimed that their employees made $80 to $100 per month, but the Colorado Bureau of Labor Statistics found they averaged $370 per year, compared with clerks, who earned $482, and bricklayers, who made $969.[35]

The Rocky Mountain states had a powerful, and sometimes divisive, radical tradition. In 1893, an organization called the Western Federation of Miners was formed among the metal miners of Butte, Montana. The WFM spread quickly throughout the West, sometimes as a rival to the UMW. Whereas Mine Workers leaders like John Mitchell tended to be conservative, the WFM had a more radical agenda. In 1900, for example, the WFM endorsed the Socialist Party ticket, including Eugene Debs for President. But the ideological distinction between the two unions should not be drawn too sharply. The UMW contained plenty of radicals and socialists who nonetheless considered their union the best hope for organizing the industry nationally. Ethnicity also divided the western miners. On top of the operators' policies of recruiting minorities and playing groups off each other, the long-standing discrimination against the Chinese in the West made racism a durable tradition. Now a growing mining industry in Mexico posed the twin threats of cheap coal and cheap labor.[36]

Despite their divisions, the twenty-two thousand miners of UMW District 15 (the Rocky Mountain states) became increasingly restive as the summer of 1903 faded, which led to growing tyranny in the mining towns, which in turn heightened interest in the union. Especially in the southeast Colorado counties of Las Animas and Huerfano, the coal operators paid for new deputies and enlarged arsenals, resources used to intimidate and spy on miners. Duncan MacDonald, a UMW organizer, recalled that when he first got off the train in Trinidad, armed thugs followed him everywhere, and workers who came up to him to shake hands were dismissed from their jobs the next day. Such strong-arm tactics created deep resentment among the mine families.[37]

Discontent also focused on the centralization of Colorado coal. In 1903, the oil tycoon John D. Rockefeller acquired controlling interest in Colorado Fuel and Iron, while the local magnate John C. Osgood gained mastery of the Victor Coal Company and the American Fuel Company. Citizens grew increasingly concerned about such concentrations of wealth, and the rhetoric (if not always the reality) of "trust-busting"—a mélange of antimonopoly laws, court decisions, and public policies—was a defining characteristic of the Progressive Era. The consolidation of business power, epitomized by J. P. Morgan's creation of United States Steel Corporation, was disturbing enough. Equally upsetting was the aggressive new tone of American companies. Businessmen across America began reinforcing their power with organizations like the "Citizens' Alliances," which fought not only unions but worker legislation such as eight-hour laws. This latter subject was particularly touchy in Colorado. In a 1902 referendum, the people of that state overwhelmingly passed an eight-hour bill, but a conference committee of the state legislature, acting at the behest of prominent businessmen, refused to enact the legislation. Here was another sign that business exercised too much control over people's lives.[38]

The WFM seized on the eight-hour issue and led a strike of ferrous metal miners at Cripple Creek. Their militancy spread to coal country. When District 15 leaders of the UMW asked for a conference to discuss outstanding issues, Colorado Fuel and Iron and the other companies declared their workers happy and refused to deal with the union. District 15 delegates met in Pueblo and voted to strike; they also passed a resolution endorsing socialism. The national office of the UMW was in a difficult spot. Organizing had not gone well, and the governor was no friend of labor. Some union leaders feared that the big operators wanted this strike as a means to crush the union. But overcaution, Mitchell and his associates knew, ran the risk of alienating the rank and file, and if that happened, the WFM was ready to step in and lead. Reluctantly, the UMW national office endorsed the strike.[39]

As it turned out, militancy ran deep. Although only a few hundred men belonged to the UMW, 95 percent of the Colorado miners walked out on November 9. Immediately, families were evicted from their homes by the companies, and they streamed into the towns of Trinidad and Walsenburg, many people carrying their possessions on their backs. Problems quickly multiplied. The costs of food and shelter alone strained the tiny District 15 treasury. Moreover, without coal, local steel mills shut down, and now steelworkers came looking for jobs in the mines. Worse, union militancy centered on Colorado; miners in the smaller Wyoming, Utah, and New Mexico fields were not as devoted to the cause, and every ton of coal they dug prolonged the strike. Meanwhile, Colorado governor James Peabody assured the operators of state protection to keep their mines running.[40]

On the positive side was surprising worker solidarity, made all the stronger by the arrival of Mother Jones. Her autobiography claims that she came to Colorado shortly before the strike disguised as a peddler, to act as the eyes and ears of John Mitchell. The story is hard to believe, not only because it is so clichéd but also because by 1903 Mother Jones had become very well known among mine families. In fact, her arrival in Colorado created quite a stir; strangers went out of their way just to catch a glimpse of her. Three months before the strike started, *The Denver Republican* published a feature story on her:

> You are surprised, astonished, incredulous to be in-
> formed that this eminently respectable and strictly con-
> ventional appearing old lady . . . should know aught of
> anything save the economy of a well ordered household.
> Political doctrines, socialist propaganda, the labor move-
> ment, the teachings of Karl Marx, strikes, lockouts, black
> lists, riots. . . . What knowledge of these belongs to this lit-
> tle old woman with the snowy hair and the soft pink
> cheeks?[41]

As the strike neared, Colorado newspapers anticipated her impact. In September, the *Republican* reported that the heroine of the Pennsylvania coal miners would instill courage among the men in the West. *The Denver Times* speculated that her influence among the miners was even greater than Mitchell's. *The Denver Post* called her the miners' "guardian angel" who "can sway thousands to a spirit of frenzy or with a shake of her head and a few soft-spoken words check the mob seeking to burn and slay." When she arrived in the southern field, according to *The Trinidad Courier*, "many nearly broke the rubber in their neck in an effort to get a good look." Even her signature on the hotel register—M. Jones, Chicago—attracted a crowd.[42]

If John Mitchell had his qualms about this strike, Mother Jones displayed no reservations, though she kept her tone moderate for the press. She met quietly before the strike with the leaders of the WFM, including President Charles Moyer and Secretary William "Big Bill" Haywood. She declared the WFM boys to be "fine fellows" and reported, rather naively, that they would stop attacking Mitchell on the pages of *Miners' Magazine.* She (again, naively) praised Governor Peabody, declared him to be a moderate man who had been misrepresented as anti-labor in the press. Mother Jones urged mine families to ignore gloomy predictions that the strike was doomed to failure. She pledged that violence and lawlessness among the miners would not be tolerated by the union leadership—"unless the thugs the coal companies have armed attempt to bully our men."[43]

It was a long strike, but the crisis came early. Barely a week after the walkout began, the Northern Coal and Coke Company proposed a generous contract with its miners in the northern field.

The company had negotiated with the union throughout the crisis, whereas the southern operators had refused to talk. Mitchell and his supporters urged acceptance of the agreement because that would allow the UMW to concentrate its resources in the south. But the more militant unionists believed that the northern field could produce enough coal to jeopardize the whole strike. As winter approached, they argued that the best bet was to keep coal supplies scarce.[44]

With her flair for the dramatic, Mother Jones introduces the story in her autobiography as a confrontation between herself and a national UMW board member, John F. Ream. Ream told her,

> "You must not block the settlement of the northern miners because the National President, John Mitchell, wants it, and he pays you."
>
> "Are you through?" said I.
>
> He nodded.
>
> "Then I am going to tell you that if God Almighty wants this strike called off for his benefit and not for the miners, I am going to raise my voice against it. And as to President John paying me . . . he never paid me a penny in his life. It is the hard earned nickels and dimes of the miners that pay me, and it is their interests that I am going to serve."

Once again, we must not take Mother Jones's version at face value. But there is a metaphorical truth here. The controversy over the northern field was a climactic moment in UMW history, and its repercussions pushed Mother Jones out of the union for several years.[45]

Ream spoke for hours before a hastily called gathering of the northern miners in Louisville, Colorado, on November 21, 1903. He explained the operators' proposal, read from a telegram sent by Mitchell, and persuaded the men to support the settlement. Before a vote, however, the other side had its turn. District 15 president William Howells spoke, but without much effect. Then Mother Jones strode to the podium. Her speech was short but brilliant. She began by reminding the northern miners of their commitments:

> Brothers, you English speaking miners of the northern fields promised your southern brothers, seventy percent of whom do not speak English, that you would support them to the end. Now you are asked to betray them, to make a separate settlement. You have a common enemy and it is your duty to fight to a finish. Are you brave men? Can you fight as well as you can work? I had rather fall fighting than working. If you go back to work here and your brothers fall in the south, you will be responsible for their defeat.

Shame and guilt—shame for betraying their own manhood, guilt for betraying their brothers.[46]

She ended with a ringing appeal to class solidarity across lines of race, region, and nationality:

> The enemy seeks to conquer by dividing your ranks, by making distinctions between North and South, between American and foreign. You are all miners, fighting a common cause, a common master. The iron heel feels the same to all flesh. Hunger and suffering and the cause of your children bind more closely than a common tongue. . . . I know of no East or West, North nor South when it comes to my class fighting the battle for justice. If it is my fortune to live to see the industrial chain broken from every workingman's child in America, and if then there is one black child in Africa in bondage, there I shall go.

Here was an open assertion of radical class consciousness, and a rejection of all those schisms—of skill level, craft, ethnicity, race—that divided workers. By referring to "my class fighting the battle for justice," Mother Jones invited her audience to see the world as she did: divided into those who created wealth and those who owned it, with all other distinctions relegated to insignificance. It was a matter of brothers and sisters not betraying each other, of workers uniting in battle to fight the common enemy that oppressed their families.[47]

Her words moved the men, and they voted to continue the strike. The next day, the *Denver Post* headline read MOTHER JONES BARS SETTLE-MENT PLANS: MITCHELL IS DEFIED. The rift with Mitchell had reopened; as he grew more respectful of businessmen, she became convinced that socialism and class-conscious unionism would be the workers' salva-tion. Her victory in Colorado's northern field was very short-lived, however. Just a week after Mother Jones went back to organize in the southern field, the northern miners, prodded by UMW officials, voted once again, and this time decided to end their strike. Their coal, along with that from the other western states, made a union victory much more difficult.[48]

As in West Virginia, the strike grew uglier as it dragged on. Slurs against leaders on both sides proliferated, and the most spectacular one was against Mother Jones. On the second day of the new year, 1904, only a few weeks after the northern miners returned to work, a story appeared in a Denver-based anti-labor magazine.[49]

Denver journalist Leonel Ross Campbell was already a local celebrity, known for her colorful reporting, when she took the pseudo-nym Polly Pry in 1903. Her new magazine, named for herself, was a scandal sheet with an anti-labor agenda. The December 26, 1903, issue declared labor leaders to be "men usually of little or no education, less principle, and no consideration either for the people they are supposed to represent, or for society at large." Accusations followed against several strike leaders: UMW district president Howells kept a mistress; national organizer William Wardjon had abandoned his wife back in Wales; national executive board member John Gehr was a con-victed murderer and an "all around thug."[50]

In the very next issue, *Polly Pry* set to work on Mother Jones. The scandal sheet repeated her life story, got much of it wrong, and then claimed to reveal her secret history. Denver's Pinkerton office, *Polly Pry* said, had a file dating back to 1889 on a "Mother Harris," who was well known in the red-light districts of Denver, Omaha, Kansas City, Chicago, and San Francisco. In May 1889, she leased a house at 2114 Market Street in Denver, completely refurbished it, brought in seven inmates said to be the "best looking girls on the row," and ran one of the most exclusive and notorious brothels in town. Wealthy mining men and corrupt politicians patronized the place, which was also known for its high-stakes gambling. Within four months, Mother Harris had saved fifteen thousand dollars, but her paramour, "Black-leg," ran off with one of the girls. Harris took to drink, was arrested several times, and by the end of the year had gone broke. She became a resident of Minnie Hall's brothel, and later held a series of illicit jobs:

> An inmate of Jennie Rogers' house on Market street, Denver, some twelve years ago. She got into trouble with the Rogers woman for bribing all of her girls to leave her and go to a house in Omaha—for which act she was paid a procuress fee of $5 to $10 apiece for the girls.
>
> She was a confidential servant in Rose Lovejoy's private house on Market street, Denver, and with her several years.
>
> . . . Lived in Eva Lewis' house on Market street at the time the Coxey Army passed through here, and took a prominent part in the Denver preparation for their care.
>
> Is known to Harry Loss, a piano player at 1925 Market street, who says he knew her first in Omaha in 1894, when she lived in a house at tenth and Douglass. She was then selling clothes to the girls.
>
> A sewing woman for the sporting class living on Lawrence street . . . says it was commonly reported that she was a procuress by trade.

Mary Harris, the Pinkertons concluded, was a "vulgar, heartless, vicious creature, with a fiery temper and a cold-blooded brutality rare even in the slums."[51]

Previous writers on Mother Jones have rejected *Polly Pry*'s charges out of hand, and they are probably right to do so. But the case is not clear-cut. For example, old friends might have exonerated her fully. In fact, Terence Powderly, Eugene Debs, and John Mitchell all equivocated. Powderly wrote years later, "My acquaintance with her began at a time when part of this alleged record of her by *Polly Pry* was being made up, and at that time to my certain knowledge, she was not the keeper of a house of ill fame, nor an inmate of such a house, neither was she a procuress for any such institution." Although Mother Jones claimed in her autobiography to have known Powderly since just after the Chicago fire of 1871, he clearly dates their friendship much later—sometime after 1889, the earliest year mentioned by *Polly Pry*—and says he can account for her activities for only part of the time in question. Debs did not meet Mother Jones until 1894, and Mitchell said that though he would like to deny the accusations against her, their acquaintance did not begin until late in the nineteenth century. Mitchell, probably still fuming at her defiance of his authority, allegedly asked her to deny the *Polly Pry* charges and sue for libel or resign from the union. She refused, saying that such action would only dignify her accuser. A UMW attorney agreed that because the accusation was somewhat ambiguous—*Polly Pry* implied rather than explicitly stated that Mary Harris Jones of the UMW was the woman named in the Pinkerton file—the case probably would be thrown out of court.[52]

Mother Jones once hinted obliquely that there might be something to the *Polly Pry* charges. The UMW organizer Duncan MacDonald wrote years later in his unpublished autobiography that when he and Mother Jones discussed the issue, she told him, "Don't you think whatever my past might have been that I have more than made up for it?" and MacDonald implied that this seemed a confession. In fact, we know so little about Mary Jones between 1871 and 1894 that it is impossible categorically to deny the *Polly Pry* accusations. Dressmaking was a trade closely tied to prostitution, and a "Mrs. Mary Jones, Dressmaker," was listed in the Denver City Directory for 1893. In a strange play on words, the phrase "the miners' angel," so often applied to Mother Jones, was also used for the prostitutes who worked the coal towns. So far as the details of the case go, the names mentioned by *Polly Pry* and the locations in Denver were real—Jennie Rogers and Minnie Hall were indeed madams, and the red-light district of Denver in 1890 centered on the 2000 block of Market Street. Moreover, when Mary Jones turned up with Coxey's Army in 1894, it was with a contingent that marched west from Denver. Finally, San Francisco, Kansas City, and Omaha all were cities to which her name had been linked during the late nineteenth century.[53]

On the other hand, there is no independent corroboration of the story. Denver city records are very incomplete for this period, but Mary Jones or Mary Harris does not show up in police or court documents. No one came forward to confirm *Polly Pry*'s account, and there are internal problems with the story. For example, in 1889, Mary Jones was fifty-two years old, a rather advanced age for a prostitute. Moreover, it is difficult to take *Polly Pry* seriously, given the magazine's absurd and vitriolic coverage of the strike (at one point, the author of the article declared that Mother Jones "controlled" both the UMW and the WFM and that she was using her base among the workers to "take over" Colorado politics). Besides, women activists often were tarred with the brush of promiscuity. Jacob Coxey, for example, discouraged women from participating in his march, knowing that the press would charge the whole movement with licentiousness, and women of the labor movement often suffered accusations of indecency.[54]

The single *Polly Pry* charge confirmed by outside evidence is that Mary Jones sewed for prostitutes. Upton Sinclair, a friend of Mother Jones's, asked her about the accusations years later:

> It appears that in those early days she was a sewing woman; she earned a precarious living, and felt herself justified in working for anyone who would pay her. She did some sewing for a girl of the streets, and this girl died of tuberculosis, and the Catholic church refused her a burial service, and "Mother Jones" wrote to a newspaper to protest against this action—her first appearance in public life, her first utterance of radicalism. And this had been remembered all these years, it was brought up against her in one labor struggle after another; only they made her the "madame" of the house where the poor girl of the streets had lived!

The Pinkerton Detective Agency, the source for the *Polly Pry* story, was highly suspect. Its Denver office in 1903 was run by James McParland, the agent who infiltrated and testified against the Molly Maguires in 1877. In 1907, McParland would assemble evidence against WFM leaders William Haywood, Charles Moyer, and George Pettibone in their trial for murder. In both cases, there is strong suspicion that McParland acted as an agent provocateur, manipulated evidence, even lied under oath.[55]

Journalistic reaction to the *Polly Pry* charges was predictable: anti-union newspapers reprinted the story; pro-union organs were outraged. Although the accusations probably were nothing more than slander, they underscore again the enigma of Mother Jones's past. Whether true or false, *Polly Pry*'s story hit a nerve. All the wholesome feelings evoked by the legend of Mother Jones were inverted by the image of mother as brothel keeper. If Mother Jones drew power from her purity, her enemies found a way of making the madonna into a whore.[56]

The accusation was part of a much larger deterioration of the situation in Colorado. Though the coal strike dragged on for almost a year, its end is quickly told. Divisions between conservative unionists and radicals, between the UMW and the WFM, between District 15 and the national union all widened. Led by dedicated organizers, the foreign miners remained stalwarts to the end; their families and communities became bastions of union strength. Mother Jones praised them in her autobiography: "No more loyal, courageous men could be found than those southern miners, scornfully referred to by 'citizens' alliances' as 'foreigners.' Italians and Mexicans endured to the end. . . . Theirs was the victory of the spirit." But solidarity was expensive; the UMW treasury hemorrhaged paying for food, shelter, and transportation out of the strike zone for workers. When it was over, the strike had cost the union half a million dollars.[57]

Meanwhile, the operators mined sufficient coal to keep afloat. And the mine guards and deputy sheriffs stepped up the violence. They bombed the homes of union activists, shot several strikers, and sent many organizers to the hospital. In March, the union called a convention to end the strike, but as it met, Governor Peabody declared martial law and ordered the Colorado National Guard to the strike zone, allegedly to preserve law and order but in reality to help escort strikebreakers into the field. The troops were paid for by Colorado Fuel and Iron, the Victor Coal Company, and the Colorado Citizens' Alliance.

The troops deported union activists, eavesdropped on conversations (all phone calls in foreign languages were forbidden), suppressed pro-labor newspapers, confiscated weapons, abrogated the right of assembly, and closed the saloons. The union could not back down now.[58]

Shortly after the *Polly Pry* charges, Mother Jones developed pneumonia, which kept her out of action for much of the winter. She recovered in time for the entry of Peabody's troops. She and the organizers William Wardjon, Adolph Bartoli, and Joe Poggiani were forcibly taken by train to La Junta on March 26 and told not to return. The next morning she went back to Denver, took a room near the capitol building, wrote a note, and had it hand-delivered to Governor Peabody: "I am right here in the capital, after being out nine or ten hours, four or five blocks from your office. I want to ask you, governor, what in Hell are you going to do about it?" Within a few days, she was taken out of circulation again, this time when doctors quarantined her in Utah—where she had gone to organize—allegedly for exposure to smallpox. Meanwhile, coal production rose, beatings, arrests, and deportations continued, and miners' wives and daughters were harassed by state troops. Finally, the national union called off the strike in June. District 15 continued on its own for a while, and Mother Jones supported the renegades, which infuriated national officials. In October, however, Colorado leaders did the inevitable and authorized a return to work.[59]

"They Will Unfurl Their Banner to the Breezes of Industrial Liberty"

Immediately after the coal strike, Mother Jones assessed the causes of the defeat. She declared that the national UMW leaders failed to understand the situation on the "field of battle," and she denounced government officials who sent thugs to kill the miners under the guise of "law and order." Then she attacked the real rulers of Colorado:

> The generations yet unborn will read with horror of the crimes committed by the mine owners of Colorado, with their hired blood hounds aching to spill the blood of

their slaves. . . . Defeated? No, you cannot defeat such brave men and women as entered into that frightful struggle. They have just retreated. They will unfurl their banner to the breezes of industrial liberty in the near future. The commercial pirates of the Colorado Fuel and Iron, and the Victor Fuel Company, with their degraded curs will go down before an outraged people in disgrace. They will yet call on the mountains to cover them from the indignation of the people.

It was Mother Jones at her most melodramatic—pirates and curs so reviled that the Rocky Mountains could not shelter them from the people's wrath. Even in defeat, she was the consummate organizer, preparing her followers for the next battle, painting for her readers with bold strokes the Manichaean struggle, promising them the bright new day of justice.[60]

Strong recriminations divided the UMW members at their annual convention in January 1905. Mitchell and the executive board believed that District 15 dragged them into this strike against their better judgment, and leaders from District 15 felt betrayed by the national office. A delegate from Wyoming named Robert Randall rose to denounce Mitchell, whom he called "the little tin labor god of the capitalistic class." He condemned Mitchell for "wining and dining" Andrew Carnegie, a man who did more than anyone else "to crush American manhood and degrade American womanhood." "I cannot find words," he went on, "to express my contempt for a man who, having raised himself to power by the sufferings of the working class, falls a victim to the flattery of his capitalistic masters and proves himself false to the working man." And the final insult—Randall contrasted Mitchell with Mother Jones: "Mother Jones' dear, white head will soon be laid at rest; her voice will soon be hushed. Her heart that beat so warmly for suffering humanity will be still in death. When she is laid in the grave no one can say she ever played false to the toiling and suffering masses."[61]

Mitchell responded in kind. Yes, he had chastised Mother Jones for disobeying the will of the national board, yes, he also castigated her for ignoring the *Polly Pry* charges. But Mitchell, too, claimed her as his own, spoke of how they had built the UMW together, described how "Mother Jones and I worked hand in hand through some of the most stirring strikes this country has ever seen." The old woman had become an icon. Mitchell branded Randall disloyal to the UMW and vowed that the union must choose between them. The convention voted to expel Randall, but Mitchell's victory proved short-lived. In coming years, he suffered financial setbacks, struggled with a drinking problem, and lost two of his children. More, his identification with businessmen undermined his support in the union. He chose not to run for reelection in 1908 and became head of the National Civic Federation instead.[62]

The UMW's national board informed Mother Jones that she must toe the line or resign. Violating the board's decisions and supporting the increasingly revolutionary Western Federation of Miners were unacceptable. She was not fired—Mitchell, in fact, reappointed her early in 1905—but she resigned anyway. She described these incidents twenty years later in her autobiography:

> John Mitchell went traveling through Europe, staying at fashionable hotels, studying the labor movement. When he returned the miners had been lashed back into the mines by hunger but John Mitchell was given a banquet in the Park Avenue Hotel and presented with a watch with diamonds. . . . From the day I opposed John Mitchell's authority, the guns were turned on me. Slander and persecution followed me like black shadows.[63]

Time had distorted her memory, for these were not her feelings as events unfolded. Immediately after resigning from the UMW, she wrote to John Walker defending Mitchell: "I *want to say right here*, I may never see him again, but one thing . . . [is] certain, I will fight to death for him against any false assertion. I know the labor movement; I know the philosophy of the *monster capitalism*. . . . John Mitchell can always depend on me. I know whatever mistakes he has made, he is right at heart." She blamed the "ring of fools," the "dirty ignoramuses"—the UMW executive board—for the defeat in Colorado. Mother Jones did turn on Mitchell after he strayed from the union and took over the National Civic Federation, but in 1905, despite their differences, she still professed her respect for him. Indeed, she defended him like a son, an errant son perhaps, but one with a good heart.[64]

Still, Mother Jones was exhausted. She was sixty-seven years old and had come through years of organizing in harsh country. Even before the Colorado debacle, she had contemplated leaving the Mine Workers union. She must have expressed her disaffection to William Mailly, then national secretary of the Socialist Party, for Mailly wrote to her in April 1903, just as the battle in West Virginia ended, "I can see by your letter that you are tired of your present work and I should like to free you from it and put you out for the Socialist party." This friend from the Alabama days offered her a job as lecturer for three dollars per day, plus expenses. She would travel the country and give four or five speeches per week. Socialist locals would put up fifteen or twenty dollars, thus covering her costs, and she would avoid the frustrations of union organizing for a while. She did not take the job immediately. But in 1905, fights within the union, the limitations she felt working in a single industry, and her hopes for change through radical politics led her belatedly to accept Mailly's offer.[65]

As she took her leave from the United Mine Workers, Mary Jones could look back on four great campaigns, in the Central Competitive Field, the anthracite region, West Virginia, and Colorado. The latter two were failures, but the first two succeeded far beyond anyone's expectations. Of the hundreds of UMW organizers who participated in these efforts, Mother Jones was by far the most famous and effective. Despite the defeats in Colorado and West Virginia, the UMW was the nation's biggest union, built in large part on her energy, courage, and charisma. In 1905, about 675,000 American men dug coal, nearly three-quarters of them worked at union scale, and 300,000 of them were UMW members. Their standard of living, their safety, and their family lives all had been improved by the strikes of 1897–1904. Mary Jones helped accomplish that. And she did it by becoming Mother Jones.[66]

★ 5 ★

The Children's Crusade

West Virginia was "a forbidden land," "the enemy's country," according to the journalist Dorothy Adams, who accompanied Mother Jones around the Mountain State in 1901 and wrote about it for *The New York Herald.* By day, local sheriffs and federal marshals harassed Mother Jones with court injunctions. At night, all of the boardinghouses and inns were closed to her:

> Thus it is that Mother Jones lies fast asleep to-night upon the hard, bare, moon-washed floor of a hovel at St. Clair. Our host's family cannot afford the luxury of a lamp. I am writing in the moonlight that streams through the sash-less windows and the low open doorway and whitens with infinite chastity the snow of Mother Jones' hair. Her head is pillowed upon her hand bag, and if she dreams at all, it is of such of her people as have fallen on evil days.[1]

Adams crafted her images with care. The hard floor in an obscure coal town, the moonlight streaming through the window, the whiteness of Mother Jones's hair, the old woman's dreams of her people—the warmth and comfort of the interior scene, with its virtuous poverty, are heightened by the sense of danger lurking outside. Most striking is the phrase "infinite chastity" to describe the whiteness of Mother Jones's hair. She radiated purity that softened the harsh lives of the poor. Her journey was a holy one, like that of an earlier Mary whom the hard-hearted turned out one night two thousand years earlier.[2]

Though Mother Jones quickly realized the power of the legend that reporters like Adams helped construct, and exploited its resonances, she certainly did not control her own image. She never would have de-scribed herself with words like "infinite chastity." Mother Jones bene-fited from the sentimental clichés about herself, and invoked them when they were useful, but she preferred the reputation of a hell-raiser to that of a saint.

The Legend of Mother Jones

Mother Jones's friend William Mailly argued that the key to her power was that she was at one with her people. Her life of suffering resonated with their struggles. " 'Mother' Jones," Mailly declared, "is above and beyond all, one of the working class. She is flesh of their flesh, blood of their blood." Mailly traveled with Mother Jones in West Virginia, and he found that everyone seemed to know her, and many even kept pic-tures of her on their walls. "Wherever she goes she enters into the lives of the toilers and becomes a part of them," he remarked. "She is in-deed their mother in word and deed. She has earned the sweetest of all names honestly."[3]

Her growing fame meant that people wanted to know her history. She seems to have told reporters certain details, held back others, and made up a few. No doubt she often gave writers the stories they wanted to hear; they closed whatever gaps remained with their own specula-tions. "My father was an Irish refugee," the New York *World* quoted her, "and I think some of his rebellious blood must linger in my veins." She came from "distinguished Irish revolutionary ancestry," according to the *United Mine Workers Journal*; "Her paternal grandfather loved Ire-land so well that he was hanged for that affection."[4]

Fact and conjecture blended into legend. *The Boston Herald,* for ex-ample, ran a long story on her in 1904 with considerable detail. Few other sources ever mentioned her younger brother, William, who by 1900 had become dean of the diocese of St. Catherine's in Toronto. Yet biography and mythology were hopelessly mixed in this article. That Mary had been an obedient and studious daughter, a modest young woman, and a faithful and loving wife was speculation, pure and simple. More tantalizing, yet still dubious, are statements attributed to her about her marriage. According to the *Herald*, Mary Jones wept when her husband had a glass of beer after work or went off to a union meeting. George found her solicitude smothering, so in later years she sought "to make women understand what she failed to understand in those early days, that the wife must care for what the husband cares for, and that every man loves freedom, even freedom from domestic tyranny." From this experience, she concluded that the "remedy for lonely wives is a broader interest in the affairs of life." Did she really think all this back in 1865? Did she become interested in the labor movement just to placate George?[5]

Even the most accurate stories were filled with errors, omissions, and contradictions. But what unites them is the assumption that Mother Jones's past reached deep into the history of social protest movements. The details mattered less than her long-standing selflessness, for the overall effect of these articles was to make her venerable. Mother Jones actively encouraged this. Eventually, she told reporters that her interest in labor went all the way back to her childhood, when her father was cheated by his employer and she marched up to the boss to demand his pay.[6]

Mother Jones was a "New Woman," declared the *National Labor Tribune* in 1897, but not the frivolous, bloomer-wearing kind who only made a "show of herself." She did more than anyone to bring the miners into the union, and, the article concluded, "Her name will go down in history as one of the martyrs to the cause of humanity." A few years later, the New York *World* argued that Mother Jones embodied a new style of female activism: "While the other women were joining women's clubs and discussing Shakespeare, she was talking with street car conductors in Chicago, the miners of Hazleton, the mill girls in Fall River."[7]

Mother Jones did not deny the negative image of women—frivolous, vain, gossipy, materialistic—but used it as a foil against which to craft her persona of militant working-class womanhood. Journalistic accounts of her merged the twin themes of warrior and saint. For example, the *United Mine Workers Journal* said in 1901 that she was as "terrible as an army with banners" to her enemies, that she roused audiences to a frenzy, that she faced Pinkertons, militias, and the rabble but was "never overmatched in any conflict." Yet the same article referred to her as "a sweet-faced, motherly old woman . . . who is revered at home, honored abroad, whose life is without reproach."[8]

The rationale behind tying militance to nurturance was a particular ideal of motherhood. "It is a big brood she mothers," the New York *World* observed in 1900, "a big, toilsome, troublesome brood, scattered all over the face of the land, delving in the earth and under the earth, swarming in mills and factories and sweatshops." This explained Mary Jones's success in the Pennsylvania coal country: "How does she do it? By the greatest of all powers, the power of love. She loves her 'boys'— be they Polish or Bohemian, or Irish or American—and she teaches them to love her. The ranks of the toilers stand firm at her bidding, and the strategy dictated by her woman's intuition does the rest." But also like a mother, she knew how to make her children behave: "Her eyes are sharp and steel gray. They are the kind that look through and through one and make deception hard in their light." It was her charismatic motherhood, then, that gave her such influence over mining families.[9]

Even though her efforts as an organizer focused on getting men into the union, she exercised extraordinary influence over women. A reporter described her speech to a gathering of mothers, wives, and daughters who marched between the Pennsylvania towns of McAdoo and Colerain to call out the men from the anthracite mines:

> Walking to the edge of the platform, "Mother" Jones stretched out her arms to them, and in her thrillingly sweet voice said, "Sisters!" A perceptible wave of emotion like that of wind sweeping the long grasses . . . passed over her audience. . . .
>
> The faces awoke, the souls back of them kindled. For

an hour the speaker walked to and fro, telling the deeds of the mothers of the past and sisters and wives. The listeners drew nearer. They leaned their elbows on the platform, and lifted their faces to drink in the words. Their bosoms heaved, and the tears rolled unheeded down their cheeks.

The operators feared Mother Jones precisely because of her influence on women: "An old colored woman ran in the dust at 'Mother' Jones' feet crying: 'Lemme jes kiss de hem of your garment.' 'Not in the dust sister to me, but here on my breast, heart to heart,' replied 'Mother' Jones, lifting the negress, and the reporter who saw this incident declares that the women went mad with emotion, crying out: 'Kiss me, too, Mother.' "[10]

Growing up in the Illinois mining country in the 1890s, Agnes Wieck remembered her own mother in terms that evoked Mother Jones. "Babies and strikes and shutdowns and blacklists," Wieck recalled, "from one mine to another, moving, always moving. . . . Before the union was firmly established my mother had stood by while my father took one reduction after another." Wieck, who later became a labor organizer and journalist, idolized Mother Jones and dated her earliest childhood memory to the great bituminous coal strike of 1897: "My mother and women like her went out among the farmers to ask for food. Each morning saw them, baskets on their arms, making their daily rounds. One morning my mother took me with her. I carried back a doll, I remember. My mother carried back a basket full of food that I'm sure she never forgot." Wieck recalled that an army of women stood behind the men who won the strike, "stood like a wall of steel that nothing could batter down." Such women took no union vows themselves, yet they pledged their lives to organized labor.[11] Mother Jones's words gave voice to such women; her speeches helped them make sense of their experience, brought shape and poetry and meaning to their lives.

The Boston Herald declared that Mother Jones was the only woman of modern times who could be compared to heroines of the ages like Joan of Arc. Her womanliness was part of her power, power the capitalists feared. The *Herald* described a mining town in West Virginia that was off-limits to her because its rich young owner forbade organizers on his property. She went to his home; he smiled and asked who she was and what she wanted:

> "I am 'Mother' Jones, the wicked old woman," replied the supplicant with her steadfastly radiant expression and her almost subtle smile, so quiet, so gentle, so intelligent, it made the words she uttered so whimsically of herself a patent libel and insult of her character.

Of course, he granted permission for her to speak.[12]

She began her address by simply describing the mining families' lives. She made them see the dirt of the coal towns and the poverty of their homes. She noted how they could not afford the food or medicine they needed, how poverty forced them to send their children to work rather than school. And she foretold their crippled and lonely old age. Why were things this way? she asked. "Because some other human beings, no more the sons of God than the coal diggers, broke the commandment of God which said 'Thou shalt not steal.' " Men and women looked shamefaced at each other with weeping eyes, as her speech ended:

> And suddenly a man pushed his way through the crowd. He was snivelling on his coat sleeve, but he cried out hoarsely:
> "You, John Walker [the organizer who had introduced Mother Jones]; don't you go to tell us that 'ere's 'Mother' Jones. That's Jesus Christ come down on earth again, and playing he's an old woman so he can come here and talk to us poor devils. God, God—nobody else knows what the poor suffer that away."

Over and over writers repeated this theme, that the poor were her people whom she knew as no one else—no one save Jesus or Mary.[13]

The pain of her past and the asceticism of her present gave Mother Jones authenticity in the eyes of hard-pressed working people. The way that she lived—a sojourner, always ready to expose herself to danger and hardship—impressed them profoundly. A letter from organizer Ben Davis to the editor of the *United Mine Workers Journal* described her in West Virginia:

> I watched the great labor leader, Mother Jones, as she walked over the mountains twelve miles and spoke to the weary miners for three long hours. . . . After she was through she again trailed back over the mountains from where she came. Oh! if the miners of this State could but picture the scene as I seen it of that aged woman, Mother Jones, going and coming over the mountains, they would certainly arise and be men and not be slaves or cowards any more.

The contrast between her grandmotherly appearance and her raw courage—braving Pennsylvania winters, West Virginia mountains, armed thugs, and prison guards—never failed to arouse awe. It was almost as if her own physical sacrifice symbolized the pain of those whom she served. Or, more evocatively, she interceded for them, took on the burden of their sorrows.[14]

Although Mother Jones professed agnosticism and scoffed at clergymen, descriptions of her were filled with religious allusions and language. A tribute in *Miners' Magazine* on the eve of her arrival in Colorado in 1903 declared that "she has borne labor's cross for more than a quarter of a century." Her heart bled for the disinherited, "whom greed has left as homeless as the Nazarene who died upon the cross to save the world." The author continued:

> "Mother Jones" has become the patron saint and the "angel of light" of the anthracite regions of Pennsylvania, and upon the summit of the hills of West Virginia the eloquent evangelist of the United Mine Workers of America has become an idol and a queen, adored and worshiped with a reverence that is as pure and as holy as ever linked together a mother and her sons.

"Her visit to the Rocky Mountains," *Miners' Magazine* concluded, "will be a sacred jewel, treasured away in memory's casket, and from the lips of thousands of strong, brawny men of the coal fields will issue the fervent prayer, 'God bless Mother Jones.' "[15]

Hers was a religious vocation. She might not have taken vows of poverty, but her asceticism resonated with the age-old Christian theme of the body as corrupt, unworthy, incapable of perfection. Writing in *The Varieties of Religious Experience* in 1902, in the shadow of Mother Jones's work in West Virginia and Pennsylvania, the philosopher William James observed of America, "We have lost the power even of imagining what the ancient idealization of poverty could have meant: the liberation from material attachments, the unbribed soul." Mary Jones had not lost that power of imagining, nor had her admirers. Her life of self-denial was a rebuke to frivolity and materialism. Even her black dresses invoked solemnity and mourning, sacrifice and suffering. Above all, in a nation that increasingly worshipped goods and measured status by material possessions—indeed, a nation that came to identify womanhood itself with consumption—Mother Jones's ascetic life in the name of the poor gave her moral power that echoed the long Christian tradition honoring martyrs and saints.[16]

Clearly, the legend of Mother Jones had a life of its own; no real individual could live up to it, no organizer could ever exercise such influence. But the legend had become a source of authority in the "real" world.

The Crusade of the Mill Children

At the beginning of 1902, Dorothy Adams wrote an article for *The New York Herald* describing a strike of mill girls in Appalachia. For ten and more hours per day, these children worked cutting velvet, a job that required them to brandish razor-sharp knives and breathe air heavy with lime dust, all for two or three dollars per week. "Oh, we do wish Mother Jones would come and help us with our strike!" one girl told Adams. "They say that strikers always win when they have Mother Jones to help them." Adams noted how Mother Jones's or any mother's heart would bleed to see such children, with their feet and ankles swollen and knotted. The little girls scanned the hills, looking for Mother Jones, whom they took to be "a sort of all-wise feminine providence who always turned up just in the nick of time." Mother Jones did not come; she was busy with other strikes, and three days later, the girls capitulated and went back to work.[17]

But within a year, Mother Jones's name would be forever linked to the cause of ending child labor. The violence of West Virginia, the intractableness of the authorities there, and the failure of the UMW to organize the Mountain State frustrated her deeply. She was not yet ready to accept William Mailly's invitation to become a speaker for the Socialists, and the Colorado struggles were on the horizon. In the summer of 1903, an important strike was brewing among eastern mill workers, many of them children. Mother Jones turned this strike into a tool of child-labor reform.[18]

According to the 1900 census, one out of every six American children under age sixteen was gainfully employed. That number seriously underestimated the total, for it was common knowledge that many parents routinely lied about their children's ages. The argument that government must not interfere in the economy carried sufficient weight that no federal laws regulated child labor. At the turn of the century, twenty-eight states had codes protecting child workers, but these laws, which set moderate age and hours goals, were easily circumvented and impossible to enforce. In some states, even weak laws offended businessmen, who lobbied successfully for their repeal. Children found employment in many trades, but mining for boys and textile milling for girls were among the most common.[19]

The reasons children worked were complicated. The idea of childhood lasting through the late teens is new. Before the 1890s, roughly 1 percent of Americans attended high school, and these were usually children of businessmen and professionals. For most Americans, the idea of youths not working was the novelty. Children worked on farms from an early age or as apprentices in traditional crafts, and as the nation became industrialized, it was assumed that children would seek gainful employment after attaining basic literacy. Before the twentieth century, in other words, it was not controversial for fifteen-year-olds to work for a living.[20]

The low salaries of working-class men often made it imperative that wives and children do something to supplement household earnings. Children deferred marriage and continued living with their parents long into adulthood to maintain the family income. Among urban ethnic groups, children contributed roughly a third to household income before the turn of the century. Occupations like mining became family trades. Textile mills hired entire families, and parents retained considerable supervision of their children on the shop floor. In cities like New York and Chicago, the needle trades employed countless children; whole families worked at home and were paid not by the hour but by the piece. Given the poverty of such people, the labor of twelve-year-olds often became essential to family survival.[21]

Textile manufacturing, which employed more children than any other single trade, was mostly carried out in small towns. Mills proliferated in the South and along the Eastern Seaboard toward the end of the century. Declining agricultural prices pushed people off the land, and this surplus labor force became an important commodity for businessmen. In Pennsylvania, mill owners sought the wives and daughters of anthracite miners. One-third of southern mill workers were under age sixteen: "We want whole families with at least three workers for the mill in each family," declared an advertisement for the Pacolet Manufacturing Company in South Carolina. Mill hands worked ten to twelve hours per day in brutal heat and noise, breathing noxious lint dust. Owners argued that families received more than just a living wage for their efforts; they also learned the habits of industry, and children grew into well-disciplined employees. Like the mine operators, mill owners often built lucrative company towns, company housing, and company stores.[22]

Child-labor legislation was an important reform during the Progressive Era (which ran from the late nineteenth century through World War I). Progressivism drew strength from the desire of the middle and upper classes to ameliorate some of the worst excesses of modern industrial society. They sought to curb corporate abuses, end government corruption, control monopoly, and democratize the electoral process. Equally characteristic of the movement was its style. Progressives were enamored of data, and statistics became a trademark of everything from government agency reports to muckraking journalism. Reformers were filled with moral zeal yet were wary of social conflict, especially between the rich and the poor. They valued order, reason, efficiency, expertise, professionalism, but their reforms tended to be moderate, not radical.[23]

Progressive influence on child labor emerged from a growing desire of many parents to send their children to school rather than to work, and during these years, rates of school attendance rose sharply. This change was in part the result of a new perception of childhood as a period of play, creativity, and preparation for adulthood. The pioneering psychologist G. Stanley Hall argued that not only were there distinct stages of development from childhood to adulthood but inappropriate activities like intense labor harmed children and threatened the evolution of society.[24]

Led by the Child Labor Committee, composed primarily of wealthy socialites and prominent church leaders, turn-of-the-century New York City was an important site in the crusade against child labor. Florence Kelley had recently moved there from Chicago, where, as Illinois's chief factory inspector, she was a pioneer in holding company owners responsible for unsafe conditions. In New York, she formed the National Consumers' League, under whose auspices she gave hundreds of speeches exposing the abuses of child labor. Important legislation limited the age, hours, and type of work that children might perform, and there was growing consensus that very young children needed protection. Just after the turn of the century, major journals of opinion like *The Independent, The Outlook, Arena,* and *Gunton's Magazine* carried several articles on child labor. In the Northeast, a strong reform impulse grew, but states passed laws only to have them struck down by the Supreme Court.[25]

During the Progressive Era, middle-class proponents of the new laws believed that childhood must be measured by its moral significance, not its monetary value. Childhood was sacred, and no commercial or material concerns should contaminate it. Reformers dismissed as pure hypocrisy the argument that children needed to make money for their families; parents who sent children out to work were monstrous exploiters, as bad as the businessmen who profited from them. Fortuitously, the reformers made these arguments precisely when child labor became less essential to the economy. The massive influx of immigrants to America before World War I provided an alternative labor supply, and the increasing mechanization of industries eliminated many simple tasks that children had performed.[26]

Mother Jones expressed her outrage over child labor in the first article she ever published, "Civilization in Southern Mills," which appeared in the *International Socialist Review* in March 1901. She began, "The miners and railroad boys of Birmingham, Alabama, entertained me one evening some months ago with a graphic description of the conditions among the slaves of the Southern cotton mills. While I imagined that these must be something of a modern Siberia, I concluded that the boys were overdrawing the picture and made up my mind to see for myself the conditions described." She took a mill job, where she witnessed six- and seven-year-olds starting their workday at 5:30 a.m., taking their scanty lunch at noon, working until 7:00 p.m., then returning home to a rushed dinner and sleep until the factory whistle blew again the next morning. "I have seen mothers," she wrote, "take their babes and slap cold water in their face to wake the poor little things. I have watched them all day long tending the dangerous machinery. I have seen their helpless limbs torn off, and then when they were disabled and of no more use to the master, thrown out to die."[27]

Innocence exploited, pure and simple. Mother Jones moved on to a job in a Tuscaloosa rope factory, and in what became a stock image that she used countless times in the future, she contrasted the blighted lives of the mill children with the coddled poodles of the masters. Anyone who tried to organize the poor, she added, was thrown into prison by judges doing the capitalists' bidding. "I shudder for the future of a nation," she wrote, "that is building up a moneyed aristocracy out of the life-blood of the children of the proletariat." Mother Jones's language here was a bit less fresh, a little more typical of the radical boilerplate of the *International Socialist Review* than of her speeches and letters. "Civilization in Southern Mills" concluded that only the overthrow of capitalism, followed by the "dawning of the new day of socialism," promised relief.[28]

As she organized miners, Mother Jones returned to the theme of child labor to reveal the brutal extremes to which operators pushed their workers. In an article called "The Coal Miners of the Old Dominion," she discussed the trap boys, who opened and closed doors deep in the mines for mules hauling out the coal. Some of the boys worked fourteen hours a day to make sixty cents, their bodies assaulted by blasts of cold air and knee-deep mud, "keeping their lone watch in the tombs of the earth with never a human soul to speak to them." She saw the exploitation stretching across generations: "The parents of these boys have known no other life than that of endless toil. Now those who have robbed and plundered the parents are beginning the same story with the present generation." She wrote also of the breaker boys, their bodies stooped and their fingers deformed, who sorted coal from slate as it all came rushing down a conveyor belt.[29]

The emancipation of children, Mother Jones proclaimed, was the

6. Textile mills employed large numbers of children, especially girls. During the Progressive Era, child labor became very controversial, and Mother Jones's "Crusade of the Mill Children" brought considerable publicity to the issue (Courtesy State Historical Society of Wisconsin)

grandest work of civilization. She pictured for a United Mine Workers audience a mother clasping her newborn son and thinking, "Some day, he will be the man of this nation; some day I shall sacrifice myself for the education, the developing of his brain, the bringing out of his grander, nobler qualities." But capitalists took boys to the breakers and girls to the mills. Now women were joining hands with the labor movement: "No more will the mother reach down into the cradle and take the babe out of it and sell it for so many hours a day to their capitalistic masters." Mother Jones declared that the labor movement must free "the little white slave":

> When I look into the faces of the little toiling children and see their appealing eyes, it touches the tender chord of a mother's heart. Think of these helpless little things with no one to fight their battles but labor's hosts! No church, no charity organization, no society, no club takes up the war in their behalf; it is only labor and labor's force that come to their rescue. I stand here today to appeal to you in behalf of the helpless children.

It was not true that only unions were interested in child labor; churches, charitable organizations, and women's clubs, as well as government and private agencies, had all begun to stir. Nor were labor's motives selfless, since children undercut the wages of adult workers. And although child labor was unquestionably evil, Mother Jones's descriptions of seven-year-olds with missing limbs working fourteen-hour days were not strictly accurate.[30]

But if we view her words metaphorically, not just literally, then a different picture emerges. Child labor, Mother Jones concluded, was not so much a moral issue, as many Progressive reformers believed, as an economic one, part of the larger problem of capital exploiting labor. In an age of corporations, working-class parents, pressed by low wages, were forced to think of their children as a source of income. Capitalists, Mother Jones declared, "have built their mines and breakers to take your boys out of the cradle; they have built their factories to take your girls." And then an image she returned to again and again in coming years: "They have built on the bleeding, quivering hearts of yourselves and your children their palaces." Child labor had become her central trope—capitalism respected nothing, including the innocence of children; workers acting alone were powerless to protect their loved ones in a wage-based economy; only a strong family of labor animated by maternal values countered capital's depredations.[31]

In 1901, Mother Jones participated in a weavers' strike near Scranton, Pennsylvania, and another one in Paterson, New Jersey. Then in June 1903, she threw herself into the textile strike centered on the Kensington district of Philadelphia. Against growing tension over control of the workplace—the National Association of Manufacturers had launched an aggressive open-shop campaign to counteract the growth of unions—the Philadelphia silk strike began on May 29 and quickly spread to six hundred area mills. A hundred thousand workers, sixteen thousand of them children under sixteen years of age—walked out. Their pay ranged from two to thirteen dollars per week, but the real issue was a Textile Workers Union demand to reduce the workweek from sixty to fifty-five hours, even if it meant a pay cut. To no avail, the union had lobbied the state legislature for a reduced-hours law, one that also prohibited night work for women and children. Mother Jones joined the strike two weeks after it began. She was there to stir up public support, but the demonstrations she held in Philadelphia gained little press attention and her initial efforts brought few results. According to her autobiography, newspapermen told her that they could not print stories about the strike because the mill owners held stock in the papers. "Well I've got stock in these little children," she told them. "I'll arrange a little publicity."[32]

The children's crusade was highly improvisational, revealing Mother Jones's willingness to keep trying new techniques until something worked. The Kensington strike was not focused on child labor, and the union leaders were skeptical about emphasizing the issue until Mother Jones convinced them of its publicity value. The wretched conditions under which the children worked, their mangled bodies, and the laxness of Pennsylvania child-labor laws were issues that might galvanize Americans and draw new supporters to labor's cause. Mother Jones told reporters that the idea for the march came from the Liberty

Bell tour, then attracting throngs of citizens who lined the railroad tracks to catch a glimpse of the icon of American freedom. But there were echoes again of Coxey's Army, and newspaper reporters quickly coined the phrase "Mother Jones' Industrial Army." The march of the mill children was a remarkable bit of street drama, most of which Mother Jones made up as she went along.[33]

On the eve of the crusade, Mother Jones told the Philadelphia *North American*:

> The employment of children is doing more to fill prisons, insane asylums, almshouses, reformatories, slums, and gin shops than all the efforts of reformers are doing to improve society. . . .
>
> I am going to picture capitalism and caricature the money-mad. I am going to show Wall Street the flesh and blood from which it squeezes its wealth.

On July 7, Mother Jones and the strike leaders revealed their plans at a rally in Philadelphia's Labor Lyceum Hall. One hundred boys and girls, along with textile workers and labor leaders, would march from Philadelphia to New York City, nearly one hundred miles. Music and speeches would grab public attention along the way, and the children would act out skits depicting the luxurious lives of "Mr. Capital" and "Mrs. Millowner" (for which they brought costume jewelry, fancy dresses, and masks). By parading from town to town and holding rallies at night, they hoped to call attention to the plight of all child laborers, while raising money and public support for the textile workers.[34]

The journey lasted over three weeks. A boy named Danny James led the way, carrying a placard that read WE ARE TEXTILE WORKERS. Some of the children were dressed as Revolutionary War soldiers, and their signs declared, WE ONLY ASK FOR JUSTICE; 55 HOURS OR NOTHING; WE WANT TIME TO GO TO SCHOOL; and PROSPERITY: WHERE IS OUR SHARE? A member of the Central Executive Committee of the Textile Workers Union swung a red, white, and blue baton, while a fife and drum corps played "Marching through Georgia" and other airs. They also carried an enormous American flag, and a reporter for the Philadelphia *Evening Bulletin* declared that the group was imbued with the spirit of the old colonial army in its fight for freedom.[35]

The children marched through towns like Bristol, Morrisville, Trenton, New Brunswick, Elizabeth, Metuchen, Rahway, and Jersey City. When thunderstorms drove them to seek shelter near Princeton, they ended up on the grounds of Grover Cleveland's estate; since the former President was out of town, the caretaker allowed them to sleep in the barn. They bathed in the Delaware River, sometimes hotel owners donated rooms, and occasionally they slept in the homes of local laborites. Farmers provided food, while trade-union locals and members of the Socialist Party offered their aid and support.[36]

At Princeton, Mother Jones lectured to a crowd that included students and professors. She declared that the rich robbed child laborers of an education in order to pay for their own sons' and daughters' college tuition. Then she introduced some of the mill children, with their gnarled hands and missing fingers: " 'Here's a textbook on economics,' I said, pointing to a little chap, James Ashworth, who was ten years old and who was stooped over like an old man from carrying bundles of yarn that weighed seventy-five pounds. 'He gets three dollars a week and his sister who is fourteen gets six dollars. They work in a carpet factory ten hours a day while the children of the rich are getting their higher education.' " When the speeches ended, the children marched out of Princeton and slept that night along the banks of Stony Brook, "where years and years before, the ragged Revolutionary Army camped, Washington's brave soldiers that made their fight for freedom."[37]

The crusade did not always go so smoothly. Disputes arose between Mother Jones and other union officials. The summer heat—most days topped ninety degrees—took its toll, as did mosquitoes. At first, the march was poorly organized. Some of the men grumbled that they had to walk while Mother Jones and the children rode in wagons, that they stayed in leaky tents while the others had roofs over their heads. When food supplies ran low, a few of the marchers started pilfering; others had to be restrained from drinking. "It's all right for Mother Jones," declared one disgruntled striker, "she sleeps in a hotel. I would rather work sixty hours a week than to endure this torture. We seem to be a kind of side show to help her get some notoriety about the country." Reports varied on how many people took part in the march, but clearly what started out as about two hundred dwindled to several dozen, partly by design, partly by attrition. In some towns, like Paterson, where an earlier mill strike had failed, the crowds were not as large nor the collections as generous as the organizers hoped. And all of these failures were reported in the press. *The New York Times* took special pleasure in pointing out the problems: " 'Mother' Jones made another speech upon the street to-night, in which she denounced capital, child labor, and things in general. She will leave here to-morrow and proceed to Rahway, Elizabeth, Newark, Paterson, Jersey City, New York, and Oyster Bay, if she has any followers by that time."[38]

Nonetheless, the march of the mill children garnered considerable publicity for the textile workers' strike and for the cause of child-labor legislation. In most towns, two thousand or more people turned out to hear Mother Jones deliver her message, and in large cities like Trenton five thousand heard her denounce the "cannibalistic plutocrats who are grinding out young lives beneath the wheels of gold":

> What is the use of bringing a lot of children into the world to make more money for plutocrats while their little lives are being ground out in the mill and the workshop? The army I am leading on to New York is composed of intelligent workmen. . . . Our cause is a just one and we propose to show the New York millionaires our grievances.

After each speech, the mill children collected contributions from the audience. Later at night, Mother Jones and her lieutenants addressed local trade-union meetings—of plumbers, carpenters, leather workers—to gain further support.[39]

The original plan called for the march to end with a monster rally in New York City, but Mother Jones casually mentioned a more dramatic denouement to a New York *World* reporter: "We will parade up and down Wall Street to show the millionaires the little emaciated boys and overworked men who have earned their millions for them. Mr.

[J. P.] Morgan may not be at home to us, but we'll give Wall Street a lesson anyway. . . . The President himself will have to be kind to us. We will march right up Sagamore Hill and dine with 'Teddy.' " At first this idea was not taken seriously, and Mother Jones even told the *New York Tribune* that she only mentioned Roosevelt's name to get people's attention. But the idea took on a life of its own, the dwindling crowds suddenly grew larger, and the sagging spirits of the group rebounded. By July 14, Sagamore Hill and an audience with the President had become the crusade's goal.[40]

On July 15, Mother Jones sent an open letter to Roosevelt, addressing the President deferentially as "our father and leader" and asking only for "advice and guidance." She told of the children's plight. She painted a vivid picture:

> These children raked by cruel toil beneath the iron wheels of greed, are starving in this country which you have declared is in the height of prosperity. . . . We who know of these sufferings have taken up their cause and are now marching towards you in the hope that your tender heart will counsel with us to abolish this crime.

She prayed that Roosevelt would heed Jesus' words "Suffer little children to come unto Me," and she concluded by asking the President—"as your children"—for an audience. Several newspapers published the letter, but Roosevelt chose not to dignify it with an answer. Mother Jones's army, the President's aides told reporters, would not be received. We are going to Sagamore Hill, the old woman responded.[41]

Mother Jones made a couple of advance trips in preparation for the "invasion" of New York. She left Paterson to attend the Social Democratic Party's annual picnic, where a crowd of four thousand cheered her for several minutes before allowing her to speak. Even though the newspapers were filled with Roosevelt's refusal to meet her, she declared her intention to find out whether he "is the President of the capitalists only, or whether he is the President of the workingmen too." She returned to New Jersey for more rallies, then crossed the Hudson again, this time to obtain a parade permit. At first the acting police commissioner refused her request. Mayor Seth Low also said no, noting that the marchers were not citizens of New York City. Mother Jones countered that the city granted Germany's Prince Henry—"a rotton piece of royalty"—a parade permit, so how could the mayor refuse American workers who contributed to the nation's prosperity? He relented. The mill children would march from their lodgings at Social Democratic Headquarters on East Fourth Street to a meeting site near Madison Square on Twenty-seventh Street.[42]

The crusaders crossed to Manhattan on the afternoon of July 23. That night, six hundred policemen kept order as thousands watched the sixty marchers parade up Second Avenue by torchlight, with banners streaming and fifes and drums playing. Unfortunately, by the time Benjamin Hanford—the first speaker and a former Social Democratic candidate for governor of New York—finished his harangue against the police and the mayor, Mother Jones was too tired and too embarrassed to make her own address. (She did not approve of Hanford's speech, especially his castigating New York City officials; she said later that the mayor and the chief of police had treated her with all possible courtesy.) With her arms draped over the shoulders of two of the mill children, she made a few remarks, and promised a speech the next evening on how child slavery in America eclipsed the horrors of Russia. Then the children took up a collection, gathering coins in their American flag. The next day, Secret Service agents visited Mother Jones at her hotel and discouraged her from going to Oyster Bay; she turned them away. That night, she gave a rousing, hour-long speech, after which the crowd followed her back to her hotel, cheering her all the way.[43]

Three days after arriving in New York, on July 26, the marchers took the train to Coney Island, invited there by Frank Bostock, an animal-show owner who sympathized with the strike. Bostock used their presence to drum up business, and at the end of the day's entertainment, he announced that Mother Jones would give an address. As she spoke, a giant picture of Roman emperors giving the thumbs-down sign hung behind the podium and lions roared in the background, while several of the mill children were locked in animal cages to represent, Mother Jones said, American employers' attitudes toward their workers. She told the large crowd that the marchers would persuade the President to "protect children against the greed of the manufacturer." She contrasted the patriotism of Civil War veterans with the venality of modern-day politicians. Just as Northern soldiers died to stop the sale of black youths into slavery, so Americans must now intervene to stop the sale of children "on the installment plan."[44]

Then she expanded her attack from child labor to poverty and powerlessness in America:

> I will tell the President that I saw men in Madison Square last night sleeping on the benches and that the country can have no greatness while one unfortunate lies out at night without a bed to sleep on. I will tell him that the prosperity he boasts of is the prosperity of the rich wrung from the poor.

If the President refused to see what was going on, she would confront him with "the wail of the children," she would bear witness to those in power:

> I saw them last Winter pass three railroad bills in one hour, and when labor cries for aid for the little ones they turn their backs and will not listen to her. I asked a man in prison once how he happened to get there. He had stolen a pair of shoes. I told him that if he had stolen a railroad he could be a United States Senator.

The division of American society into the rich and powerful, on the one hand, and the poor and dispossessed, on the other, was all but complete:

> You are told that every American-born male citizen has a chance of being President. I tell you that the hungry man without a bed in the park would sell his chance for a good square meal, and these little toilers, deformed, dwarfed in body, soul, and morality, with nothing but toil before them and no chance for schooling, don't even have the dream that they might some day have a chance at the Presidential chair.

She concluded, "One hour of justice is worth an age of praying," and that was why they were on their way to see the President.[45]

They never met Roosevelt. As the mill children marched across Long Island, the Secret Service kept a lookout, the press speculated that police would block the roads, and Roosevelt's personal secretary, B. F. Barnes, warned that Mother Jones would not be permitted to enter the grounds with an "invading army." Discreetly, Mother Jones, two organizers, and three mill children approached Roosevelt's home on July 28. The President's secretary met them at the executive office and told them that Roosevelt was not in. He advised Mother Jones to submit her request in writing. The group quietly took the next train back to New York City.[46]

Mother Jones wrote her letter to the President. She told him that child labor jeopardized the republic, for ill-formed, uneducated children could not grow up to be true citizens. She noted that state laws went unenforced, thus the need for federal legislation. She made her appeal as *Mother* Jones: "I have seen little children without the first rudiments of education and no prospect of acquiring any. I have seen other children with hands, fingers and other parts of their tiny bodies mutilated because of their childish ignorance of machinery. I feel that no nation can be truly great while such conditions exist without attempted remedy." Although the President's secretary told Mother Jones that Roosevelt would read her letter, there is no evidence that he did. Barnes wrote the reply, assuring her that the President had the "hardiest sympathy" with efforts to prevent child labor but that the Constitution empowered only the states to deal with the problem.[47]

Mother Jones scoffed at the President's hearty sympathy, wondered aloud to reporters why he would not see three boys who represented thousands, and warned workers not to vote for Roosevelt in 1904. She said she would keep the group together, made more speeches in New York City, and considered organizing even larger children's marches to Washington, D.C. But the Colorado coal strike beckoned Mother Jones before such demonstrations ever took place. Besides, the textile strike was soon broken, and everyone returned to Philadelphia. The children went back to work.[48]

"To Give Child Labor a Mortal Stab"

The children's crusade grew in reputation as time passed, and it is often mentioned as one of Mother Jones's great triumphs. The event made indelible the image of her as defender of children everywhere. But the legacy of the children's crusade was not clear immediately. A certain sourness poisoned the event from beginning to end. Summer heat and poor planning shortened tempers. Much of the press was distinctly unsympathetic to labor, even to the cause of ending child labor. *The Cincinnati Enquirer,* for example, dismissed the marchers as "a gang of lunatics." Some reporters chastised Mother Jones for sending an "invading army" to see the President, forgetting that the metaphor was largely of the press's own making. Other newspapers used the rocky start and unclear initial goals of the children's crusade to portray its leader as a crank. And Mother Jones's melodramatic language, always so effective in person before working-class audiences, must have appeared overwrought to those who read her words in the morning papers over coffee and rolls.[49]

There were deeper problems. Ten-year-olds working twelve hours a day for a pittance made great drama. But most of the youths were much older, and while they surely were exploited, their situation in the labor market was complex. We see this clearly in the textile strike of 1900–1901, a tune-up for the children's crusade two years later. The very year Mother Jones was named an international organizer for the UMW, she became involved in the silk strike near Scranton, Pennsylvania. Here, a single owner, Henry D. Klots of New York City, ran several mills that employed over five thousand workers. Mother Jones described the situation: "Most of them are little tots, ranging from 8–14 years of age. The poverty of the parents compels them to swear that these babies are of the age when they can be legally worked by the master class. . . . This is capitalism with a vengeance, the robber system that is upheld by those who vote Republican and Democratic tickets." In fact, in Carbondale, the center of the strike, roughly two-thirds of the children were between the ages of fourteen and seventeen, three-fifths of them female, and only about 10 percent under age thirteen. Mother Jones exaggerated the numbers of very young children working in the mills for dramatic effect, but by doing so, she obfuscated the larger issues of the strike.[50]

Most Klots mill girls were daughters of UMW members, men who wanted to control their families' labor and income. The UMW and Mother Jones supported a settlement of the silk strike that raised wages a little but left the terms of employment untouched. The textile workers were not satisfied with the agreement, but the UMW, a far more powerful union, pressured them to take it. The settlement did nothing to curb child labor and failed to consider that many of the strikers did not even come from homes headed by men. They needed a better settlement, not one that caved in to the UMW's paternalist assumptions that men must protect their daughters. By backing the UMW, Mother Jones simply avoided these larger, thornier issues, issues of family control, independence for youths, and women's need to make their own money and lead their own lives.[51]

Still, the positive results of the children's crusade outweighed the negative. After the rocky beginning, Mother Jones showed real leadership in articulating the meaning of the march for her various audiences, and in her handling of New York City officials. She insisted that only textile workers be allowed to participate, rejecting the idea of a larger and potentially more unruly parade of all aggrieved laborers. Her intent always was a symbolic show of the miseries inflicted by capitalism, not an assault on its bastions (although journalists' accounts of the impeding "invasion" by this "army" made it sound like a second Paris Commune). She reached Sagamore Hill and handled the President's refusal to see the marchers with dignity. Above all, she gained invaluable publicity for the issue of child labor. In cities where many people had never thought about the subject, enormous crowds turned out for speeches and parades, while local editorials emphasized its importance. As the *United Mine Workers Journal* put it, "The New York press, and indeed the press of the whole country, has given the child labor problem columns where they would not otherwise have devoted lines to this subject."[52]

The march of the mill children was an early moment in a long change of consciousness that led to the abolition of child labor in America. Although the states continued to tinker with the problem—

raising the legal age for employment or requiring stronger evidence from parents of their children's birth dates—no national legislation was even introduced until 1907. In 1916 and 1919, Congress finally passed laws, which were struck down by the Supreme Court; efforts at a constitutional amendment in the 1920s failed to gain approval of three-fourths of the states; only when Congress passed the Fair Labor Standards Act in 1938 as part of the New Deal, and the Supreme Court ruled it legal in 1941, did America have a nationwide law regulating child labor.[53]

It is easy to slight Mother Jones's courage in 1903, for hindsight makes her stand against labor by children appear unassailable. At the beginning of the century, however, the voices of powerful people (and many working-class ones as well) still supported child labor. No consensus on the inviolability of childhood yet condemned the practice as barbaric. So although the children's march had only mixed results in 1903, Mother Jones did take an important step on the road to significant social change. As the *United Mine Workers Journal* expressed it, her crusade "helped to give child labor a mortal stab, and though it will take plenty of time to kill the cruel monster that insists on feeding off the flesh and blood of little children, yet it is doomed."[54]

Although the march of the mill children catapulted Mother Jones to new fame, she never saw abolishing child labor as a social panacea. Rather, the plight of the mill children was part of the much larger problem of labor's exploitation. The logic was simple: the aim of capitalists was to produce goods as cheaply as possible; desire for profits and fear of losses to competitors enforced such behavior; therefore, businessmen would do whatever was necessary to survive and prosper, even exploit eleven-year-olds. Children worked because parents could not make enough money for their families. Mother Jones's ultimate goal was a living wage for working families, better yet, sufficient pay for men so that women could stay home and children go to school. With this larger purpose in mind, she turned her attention to politics.

★ 6 ★

"Faithfully Yours
for the Revolution"

"Like a mother talking to her errant boys she taught and admonished that night in words that went home to every heart," Kate Richards O'Hare recalled of the first time she heard Mother Jones speak. The old woman exhorted unionists to become Socialists: "She told them that a scab at the ballot-box was more to be despised than one at the factory door, that a scab ballot could do more harm than a scab bullet; that workingmen must support the political party of their class and that the only place for a sincere union man was in the Socialist party." Mother Jones's speech was one of the reasons O'Hare became a Socialist. Ten years later, Elizabeth Gurley Flynn, eighteen years old and a rising star as a "jawsmith" for the Industrial Workers of the World, was inspired by hearing Mother Jones speak in New York City. This "greatest woman agitator of our time" was giving city folks hell: "Why weren't we helping the miners in the West? Why weren't we backing up the Mexican people against Díaz? We were 'white-livered rabbits who never put our feet on Mother Earth.' " So vivid were Mother Jones's descriptions of bloodshed in the mine country, and so virulent her attacks on Democrats and Republicans, that Flynn, already a bit light-headed from standing so long, fainted.[1]

Mother Jones engaged in a number of struggles between 1905 and 1912 after she left the United Mine Workers. She earned her bread as

143

a speaker for the Socialist Party, which kept her on the road constantly. Along the way, she took up the cause of Milwaukee brewery workers, Arizona copper miners, Chicago telegraphers, Alabama textile workers, New York City garment workers, exiled Mexican revolutionaries, and imprisoned American labor leaders. For someone who thrived on great dramatic struggles, however, these years offered no singular crisis. Mother Jones was less in the public eye than during the previous coal strikes, and certainly less than she would be in the coal wars of 1912–1915. But even if she spent no time in jail, these years challenged her in important ways. She emerged from them still faithful to socialist ideas but wary of the Socialist Party and its middle-class supporters. In the end, her commitment to a democratic, class-conscious labor movement grew stronger than ever.[2]

"Go to Your Homes, Workers, and Study the Question"

Pneumonia hospitalized Mother Jones toward the end of 1903 during the Colorado strike, and many of her friends helped nurse her back to health. Bertha Howell Mailly, a Socialist and journalist and the wife of William Mailly (who first wrote to Mother Jones offering a position in the Party), spent time with her in Trinidad, Colorado, then brought her home to Omaha, Nebraska, for further convalescence, as well as more coaxing to become a speaker for the Socialists. Mother Jones's frustrations with the United Mine Workers—the conservatism of John Mitchell, the disagreements over tactics, the defeats that she believed could have been avoided, the stigma over the *Polly Pry* charges—finally caused her to accept the Maillys' offer.[3]

The early years of the twentieth century were marked by great political ferment, but progressivism, the dominant political trend at the time, was more reformist than radical. Progressives tended to be middle-class, native-born Americans from Protestant backgrounds who tinkered with the system in order to save it. Muckraking journalists attacked enormous businesses like Standard Oil, or corrupt municipal institutions like urban transportation companies, to call attention to their abuses and thereby foster change. Many progressives advocated modifying the electoral system—implementing the initiative, referendum, and recall, even allowing women to vote—to bolster democracy and make politicians more responsive to the public will. They challenged the autocratic power of political machines but usually worked within the two-party system. If most progressives were disinclined to storm the barricades of industrial capitalism, they humanized things with new antitrust laws and business regulations, legislation protecting women and children in the workplace, some rudimentary workmen's compensation laws, and new codes for factory safety.[4]

Many Americans wanted more dramatic change. The rise of industrial capitalism produced some militant radicalism and bred a number of revolutionaries, syndicalists, and anarchists. The left grew dramatically around the turn of the century, but it also became more factionalized. Socialism never became a single unified movement in America. It was a mixed bag of middle-class people dissatisfied with progressive moderation and working-class folk who felt that what unions accomplished in the economic sphere, socialists might do in politics. The movement attracted advocates of diverse causes such as birth control, international peace, and prison reform. The Socialist Party was America's single largest radical organization, and electing candidates to office was its goal. An older and much smaller group, the Socialist Labor Party, was doctrinally sophisticated, strongly Marxist, and heavily German. More conservative "gas and water" socialists advocated little more than public ownership of municipal utilities. The broad rubric of socialism encompassed former populists from southwestern farm states, immigrants, and militant western radicals. The bonds between factions threatened constantly to come undone, but during the years Mother Jones worked for the Socialist Party, growing numbers of disaffected Americans made it their political home. Broadly speaking, the organization denied the legitimacy of corporate power and sought public ownership of basic industries, while at the same time working within America's traditions of democratic politics and civil liberties.[5]

Socialist ideas originated in the class wars of Europe, but Eugene Debs of Terre Haute, Indiana, domesticated the movement. Even as he inveighed against plutocracy, Debs did so with an American accent, calling for collectivization in the name of republican ideals and Christian brotherhood. For Debs, socialism meant a return to the mutuality of his beloved Terre Haute, before national and international corporations replaced human bonds with monetary ones. And many of Debs's countrymen—prominent Americans such as Florence Kelley, Theodore Dreiser, Frances Perkins, Jack London, Helen Keller, and Upton Sinclair—joined the Party. Not only did Debs gain a growing percentage of the presidential vote in 1904, 1908, and 1912, but the Party elected several mayors in towns across the country and a handful of congressmen, as well as countless state and local officials. Even while the vast majority of American workers remained loyal to the Democrats and Republicans, the Socialist Party grew so rapidly that many businessmen feared it might dominate American politics someday.[6]

Radical movements often evoke frantic responses, and socialism was no exception. One gets a sense of the anxiety that the Party engendered from a 1908 article, "America's Trouble-Makers," written by James Creelman and published in the popular journal *Pearson's Magazine*. Creelman described a bomb explosion in New York City, compared the (allegedly) growing number of such incidents to an epidemic, and offered a list of those accountable. He mentioned dozens of individuals and organizations—some militant, some moderate, but "all serving, directly or indirectly, openly or secretly, toward the destruction of American civilization." Socialists were the biggest culprits, and Creelman spoke of their "sleepless propaganda," of how the leaders were "orderly, patient, persistent and capable of great effort and supreme suffering." The movement was "anti-American to the marrow of its bones and its heart's core," for it sought nothing less than the destruction of the government designed by the forefathers. Instead of embracing the American belief that there must be no class divisions, the Socialists constantly attempted to pique workingmen's class consciousness and goad their hatred for the rich. The enemy was sneaky and persistent: "One defeat means nothing to the socialist. He is at it all the time, night and day, mining and sapping, openly and secretly." The Party was an insidious, unmanly, violent foe of America, fomenting a "deliberate war of extermination of the capitalists."[7]

That her adversaries believed socialism to be so powerful gave Mother Jones considerable pleasure. Her lectures endorsed Socialist candidates, advocated social revolution, and promoted the labor movement. But mostly she told stories about her own exploits. Her technique was not to persuade by cool argument but to ridicule her opponents, canonize labor's heroes, and invoke her own iconic status. After each address, she peddled Eugene Debs's new book, *Unionism and Socialism,* in which he advocated a two-pronged approach to radical change, organizing on the shop floor *and* working for Socialist candidates.[8]

Mother Jones started work with the Illinois Socialists in January 1905. She had long espoused fundamental socialist ideas—that capitalist societies create two classes, one in control of productive property, the other impoverished by its dependence on wage labor; that class struggle was a fact of American life; that the working class could take control of government back from the capitalists at the ballot box; that large industries should be publicly owned and that workers must act in solidarity toward that goal. She wrote of the two-party system with characteristic scorn in the *International Socialist Review*: "The father who casts a vote for the continuance of that system is as much of a murderer as if he took a pistol and shot his own children." Evils such as child labor would only end with the overthrow of capitalism and "the dawning of a new day of socialism." With Socialist electoral victories, she promised an audience in Washington, "the wealth of the country will eventually get back into the hands of the people."[9]

For Mother Jones, as for many Americans, socialism was a moral imperative, infused with almost religious significance. She described to fellow Party member Jack London how she spent her days in the winter of 1905 organizing "factory slaves" in the South, then industrial workers in Troy, New York; and every night she made her pitch for socialism. "My Dear Comrade," she wrote London, "How sad it is . . . the earth filled with wealth! So many of God's children suffering! What is it to us if the church bell tolls each Easter morning and announces the resurrection of the Christ? It has never yet tolled for the resurrection of Christ's children from their long dark tomb of slavery." Most of her personal letters in these years were signed under phrases like "Fondly and loyally yours for the emancipation of the race" and "Faithfully yours for the revolution."[10]

She kept a very busy schedule, but no full texts of her speeches survive. She never spoke from notes, so her content varied from place to place. Although she always tailored her presentations to the particular locale and to current events, certain themes emerged.[11]

A newspaper report of a speech she gave in Helena, Montana, on June 13, 1905, gives us a sense of what she told her listeners. She began by declaring that "we are face to face with a conflict of the classes." Her fundamental assumption was the labor theory of value—that the worth of goods comes from workers combining their toil and skill with natural resources. From this followed the belief that capitalists unjustly deprive workers of the product of their labor, that the earth's treasures rightfully belong to the people, that the primary identity of those who toil for a living is with each other, and that out of such awareness will come change. Government, she insisted, was a prisoner of capital: "You assume that you live in a republic, but it is a mistake; you live under the flag of an oligarchy. Your President and Congress do not represent the people. They represent the robber class, and do not represent the working class." For Mother Jones, the conclusion was obvious: "The wealth that I produce is mine and it does not make any difference to me how I am robbed." The working class must take back at the ballot box what was rightfully its own.[12]

Although her ideas were far from original intellectually, the way she spoke to her listeners, her relationship with them, her language and metaphors made her singularly effective. In good republican fashion, she invoked the wastefulness of the upper class: "Why, my working brothers, the rich class cur dog has a better time than you. A short time ago they had a dog marriage and paid the preacher $100." She went on to juxtapose her own dedication to the indifference of her audience: "I have faced the capitalist government of to-day; I have faced the bayonets; I have held your bleeding heads in my lap. . . . My days are not long on this earth, but I shall continue the fight for your children if you are too bigoted or too cowardly to do it yourself." She invoked America's revolutionary history: "Brace up for the fight, and in the words of a patriot, 'Give me liberty or give me death.' " She told the women that they were as guilty as the men, that they must organize and think about real issues rather than losing themselves in musical shows and dime novels. She concluded with an image that brought politics into the household: "Go to your homes, workers, and study the question. Don't go to the saloons, don't go to the gambling rooms, but go to your own firesides and study the question."[13]

The Western Federation's publication, *Miners' Magazine*, followed her exploits around the country and reported them in deep purple prose. Arkansas, 1906: "The fire of her eloquence is arousing the exploited slaves from their slumber of lethargy." Utah, 1907: "Millions of men and women will revere the memory of this dauntless woman, whose heroism upon the industrial battlefield nerved faltering men to action in the cause of human liberty." Texas, 1908: "Her hearers everywhere are declaring themselves for the remedy of Socialism. . . . She has learned the truths of Socialist philosophy not from academic discussion and study of scientific lore, but from actual contact with the people." South Dakota, 1909: "Mother Jones in her speeches in the Black Hills wore no gloves but rapped capitalism with bare knuckles."[14]

Mother Jones agreed that experience, not theory, was the source of her authority. Thus, on January 12, 1907, she wrote an open letter to Bertha Honoré Palmer, a socialite and reformer and the wife of a prominent Chicago businessman. Mrs. Palmer was about to host a meeting of industrialists and workers at her mansion, with the goal of harmonizing their conflicting interests. Mother Jones praised Palmer's sincerity but argued that a woman of wealth had no chance to understand the "grim reality" that made such reconciliation impossible. Then she explained her own perspective:

> I am a workman's daughter, by occupation a dressmaker and school teacher. . . . During the past seventy years of my life I have been subject to the authority of the capitalist class and for the last thirty-five years I have been conscious of the fact. With the years' personal experience—the . . . best of all teachers—I have learned that there is an irrepressible conflict that will never end between the working-class and the capitalist-class, until these two classes disappear and the worker alone remains the producer and owner of the capital produced.

She described the horrors she had witnessed firsthand. Depredations, she concluded, would not end until "the working-class send their representatives into the legislative halls of this nation and by law take away the power of this capitalist class to rob and oppress the workers."[15]

Speaking from life experience gave Mother Jones's words great power, but the Socialist Party never fully engaged her imagination. Class consciousness was the rock of her faith, yet she grew weary of the hairsplitting doctrinal debates and dispirited at the inflated egos of her colleagues (or at the clash of others' inflated egos with her own). Her all-or-nothing commitment to the cause gave her great power as a speaker but also led her to question the purity of others' motives and the depth of their commitment. Most of all, she increasingly scorned anyone not from the working class, a problem because socialism attracted large numbers of middle-class, even wealthy, Americans, and Mother Jones did not usually bother hiding her disdain for them.[16]

Perhaps Mother Jones felt ill at ease because she lacked their education and social polish, but also, beneath her hostility lay a growing conviction that social transformation depended on the working class itself. For all of these reasons, she was never fully satisfied working for the Party. Mere speechmaking lacked the drama on which she thrived. Like most others involved with radical politics, she was clearer about what she did not like than about specific remedies for the future. Would it be a centralized socialist state, a decentralized anarchist one, a syndicalist government run along industrial lines? She seemed to prefer any radical alternative to the poverty and powerlessness that modern industrial capitalism inflicted on so many people.[17]

Although Mother Jones never fully embraced anarchism or syndicalism, her name became associated with an organization that did. At the beginning of 1905, just as she started her work for the Socialist Party, she joined twenty-two other radicals in Chicago to hammer out a manifesto calling for the gathering of all industrial workers into one big union. They reconvened with dozens more kindred spirits six months later and formed the Industrial Workers of the World, better known as the Wobblies. Many Socialists participated, but the Wobblies emphasized labor organizing over politics. They welcomed all who toiled, including African Americans, immigrants, women, unskilled and migratory laborers, under the assumption that they were workers first and foremost. And because many among the dispossessed were barred from voting anyway, industrial organization made far more sense than the Socialists' electoral ambitions. The IWW, dedicated to revolutionary social transformation, quickly became America's most prominent syndicalist organization.[18]

Because she was the only woman at the initial planning meeting, Mother Jones might be called the "founding mother" of the Wobblies. They captured her imagination, and the IWW's manifesto echoed her own most radical moments:

> The working class and the employing class have nothing in common. There can be no peace as long as hunger and want are found among millions of working people, and the few who make up the employing class have all the good things of life. . . . Between these two classes a struggle must go on until the workers of the world organize as a class, take possession of the earth and the machinery of production, and abolish the wage system.

Yet after her initial involvement with the Wobblies, she held aloof. Indeed, she hardly spoke during those first two meetings, and it seems she never attended another one. Although a charter member of the IWW and a friend of many of its leaders, she said little about the organization in coming years except for an occasional rebuke, and she chose not to mention her presence at its founding in her autobiography.[19]

Mother Jones was never very explicit in her criticism, but she clearly grew mistrustful of the IWW's romanticism. She entered strikes intending to win, not just to make defiant gestures and pose as a revolutionary. Like many other unionists and socialists, she believed that the Wobblies grew more intent on posturing than on victory, and though she had her utopian moments too, she knew when to settle for incremental change. Because the IWW was so open-ended, what it gained in spontaneity it more than gave up in coherent strategy. Moreover, Mother Jones looked askance at the Wobblies' fascination with violence. Personally fearless, even an occasional advocate of workers taking up arms, she generally counseled against force. Although thoughts of armed rebellion sometimes beguiled Mother Jones, democratic transformation was usually more compelling to her. Besides, the IWW was formed to heal rifts among radicals, but the group only seemed to multiply them, as various factions took to attacking each other. Finally, most Wobblies were single, unattached men, and their working-class machismo did not fit well with her insistence on the metaphorical and literal *family* of labor.[20]

Mother Jones cooled to the Wobblies before the ink dried on their manifesto, but her life became enmeshed with two of their most prominent leaders only a year after the IWW's initial meeting. On December 30, 1905, a bomb exploded at the front gate of the house of Idaho's former governor Frank Steunenberg, killing him. Police rounded up the usual suspects, a man named Harry Orchard prime among them. Orchard had stalked Steunenberg, and detectives found bomb-making paraphernalia in his quarters. He confessed to the murder, and to a score of others, but Idaho officials were not satisfied. As governor, Steunenberg had fought the Western Federation of Miners bitterly at Coeur d'Alene; he broke the union's efforts there, drove members out of the mines, and imprisoned their officers. Steunenberg's murder, some said, was payback by the WFM's "inner circle." Idaho governor Frank Gooding appointed James H. Hawley and William Borah, the attorneys who had prosecuted the union at Coeur d'Alene in 1899, to handle the case, and they retained the Pinkerton Detective Agency to find evidence linking the murder to the WFM. Idaho came under the purview of Pinkerton's Denver office, headed by James McParland.[21]

With McParland's coaching and promises of immunity, Orchard gave testimony against the WFM leaders. President Charles Moyer, Secretary-Treasurer William "Big Bill" Haywood (both IWW members), and George Pettibone (a former member of the WFM's executive board) were seized in Denver and shipped secretly by special train, clearly in violation of federal and state law, though no court overruled their rendition to Idaho. They waited in prison for a year while McParland gathered evidence. Meanwhile, the story raged in the headlines, and Boise became a circus. Reporters from all over America came to town; both sides recognized that Moyer, Haywood, and Pettibone, indeed, the American left, were on trial as much in the press as in the jury box. Eugene Debs warned that Idaho's outrageous tactics threatened to bring down the wrath of American workers, and even Samuel Gompers denounced the machinations of mine owners and government officials. President Theodore Roosevelt got into the act when he publicly called the accused (as well as Debs) "undesirable citizens." Colorado Socialists demonstrated their contempt for Idaho officials by nominating Big Bill Haywood for governor. And if all that were not enough, the defense hired America's most famous trial lawyer, the Socialist Clarence Darrow.[22]

Mother Jones was sidelined with illness early in 1906 and again in the summer, but Darrow told her that the defense needed cash for a long and expensive trial. As soon as she was able, she went back on tour, giving speeches and organizing rallies. She wrote to Terence Powderly from Bisbee, Arizona, that the arrests in Idaho proved that "capitalism has no soul," and she mocked Theodore Roosevelt for his remarks about the defendants before the trial had even begun: "How the spectacular performer in Washington has put his foot in it. The word 'undesirable citizen' will go down in history. He and his crew of pirates would no doubt give a great deal to undo that." She believed that Governor Gooding had no intention for Moyer, Haywood, and Pettibone ever to leave Idaho alive, because they were "a menace to the capitalist anarchists that ruled with blood and iron." McParland, she declared, was the real mastermind behind the plot to frame the WFM leaders: "He put up the job with Guggenheim and his crowd to back him up, supply the funds, the special train and the hundred other factors in the conspiracy." Nonetheless, Mother Jones was optimistic for the future: "Go where we will the workers are beginning to stand up and talk out loud. They are feeling the thrill of manhood; they are tired of cringing and crawling; they are just realizing what they are and what they can be; and the change from slavery to freedom, from misery to splendid manhood is coming more swiftly than we know or the plutocrats dream."[23]

Both defense and prosecution skirted the law as they gathered evi-

dence and selected jurors. Finally, on May 9, 1907, a jury of elderly
Idaho farmers heard testimony. The prosecution chose to try Haywood
first, since he was the most outspoken, the most radical, the easiest to
convict. Harry Orchard proved a willing witness—too willing, since he
confessed to crimes that the defense easily demonstrated he could not
possibly have committed. A murderer, thief, perjurer, and bigamist, he
also had been a paid agent provocateur for the Pinkerton agency during the Cripple Creek strike. The prosecution's case collapsed, and a
year and eight months after Steunenberg's murder, the jury found
Haywood innocent. Pettibone was exonerated a few months later, and
the charges against Moyer were dropped. It was a Pyrrhic victory. The
trial drained finances and divided loyalties, with Haywood taking the
IWW toward revolution and Moyer leading the Western Federation to
the AFL. For those who sided with the prosecution, the acquittals
merely proved the conspiratorial powers of the WFM inner circle.[24]

The state's eagerness to prosecute Moyer, Haywood, and Pettibone
simply confirmed radicals' belief that dissent brought persecution and
that governments were bought and paid for. Shortly after Haywood's
acquittal, but before the Idaho trials ended, a new series of events began that underscored for people like Mother Jones the power of business to assert its prerogatives and the necessity for everyone else to
fight back.[25]

Revoltosa

Corporate expansion did not stop at the nation's borders. America had
become an empire by the end of the nineteenth century, controlling is-
lands such as Cuba, Hawaii, the Philippines and thereby securing trade
throughout the world. But before the Caribbean and the Pacific, there
was Mexico. By 1890, American companies had invested $130 million
there; as of 1900, $200 million; a decade later, $500 million. In 1910,
seven of Mexico's largest businesses were owned primarily by American
interests, and two of the three richest enterprises in the country were
American. Especially in the northern provinces, the names Rockefeller,
Guggenheim, Harriman, and Morgan were well known. Extractive

industries like mining and petroleum led the way, and the owners of these companies usually hired Americans as managers, Mexicans as laborers. Presidents from William McKinley to Woodrow Wilson nurtured the expansion of American capital and took pains to ensure its protection. This included supporting the autocratic government of President Porfirio Díaz (ruler of Mexico from 1877 to 1880 and again from 1884 to 1911), who encouraged foreign investment through low taxes, compliant courts, and friendly police. Mexicans, however, were growing restive; peasants, industrial laborers, and middle-class intellectuals formed a revolutionary movement. The Partido Liberal Mexicano was the largest *revoltoso* group, but between 1905 and 1911, the Díaz government made life increasingly difficult for PLM leaders. To avoid arrest and persecution, many relocated in America. They plotted a series of strikes and uprisings against Díaz from San Antonio, St. Louis, and Los Angeles.[26]

Ricardo Flores Magón was the most charismatic leader of this movement, and his followers were called Magonistas. Other leaders included his brother Enrique Flores Magón, Juan and Manuel Sarabia, Antonio Villarreal, Librado Rivera, and Rosalio Bustamante. Their politics moved gradually left over the first decade of the century from anti-Díaz and anticlerical reformism, through nationalist revolt, to anarchism, and even communism. Although their strongest base of support was in northern Mexico, where modernization brought deep labor strife, many supporters also lived north of the border, in Texas, Arizona, and California, where dozens of Spanish-language newspapers spread the word to Mexican Americans and to recently arrived immigrants. Many Americans, especially IWW and WFM activists, began to find common cause with expatriate PLM leaders.[27]

When Mother Jones praised Mexican men for standing with their American brothers in the Colorado coal strike, she alluded to an issue of growing importance. Coal was an international commodity, and exploited Mexican workers mined it cheaply, undercutting Americans. Equally important, many of those who crossed UMW picket lines came from south of the border. By 1903 in Arizona, a two-tiered system had developed for American and Mexican miners, with the latter working longer hours for lower pay. White American labor had a history of enhancing its own solidarity by cultivating anti-Mexican sentiment, yet there were signs of change in the border states. In 1905, the WFM, fed up with operators exploiting Mexican workers then using the ethnic issue to divide miners, began organizing workers on both sides of the border in Bisbee, Arizona, and in Cananea, Sonora. By 1907, the Western Federation openly opposed AFL policies of racial exclusiveness.[28]

On July 1, 1907, the eve of Big Bill Haywood's acquittal in Idaho, Manuel Sarabia was seized in Douglas, Arizona, and transported across the border. He was released, but six months later, a U.S. district court in Arizona handed down indictments of PLM leaders Sarabia, Villarreal, Rivera, and Magón on charges that they conspired to launch a military attack against the Díaz government from American soil, thereby violating neutrality laws. The four were arrested and detained in Los Angeles. *Miners' Magazine* declared in its most melodramatic tones that because "they have lifted up their voices against Cossack barbarism in Mexico they are hounded by the vultures of capitalism and treated with no more consideration than wild beasts of the jungle."[29]

Many Americans spoke out on the Mexican Revolution, including Samuel Gompers, Eugene Debs, and Emma Goldman, but none were more active than Mother Jones. She was speaking in Douglas, Arizona, to striking copper smelters when American officials arrested Sarabia, then shipped him to a Sonoran jail. The kidnapping touched a nerve among American unionists, and Mother Jones immediately seized on Porfirio Díaz as the symbolic enemy. She denounced "the idea of any bloodthirsty pirate on a throne reaching across these lines and crushing under his feet the Constitution which our forefathers fought and bled for." She organized letter-writing campaigns and held rallies to protest the kidnapping. Her efforts and those of others apparently got results; Mexican authorities released Sarabia after several days. When he and the other three were later arrested in Los Angeles, beaten by the police, and imprisoned, American labor leaders launched a public campaign to have them freed, with Mother Jones taking a leading role. Keeping up the publicity, she argued, prevented the government from simply turning them over to Díaz for execution.[30]

Between 1907 and 1910, Mother Jones spent much of her time raising money for the defense of the PLM leaders. On January 27, 1909, she returned to the UMW annual convention to appeal for funds. It was a homecoming, with her at the peak of her oratorical powers. She began by noting that nothing would have pleased King George III more than to reach across the ocean in 1776, kidnap George Washington, and hang him, which was precisely what Díaz now proposed to do to Mexican patriots. International economic interests dictated the policies of the American government, she declared; Wall Street, not Washington, ruled.[31]

Mother Jones made her pitch for the PLM leaders, then charmed the men with her stories. She told them that just one woman in Washington would make House Speaker Joe Cannon shake on his throne, how if she were there she would tell Teddy Roosevelt to shut his mouth. Then she described an incident in El Paso:

> We saw a gang coming down the street and they were hammering each other. I asked a policeman what the trouble was. He said . . . "The Salvation Army and the Volunteers [for Christ] are fighting about Jesus." I said, . . . "Why don't you arrest them?" He said it would not do because they were fighting for Jesus. . . . While they were hammering each other the collection that had been taken up rolled on the street. I jumped in and rescued the coin. . . . I said to the policeman: "Don't you want a drink on Jesus?" He said, "By God, I do!" so we went to a restaurant and got supper and some beer, and if any fellow wanted to get an extra jag on we were ready to pay for it because we had Jesus's money.

Do-gooders all had separate agendas; workers must take care of their own.[32]

Mother Jones finished her speech holding out the hope of future victories by telling her listeners of past ones. When Sarabia was first seized, many assumed he would be killed. She described holding rallies to keep the pressure up for his release. The boys along the border promised to follow her south and make Díaz give him up. "There isn't a Pinkerton between here and hell we won't go hang," she told them.

Sarabia was freed. She told how Chicago activists secured the release of two Jewish radicals just before their extradition to Russia. The lesson was clear: activism worked. Or as Mother Jones put it, "I long ago quit praying and took to swearing. If I pray I will have to wait until I am dead to get anything; but when I swear I get things here." Having sworn her way through the evening, she repeated her plea for funds to defend the Mexican rebels: "I am not here to beg. I hate beggars. . . . I want to fight and take what belongs to us." She left the convention with a pledge of one thousand dollars.[33]

Still the four *revoltosos* remained in a Los Angeles jail, and other Mexican nationals were harassed and imprisoned. Mother Jones's rhetoric reached new heights of indignation: "From out the bastiles of capitalism in California and Arizona," she began an open letter to the socialists and unionists of America, "comes the appeal of our Mexican comrades and brothers, Magón, Villarreal, Rivera and Sarabia." These four had now spent over a year in American custody. According to Mother Jones, "Rockefeller, Morgan, Harriman and other Wall Street pirates are backing up the persecution of these Mexican patriots. They are the holders of Mexican bonds and the owners and exploiters of Mexican interests and they, of course, lend a ready hand to Díaz in keeping his hordes of peons in slavish subjection." By paying Mexican workers less than twenty-five cents a day, capitalists amassed fortunes, making it clear why "the rising spirit of revolt is to be crushed and why Magón and his compatriots are to be shot to death or buried alive in some hellish dungeon." The Mexican rebels, she concluded, fought for the same cause as American unionists and socialists.[34]

She continued her attack in an article in the *Appeal to Reason*, referring to Díaz as "this tyrant, this fiend, beside whom King George was a gentleman and lover of the poor." But her main point of comparison now was not America's liberation from England but the freeing of the slaves. She reminded her readers of the issue that galvanized the nation on the eve of the Civil War. The *revoltoso* question, she argued, was the same as the fugitive-slave controversy of the 1850s—should free Americans remand captives to their oppressors, as the Supreme Court insisted in the Dred Scott decision? "Men of America, women of America," she pleaded, "rouse as you never roused before. Wipe from our jurisprudence the infamous fugitive slave law of this later day."[35]

The issue became so large and Mother Jones's role so visible that President William Howard Taft agreed to see her. She made her case for a pardon, to which Taft said that if Mother Jones had that power, the jails would be empty. If America spent as much on making good citizens as it did on making criminals, she replied, there would be less need for penitentiaries. The President acknowledged her point and promised to review the case. Taft, she decided, was a different sort of man from his predecessor, the hated Roosevelt. At least "I don't think when he retires from office he will go out to kill monkeys way off in the jungles of Africa." But another half year passed without a response from Taft, the prisoners continued to languish, and she wrote the President a letter. The *revoltosos*, she told him, "were moved by exactly the same motives which were felt by Washington, Jefferson, Adams, Patrick Henry and the fathers of our own American Revolution"; their goal was to bring to Mexico "the same free institutions which we presumably enjoy in this country." She failed to mention their sympathy for anarchism and syndicalism.[36]

Taft neither responded nor intervened, and Mother Jones took her anger out in the pages of the *Appeal to Reason*. In language redolent of the old jeremiad, she declared, "Does God sleep? No, he does not. He will wipe out injustice with suffering, wrong with blood, and sin with death." American capitalists had forced their government to shill for Díaz, the "most ferocious murderer on the face of God's earth." President Taft did nothing; even if he were so inclined, the "money power of Wall Street" would not allow him to. "His independence is gone, his manhood is sacrificed and his love of liberty if he ever had any must be offered up on the altar of selfish ambition." Playing on her age, on how her life reached back into American history, she declared, "I know what Lincoln would say to that crew on Wall Street: 'The nation first and you last.' " If manhood was in such short supply, then women must carry the day: "Women win all strikes! Women support all strikes! They keep their husbands in good standing in the union; they give them the courage to fight. We need the women in this fight against the tyranny of Mexico."[37]

William Wilson, Mother Jones's old friend from the anthracite battles and now a congressman from Pennsylvania, parlayed labor's protests into an investigation by the House Rules Committee. John

Kenneth Turner, the author of *Barbarous Mexico*, and John Murray of the Political Refugee Defense League testified on the horrors of the Díaz regime, then Mother Jones closed the proceedings. Harking back to the old republican tradition, she raged against judges and politicians "feasting and eating and drinking with those who own the fleshpots of Egypt." The wealthy, she thundered, might have callous disregard for plain people like herself, but Americans still had the right to investigate violations of human liberty. Indeed, sharing freedom with others was the American way, a point she made by telling the congressmen about her experience as an immigrant and how her own family came here "under the shelter of this flag," for America was the "cradle of liberty." Just as Irish Americans founded the revolutionary Fenian society in the 1860s to secure an independent Irish republic, just as they supported the Irish nationalist Charles Parnell with thousands of dollars to wrest Ireland from England, so the *revoltosos* and sympathetic Americans must be free to bring liberty to Mexico.[38]

In November 1909, after two years in jail, the *revoltosos* were found guilty of violating America's neutrality laws and sentenced to eighteen-month prison terms in Florence, Arizona. From their cells, they wrote Mother Jones a message of thanks for her labors:

> You are setting a noble example, and teaching a lesson humanity should not forget. You, an old woman, are fighting with indomitable courage; you, an American, are devoting your life to free Mexican slaves. . . . And they will be freed in the near future, and they will learn to call you Mother. . . . You are the woman at the foundation of this tremendous struggle for the emancipation of our country and you will live forever in the hearts of all liberty loving Mexicans.

They were released from prison in August 1910.[39]

A few months later, an armed revolt deposed Porfirio Díaz. Francisco Madero succeeded him, restored civil liberties to Mexico, and granted workers the right to organize unions. In October 1911, he welcomed Mother Jones and officials from the United Mine Workers and the Western Federation of Miners to Mexico City, where he pledged to help them organize Mexican miners. Madero was not as radical as the Magonistas, but he was serious about reform, and most *revoltosos* decided to work within his government. Ricardo Flores Magón, however, along with a handful of other Mexican nationals, refused. Mother Jones tried to persuade him to join with Madero, to give up his insane dream of launching military raids against Mexico with the aid of a few American Wobblies, anarchists, and adventurers. That failing, she denounced him and his followers: "I consider them one and all a combination of unreasonable fanatics, with no logic in their arguments."[40]

Mother Jones's reaction to Magón reveals once again her distaste for those seeking ideological purity. She could be naive about the ins and outs of radical ideologies, but her lack of sophistication regarding doctrinal squabbles gave her great flexibility. She was less interested in ideas than in working from within mass movements and leading them in progressive directions. Just as she turned away from the Wobblies because they alienated the mass of American workers with their radical posturing, she finally dismissed Magón as an ideologue who ignored a real opportunity for radical change.[41]

"It Is a Little Lonely for Me"

Mother Jones devoted much of her attention to the *revoltosos* in part because her relationship with the Socialist Party had grown so tense. The Socialists' tepid response to the Mexican rebels' plight angered her. More important, many of the Party's new members were middle-class professionals—lawyers, doctors, journalists, ministers—people who Mother Jones believed lacked real commitment to social change. Although she remained on the road for the Socialists, she diverted increasing amounts of time to other causes.[42]

Since her break with the UMW, she spent more time than ever working with the Western Federation of Miners. Back in 1905, she had traveled to Michigan's Upper Peninsula to help them organize a copper strike. There, she praised the miners' wives and heaped scorn on non-union men: "How a woman can degrade herself by marrying a measly man who does not dare to join a union is beyond my comprehension. You say you cannot join the union because you would lose your job. Poor, dreamy wretch. You never owned a job, for those who own the machinery own the job and you have got to get permission to earn your bread and butter." In 1907, she organized for the WFM in Arizona's copper country, where she first encountered the Mexican exiles. Then she went north again to help them unionize ironworkers in Minnesota's Mesabi Range. She continued to branch out. Late in 1908, she returned to Alabama to expose pay cuts and speedups in the cotton mills. In 1909, she gave speeches to striking Jewish shirtwaist makers in Philadelphia and New York City. The following year, she organized women bottle washers in Milwaukee breweries and persuaded the UMW to boycott Pabst and Schlitz until the brewers gave in.[43]

She also wrote a number of short essays during these years. Articles in *The Cincinnati Post* recounted her triumphs in the coalfields. More pointed essays published in the *United Mine Workers Journal* addressed contemporary crises. One article, "Mother Jones' Plea for Babies," claimed that in Illinois overwork caused mothers to bear anemic children. She lashed out at the rich: "Some day we will have the courage to rise up and strike back at these great 'giants' of industry, and then we will see that they weren't 'giants' after all—they only seemed so because we were on our knees and they towered above us." In another article, she criticized the schools because they forced children to "memorize a lot of stuff about war and murder," then taught them nothing of economic conditions. Mothers must become educators, must spend less time thinking about their clothes and more time teaching their children about the reality of class conflict.[44]

Mother Jones's disaffection from the Socialists reached the boiling point around 1910. Just as with the UMW five years before, she complained in letters to friends that some Party members were more interested in soft jobs and fat fees than in fighting injustice. She told Thomas Morgan, a Chicago attorney with whom she worked in the 1890s, that just thinking about Party corruption made her sick. Morgan was a kindred spirit, a dissident among dissidents, who edited a socialist newsletter appropriately named *The Provoker*.[45]

Mother Jones's disaffection came to a head during a very ugly confrontation with the Socialists' national secretary, John Mahlon Barnes. She claimed to have loaned Barnes two hundred dollars in 1905 when he first came to Chicago. He needed the money for his family, and in the next few years, she loaned him more. She also sent the funds she collected at rallies across the country back to the Chicago office, money that mysteriously disappeared. Of course she never kept records—small amounts of cash came into her hands from speaking fees, monthly stipends, reimbursements, contributions; she quickly spent the money for living expenses, travel, organizing costs, donations. When the Socialists offered what she considered insufficient support for the Mexican prisoners, she asked Barnes for her money back so she might donate it to them. He claimed he had already paid her. She asked attorney Morgan to try to collect the money for her, and the dispute became public. Others then accused Barnes of sexual improprieties, and *The Provoker* spread charges of financial misconduct against other Party members.[46]

Behind the bickering were fundamental issues. Mother Jones wrote Morgan, "If this movement is going to move onward for the benefit of the workers we must take our stand boldly and fearlessly with the working class." The Party's lofty internationalism, she believed, masked the leadership's distance from American labor. Moreover, she condemned the Socialists' inner circle, the executive committee, as a gang of fame chasers and self-seekers. She exploded at the Party's spending enormous sums to send eight leaders to an international conference in Copenhagen when not a single one of them was from the working class. She bristled at the Party's sudden interest in immigration, the "sex question" (birth control), woman suffrage, and temperance ("we're not building a movement for free-lovers and job hunters," she wrote Morgan), and its silence on the Mexican Revolution and the implications for labor and civil liberties. The way the Party was going, she concluded uncharitably, the executive board members might soon be dining with the National Civic Federation.[47]

Mother Jones, Morgan, and their supporters publicly questioned the integrity of such prominent Party leaders as Morris Hillquit, John Spargo, and Victor Berger. Berger responded that Mother Jones had a

drinking problem, that on one occasion she had left a hotel room lit-
tered with empty whiskey bottles, that liquor made her tongue intem-
perate. Barnes accused her of bribing Party officials to back her
charges against him. He also wrote in the Party *Bulletin* (the organ of
the Socialists' National Executive Council) that she made a fortune as
a lecturer. Then he revisited the old charge that she had run a brothel
before joining the labor movement. As the Party moved toward an official investigation of Barnes, Mother Jones denied all of the attacks in
sworn affidavits that Morgan filed with the Cook County courts, and
made some new accusations of her own. She demanded that Barnes
produce his evidence against her but also indicated that she was too
busy with new coal crises in Colorado and Pennsylvania to be bothered
with the investigation. Barnes resigned as national secretary when evidence confirmed his affair with a young woman in the Party—but not
before the investigating committee declared Mother Jones's charges to
be without foundation and accused Thomas Morgan of instigating the
trouble in order to embarrass Barnes. Mother Jones ceased being a
Party member in 1911. She claimed she resigned; others declared she
had been expelled.[48]

These battles rocked the Party just before its greatest triumph, the
1912 election, when a million Americans, nearly 6 percent of the elec-
torate, voted for Eugene Debs for President. Debs had always been one
of Mother Jones's staunchest supporters, and his loyalty to her never
wavered. When George H. Goebel wrote Debs in 1912, "No one knows
better than you, that Mother Jones has nothing but vile language for almost every well known worker in the movement, particularly the
woman comrades. . . . And Mother Jones is the only woman I ever purchased whiskey for, and at her request," Debs's anger exploded:

> It does not matter to me that Mother Jones has used vile
> language and that you have bought whisky for her, she
> has spent weeks and months in the bleak hills of West Vir-
> ginia, Pennsylvania and other states, where the official
> machine that maligned her dare not go, standing on the
> firing line, face to face with guns and bayonets, fighting
> the battles of the workers; she has been in jail all over this

country and again and again enjoined by the courts; she has gone to prison where strikers were locked up, "ignorant foreigners," afflicted with the smallpox and nursed them as tenderly as if they had been children; she has been routed out of her bed at midnight by armed ruffians, corporation murderers, and made to leave a coal camp alone at that hour.

Debs denounced Socialist leaders who would "beslime this grand old woman to keep their own power intact and perpetuate their own machine rule in the party." Long after Mother Jones left the Socialists, he continued defending his old friend.[49]

Once Mother Jones made her break from the Party, she moved decisively back toward the labor movement. Thomas Lewis succeeded John Mitchell as president of the UMW in 1908. Cautious and conservative, he was much like Mitchell, but once he took over, Mother Jones became a regular speaker again at United Mine Workers conventions. By 1910, she had returned to the anthracite fields of Pennsylvania. "I have been up to my ears in a strike of the miners here I have not had a moment to spare," she wrote Thomas Morgan from Greensburg, Pennsylvania. "I have just got back after ten miles going and coming in a blizzard to a house away from Civilization. I find the father down with Typhoid fever the mother and six children shivering with cold no clothing not a thing to eat. . . . The little ones ailing with cold." She was once again in her element, "the Class War in its reality," as she called it, the struggle that made her feel most alive. When her old friend John P. White became the Mine Workers' president in 1911, she went back on the payroll as an organizer.[50]

Still, a note of sadness crept into her voice. She wrote Morgan on Christmas Day, 1910, "I am here in an industrial battle against the powers that oppress my class." To underscore her oneness with the miners, she remarked of the Socialists, "I have neither time nor strength to waste with that bunch of middle class dictators. . . . They can put me out of the party but out of the movement never." She imagined their scorn for her: "To Hell with old Mother Jones. She's getting old. We will make her shut up. She must go off and die." She noted that the

7. Although Mother Jones was no longer a member of the Socialist Party, this photograph appeared on the cover of the *International Socialist Review*, June 1913 (Courtesy Newberry Library)

capitalists did not think she was getting old, though they wished she was. Then after raging at her enemies, she ended her letter, "Well, Merry Xm. it is a little lonely for me." And she signed herself "Always yours until I rest in the [illegible] earth, Mother."[51]

Perhaps it was just the lonesomeness of the season for one on the road without a family of her own. But the sadness was not new. It emerged, for example, when she told and retold the story of Martin Irons. Irons was a regional leader in the Knights of Labor during the 1880s. Master Workman Terence Powderly disapproved of strikes, but Irons led his men out against Jay Gould's Missouri Pacific Railroad in 1886. The strike was a disaster: Gould refused to negotiate, state militias killed several workers, the Knights' national leadership gave inadequate support to the strikers, who were forced to return to their jobs. As Mother Jones told it, Irons was disgraced before his own men and blacklisted by the railroad. He wandered the Southwest looking for work, was arrested for vagrancy, and ended up in a labor camp. He died alone in Bruceville, Texas.[52]

Mother Jones visited Martin Irons's grave in April 1907 and wrote Powderly about it. She told Powderly that he and Irons "were rocking the cradle of the movement," that they "made it possible for others to march on." Then she said of Irons: "He sleepeth well, Jay Gould cannot awaken him now. His grave was marked by a piece of iron, it is his only tombstone. . . . No tender hand seemed to care for it, but the wild flowers did not forget to plant their perfume around his grave. . . . I enclose a few leaves from his grave, knowing how deeply you will appreciate them, and how poor Martin would feel if he saw you press your lips to them." She repeated Martin Irons's story many times in coming years and always ended by declaring that such heroes would never be forgotten. She knew it was a lie.[53]

Thoughts of martyrdom, comparisons with Christ or Joan of Arc, intimations of final days, were all staples of the Mother Jones persona. And for *Mary* Jones, too, death's visage stayed near at hand, never more so than in Cork and Memphis, inescapable in memory. Always in the past, death had appeared without justice or reason, leaving only numbness or rage in its wake. She was old now, and her health was not so good. The end could not be far off for someone three-quarters of a century old. Would Mother Jones be forgotten like Martin Irons, her soul as homeless as her body, wandering the world in search of rest? At least martyrdom meant a meaningful end, one that brought order to life's anarchy. And martyrdom meant living on in memory to inspire new assaults by new crusaders. She feared death, of course, but wished for it too, a meaningful death, one filled with absolution. Her inclination to find betrayal in the world—not just among businessmen and politicians but also among comrades—fed the ideal of martyrdom. She needed to feel more virtuous than others, alone in her righteousness. Part of being Mother Jones was living on the fringe, denying comfort; she must be the most pure, the most dedicated. Thus the sadness that always lingered beneath the turbulent surface. She countered that sadness by losing herself in the turbulence with spectacular acts of courage and moral righteousness that courted danger, even death. And so she returned to West Virginia and Colorado.

★ 7 ★

"Medieval West Virginia"

In 1913, Mother Jones reached the height of her fame and influence. She thrust herself into the spotlight during a violent strike in West Virginia. By the time the strike ended, she had become one of the most famous women in America, and her legions of admirers and detractors would never again be so vociferous in her praise and damnation. "Medieval West Virginia," Mother Jones concluded of the Mountain State. "With its tent colonies on the bleak hills! With its grim men and women! When I get to the other side, I shall tell God almighty about West Virginia."[1]

"The Revolution Is Here"

When Mother Jones left the Socialists and rejoined the UMW, more coal came from West Virginia than ever before. Coal production in southern Appalachia multiplied fivefold between 1900 and 1930, and by 1912, the flow of West Virginia coal crossing the Central Competitive Field into the Great Lakes market had become a flood. It was a high-quality product, mined out of rich veins and shipped at especially low freight rates.[2]

Above all, West Virginia coal was cheap because the miners worked more for less pay than their counterparts in the unionized Middle West. In 1912, coal miners in West Virginia's southern field earned a little over thirty-eight cents per ton, only about two-thirds the amount of the Central Competitive Field's lowest-paid men. Still, more impoverished Appalachian farmers, more African Americans, and more immigrants came looking for work.[3]

Coal operators believed that success in business justified their control over the mining communities. They paid deference to the ideal of social mobility but felt that miners were a shiftless lot on whom freedom and opportunity were wasted. The operators wanted hard work and steady habits from their men but thought of mining folk as "uncivilized" people who must be educated or coerced into modern ways. Above all, mine owners and managers were anti-union. The labor movement, they believed, was a conspiracy to disrupt the natural harmony of interests between labor and capital.[4]

Anti-union repression was the most important reason for the United Mine Workers' failure in West Virginia, but there were other factors. Organizing efforts also foundered because mine families still had space to carve out decent lives for themselves, so many felt they did not need the union. Life in the mining camps, though far from ideal, was not desperate. Miners received low pay, but coal was plentiful and relatively easy to mine. As long as market demand remained high, families could scrape by. They supplemented their incomes by raising produce and livestock, by taking in boarders, and even by distilling and selling bootleg liquor. And operators had not yet imposed such discipline that the men were invariably forced to work ten or twelve hours per day.[5]

But life in the company towns had started to change by 1912. Despite growing ethnic diversity, a rough awareness of shared class identity permeated the camps. Whites might look askance at blacks, and blacks at immigrants, but beyond that was a work culture that bound them together as miners, a mining-camp life that united them as families. There was a developing consciousness of a common set of grievances. That the companies preferred to hire miners with families proved especially important, because such men were more likely to join the union than simply move on to the next mining town in hopes of a better deal. Families gave men a stake in their communities and something to fight for.[6]

The unique religion of the mines flowed into unionism. Most communities had churches owned by the companies and preachers hired by the operators. Catholic immigrants, mountain Methodists, and black Baptists all brought different Christian outlooks to the mine camps. The company churches failed to recognize denominational differences and therefore garnered only limited loyalty. The official ministers had to toe the company line, but an underground religious tradition offered much more latitude. This sometimes included the conflation of Christian and union imagery, as the community of saints and the community of labor merged. Declared one miner-preacher, "I say to you that any man in this gathering today . . . who does not join this strike and stand by it, even until death—for the sake of the children, is not worthy to call himself a Christian because he is not willing to stand up for the Kingdom of Heaven." In the hands of such men, Christianity and labor organizing became part of a single prophetic tradition; Scripture offered a vision of social justice and a charter for belief in the movement.[7]

By 1912, then, change had come to West Virginia. Mine families from diverse backgrounds felt a growing identity with each other, and coming events only deepened the sense of solidarity. The operators, too, increasingly identified with one another as a distinct group. Many of them believed—falsely—that mine companies in the Central Competitive Field now financed UMW efforts to organize West Virginia and thereby keep cheap coal out of the marketplace. Such fears reveal just how embattled the operators felt. So when the time came to discuss new terms in 1912, the division between labor and management already ran deep.[8]

Paint and Cabin Creeks are two small parallel streams that roll north toward the Kanawha River. They cut sharp valleys—no more than twenty-five miles long and often barely wide enough for train tracks and a road—that held rich reserves of coal. The mines were generally small operations, run on thin profit margins. Since the 1904 strike, most of the mines on Paint Creek had remained organized, making the area one of the few UMW strongholds in the state.[9]

In March 1912, the UMW asked that the new contract for union miners in the Kanawha River Valley include a small raise and an automatic payroll deduction for union dues. At first the operators balked, then many conceded after sporadic work stoppages. But some refused to give in out of fear that even a small increase in costs would drive their product from the marketplace. Led by Quinn Morton, the manager of the largest Paint Creek mines, they ended negotiations and withdrew recognition of the union. The miners, including hundreds previously not UMW members, went on strike. Morton evicted families from their homes, forcing the displaced to set up a tent colony at Holly Grove near the mouth of Paint Creek. Soon miners on non-union Cabin Creek demanded union recognition, the restoration of the rights of free speech and assembly, an end to the blacklisting of discharged workers, accurate scales with the miners' own representatives guarding against short-weighting, and freedom to trade outside the company stores. Once again, the operators refused.[10]

Tensions escalated as the companies brought in thousands of strikebreakers and hired more armed guards, who began a campaign of intimidation. The strike originated with the rank and file, and their leaders came not from the national office but from the mines themselves, men like Frank Keeney and Bill Blizzard, two miners in their early twenties. As the strike spread, company guards loaded families and their belongings onto railroad cars, rode them out of the valleys, and dumped them along the tracks. The mine folk lived in tents; hunger and unsanitary conditions spread diseases throughout the community. Meanwhile, the companies built concrete fortresses to guard the mines and began advertising in eastern papers for new workers: "Steady Employment at Good Wages in the Mines of West Virginia, No Strikes, Free Transportation." Before it was over, the strike named for two small West Virginia streams became one of the longest and bloodiest labor conflicts in American history.[11]

Mother Jones came back to West Virginia just as the crisis began to boil. She had kept her usual hectic schedule as her rift with the Socialists deepened. A lively speech before the UMW convention in January 1911 signaled her full-time return to the labor movement. She was her feisty old self. She described judges whose bodies, souls, and brains—

"though they never had much brains"—were owned by the corporations, and promised that the day was not far off when the workers would throw them in prison rather than the other way around ("Put that down, Mr. Reporter, so the judges will know it!"). She told the men about strikebreakers:

> I know how a scab is made up. One time there was an old barrel up near heaven, and all of heaven got permeated with the odor. God Almighty said, "What is that stuff that smells so?" He was told it was some rotten chemical down there in a barrel and was asked what could be done with it. He said, "Spill it on a lot of bad clay and maybe you can turn out a scab."

Then she was off again, to New York, Ohio, California.[12]

She was in Butte, Montana, speaking on behalf of copper miners when she heard about the walkout on Paint Creek, a site she had helped organize in 1904. According to her autobiography, she canceled her speaking engagements, tied up all of her possessions in a black shawl—"I like to travel light"—and headed for West Virginia. She arrived in early June. Near the tent colony at Holly Grove was a fort armed with a machine gun and manned by Baldwin-Felts guards to defend the Paint Creek Collieries Company office. The two sides engaged in virtual open warfare, with pitched battles and military-style maneuvers.[13]

A reporter for *The Charleston Daily Gazette* who covered Mother Jones's first speech observed how she climbed a steep hill unassisted to the meeting ground, where she spoke for an hour with more animation than others half her age. He interviewed her afterward, and despite her break with the Socialists, her ideas still echoed theirs: "I am simply a social revolutionist. . . . I believe in collective ownership of the means of wealth." She added, "When force is used to hinder the worker in his efforts to obtain the things which are his, he has the right to meet force with force." Some of the most effective UMW organizers in West Virginia were socialists with whom she worked closely, and the radical press gave her respectful coverage.[14]

Mother Jones was ubiquitous in West Virginia over the next year. Sometimes she spoke in the no-man's-lands, where most organizers feared to go. When the companies owned the roads, she walked in the creeks to get to "free soil" where civil liberties were still in force. Her rhetoric grew increasingly militant, incendiary in the eyes of the operators. According to one report, she invited the mildly progressive Republican governor William E. Glasscock to a rally she held in the capital. When the governor failed to attend this "living petition," she denounced him to the crowd: "You can expect no help from such a goddamned dirty coward . . . whom, for modesty's sake, we shall call 'Crystal Peter.' But I warn this little Governor that unless he rids Paint Creek and Cabin Creek of these goddamned Baldwin-Felts mine-guard thugs, there is going to be one hell of a lot of bloodletting in these hills." The source of this story was a mine operator, who claimed that Mother Jones then told her audience, "Arm yourselves, return home and kill every goddamned mine guard on the creeks, blow up the mines, and drive the damned scabs out of the valleys." He added that once, on Cabin Creek, she held up the bloodied jacket of a Baldwin-Felts agent and declared, "This is the first time I ever saw a goddamned mine guard's coat decorated to suit me," and she had swatches of the garment cut up and distributed to the crowd.[15]

Although she did not shy away from strong language or invective, and she increasingly encouraged the miners to respond to violence with gunfire of their own, this report distorts her words. Her most militant calls generally were couched in defensive terms, and there is plenty of evidence that she directed miners to obey the National Guard and to respect private property. Still, she did urge the men to acquire guns. And though she may not have been the crazed incendiary her enemies portrayed, her rhetoric was escalating.[16]

During August and September 1912, the Coal Operators Association hired a stenographer to follow Mother Jones and record her words, so although most of her speeches have not survived, half a dozen verbatim transcripts reveal the core of her message. These were open-air meetings with thousands of listeners, held in public places like the levee in Charleston, on the capitol steps, and at a baseball park in Montgomery. On July 26, after sixteen perished in a battle between guards and miners at Mucklow, Governor Glasscock sent in three companies of the state militia to restore order. In response, Mother Jones insisted that the brutal mine guards no longer be tolerated: "We are law-abiding citizens, we will destroy no property, we will take no life, but if a fellow comes to my home and outrages my wife, by the Eternal he will pay the penalty. I will send him to his God in the repair shop. (Loud applause.) The man who doesn't do it hasn't got a drop of revolutionary blood in his veins."[17]

Because workers produced the wealth that paid the guards, those same workers had the right to get rid of them. Still, there was a studied ambiguity to her words: "I am not going to say to you don't molest the operators. It is they who hire the dogs to shoot you. (Applause.) I am not asking you to do it, but if he is going to oppress you, deal with him." At her most militant, she came very close to declaring war on the private detectives: "Now when you kill a handful of guards they raise a great howl. You are to blame because you didn't clean them up. (Loud applause.) When you go at it again, do business." And later, "IF THE GOVERNOR WON'T MAKE THEM GO THEN WE WILL MAKE THEM GO." She added that if Glasscock declared martial law, the men should bury their guns in the woods rather than give them up.[18]

Mother Jones's speeches were powerful tools of persuasion. She not only addressed the immediate issues at hand, she helped give shape to the larger ideas and feelings of her listeners. Reproduced on the printed page, however, her words lose some of their power. Without the music of her voice—her brogue, her cadence, her gestures, her interactions with the audience—the speeches seem a bit flat. Sometimes stenographers garbled her words, and because her style was so emotional, Mother Jones's sentences often grew sloppy, her syntax careless. Still, we can feel her oratorical power.

She told her listeners that they were on a crusade: "We are doing God's holy work, we are breaking the chains that bind you, we are putting the fear of God into the robbers." The union's mission and the Lord's were one: "We marched the mountains, every one who took up Christ's doctrine—not the hypocrites but the fighters." She still rejected institutional religion, still called clerics "sky pilots," still said that YMCAs and churches and the Salvation Army were built on the "bleached bones of workers," for they did nothing but give people a false sense of contentment. The miners cheered as she described how the "big fellows" always sat in the front pews, singing "All for Jesus," when in fact they "robbed for Jesus, murdered for Jesus." You could hear them forty miles away, praying for their daily bread, but then muttering, "Oh, Lord Jesus, fix it so I can get three or four fellows' bread."[19]

She invoked the Old Testament to show that true religion and the labor movement came from God: "He commanded the prophets thousands of years ago to go down and redeem the Israelites that were in bondage, and he organized the men into a union." She contrasted the institutional religion of the bosses with the open-air religion of the workers, an immanent faith manifesting itself right where they stood:

> The star that rose in Bethlehem has crossed the world, it has risen here; see it slowly breaking through the clouds. The Star of Bethlehem will usher in the new day and new time and new philosophy—and if you are only true you will be free—if you are only men.

The good fight on earth and the good fight in heaven were one:

> We have fought together, we have hungered together, we have marched together, but I can see victory in the heavens for you. I can see the hand above you guiding and inspiring you to move onward and upward. No white flag—we cannot raise it, we must not raise it. We must redeem the world.[20]

Above all, Mother Jones's speeches gave working people faith in themselves. Neither bosses, ministers, nor politicians would change things—"we, the people, have got to do it." When she berated the miners for their cowardice and questioned their masculinity, the message behind her scolding was always to take heart and to do their manly duty. To those betrayed by the promise of American life, for those whom the gleaming consumer world presented in all the magazines and newspapers of the day seemed so distant, her speeches pledged dramatic transformations: "Take possession of that state house, that ground is yours." Or, "We build the jails, and when we get ready we will put *them* behind the bars. That may happen very soon—things happen overnight." And again, "Go with me up those creeks, and see the blood-hounds of the mine owners. . . . I went up there and they followed me like hounds. But some day I will follow them. When I see them go to Hell, I will get the coal and pile it up on them." She spoke of earlier strikes, told her people that defeats never lasted, that a new day brought victory: "You have suffered, I know how you have suffered. I was with you nearly three years in this state. I went to jail, went to the Federal courts, but I never took any back water. I still unfurl the red flag of industrial freedom, no tyrant's face shall you know, and I call you today into that freedom."[21]

This was no mere trade-union fight for a little more money; it was a principled struggle for human dignity, for the rights of American citizens. Oppression, Mother Jones reminded her listeners, not only crushed the poor, it perverted the rich. She told the operators to come out of hiding, visit the tent colonies, and see how the women and children lived. How could capitalists sleep at night? she asked. Then she turned to one of her stock sketches, the society lady with her dog:

> I saw her coming down the street the other day in an automobile. . . . I looked at her and then looked at the poodle. I watched the poodle—every now and again the poodle would squint its eye at her and turn up its nose when it got a look at her. (Laughter and applause.) He seemed to say: "You corrupt, rotten, decayed piece of humanity, my royal dogship is degraded sitting beside you."

The high-class burglars created ladies, she concluded, but God Almighty made women. She repeated her old story of the mine owner who, when asked why he failed to use sufficient timber to prop up the ceilings, resulting in a fatal cave-in, replied that "dagos" were cheaper than props. Then she imagined for her listeners a better day, when they would own the mines, when the first would be last, and they would say to the likes of William Howard Taft and Teddy Roosevelt, "You have had a devil of a good time, [now] go in and dig coal."[22]

Her authority came from her dedication to the cause, from "measuring steel in the dead of night with the blood-hounds of the ruling class." She always exaggerated her age now, claiming to be eighty years old when in fact she was seventy-three. The greater age made her vigor and courage all the more remarkable, as she pledged to her listeners, "I will be eighty more, for I have got a contract with God Almighty to stay with you until your chains are broken." She told her boys that she had worked in the mines on the night shift and the day shift for twenty-five years, even helping load coal sometimes but always passing out literature and talking union. She used her own life as an example of courting danger and never backing down: "I have been in jail more than once, and I expect to go again. If you are too cowardly to fight, I will fight. You ought to be ashamed of yourselves, actually to the Lord you ought, just to see one old woman who is not afraid."[23]

It was her lived struggle, made palpable by her stories, that gave her the authority to say to working families, "Take this advice from Mother." She scolded, coaxed, comforted, and she upheld standards to which her children must measure up. She spoke the miners' language, cursing, fulminating, weeping, cajoling. And as always, she embodied fearlessness in labor's cause, fearlessness that grew out of faith in ultimate justice: "When I know I am right fighting for these children of mine, there is no governor, no court, no president will terrify or muzzle me." She made her fighting spirit their own. "Be good," she told her people at the end of one speech, "Mother is going to stay with you."[24]

The theme of a brighter day coming permeated her addresses. She gave expression to the mine families' grievances, their rage at the companies, but over and over again, she emphasized that the struggle was for a better life for their children. To Charleston she brought one hundred little ones, who marched the streets with banners reading WE ARE THE BABES THAT SLEEP IN THE WOODS and WE WANT TO GO TO SCHOOL AND NOT TO THE MINES. She organized the women: STRIKERS' WIVES ARE NOW INCITED, read a headline in the *Wheeling Register* after one of her meetings. Above all, she gave her audiences a vision of the future based on

8. Mother Jones in a West Virginia mine camp, helping out with the children. Her name became associated with "Medieval West Virginia" more than with any other state (Courtesy Newberry Library)

solidarity, not selfish individualism. Together they would transform their lives: "I will be with you at midnight," she told her children, "or when the battle rages, when the last bullet ceases, but I will be in my joy, as an old saint said:

> *Oh, God of the mighty clan,*
> *God grant that the woman who suffered for you,*
> *Suffered not for a coward, but Oh, for a man.*
> *God grant that the woman who suffered for you,*
> *Suffered not for a coward, but Oh, for a fighting man."*

When she finished and they passed the hat for those most in need, an old miner came up to Mother Jones: "Here is ten dollars, I will go and borrow more. Shake hands with me, an old union miner. . . . I don't care if this was the last cent I had, I will give it to Mother."[25]

But some discordant notes sounded too in these otherwise moving speeches. Most jarring was the extent to which Mary Jones seems to have believed her own mythology. Even granting her enormous influence over mine families, she indulged in some striking self-puffery, blurring the line, for example, between herself and the "old saint" who invoked the God of the mighty clan. "That is my mission," she declared at the end of one speech, "to do what I can to raise humanity." She went on, "The miners are close to me. The steel workers are. I go among them all. One time when I took up the Mexican question I went to Congress to save some lives. . . . [T]hey appealed to me and said, 'It's up to you, Mother, to save our lives.' " Mother Jones clearly had influence and was an extraordinary organizer. By creating herself as a mythic figure, she gave the powerless someone to rally around. But was Mary Jones starting to believe her own fiction? Biblical cadences about herself—"I will be in my joy" and "I go among them all"—were more than a little presumptuous.[26]

Perhaps in all of the children's cries and the workers' pleas for aid she heard echoes of her past. It was, after all, the helplessness she felt in 1867—the horror of watching her husband and children die—that sent her on the road. Whereas she stood powerless and alone before yellow fever, now she was an all-powerful, life-saving mother. But the relationship of a mother and her children is always a difficult one. Children grow up, resent being scolded, lead their own lives. And mothers, finally, have more influence than control. With her magnificent words as *Mother* Jones, she reached for power that society had denied her as a woman. Her persona gave her far more influence than she might otherwise hope to have. The metaphors she deployed, however, also suggested the confines of her situation, for they placed her and her "boys" in a relationship that offered them only limited control of their condition.[27]

Still, there is no denying the effectiveness of this iron-willed working-class woman. Ralph Chaplin, the Wobbly poet, shared the podium with Mother Jones in Charleston:

> She might have been any coal miner's wife ablaze with righteous fury when her brood was in danger. Her voice shrilled as she shook her fist at the coal operators, the mine guards, the union officials. . . . She prayed and

cursed and pleaded, raising her clenched and trembling hands, asking heaven to bear witness. . . . The miners loved it and laughed, cheered, hooted, and even cried as she spoke to them.

Lawrence Lynch, a writer who supported the operators' position and described the Cabin Creek strike in words not complimentary to the union, declared:

Head and shoulders above all the other agitators in ability and forcefulness stands "Mother" Jones. . . . She is the woman most loved by the miners and most feared by the operators. . . . She knows no fear and is as much at home in jail as on the platform. In either situation she wields a greater power over the miners than does any other agitator.

And Fred Mooney, a miner who became secretary of West Virginia's UMW District 17, wrote:

She could permeate a group of strikers with more fight than could any living human being. She fired them with enthusiasm, she burned them with criticism, then cried with them because of their abuses. The miners loved, worshipped, and adored her. And well they might, because there was no night too dark, no danger too great for her to face, if in her judgement "her boys" needed her.

She knew the mine families' sorrows, bore their burdens, shared their hopes. And she was as tough as the steel their coal produced.[28]

"Organize Us! Organize Us!"

Charles Cabell, one of the largest operators on Cabin Creek, was a classic paternalist. Living conditions for his miners were relatively good, but he was virulently anti-union. Cabin Creek—"Russia," as Mother

Jones called it—was even more isolated than Paint Creek, and mine guards had effectively cut off access to it for years. Union men told legends of organizers who got in but came out in a box. No one, Mother Jones later recalled, "was allowed in the Cabin Creek district without explaining his reason for being there to the gunmen who patrolled the roads, all of which belonged to the coal company." She asked some sympathetic railroad men to spread the word that she would hold a meeting in Eskdale on August 6, 1912. Mine Workers officials warned her not to organize on Cabin Creek, but she went in anyway.[29]

At Eskdale, according to her autobiography, she listened as a member of the national board of the UMW counseled moderation. She rose and addressed the miners:

> "You men have come over the mountains," said I, "twelve, sixteen miles. Your clothes are thin. Your shoes are out at the toes. Your wives and little ones are cold and hungry! You have been robbed and enslaved for years! And now Billy Sunday comes to you and tells you to be good and patient and trust to justice! What silly trash to tell to men whose goodness and patience has cried out to a deaf world."
>
> I could see the tears in the eyes of those poor fellows. They looked up into my face as much as to say, "My God, Mother, have you brought us a ray of hope?"
>
> Someone screamed, "Organize us, Mother!"
>
> Then they all began shouting . . . "Organize us! Organize us!"
>
> "March over to that dark church on the corner and I will give you the obligation," said I.
>
> The men started marching. In the dark the spies could not identify them.
>
> "You can't organize those men," said the board member, "because you haven't the ritual."
>
> "The ritual, hell," said I. "I'll make one up!"
>
> "They have to pay fifteen dollars for a charter," said he.

"I will get them their charter," said I. "Why these poor wretches haven't fifteen cents for a sandwich. All you care about is your salary regardless of the destiny of these men."

On the steps of the darkened church, I organized those men. They raised their hands and took the obligation to the Union.

This story is greatly embellished, of course. The version Mother Jones told ten years earlier to the Commission on Industrial Relations had no craven stooge interested only in his salary, warning her that she lacked authority to organize the men. But once again, her autobiography contains metaphorical, if not strictly literal, truths. The whole passage reads like an ecstatic religious service. Metaphor became fact as men listened to her speeches, put aside their tools, and joined the strike.[30]

The Cabin Creek operators feared Mother Jones more than pestilence, according to the reporter Harold West of the Baltimore *Sun*, and they accused her of everything from using profane language to inciting riot. Above all, management charged that she bred discontent and that her words provoked violence. J. R. Thomas, a vice president at Carbon Coal Company, testified that his miners were happy until Mother Jones arrived on Cabin Creek. His boss, Charles Cabell, added that by mid-August, shortly after she arrived, previously contented men were at fever pitch. L. D. Burns, the superintendent of the Dry Branch Coal Company, told a state investigating committee that Mother Jones offered to supply guns to three or four men, who then intimidated two hundred others into striking. The operators understood the problem as a contagion spreading through the coal camps: outside agitators made incendiary speeches; a handful of malcontents intimidated the men into quitting work; lawlessness and violence followed.[31]

They were wrong that outsiders' bitter words alone made their workers unhappy, but they were right that organizers—"the notorious 'Mother Jones'" prime among them—held great power over mine families. Mother Jones's speeches articulated the discontents of the coal towns; her body offered a model of physical courage; her spirit taught hope and perseverance. On one level, she turned the symbolism of old age on its head; rather than being an emblem of the past, of bygone days, she made herself into the voice of transcendence. But at the same time, Mother Jones's age and her long history in the movement gave legitimacy to her claims that the union represented a return to true patriotism, to authentic Christianity, to the genuine ways of old. She turned American civil religion to the cause of radical social change.[32]

One of her stories in particular shows how she shaped narratives to her purposes. A few days after the speech at Eskdale, she moved with several of her boys to the town of Red Warrior. They started down the road but soon found their way blocked by mine guards armed with rifles and a machine gun. Mother Jones spoke quietly to the guards and persuaded them to let her pass. Within a short time, however, she turned this small incident into a legend. When she told about it to the Commission on Industrial Relations in 1915, she emphasized how she put her hand on the barrel of the machine gun, how one of the guards, his lip quivering, ordered her to take her hand off, how she refused and said to the Baldwin-Felts men, "You have yourselves mothers and wives and children probably, and I don't want to hear their groans; and I don't want to hear the groans of the mothers and wives and children of my boys; don't you hurt them." She told the detectives she had work to do up the creek, and she persuaded them all to shake hands, saying, "Let us have peace on this creek."[33]

She continued to work this story into her speeches, and by the time it found its way into her autobiography, she had inflated it to epic proportions:

> I walked up to the gunmen and put my hand over the muzzle of the gun. Then I just looked at those gunmen, very quiet, and said nothing. . . .
>
> "Take your hands off that gun, you hell-cat!" yelled a fellow called Mayfield, crouching like a tiger to spring at me.
>
> I kept my hand on the muzzle of the gun. "Sir," said I, "my class goes into the mines. They bring out the metal that makes this gun. This is my gun! . . . My class is not

fighting you, not you. They are fighting with bare fists and empty stomachs the men who rob them and deprive their children of childhood."

Her words shamed the guards, according to this 1925 account, but Mayfield still threatened to turn the machine gun on her. She told him that if he did, his own blood would redden Cabin Creek, and she pointed to the hilltops: "Up there in the mountain I have five hundred miners. They are marching armed to the meeting I am going to address. If you start shooting, they will finish the game." There were no armed men in the hills, just a few rabbits, but the ruse allowed her and her boys to move on to Red Warrior, which they organized that night. Although Mother Jones's work did not really proceed with such dramatic triumphs of good over evil, the drama of her language persuaded more and more men to join the union. Before August was over, the UMW had brought most of the Cabin Creek miners into the strike.[34]

In the midst of Mother Jones's efforts, as the confrontation deepened, Governor Glasscock made a personal tour of the strike zone, appointed a commission to recommend a settlement, then declared martial law on September 2. To counter the state of "insurrection" that threatened life and property, twelve hundred troops entered the area to disarm the guards and the miners. They seized hundreds of guns and thousands of rounds of ammunition. Glasscock authorized the military to court-martial citizens despite the fact that the regular civil courts continued operating, a clear violation of constitutional liberties but one that the West Virginia Supreme Court upheld. Sixty-six individuals—almost all of them union officials, striking miners, and members of the Socialist Party—were arrested, tried by the military court, and imprisoned. Glasscock's declaration of martial law became an excuse for a massive abuse of power. The military took jurisdiction over cases that began before a state of insurrection was declared and that occurred far outside the martial-law zone. Equally important, prisoners' rights to legal counsel, to not incriminate themselves, to habeas corpus, and to trial by jury were suspended.[35]

Despite martial law, Mother Jones continued her work. She organized mine women to harass strikebreakers, and she rallied children of the tent colonies into protest parades. She traveled throughout the region, then on to New York City to explain the strike, raise funds, and gain publicity. Then she and UMW vice president Frank Hayes went to Washington to testify that employment agencies violated state laws against peonage by importing thousands of men into West Virginia and forcing them to labor against their will. Several of these strikebreakers fled the mines and were secreted away at night by union men who knew the hills. Sometimes the Baldwin-Felts guards waited in ambush, brought the workers back to the mines, then killed their deliverers; sometimes other union men lay in wait for retaliation.[36]

While Mother Jones was out of state, Governor Glasscock's commission produced its report. The group consisted of Bishop P. J. Donahue of the Wheeling Diocese, state militia captain S. L. Walker, and state tax commissioner Fred O. Blue—a sky pilot, but no miners or working men, Mother Jones observed. The commission criticized the mine-guard system for its violations of American liberties, argued that company stores charged exorbitant prices, agreed that the companies cheated the men at the scales. But it also declared miners to be well paid in West Virginia and accused the UMW of stirring discontent and intimidating nonmembers. The commission ignored the key issues: the right to organize, union recognition, and the abolition of the guard system. With the commission offering no solutions and the operators still refusing to negotiate, the situation could only decay. Glasscock quietly withdrew the troops early in the new year, and the shooting recommenced. With things heating up once more, Mother Jones returned just in time for the most dramatic moments of the strike.[37]

On February 7, a Paint Creek strikebreaker was injured on the job. Union men shot at him and his doctor as they made their way to the hospital in Holly Grove. A group of heavily armed mine guards moved in, but the strikers repulsed them, then kept up a steady barrage against the fort at Mucklow. The mine operator Quinn Morton quickly gathered weapons, contacted local sheriffs, who raised a posse, and with the cooperation of the Chesapeake and Ohio Railroad rode a darkened armored train that night, the Bull Moose Special, toward the strikers' tent colony. Morton and the posse fired rifles and a machine gun into the miners' tents, killing one man and wounding a woman.[38]

Violence escalated, there were several casualties at Mucklow, and Governor Glasscock once again sent in the National Guard. Mother Jones called for a meeting with Glasscock to protest the troops' arresting union men and no one else. Bearing a petition, she headed for Charleston with a few dozen supporters. When they arrived on February 13, *The Charleston Daily Gazette* warned that she came at the head of five hundred armed miners to assassinate the governor. City Hall's bell tower rang out a riot warning, while local police and National Guard troops massed to defend the capitol. Mother Jones never made it past the Charleston train station. She was arrested by the military authorities, then transported back into the strike zone, to the town of Pratt, West Virginia, where the military prosecutor indicted her and forty-seven others. No mine guards were charged.[39]

Most of the union men were held in a bull pen, a converted railroad warehouse. The militia commandeered a boardinghouse, confined Mother Jones there, and posted two sentries to guard her. She was allowed to send and receive censored mail, to go for an occasional walk (she persuaded one of the guards to accompany her to a nearby village for beer), and to give a few closely watched interviews (under martial law, most news from the strike zone was embargoed). Arrested along with Mother Jones were the editor Charles Boswell of the socialist *Labor Argus* and UMW organizers Charles Batley and Paul J. Paulson. Attorneys for these four brought habeas corpus proceedings before the West Virginia Supreme Court. In the case *In re Mary Jones, et al.*, the court refused to limit the power of the governor to declare martial law or the right of the military tribunal to arrest and detain individuals. The judges went further, ruling that a state of war existed in the strike zone and that good evidence linked Mary Jones and the others to riot and insurrection, justifying their detention. Defense attorneys advised their clients not to enter a plea or testify before the military court, whose jurisdiction and legitimacy they continued to deny.[40]

The trial began on March 7, just three days after a new governor, Republican Henry D. Hatfield, took office. The charge was conspiracy that resulted in murder, and then further conspiracy to aid the killers in their escape. These were capital crimes under martial law, punishable by death if the court so ruled and the governor agreed. Mother Jones told the tribunal that she would make no defense in her own behalf: "Whatever I have done in West Virginia I have done it all over the United States, and when I get out, I will do it again." The others also refused to plead.[41]

The trial focused on Mother Jones's alleged incendiarism, and the state had only inconclusive evidence against her. The most detailed documents entered into the record were transcripts of the speeches she gave in August and September, which were far from unequivocal calls to violence. She had urged the miners to defend their families with guns if necessary, but she had also told them to remain sober, obey the law, protect property, and respect the militia. All of her speeches, rallies, marches, and petitions were well within the established limits of American civil liberties.[42]

What Mother Jones had been guilty of was flagrant disrespect for the governor, disdain for public officials, and contempt for property owners. Her swearing was not ladylike, her attacks on clerics blasphemous. She was an elderly woman who failed to observe social niceties in public places. Her characterization of West Virginia as a police state and her attacks on mine operators as rapacious murderers defied the national mythology of free enterprise. And worst of all, the miners listened. Her enemies were right—she was a prodigious troublemaker. In his closing remarks to the military court, the prosecutor, Judge Advocate and Lieutenant Colonel George S. Wallace, argued that Mother Jones held a large share of responsibility for the recent violence but added, "I frankly say that I do not think the evidence is very strong against her."[43]

No record survives of the military tribunal's decision, but we know that twenty-five prisoners were released unconditionally by Governor Hatfield on March 20 and nineteen more on the promise of good behavior two days later, while eleven were remanded to local jails or the state penitentiary. Mother Jones must have been found guilty, for she was kept under house arrest. No one knew how long the prisoners would be held—or even if they might be executed—but it was clear that the government had singled out the most radical and effective leaders. If the state's aim was to silence the outspoken, it succeeded for a while, but it failed in the long run. For a month, a news embargo meant that little was heard from the military zone, a major setback for the union because publicity had been an important weapon. Once the trial began on March 7, however, the dam started to crumble. What could make better copy than the court-martial of an eighty-year-old woman? On March 11, *The New York Times* ran a story on page 1, " 'Mother Jones' Defiant," emphasizing the possibility of death by firing squad: " 'I am 80 years old and I haven't long to live anyhow,' she said. 'Since I have to die, I would rather die for the cause to which I have given so much of my life.' "[44]

In the pages of *Collier's*, Mother Jones told the journalist Cora Older, "I can raise just as much hell in jail as anywhere," and she did. "While one of these, my boys, are in prison, I am in prison," she declared in the *United Mine Workers Journal*; "If they want to stop my protest against the unjust conditions, the brutal use of force and murder . . . let them stand me against a wall and shoot me." She told *Miners' Magazine* that West Virginia officials offered her freedom if she would leave the state and not come back. "You bring your guns," she replied, "and put me up against that tree outside of this bastille and riddle me with bullets, but I will never surrender my rights to remain in this state as long as it suits my business to do so."[45]

Even her prison correspondence was written for dramatic effect. To Idaho senator William Borah, who called for an investigation when the troubles first erupted on the creeks, she offered her gratitude on behalf of "the crushed and persecuted slaves of the coal mines." She added, "This is just what the old monarchy did [to] my grandparents 90 years ago in Ireland." Writing to Caroline Lloyd, Mother Jones compared conditions in West Virginia to the Spanish Inquisition and called the military tribunal the most infamous court since the Middle Ages. At the end of her note, she appended, "I am scratching this off in a hurry. It goes out underground. I am watched on all sides of my room. . . . I am writing it blindly for I have to watch the window." In a second letter to Lloyd, she wrote, "When I know my doom I will Tell I was tryed 4 weeks ago by the Drum Head Military Court. I have not recd. my Sentence yet. . . . I'll die fighting the Crew of Pirates." Her return address: "Pratt W. Va., Military Bastille (In Russianized America)."[46]

Others began beating the drums for her. Writing in the *Appeal to Reason*, Eugene Debs remembered his old friend—this "heroine of a thousand battles . . . this intrepid old warrior in labor's cause, this scarred old soldier of the revolution"—as a commanding general and called for the left to rise in revolt if the "corporate brigands" murdered her. He concluded, "Mother Jones, we salute you, and we swear that the bullpen shall not be your grave!"[47]

Letters from individuals, petitions from socialist clubs, resolutions from union locals poured into the White House and the Labor Department. T. J. Llewellyn wrote from Missouri to the new Secretary of Labor, William Wilson, "I have carried a gun three times in industrial wars in this country, and by the eternal, if any harm comes to the old Mother, I'm not too old nor by the same token too cowardly to carry it again." He signed himself "one of 'Mother Jones' boys." Margaret R. Duvall warned Secretary Wilson to expect an aroused working class "more dreadful than this country has ever seen" if their "brothers and sister" died in prison. A. Van Tassel of Conneaut, Ohio, begged the President to restore republican government and free the miners' angel: "This beautiful hero of the labor movement has committed no crime, but is being slowly murdered because she insisted on agitating and educating the workers to realize their true status in society."[48]

In the old song-poem tradition, J. A. Bradley of Lancaster, Ohio, wrote in the *United Mine Workers Journal*:

> *We love her for her constant voice.*
> *Raised ever 'gainst wrongs and ills,*
> *For healing the bodies, bruised and torn,*
> *In the factories, mines and mills. . . .*

> *No truer words than those last words,*
> *"They know not what they do,"*
> *They nailed a Son upon a cross,*
> *And would smite a Mother, too.*

Not only workers but middle-class Americans—merchants, insurance agents, auto dealers, booksellers, accountants, even real estate brokers—expressed their outrage at the cavalier treatment of constitutional liberties in West Virginia and the trampling on women's protected status.[49]

Popular outrage made its way into the press. In May, Harold West published a long article, "Civil War in the West Virginia Coal Mines," in *The Survey*. West wrote that he entered the mine country a neutral observer but came away pro-labor. There had been plenty of violence on both sides, he noted; the operators genuinely were squeezed by market pressures in their efforts to get coal into the lake trade at a profit. Nonetheless, West sketched in broad outline a system of peonage—making workers perpetually indebted to the companies, gouging on rents and goods, retaining private guards to keep workers in line. West charged that families were kept poor and their rights denied because it paid. He concluded by quoting former governor W. M. O. Dawson—Glasscock's predecessor—that many West Virginia mines practiced "robbery of the poor and oppression of the weak."[50]

Protests notwithstanding, the state kept Mother Jones under arrest as part of a larger strategy of quashing dissent, shutting down the strike, and imposing a settlement. She remained incarcerated for nearly three months, much of the time in poor health. The use of martial law on a hitherto unheard-of scale set a precedent for state intervention in labor affairs frightening in its implications. Civil liberties as embodied in the right of habeas corpus, the use of arrest warrants, the U.S. Supreme Court decision in *Ex Parte Milligan* (which strictly limited the scope of military tribunals) were ignored. The state court-martialed over one hundred individuals, almost all of them unionists, and when two socialist newspapers urged miners to reject a compromise settlement, Governor Hatfield sent troops to shut them down, jail the editors, and destroy their presses. In contrast, the guards who rode the Bull Moose Special, shot up Holly Grove, and committed countless other acts of terrorism were never even detained.[51]

As it turned out, the governor's strategy failed. Hatfield began "negotiations" while Mother Jones and the others were still under arrest. The operators agreed to a nine-hour day, the workers' right to select their own checkweighmen, semimonthly pay, and no blacklisting of union miners, concessions that had been won in previous strikes or were part of state law but were never enforced. The points uppermost for the mine families, union recognition and an end to the guard system, were not addressed. Although hesitant to make any concessions, the operators knew a good deal when they saw it; besides, the strike was a year old and getting costlier all the time. UMW president John White attempted to hold out for union recognition. Hatfield responded that he would imprison anyone not cooperating with his settlement plan on grounds that they abetted the insurrection. In late April, both sides agreed, and the UMW ratified the pact, not with a rank-and-file vote, which probably would have failed, but through a district convention.[52]

The settlement outraged miners on Paint and Cabin Creeks, but when they threatened to continue their strike, Hatfield issued an ultimatum ordering them to return to work or face deportation from West Virginia. Not only did the national UMW leadership endorse the settlement, but a special committee of the Socialist Party consisting of Eugene Debs, Victor Berger, and Adolph Germer also praised the agreement and exonerated Governor Hatfield of wrongdoing. Local militants and radicals were furious, especially when their newspapers were shut down by the state. Mother Jones heard about the settlement while still under confinement. Though willing to accept these terms as the best outcome of a bad situation, she was appalled at the Socialists' whitewash of the government, and she would continue to nurse her grudges against them. But with the militia in place to enforce the governor's policies, the men went back into the mines.[53]

A few days later, the U.S. Senate debated conditions in the coalfields. Senator John Worth Kern of Indiana, the majority leader, asked for an investigation into violations of immigration, contract-labor, peonage, and civil liberty laws. Senator Nathan Goff of West Virginia argued that an investigation was unnecessary, called Mary Jones the mother of agitators, and seconded Governor Hatfield in declaring that she was not incarcerated but merely confined to a pleasant boardinghouse. Senator Kern pulled out the telegram Mother Jones had sent him on May 4 and read it aloud: "From out of the military prison walls, where I have been forced to pass my eighty-first milestone of life, I plead with you for the honor of this Nation. I send you the groans and tears of men, women, and children as I have heard them in this State, and beg you to force that investigation. Children yet unborn will rise and bless you." Kern timed the moment perfectly; the Senate authorized the investigation amid a flurry of national publicity.[54]

On May 8, embarrassed by the attention Kern's move generated, Hatfield freed Mother Jones, convinced that his settlement still would hold. Less than two weeks after her release, she addressed an auditorium of well-wishers in Pittsburgh, Pennsylvania, and already West Virginia stories had become part of her repertoire. She told how she ignored warnings not to go to Cabin Creek: "I didn't come out on a stretcher. I raised hell." She advised the miners to stay armed: "The Governor wants your guns. Don't you dare give up any of them. If you are forced to use them, you use them." She pleaded for unity in the labor movement: "You trades unions must stop wrangling with the I.W.W., and the I.W.W. must stop wrangling with the trades unions. . . . I know Industrial unionism is coming, and you can't stop it."[55]

Less than a month after the settlement, hearings before a U.S. Senate subcommittee publicized the outrages that martial law concealed. Meanwhile, miners chafed at the Hatfield-imposed settlement. Wildcat strikes broke out at the end of June on Paint and Cabin Creeks. With the Senate investigation exposing the abuses of the previous year, the state had little leverage to compel the miners back to work. The operators conceded the dues checkoff at Paint Creek and the right to arbitration at Cabin Creek, de facto recognition of the union. Soon, the entire central portion of the state was organized by the United Mine Workers. Though the mine guards were not eliminated, and operators in West Virginia's southernmost fields remained adamantly anti-union, it was a major victory.[56]

Mother Jones's role had been an important one. She brought national publicity, even congressional intervention, at the crucial moment. More important, her words and fearless presence rallied the rank and file, who were ripe for strong action. Her salary was paid by the national office of the UMW, but her ideas fit better with local militants. By the time the final settlement came, the mine families had gained a new sense of themselves. On the surface, when the miners' contract expired at the beginning of April 1912, money was their main concern. But they moved toward much larger issues of freedom, dignity, and the rights of citizens. They would not relinquish their liberty as Americans to the owners of property, they would demand decent material lives for themselves and their children, and they would do it together. They would indeed question the legitimacy—the Americanness—of a system that gave everything to a few, nothing to many.[57]

The dramatic scenes in West Virginia's mountains added the most spectacular chapter yet to the legend of Mother Jones. Her crowning moments were played out on the national stage, but as always, it was the radical and unionist press that lavished the most praise on the old woman. Declared *The Christian Socialist,* "She is God's great ministering angel, the incarnate spirit of motherhood, a mighty prophetess of the coming reign of justice, love and joy." *Miners' Magazine* observed, "A few years more, and 'Mother' Jones will be sleeping in the bosom of Mother Earth, but when the history of the labor movement is written and there is recorded the glad tidings of labor's emancipation, the name of 'Mother' Jones will shed a halo of lustre upon every chapter." "Martyrdom," the *International* added, "would be her apotheosis."[58]

"Search for the Mosquito!"

Passing through New York City just three weeks after her release, Mother Jones gave lengthy, reflective interviews. *The Brooklyn Daily Eagle* called her "perhaps the most remarkable woman in America" and devoted a long story to her. She described living with the mine families on Paint and Cabin Creeks. She told the story of the strike, but when she turned from these events of the moment, she gave a thoughtful assessment of the labor movement. Mother Jones criticized the Socialists as too idealistic, the IWW as reckless, the AFL as hidebound; but she added that socialism was inevitable, praised the Wobblies for bringing countless dispossessed workers into an industrial union, and commended the trade unionists for their tireless work and powerful organizations. She mused on how to heal divisions and build on the movement's strengths. Perhaps not coincidentally, in calling for unity among American workers, she also made the most blatantly racist comment of her long career, complaining that both the "Japs" and the "Hindus" were entering the country in large numbers and becoming a serious menace to labor in the western states.[59]

That same day, *The New York Times* also featured her in a long interview. The reporter was startled at her moderate tone: "I had expected much incendiary talk in uncouth English and found an educated woman, careful of her speech and sentiments. If she had a red flag with her, she kept it in her satchel with her comb and brush and powder puff. She has a powder puff. That too astonished me." Clearly, Mother Jones decided to let the coal operators and West Virginia officials look like the extremists while she took the high road. She criticized fanaticism, praised all moderates, including a few government and business leaders. She seldom exposed her private feelings to anyone, not even in personal letters, so it was a rare thing for the *Times* to catch her in a moment of introspection.[60]

She said something remarkable in this interview: "My husband died of yellow fever in the South . . . and the same disease made other widows by the tens of thousands. It is making no more widows, because we now have mastered it. The world is suffering, today, from an industrial yellow fever, not less fatal, but I am certain, as preventable." The cause of yellow fever had only been discovered a few years before. Mother Jones rarely mentioned the deaths of George and her children to that disease back in 1867, and then only in passing. But now she turned the scientific breakthrough that might have saved them thirty years earlier into a metaphor: "Search for the mosquito! That ought to be a slogan with investigators on both sides of the labor question." Child-labor legislation was science's first triumph, and people like herself were simply trying to "drain the industrial swamps." There it was: her mission was to conquer yellow fever. Mother Jones would do the work Mary Jones could not; she would save the children.[61]

She probed even more deeply into her own past for the *Times*. She told her old story about going south to investigate conditions in the cotton mills, but this time the story took a new turn. She described meeting a widow and three children who worked fourteen hours a day, seven days a week, all powerless to escape their peonage. "I abducted the whole family," Mother Jones recalled:

> It was a real abduction, for they went almost against their will. They could not believe escape to be a possibility. I

shall never forget that night. . . . We drove along the miles
of road, my charges shivering in fear, although the night
was moist and hot, with all the qualms which might have
thrilled us had we been a party of the antebellum aboli-
tionists and escaping negro slaves. Always listening for the
baying of bloodhounds, we reached the station, climbed
furtively aboard the train, and started off. My charges all
broke down then, quite hysterically. The strain had been
so great!

The story, Mother Jones concluded, revealed the possibility of change,
and she observed how genuine progress was being made now that
many states had passed child-labor legislation.[62]

At her greatest moment of fame and triumph, Mother Jones chose
to bring up—albeit obliquely—the subjects she mentioned so rarely,
yellow fever and the death of her family in Memphis. Her call to find
the mosquito causing industrial ills made explicit the tie between
watching her family die and her need to save others. She made the
connection even clearer by linking those horrifying days almost a half
century ago to a story about leading a widow and children out of the
South. Later in the interview, she went on at length about neglectful
mothers and about how women must stay at home and raise their families. She declared that "the average human being only wants a quiet
home, a well-fed, comfortable family, so situated that its happiness is
possible." She might well have been describing herself, George Jones,
and their children in autumn 1867. Clearly, in this *Times* interview, she
made a leap of fantasy. For a moment, she imagined her personal history magically changed. Rather than passively watch her babies die in
the Old South after the Civil War, she returned, strong and transformed, to rescue them. No longer the "spiritless and hopeless" widow,
"bowed by the weight of misery impossible to describe in words," Mary
Jones came back to deliver her family. The woman warrior whose
strength of purpose saved the day supplanted the heartsick mourner of
1867.[63]

It was pure fantasy, of course. Nothing could rescue her long-dead
loved ones. But saving Mary Jones was not a fantasy, and the character

she created, Mother Jones, was no fantasy either. Out of famine, plague, and fire, out of grief and helplessness, dauntless Mother Jones had emerged and triumphed. Martyr and savior, the old woman of the labor movement was real enough to help save those who could not save themselves—workers, their families, and Mary Jones herself.

★ 8 ★

The Colorado Coal War

"I hate violence," Mother Jones declared in a long interview in *The New York Times*, "I favor drama." But violence and drama were not mutually exclusive. She mentioned Coxey's Army as a good example of political drama, but even though Coxey's followers were quite peaceful, it was the implicit threat carried by thousands of unemployed men that gave the event drama. One of the keys to understanding Mother Jones's power as a dramatist is the way she played at the edge of violence. She juxtaposed images: sacred motherhood and mass marches of women, black Victorian dresses and hellfire speeches, phrases like "listen to Mother" and "every bloody murderer of a guard has got to go." The drama of the mine wars came from force, whether real or imagined. And the threat of force was magnified by Mother Jones's moral claims to protecting that which was sacred—women, children, families.[1]

Others came to understand her in precisely these terms. Kate Richards O'Hare, for example, one of the Socialists' most charismatic organizers, published a tribute to Mother Jones in 1913 filled with theatricality and militance. "Out of the blackness of the working class night," O'Hare wrote, "she has flashed across our nation, a portent of the rising tide of revolution." O'Hare described the first time she heard her: "Here was one woman in a million, a personality that was fire tempered, a soul that had been purified in world travail, a voice whose call I could follow to the end of the road." O'Hare concluded with the now-obligatory death scene: "She will die fighting with her face to the enemy and when at last her voice is stilled by the touch of death her spirit of revolt will live and grow in the hearts of men until at last we finish the work her hands were compelled to drop."[2]

In the bleak landscape of southeast Colorado, Mother Jones, the woman warrior, fought again. Public praise songs like O'Hare's were the very fuel of the old woman's authority. Although Mary Jones had cast her lot with the workaday world of organized labor, it was only through the mythopoeic persona of Mother Jones that she held sway. Unlike other labor leaders, she did not exercise powers of office, administer a budget, secure the loyalty of assistants through patronage, or give orders to subordinates. As a woman, she could never move up the union hierarchy. Her success depended on how well she played the part of Mother Jones and how responsive her audiences were to that role. In 1913, she was at the peak of her powers because she was at the peak of her fame. But Colorado, with its Rockefeller-controlled mines, took her measure.[3]

"Let the Fight Go On"

There were important differences between Colorado and West Virginia. Western coal country was less mountainous, with wider horizons but a harsher climate. Immigrants were a majority in Colorado, with large Greek, Italian, and Mexican populations. And, unlike West Virginia, a few enormous companies rather than an array of smaller firms dominated the market. Still, there were striking similarities. Operators in both states were in a position to produce coal cheaply and thereby threaten competing suppliers. Colorado received not only many of the same families that had worked the West Virginia fields but some of the same Baldwin-Felts detectives as well. Both states suffered from similar maladies—election fraud, local governments controlled by the operators, industrial espionage, brutal mine guards, lack of union checkweighmen, payment in scrip, company towns, and rising costs of living. Above all, both states felt the brunt of raw industrial warfare. Owners and managers demanded autonomy; the United Mine Workers insisted on the workers' right to organize; and each side resorted to violence to enforce its position.[4]

In the years after the defeat of 1903–1904, UMW membership in Colorado dwindled to a few hundred men. The union was broke and the leadership exhausted. Three firms still dominated the market, Victor, Rocky Mountain, and the largest of them all, Colorado Fuel and Iron, controlled by the Rockefeller family. Led by President Jesse Welborn and Vice President Lamont Montgomery Bowers, Colorado Fuel and Iron remained aggressively anti-union. Bowers reduced costs by cutting pay and scrimping on mine safety. By 1910, Colorado had become the nation's most dangerous state for coal miners.[5]

The years following the 1903–1904 strike were far from quiet, but the UMW was unable to mount a full-scale campaign in Colorado. On April 4, 1910, for example, miners in the northern field walked out when the operators refused to negotiate a new contract. The strike proved disastrous. Operators fenced the mines with barbed wire and replaced the old British-ancestry miners with immigrant strikebreakers. The UMW refused to concede defeat, sending in thousands of dollars of strike relief every month and draining precious resources. Meanwhile, miners in southern Colorado remained distrustful of the UMW and hesitant to support the strike, especially when they recalled how the northern miners betrayed them by voting for a separate settlement in 1903.[6]

The union faced other problems. Thomas Lewis, who followed Mitchell as UMW president in 1908, proved incompetent at best. He was defeated for reelection in 1911, then went to work for West Virginia's Kanawha Coal Operators Association (to which he turned over union records). Meanwhile, the national office was $300,000 in debt, and only loans from Central Competitive Field locals kept it afloat. In the Rocky Mountains, District 15 was broke, spies had infiltrated the union, and the operators spread stories of union corruption.[7]

But as the strike commenced halfway across the continent in West Virginia, things began looking up for the UMW in Colorado. New leadership emerged in the union, including John P. White, who rehired Mother Jones as an organizer when he assumed the presidency in

1911. Frank Hayes became vice president, and, as Mother Jones's immediate superior, he pretty much let her do what she pleased. Moreover, workers in the southern field were growing restive, and the victory in West Virginia emboldened them still further. The UMW opened an office in Trinidad for the first time in five years. The union also hired talented organizers like Louis Tikas, a Greek, and Mike Livoda, a Slav, who had remarkable success organizing those two-thirds of the Colorado miners who were not native-born Americans.[8]

The operators reacted by stiffening their resistance, and Colorado Fuel and Iron led the way. To mollify workers, the company raised pay rates per ton slightly, and got more coal cars into the mines to avoid delays. Correspondence between Welborn, Bowers, and controlling shareholder John D. Rockefeller, Jr., however, indicates unyielding opposition to the UMW. Bowers wrote Starr J. Murphy, Rockefeller's legal adviser, that the only real issue was recognition of the UMW, and he added, "We flatly refuse to even meet with these agitators." As worker restiveness grew, Colorado Fuel and Iron recruited more detectives, and retained the services of employment agencies to supply strikebreakers. Then on August 16, 1913, George Lippiatt, an Italian organizer, was accosted on the streets of Trinidad by two mine guards. When Lippiatt drew his gun to defend himself, they shot and killed him. His death galvanized labor.[9]

Mother Jones returned to Colorado on September 2 and immediately began working the coalfields, always accompanied by organizers who could translate her words for the crowds. She received menacing letters for her pains. "They are sending me all sorts of threats here," she wrote Terence Powderly; "They have my skull drawn on a picture and two cross sticks underneath my jaw to tell me that if I do not quit they are going to get me. Well they have been a long time at it." District 15 called a convention for mid-September to decide a course of action. In the Trinidad Opera House on the night before the convention began, Mother Jones addressed an overflow crowd. She called for arbitration, urged Governor Elias Ammons to persuade the operators to negotiate, but finally declared that if the choice was strike or submit, "why, for God's sake, strike—strike until you win." She left the crowd screaming its approval.[10]

The next day she spoke at the convention. She opened with a story about an operator who declared after an explosion, "A miner is cheaper than a mule to a coal company." She emphasized her longevity in the movement, pointing out that she had known many of the men in the audience since they were trap boys. She told them that they only got one dollar for every ten dollars' worth of coal they dug but that without their efforts, the coal had no worth at all. Above all, Mother Jones recounted stories of how the West Virginia miners made the whole world stand up and take notice, how they asserted their freedom as Americans. She described to the Coloradans how she sent a committee to Governor Glasscock: "Take this document to the Governor's office, present it to him yourselves and don't go on your knees; we have no kings in America. Stand erect on both feet with your head erect as citizens of this country and don't say 'Your honor,' very few have honor. They don't know what it is."[11]

As always, the lesson was to take courage: "Don't be afraid boys; fear is the greatest curse we have. I never was anywhere yet that I feared anybody." She pledged her devotion to the Colorado miners, declaring, "I would rather be shot fighting for you than live in any palace in America":

> Keep away from the saloon, the pool room, the gambling den. . . . Develop your brain and heart by serving humanity and reading human history. Be true to your fellow men and stand loyally to the cause of the worker. No power on earth can dissolve us and we will get what we want if we are loyal . . . . The United Mine Workers of America will never leave the state of Colorado until the banner of industrial freedom floats over every mine in the state. It is up to you my boys to gain the victory.

"Let the fight go on," she added; "if nobody else will keep on, I will."[12]

The strike was set for September 23, 1913, and the union's demands reveal how closely the Colorado situation paralleled that of West Virginia. The UMW asked for the enforcement of state law, an eight-hour day, an improved wage scale, the abolition of the guard system, and union recognition. Management refused to budge, genuinely believing that their workers would remain loyal, but on September 23, over 90 percent of the miners walked off the job. Mine guards forced families out of their homes, and amid wind and rain, ice and mud, thousands streamed toward the makeshift towns built by the UMW with tents shipped west from Paint and Cabin Creeks. The largest colony was located at a depot called Ludlow. There, twelve hundred families speaking two dozen languages reassembled their lives. Despite the differences that divided them, blacks and whites, Mexicans and Anglos, Italians, Greeks, and Slavs were brought together by the strike. The union supplied water and coal, as well as a few dollars per week for each family. Men hunted and fished to supplement scant rations, women shared the household chores, children did their lessons. Baseball helped pass the days, and at night there was music—polkas, corridos, tarantellas, mountain ballads, spirituals.[13]

Trouble quickly escalated. Sometimes it was just verbal—pickets jeering at the bosses as they approached the mine each day, women harassing, even assaulting, scabs. In his correspondence with New York, Lamont Bowers insisted that the UMW was an outlaw group, that only terrorist intimidation kept men out of the mines, that the organizers were outside agitators, and that Mother Jones was a former brothel keeper, a lewd and immoral woman. President Woodrow Wilson's personal emissary, Ethelbert Stewart, head of the Bureau of Labor Statistics, toured the strike zone and tried to mediate but, after sitting through a diatribe by Bowers, wired Washington that he could do no good and returned home.[14]

Both sides purchased thousands of dollars' worth of guns and ammunition and soon put their weapons to use. A few days after George Lippiatt's death, a group of Greek strikers ambushed and killed the Baldwin-Felts detective Bob Lee, a man widely regarded as a rapist and a bully. Terror escalated further when the mine guards trained machine guns on the tent colonies, then installed electric searchlights, whose beams swept the grounds all night. Albert Felts himself designed an armored automobile, the "Death Special," from which his employees could shoot with impunity. On October 7, after speeches by Mother Jones and John Lawson (now president of District 15) at the Ludlow tent colony, shooting broke out and continued until dark. Ten days later, mine guards fired four hundred machine-gun rounds into the Forbes tent colony; a miner was killed, a guard wounded, and a young boy crippled for life.[15]

As always, Mother Jones goaded the miners, belittled their manhood:

> You have allowed a few men to boss you, to starve you, to abuse your women and children, to deny you education, to make peons of you, lower and less free than the Negroes before the Civil War. What is the matter with you? Are you afraid? Do you fear your pitiful little bosses? . . . I can't believe it. I can't believe you are so cowardly, and I tell you this, if you are, you are not fit to have women live with you.

In late October, she hired a band and organized fifteen hundred children for a parade in Trinidad that coincided with the arrival of Governor Ammons. Four thousand people came and marched before the Hotel Cardenas in a show of strength. The children led the demonstration carrying signs reading, MOTHER JONES' FAMILY and A BUNCH OF MOTHER JONES' CHILDREN; other banners declared, WE WANT FREEDOM, NOT CORPORATION RULES, and IF UNCLE SAM CAN RUN THE POST-OFFICE, WHY NOT THE MINES? Over the years, Mother Jones embellished the story of this Trinidad rally. She described marching the women and children through the hotel lobby right up to the governor's room. She knocked on the door, but he hid from them and refused to come out. "Unlock that door and come out here," she claimed to have told the governor, "these women aren't going to bite you."[16]

As tensions grew, the coal companies pressured Governor Ammons to send in the Colorado National Guard, claiming that most miners would return to work once they were protected from the "troublemakers." But the men remembered that deportations carried out by the soldiers in the 1903–1904 strike helped defeat the union, and they opposed the militia now, believing that, as in West Virginia, it would become a tool of the operators. With violence escalating, however, Ammons sent in the troops on October 28. Although the governor did not declare martial law, General John Chase simply arrogated those powers. Soldiers escorted strikebreakers into the field, hung around the operators' offices, rode in company cars, were paid with company money, and brandished company weapons. Fear alternated with rage in the tent colonies, as it became clear that local sheriffs, private detectives, and state troops operated as a single unit to intimidate mine families and break the strike. Ten days after the army arrived, miners ambushed and killed three guards and a strikebreaker, then two weeks later assassinated George Belcher, Lippiatt's killer. Next, rumors of a trainload of strikebreakers headed for the Ludlow depot brought out dozens of mine women armed with clubs and tree limbs; the rumors proved false. Later, an armored train approached Ludlow with machine guns blazing but was turned back by rifle fire.[17]

President Wilson's man, Ethelbert Stewart, argued that the situation was unraveling because the operators tried to force tenth-century despotism onto a twentieth-century industrial situation. "The companies created a condition," Stewart wrote to Assistant Labor Secretary Louis Post, "which they consider satisfactory to themselves, and ought to be to the workman, and jammed the workman into it and thought they were philanthropists. That men have rebelled grows out of the fact they are men, and can only be satisfied with conditions which they create, or in the creation of which they have a voice and share." The managers in Colorado refused to make any concessions to the union, and Woodrow Wilson chastised Lamont Bowers: "A word from you would bring the strike to an end, as all that is asked is that you agree to an arbitration by an unbiased board." The President's ire notwithstanding, the operators' policies remained unchanged.[18]

Secretary of Labor William Wilson painted a gloomy picture for the President in a memo dated December 10. The union sought arbitration, but the operators agreed only to obey the state laws, which they had always flagrantly violated. Ammons was too intimidated by the operators to intervene. Secretary Wilson saw no way out:

> A condition of guerilla warfare exists and many people
> have been killed. Each side places the responsibility upon

the other. It is freely asserted amongst citizens of Colorado other than those engaged in mining that a feudal system exists in these coal fields, sometimes benevolent and sometimes otherwise; that the power of the coal companies has been absolute in those camps and so great that it has dominated not only the industrial but the political and social conditions of the mining communities.

Wilson added that the operators denied all of these allegations, and he concluded that only a congressional investigation might help break the deadlock. Meanwhile, General Chase detained more organizers and union sympathizers, often without charges.[19]

As the impasse deepened, Mother Jones took to the road. She lobbied Congress for an investigation proposed by Colorado representative Edward Keating. She moved on to Boston, New York, and back to Washington to raise money for the strike. Then she rode the rails to the opposite coast and made appearances in Seattle and Vancouver. At year's end, she returned to Denver and addressed the Colorado Federation of Labor convention. There she challenged delegates to follow her to the state capitol. Two thousand unionists marched in the snow behind Mother Jones and an American flag. They confronted the governor about misconduct of state troops, a charge he denied but invited them to document. They sent him a detailed report the following month, but to no avail. From Denver, Mother Jones went to El Paso, Texas, for two weeks in an effort to stop state troops from escorting Mexican strikebreakers into Colorado. She also went to Juárez to meet with the Mexican revolutionary Pancho Villa, who pledged to help stop the flow of strikebreakers across the border.[20]

Governor Ammons and General Chase were happy to have Mother Jones away from Colorado, and they decided to keep her out of the strike zone. Chase issued an edict banning her return to Trinidad. She responded that, as a citizen, she would go anywhere in the United States she pleased. Using the sort of hyperbole that always gained the desired publicity, she added that if Chase had her killed, it would only speed the union victory. Chase told reporters that Mother Jones "is dangerous because she inflames the minds of the strikers." She baited the pompous general in her response to newspapermen: "Tell General Chase that Mother Jones is going to Trinidad in a day or two and that he'd better play his strongest cards—the militia's guns—against her." She added, "He had better go back to his mother and get a nursing bottle. He'll be better there than making war on an 82-year-old woman in a state where women vote."[21]

Mother Jones entered Trinidad on January 4, 1914, and was immediately detained, then sent to Denver. When her train stopped at the Walsenburg station, miners carrying a large American flag serenaded her with the song "The Union Forever." She promised to return, but General Chase vowed to reporters that if she came back, she would be jailed and held incommunicado. The *United Mine Workers Journal* urged others to take up her fight: "The chief rebel has been exiled. But the spirit of rebellion is still there. . . . Her children will continue the battle, and they will win." In Denver, she pledged to the Trades and Labor Assembly that she would not be silenced. The next day, she bought and distributed five hundred dollars' worth of shoes for children of the mines; then she sneaked back into Trinidad on January 12.[22]

Across the street from Chase's headquarters, she took a room; Chase sent his men to arrest her. She told the Commission on Industrial Relations, "There was 150 cavalry, 150 infantry, 150 horses with their heads poked at me, 150 gunmen of the Standard Oil Co., and the old woman." Troops rushed her by automobile to Mount San Rafael Hospital, run by the Sisters of Charity. For nine weeks, round-the-clock guards held her under house arrest, allowing no one but the union attorney to visit and preventing her from reading newspapers or sending mail. The governor declared she would be held until she promised to leave the strike zone for good. Her detention was of dubious legality, as was the arrest of twenty-seven other union supporters that week alone. General Chase acted as if the full power of the courts now rested with him, but Ammons had never officially declared martial law. Sometimes Chase denied that the militia held Mother Jones at all (her staying in the hospital was a publicity stunt, he said), then contradicted himself, declaring that she must be detained lest she cause more violence.[23]

As in West Virginia, Mother Jones got more attention in prison than out. In Denver, the Equal Suffrage Association denounced her detention as a violation of the right of free speech. In Rockvale, nine hundred miners threatened to march to Trinidad and free her by force. A group of two hundred mine women, waving flags and singing union songs, marched from the Trinidad union hall to militia headquarters, accosted General Chase in his hotel, and demanded her freedom. He refused. What came to be known as "the Mother Jones riot" occurred a week later. One thousand women and children, wearing their Sunday best, marched in protest, carrying signs that read, MOTHER JONES HAS NOT DONE ANYTHING THAT WE WOULD NOT DO. They encountered one hundred armed and mounted troops, led by General Chase. Rather than halt when ordered to, the marchers advanced slowly. At this tense moment, Chase lost control of his horse and fell off, bringing much derisive laughter. He ordered his troops to charge, which they did, swinging their sabers and rifles. Six women were badly injured.[24]

Meanwhile, the Colorado Supreme Court heard UMW attorneys' request for Mother Jones's release on a writ of habeas corpus. General Chase claimed that the Greeks, Montenegrins, and Italians who packed the court's hearing room on March 6 were there to precipitate a riot and assassinate state officials. Only his timely order to surround the courthouse with soldiers, he declared, prevented disaster. The Colorado Supreme Court agreed to hear Mother Jones's case on March 16. Wishing to avoid a precedent-setting decision that would force the release of other prisoners, the militia freed her on March 15. Chase declared that she had always been free to go but that she would be re-arrested if she came back. Mother Jones returned to Denver, made some speeches against military despotism, conferred with her colleagues, then headed back to Trinidad on March 22.[25]

Just before boarding the train from Denver, she posted a letter to "my own dear son," Terence Powderly. She told him that the troops were looking for her, she predicted they would arrest her again, and she asked him to check the newspapers for word of her fate. Then she bitterly attacked local Catholic officials. She called the Sisters at the convent hospital where she had been detained "moral cowards," blasted them for allowing a religious institution to be turned into a military prison, and said they were all owned by the Rockefeller interests. "How they prostituted Christ's holy doctrine," she declared; five "big, burly, uniformed murderers" guarded her door every night, and the Sisters and priests did nothing to protest. The hypocrisy of it stunned her: "Right on the ground with that convent those uniformed members drilled every afternoon to learn how to become experts in the shedding of human blood. The military now is turned on the working class and priests and presidents and ministers endorse the crime."[26]

Before her train ever got to Trinidad, troops boarded it, arrested her, and confined her to a cell in the basement of the Huerfano County Courthouse in Walsenburg, a prison that the Colorado State Board of Charities and Corrections had previously condemned as unfit for human habitation. Despite the pleadings of union officials, Chase refused to move her out of these quarters. "It was cold, it was a horrible place," she told the Commission on Industrial Relations months later. "I had sewer rats that long every night to fight, and all I had was a beer bottle; I would get one rat, and another would run across the cellar at me. I fought the rats inside and out just alike."[27]

Although held incommunicado, she managed to smuggle out a letter, another masterful piece of propaganda. Once again addressing her friends and the public at large from the "Military Bastille," she declared that no amount of punishment would make her give up the struggle, any more than imprisoning John Brown and John Bunyan brought their surrender. Her arrest was just one more example of Colorado's disregard of civil liberties, she wrote, emblematic of capitalism's assault on American freedom, proof that citizens' rights had no protection against the "national burglars of Wall Street."[28]

Mother Jones's arrest once again brought a wave of outrage. Eugene Debs asked Americans to imagine Mother Jones in her dark cell and Ammons in the governor's mansion: "Behold them both, the one the inspired liberator of the masses, the other the servile lackey of the princes of plunder and assassination; the one as glorious in her guarded cell as the other is despicable in his guarded sanctum!" *The Denver Express* wrote, "The fire of MERCY is in her eye, the love of HUMANITY in her heart, the TRUTH upon her tongue, FEAR of nothing this side of God within her heroic soul." Petitions and letters flooded the White House, as well as the Justice and Labor Departments, from union locals and progressive organizations all over America. A mass meeting of women from Las Animas County called for Chase's removal, Ammons's impeachment, and Mother Jones's freedom, adding, "If the men of the state of Colorado are going to stand idly by and see the motherhood of this state plundered, profaned, and disinherited, then we, the women of Colorado, shall exercise our prerogative as citizens and take whatever actions are necessary to secure the liberation of Mother Jones, the abolition of military despotism, and the restoration of the constitution to the people of Colorado."[29]

Letters too poured in. Miners from Dekoven, Kentucky, wrote to their congressman, "Our poor old Mother Jones . . . has been arrested and landed in prison at Trinidad, Col. by murderers and scoundrels of the earth. . . . We ask you, as a body of honest, working and producing people to take this case up." One Britt Adams wrote to President Wilson from Sheridan, Arkansas, that the situation in Colorado proved "that the old lady is right when she says that the worker has no protection from our Government, and that the Government is run by and for the wealthy." Even Pancho Villa wrote to Woodrow Wilson, reminding him that Mother Jones had been an honored guest of President Madero in Mexico and suggesting an exchange of political prisoners, Mother Jones for one of Villa's captives.[30]

The state of Colorado kept Mother Jones locked up for twenty-six more days, over three months total of incarceration. General Chase justified her imprisonment in a statement he wrote for a congressional investigating committee. He alluded to the *Polly Pry* charges, then accused Mother Jones of inciting "the more ignorant and criminally disposed to deeds of violence and crime." He said that her speeches were "couched in course, vulgar, and profane language, and address themselves to the lowest passions of mankind." She used her age and her sex like a shield, manipulating them to gain popular support. Chase stated it baldly: "I confidently believe that most of the murders and other acts of violent crime committed in the strike region have been inspired by this woman's incendiary utterances." But he never charged her with a crime. Once again, it was her impending appearance on habeas corpus proceedings, before Colorado's Supreme Court, that forced him to free her. She left the state exhausted.[31]

Ludlow

Mother Jones's imprisonment gave the UMW fine publicity and the moral high ground, but the winter of 1914 was a desperate time. The operators took their losses, ignored federal mediators, and refused to negotiate with the union. While Mother Jones sat in the Huerfano County Jail, strikebreakers produced coal at about two-thirds of the mines' capacity. As in 1903–1904, the UMW's national treasury ran dangerously low; only loans from the rich Midwestern districts kept the strike going. Recriminations mounted, particularly between District 15 and the national office. Meanwhile, hunger and cold gnawed at the mining camps during the hard winter, and with two dozen people already dead, the threat of more violence grew daily.[32]

To make matters worse, the state of Colorado failed to meet the payroll for its militia troops and sent them home. Their places were taken by private detectives, paid by the coal companies. "All that is left now," one striker declared, "are the gunmen, the scum of the earth, barrel house bums, professional killers from every part of the country who think nothing of human life." On a sleety March day, acting on or-

Drawn by Arthur Young.
From the Masses.   MOTHER JONES: "COME ON, YOU HELL-HOUNDS."

9. While Mother Jones was under arrest in Colorado, the artist Arthur Young depicted her moral and physical courage in this drawing from *The Masses*, reprinted in the *International Socialist Review*, March 1914 (Courtesy Newberry Library)

ders from General Chase and wearing the uniform of the Colorado National Guard, the detectives tore down tents at the Forbes camp, throwing mine families on the road, including one woman who had just given birth to twins. Purely for intimidation, the guards surrounded the remaining camps each night. April arrived, but rather than looking forward to a springtime lifting of spirits, both sides expected an attack on the Ludlow camp, and underneath their tents miners dug pits, in which women and children could hide from flying bullets.[33]

Meanwhile, the House Subcommittee on Mines and Mining began hearings on the strike. Newly freed from prison, Mother Jones went to Washington to testify, and Governor Ammons also headed for the nation's capital. The most important testimony, however, was given by John D. Rockefeller, Jr., early in April. Rockefeller declared he would lose his entire fortune before recognizing organized labor. This was a matter of principle, he declared, the principle of the open shop. Even as Rockefeller made company policy clear, soldiers took their positions at Ludlow. Troop A of the Colorado National Guard was composed mostly of company employees, and Troop B consisted almost entirely of mine guards commanded by the hated Lieutenant Karl Linderfelt. On Sunday, April 19, Greek mining families celebrated Easter according to the customs of the Orthodox Church, and all of the ethnic groups at Ludlow partook of the festivities.[34]

Gunfire began early that day, and it poured steadily from both sides. Men, women, and children hunkered down behind anything solid or clambered into pits dug underneath the tents. Strikers ran out of ammunition by late afternoon; most of them fled along an arroyo, into the hills. At nightfall, troops entered the camp, torching and looting it. They took several prisoners and executed three of them, including Louis Tikas, the acknowledged leader of the Greek miners and their families. Tikas's death can only be described as an assassination: Lieutenant Linderfelt smashed his head in with a rifle butt, then shot him at point-blank range. Daylight revealed even greater horrors. As legend has it, a telephone lineman working in the ruins discovered a trapdoor. Underneath lay the asphyxiated bodies of two women and eleven children. Lamont Bowers wired young Rockefeller, "Unprovoked attack upon small force of militia yesterday forced fight resulting

in probable loss of ten or fifteen strikers, only one militiaman killed."
Bowers added, "Suggest your giving this information to friendly papers." But there was no way to gloss over the Ludlow Massacre. Twenty
on the union side died, mostly women and children.[35]

When the enormity of the tragedy became clear, union miners
vented their rage. UMW District 15 officials issued a "call to rebellion,"
and Colorado labor organizations openly distributed guns. Men organized themselves into companies, camped in the hills, and began a
campaign against mine property and the guards who protected it. By
midweek, miners had taken control of a swath of territory roughly fifty
miles long and five miles wide, including the town of Trinidad. Guerrilla warfare was on. Strikers sniped at mine officials whenever they saw
them, and burning mine tipples lit up the night. A brief truce in the
hills lasted long enough for the emotional funeral of the Ludlow victims, but before the shooting ended, over fifty people died.[36]

Petitions and letters swamped Washington, mass meetings were
called in Chicago, San Francisco, and New York, newspapers across
America carried angry letters to the editor. Led by Upton Sinclair,
demonstrators outside Rockefeller's offices at 26 Broadway kept a
silent vigil for two weeks. Others marched on Sunday mornings at the
Manhattan church where Rockefeller worshipped. Angry miners from
across America threatened that if the federal government did not intervene, they would. UMW locals called for a nationwide strike to
protest the killings, and, given the depth of public sympathy for the
miners, it might have succeeded. But the national UMW leaders, always
insistent on maintaining their image as sober business unionists, refused to pursue this option. Meanwhile, the Colorado National Guard
set up a committee to investigate Ludlow. It interviewed no miners, declared that the strikers planned and caused the entire incident, and
added that most union members were "ignorant, lawless, and savage
South-European peasants," aliens who did not understand the concept
of American liberty.[37]

Just four days after the Ludlow Massacre, Mother Jones returned to
Washington to testify before the House Subcommittee on Mines and
Mining. Her tone was restrained, the congressmen polite. She argued
that education, not violence, would solve labor troubles, but she also

warned of impending rebellion if incidents like Ludlow continued. She urged that the guards must go, workers must be allowed to organize, and the federal government must enforce both demands. A few congressmen asked if she had not made incendiary speeches; she responded with evasive answers about earlier strikes in West Virginia and Pennsylvania and added that she might have helped prevent bloodshed had she not been imprisoned. Overall, the questions were friendly, her answers vague, and her testimony brief.[38]

She was more forthcoming when she spoke before a meeting of UMW District 14 in Pittsburg, Kansas. She told her listeners that "every man should shoulder his gun and start to Colorado to stop the war there." She praised the miners for their fight against the owners and placed herself at Ludlow. She described talking to Louis Tikas just before the battle. He cried as he told of leaving his homeland to avoid fighting in a capitalist war. "I am here now," he went on, "and this is my battle, the battle of right for the class that I belong to." There, Mother Jones declared, was the whole philosophy of the labor movement. "Mother, I need a gun," he told her. "You will have one, Louis, if Mother has to take her hat off and sell it, you will get the gun."[39]

Mother Jones was not even in Colorado in the days before Ludlow, so this conversation could not have taken place. But once again, she shaped her story to make a larger point. During the 1903–1904 strike, shipping agents paid by the operators brought many foreign miners (Tikas included) to America as strikebreakers. When these men discovered how the coal companies exploited them, many tried to resist, only to have their lives threatened. A gun for Louis Tikas symbolized the miners' need to defend their families against an evil system. And for Mother Jones, young Rockefeller, inheritor of a ruthless monopolist's fortune, now personified that system: "He has been able to crush them, rob them, persecute them until he has made his millions out of their precious blood, and then he goes into church on Sunday and is hallowed by the people of this great nation." Precious blood of the persecuted on one side, a hypocritical show of faith on the other.[40]

This Kansas speech, as much as any other Mother Jones ever gave, depicted a class-riven world. Why were some miners jeopardizing solidarity by keeping women out of their organization?

> Every woman should arise . . . and stand shoulder to
> shoulder as the women of the old Romans did 2,000 years
> ago, when they marched barefooted through the desert
> to carry the message of hope to their sister women and
> their brothers. That is the type of woman that has seen
> the jail and the scaffold and has stood side by side with
> her brother, working on the battlefields, urging him to
> keep on in this desperate struggle until victory is ours.

Only an all-embracing solidarity that excluded no one would allow them all to fulfill their historic destiny: "You are the revolutionary forces of the labor movement in America. You are the power they are afraid of. You are the power that the invisible government is after."[41]

Her images were striking—Rockefeller's paid goons roasting women and children alive; the voices of Ludlow's martyrs calling out to the living. She described prominent and well-meaning bourgeois women who went to the great magnates of Chicago like Marshall Field to beg them to pay their employees a bit more: "These women never thought of making Marshall Field produce their books to see the profit they made out of the life and blood of these girls. They didn't think that far. They don't belong to the class who is crucified. They belong to the sentimental class, and they must not hurt the feelings of the blood-sucking pirates." She told working-class women to forget about things like temperance and organize for labor; she told men they built the railroads and ocean liners, the streets and subways, and now must stand together against their oppressors; she told them all, "We don't want sympathy, we want to stand up straight before the world that we are fighting the battle for our own cause."[42]

Seventy-seven years old now, she crisscrossed the continent to share her rage. The plutocrats, not the poor boys in the National Guard, were the ones responsible for Ludlow. "What does all this strife and turmoil growing out of the coal strike and the Ludlow Massacre mean?" she asked. "It means that the workers would rather die fighting to protect their women and children than to die in death-trap mines producing more wealth for the Rockefellers to use in crushing their children. . . . It means that the whole nation is on the verge of a revolution."[43]

Yet she stopped far short of calling for revolution. Despite her harsh words for the operators, her dominant tone when she returned to Colorado was conciliatory. She told one gathering, "Don't commit any depredations. . . . Go home boys. Mind me now and keep cool. Stay out of the saloons, save your money, and when I want you I'll call you." Clearly, she still hoped public opinion would turn the tide for the union. Nonetheless, her enemies saw only red. U.S. congressman George Kindel blasted Mother Jones on the House floor as a "notorious and troublesome woman." To destroy her effectiveness, he read into the *Congressional Record* the old *Polly Pry* charges, ensuring that now they could be repeated at any time by her enemies under the imprimatur of Congress.[44]

Mother Jones's calls for moderation came in the context of a touchy situation. A week after Ludlow, as guerrilla warfare raged across Colorado's southeastern counties, Woodrow Wilson bowed to pressure from unions, businessmen, and the state; he ordered the U.S. Army into the coalfields. UMW leaders knew that defying federal troops would bring a wave of public revulsion. Besides, federal intervention was their only hope of avoiding abject defeat. Although the Wilson administration acted with relative impartiality, it refused to impose arbitration, and the stalemate ground on for months. At the end of summer, with federal troops still policing the coalfields, the President suggested a settlement that granted no union recognition or raises and that imposed a moratorium on strikes for three years. These were insulting terms, yet with funds exhausted, and strikebreakers operating the mines, UMW leaders endorsed the plan, seeing it as better than abject surrender. In her speech at the special convention in Trinidad, Mother Jones spoke for the President's proposal, compared him to Lincoln and Jefferson, and observed that only Wilson had the courage to rise with the miners against John D. Rockefeller. This was the stuff of fantasy, but her advice to the boys was pure pragmatism: "Take what you can get out of the pirates." The men voted to settle.[45]

The operators rejected Wilson's plan. They hoped permanently to destroy the UMW in the West. In October, Mother Jones wrote to the President, urging that the federal government give Rockefeller and the others five days to settle the dispute or face a federal takeover of the mines. She met with Wilson and again urged him to seize the mines if the owners failed to act. *The New York Times* castigated Wilson for even seeing her and cited General Chase's official report to Governor Ammons and the *Polly Pry* charges in the *Congressional Record* as evidence of her tarnished character. With remarkable callousness for the plight of the miners, the *Times* concluded, "It is to be remembered that there is no trouble in Colorado now, because the law is being obeyed."[46]

Despite considerable public sentiment favoring a settlement, Wilson argued that he had no authority to impose one or to take over the mines and that the courts would reverse any federal intervention. He was livid at the operators, but he would not block their drive for the union's surrender. He appointed a special commission to investigate and make recommendations, and the UMW seized on this face-saving gesture. With its treasury and all hope of mediation exhausted by early December, with mass starvation a very real possibility as the winter deepened, the miners voted to call off their fourteen-month-long strike. State courts continued to prosecute union leaders by the hundreds. It was a bitter defeat in every way.[47]

The only saving grace was that the Ludlow Massacre forced many Americans to recognize for the first time a painful reality—corporate power enforced at the point of a gun on one side, American citizens impoverished and deprived of civil liberties on the other. In Ludlow, there was enough drama even for Mother Jones.

"I Have Been Working the Game Very Quietly"

Victory had its price for the operators. Guards and munitions cost tens of thousands of dollars; idle mines had bled hundreds of thousands more. Perhaps worst of all was the tarnished image of the mine owners, of the Rockefellers, indeed, of American capitalism. In contrast, every time mining families marched under the American flag, every time their leaders invoked the ideals of Washington and Lincoln, working-class patriotism stood out in bold relief. The intransigence of capitalists, the denial of civil liberties, the murders at Ludlow, all suggested that dissident workers upheld American rights while corporations felt no such loyalties. Amassing wealth and trampling liberty, it seemed, went hand in hand.[48]

These ideas had been staples of radicals and militant laborites for decades, but now they made inroads into mainstream political consciousness. Just two years before Ludlow, after all, a million Americans voted for Eugene Debs, the Socialists elected twelve hundred candidates to public office, and two million citizens subscribed to one or more of the nation's three hundred socialist publications. Criticism of business continued to seep into the middle class through the investigative reporting of the muckrakers. The story of Ludlow piqued anew the suspicion that corporate capitalism threatened American freedom. Despite all the bad publicity, Ludlow failed to bring substantial change except in one very important sense. The earnest young Sunday school teacher John D. Rockefeller, Jr., experienced feelings of regret after the Colorado mine war. In the next two years, he and his empire underwent not so much a change of heart as a change of image.[49]

During the hearings of the House Subcommittee on Mines and Mining, Rockefeller's main defense when cross-examined about day-to-day operations at Colorado Fuel and Iron was to plead ignorance. Although his family owned a controlling 40 percent interest in the company, he declared that he had not visited the mines for a decade, nor had he attended a single meeting of the board of directors. He denied all responsibility for events in Colorado, placing that burden solely on the managers in the field.[50]

But when Rockefeller testified a few months later before the Commission on Industrial Relations, Frank Walsh, head of the commission, skewered the young tycoon on the witness stand. To Rockefeller's convenient memory lapses, his declarations that he had no notion of daily business operations, his insistence that most of his time during the great coal strike was taken up with his philanthropies, Walsh countered with internal company memoranda proving Rockefeller's knowledge and control of events in Colorado. For example, Walsh entered into the record Lamont Bowers's memo informing Rockefeller that the operators used their financial clout to keep newspaper editors, bankers, even the governor in line. Equally damning, the testimony of Colorado

Fuel and Iron president Jesse Welborn corroborated Walsh's depiction of Rockefeller's close scrutiny of daily events. Worst of all, it was revealed that Rockefeller knew in advance of the formation of Troop B—commanded by Lieutenant Linderfelt and manned by mine guards under the guise of the state militia—for duty at Ludlow.[51]

Newspapers overflowed with the revelations. Something had to be done, and Colorado Fuel and Iron promised reform. The changes turned out to be more concerned with improving the company's image than with ending worker exploitation. Lamont Bowers, the hardline defender of the capitalist faith, found himself out of a job. Rockefeller increasingly entrusted his company's management to new men like Ivy Lee and William Lyon Mackenzie King, who believed that a pleasing company image, good press, and public relations worked better than force. Managing consensus—among employees, consumers, the public in general—was more efficient, and in the long run more profitable, than trying to win every possible confrontation.[52]

Ivy Lee has been called the father of modern public relations. Just seven weeks after Ludlow, Rockefeller told his officers in Denver that Lee would begin a major publicity campaign to rehabilitate the image of the family and its interests. This Lee did with a series of posters, news releases, and especially pamphlets called "The Struggle in Colorado for Industrial Freedom." Lee publicized how companies like Colorado Fuel and Iron brought prosperity to the state and the nation. Although less important than presenting a positive company image, denigrating opponents was also part of the public relations regime, and Lee found creative ways of reviving the old *Polly Pry* charges against Mother Jones. Overall, Lee's work was a remarkable pastiche of lies, half-truths, and slanted reporting, all posing as hard news.[53]

Building consensus, however, went beyond mere propaganda. The labor expert Mackenzie King urged Rockefeller to seek a position between the union's demand for a closed shop and management's insistence that each employee bargain as an individual agent. He outlined a form of company unionism for Colorado Fuel and Iron. His "Industrial Representation Plan" set up a system to mediate grievances between employees and the company. Mackenzie King nonetheless made it clear to Rockefeller that, like Ivy Lee, he was mainly concerned about manipulating images: "The machinery to be devised should aim primarily at securing a maximum of publicity with a minimum of interference in all that pertains to conditions of employment."[54]

Colorado Fuel and Iron's makeover was the beginning of a much larger transformation. By the early twentieth century, American corporations had reorganized manufacturing, distribution, finance, and management. Now, with the Rockefeller interests leading the way, they sought to reorganize how citizens *perceived* business. Securing consent by manipulating public trust became a bulwark of corporate power, and Rockefeller was a pioneer in that endeavor. Whole new industries—advertising, public relations, opinion research—were born. Increasingly, companies sold not just their products but themselves; the velvet glove of publicity masked the iron hand of corporate power. Thus even as Colorado Fuel and Iron's advertising and labor relations campaigns went into high gear, the company supported the prosecution of hundreds of union leaders on a range of absurd charges. District 15 president John Lawson, for example, was indicted for murder, but no company representatives were charged with any crimes.[55]

Rockefeller's public relations men served him well. Lee and Mackenzie King managed to neutralize much of the bad press with declarations of Rockefeller's sincere goodwill and his company's new openness. Mackenzie King even arranged for Rockefeller to visit the Colorado mines, where he spoke to the men, danced with their wives, hugged their children, and declared that the "Industrial Representation Plan" meant a new day of cooperation between labor and management. Rockefeller was not being entirely cynical with this new strategy. The rhetoric of industrial partnership and harmony of interests resonated with his deep Christian beliefs. He argued that in modern corporations, with their thousands of shareholders and hierarchical management, only genuine feelings of brotherhood might humanize relations between labor and capital. What organized labor wanted, however, was justice, equality, sharing power and wealth, not brotherhood with the rich; only structural changes that broke down inequities could humanize relations between labor and capital.[56]

Colorado Fuel and Iron's *Industrial Bulletin* carried long stories on Rockefeller's trips to Colorado in 1915 and 1918, describing how he

visited homes and churches, broke bread with the men, and made lasting friendships. Even Mrs. Rockefeller was photographed with the
mothers and children of the mines. The UMW opposed the "Industrial
Representation Plan" as an anti-union ploy, but with the strike broken
and membership in the western states in steep decline, they were in no
position to resist.

The new order did change a few things. The mines would be run
without guards beating anyone who uttered the word "union," new
grievance procedures offered a way of adjudicating small problems,
checkweighmen measured the coal, and each mine elected worker-
representatives to discuss issues such as health, safety, and education
with management. Fundamentally, however, the new regime relinquished only the appearance of the mine owners' power.[57]

Mother Jones hated company unions, yet she was momentarily
charmed and disarmed by young Rockefeller. A few weeks after Ludlow, she sent him a registered letter proposing that they meet to discuss
things. The letter was returned unopened and marked REFUSED. But
eight months later, after a flurry of bad publicity, Rockefeller spotted
Mother Jones across the Commission on Industrial Relations hearing
room, went over to her, and within earshot of reporters asked her to
come to his offices and tell him what she knew about the situation in
Colorado. Always flattered by powerful men who sought her counsel,
she declared, "When I have a good motherly talk with him I believe I
can help him take another view of the situation among the miners out
west." The next day, they met at Rockefeller's office, where she apologized for calling him a high-class burglar, then advised him on the in-
justices of the mining camps. She accepted at face value his profession
of ignorance and declared after their meeting, "I don't hold the boy responsible." Her colleagues were appalled. Upton Sinclair advised her
gently not to be so easily swayed. No doubt, the subsequent grilling of
Rockefeller by Frank Walsh discredited in her eyes much of the magnate's pious goodwill.[58]

When Mackenzie King's company union plan was unveiled a few
days after her meeting with Rockefeller, Mother Jones lined up with
other union leaders and denounced it as "a sham and a fraud," "the
shadow and not the substance" of true industrial democracy. In a

widely reported speech at Cooper Union in New York City, she stated that Rockefeller gave only lip service to industrial democracy, for if a few miner-representatives could meet with company officials once in a while but had no organization behind them to enforce their requests, then no real change was possible. She added that while she liked Mr. Rockefeller's apparent change of heart, she now awaited a real transformation of policy. "You can't fool my boys," she admonished him, and might have added that her own gullibility had its limits too. When it was Mother Jones's turn to testify before the Commission on Industrial Relations, she insisted that no individual should own the resources that God put in the earth, that they must belong to future generations, and that only nationalizing basic industries would ensure decent wages and hours for workers.[59]

Mother Jones attained remarkable fame in the Colorado coal strike, but that event also revealed the boundaries of her influence. On the one hand, she commanded audiences with the President of the United States and with one of the wealthiest men in the world. Yet in both cases, all she could do was to state her case and hope for the best. President Wilson was not prepared to act in labor's behalf; and Rockefeller had a business to run and profits to protect. We see the limits of Mother Jones's influence most clearly after the strike ended. She tried to keep the miners' problems in the press so that Rockefeller would know that "working people are demanding to be heard." She met with Mackenzie King in Colorado and warned him against local conservatives who thought that his schemes smacked of radicalism. "I have been working the game very quietly," she wrote James Lord, head of the AFL's division of mining. "I am inclined to think that a good many of the Rockefeller representatives will get their walking papers. [King] is digging into things here and I have got the right people going to see him, not out of the Labor Movement. I think before I get through we will be able to organize the southern coal fields."[60]

It was a pipe dream born of powerlessness. Not only was the strike lost, but the UMW had been crushed in Colorado, and only the demand for coal created by World War I revived it. Rockefeller and King put their company union plan into effect, and Mother Jones's efforts behind the scenes were meaningless. "I sent young Rockefeller a letter of sympathy on the loss of his mother," she wrote Lord later. "I believe we should touch the human side every where we can." Her note to young Rockefeller began, "The sympathy of one whom thousands of men have called 'Mother' is with you at this time when your heart is filled with sorrow for her who called you 'Son.' . . . I voice the hope that you will pay the highest tribute to a mother's love by being all she prayed for you to be." Mother Jones went on to describe the power of mothers: "The mothers of the race fix all standards of life. The mother love preserves it. He who justifies that love will find consolation for every sorrow of life. I am sure that you will not resent these few words from one who has felt a mother's love for all boys and men, who has shared the sorrows of those in the ranks of toil, and finds in her heart the same sympathy for you, in this, your hour of greatest grief."[61]

No doubt Mother Jones's empathy for Rockefeller was genuine, but it was also manipulative. Even as she consoled him for his loss, she invoked her authority, the authority of motherhood. For years now, she had conflated the trope of family with labor radicalism. For most American men, however, motherhood was about love and sentiment; they paid homage to women in the home but otherwise failed to take them seriously. Certainly wealthy men found in women's claims to moral superiority not a challenge to their power but a slight modification of it. In no sense did embracing the ideal of motherhood necessarily lead to accepting a radical social agenda. On the contrary, by exploiting motherhood's conventions, Mary Jones attempted to bend a very conservative concept to her own radical cause.[62]

Rockefeller surely appreciated Mother Jones's condolences. And judging from a letter she sent two days later to his associate Walter Watson Stokes, she thought that young Rockefeller might yet see the light: "I believe the human is very deeply planted in his breast and when he understands the conditions under which his people suffered here, he will do everything to remedy the wrongs." She described to Stokes a child of the mines dying of pneumonia and declared, "I know Mr. Rockefeller would not stand for this for one moment, if he knew it."[63]

For someone who prided herself on clear-eyed realism, this was almost delusional. Mother Jones persisted in her belief that disingenuous advisers had led the young magnate astray, despite the fact that the

Commission on Industrial Relations clearly established that Rockefeller was an active shaper of Colorado Fuel and Iron policy. He knew
the conditions of the mines, knew that his corporation hired brutal
thugs, directed his subordinates to keep the union out at all costs, and
justified his acts with his utter faith in the beneficence of American
capitalism. Touching his "human side" got the miners no closer to ending hunger, suffering, and misery. The limits of Mother Jones's influence became clear in her dealings with Rockefeller. She staked her
claim to authority on her symbolic role as mother. Rockefeller flattered
her, but never quite took her seriously. She had come up against someone with real power. Aided by Mackenzie King and Lee and their min-
ions, Rockefeller was even better equipped than Mother Jones for
publicity and public relations. She had met her match.

"The Walking Wrath of God"

"There broke out a storm of applause which swelled into a tumult as a little woman came forward on the platform. She was wrinkled and old, dressed in black, looking like somebody's grandmother; she was, in truth, the grandmother of hundreds of thousands of miners." So Upton Sinclair introduced "Mother Mary" in his lightly fictionalized history of the Colorado strike, *The Coal War.* Mother Mary told of battles for the union, of how she faced down the gun thugs. She explained to her audience that only fear stood in the way of victory. "Hearing her speak," Sinclair wrote, "you discovered the secret of her influence over these polyglot hordes. She had force, she had wit, above all she had the fire of indignation—she was the walking wrath of God." Mother Jones gave voice to workers' rage, and stories were her weapons: "She would tell endless stories about her adventures," Sinclair concluded, "about strikes she had led and speeches she had made; about interviews with presidents and governors and captains of industry; about jails and convict camps. . . . All over the country she had roamed, and wherever she went, the flame of protest had leaped up in the hearts of men; her story was a veritable Odyssey of revolt."[1]

Mother Jones was certainly one of the most famous women in America now. New accounts of her life crossed the border between biography and hagiography. Peter Michelson, writing in *The Delineator,* retold all the old stories and added a few new ones: as a young dressmaker in Chicago, she sewed Mary Todd Lincoln's inaugural gown; she directed her first strike in 1882 in Ohio's Hocking Valley and, as a result, met a young attorney named William McKinley. Even some of her enemies found much to admire. An essay in *The New Republic* criticized her speeches for their hyperbole and vulgarity, for depicting the world in simplistic, Manichaean terms. Yet the author conceded that her transgressions often were in the cause of larger truths. She acted out of a clear vision of the world's injustice and effectively mobilized action against oppression. In its April–May 1914 issue, *Everybody's Magazine* devoted to her a poem, an artist's sketch, and an article by Leonard Abbott titled "The Incarnation of Labor's Struggle." Abbott called Mother Jones "a John Brown in petticoats," an "epic figure," and he concluded, "She is primitive, simple, direct as a child."[2]

Mother Jones's iconic status among workers was nothing new, but her legend now had spread widely among the middle class. When the coal wars ended, she was eighty-five years old by her own reckoning, seventy-eight in actuality. She would keep the stage for only a few more years. Starring roles in dramatic strikes with opponents foolish enough to incarcerate her grew scarce. More important, her lack of institutional resources—money, a commanding job, political clout, all denied her as a woman—severely restricted her influence. With the Mother Jones persona as her main asset, the limits of her power were clear.

"God Almighty Made the Woman"

The writers who heaped accolades on Mary Jones often presented her as the embodiment of authentic motherhood. The irony was that she played a role as *Mother* Jones, a role that required an uneasy reconciliation of two ideals. On the one hand was the old cult of true womanhood, which required devoted, nurturing, asexual mothers. On the other hand was working-class motherhood, with powerful women who held families together; Mother Jones's boys were accustomed to outspoken, physically tough wives and mothers. Reconciling these two halves of motherhood created problems. Domesticity was central to

Mother Jones's persona, but while conveniently masking her fire-and-brimstone radicalism, it could also be a trap. The nurturing image invited people to ignore Mother Jones's radical message, to embrace and dismiss her at the same time. The problem got worse as she grew older and became a grand eminence.[3]

Mary Field's "She 'Stirreth Up the People,' " for example, published in *Everybody's Magazine* in 1914, presented Mother Jones through the prism of authentic motherhood. Among workers, Field declared, she was the most beloved woman in America; ask any miner about her, and "his eyes will kindle, the pale face will relax, the mouth will smile." The very name *Mother* "sprang like the folk song . . . out of the hearts of simple people." Field described a train ride she took with Mother Jones from Los Angeles to Fresno, California: "At every stop of the train, brakemen, roadmen, laborers came aboard just to shake their Mother's hand, to bless her, to bring her baskets of fruit and boxes of candy."[4]

According to Field, Mother Jones was a treasured character of American folklore, one whose name was spoken with veneration by hundreds of thousands of common people. But even as she mythologized her, Field recognized that much of the old woman's power grew out of such mythology. Owners dreaded Mother Jones, Field wrote, not just because she organized their workers but because her courage was infectious and her devotion brought great public sympathy to labor's cause. The character *Mother* Jones—selfless, long-suffering, filled with the faithfulness of the biblical Mary—gave *Mary* Jones's words and ideas their emotional charge. Her iconic power flowed from her audiences' assumptions about sacred motherhood and from how well she played her role.[5]

So here was the problem: Domestic motherhood increasingly locked Mother Jones into advocating very conservative ideals of women and family, but Mother Jones the rebel constantly violated those very ideals. She thundered her message of labor solidarity from a thousand rostrums, then told women that their most important tasks were being good wives and mothers. She organized women for aggressively pro-labor actions, then advised them to stay home and take care of the children.[6]

Woman suffrage reveals her divided thoughts. Early in the twentieth century, in good Victorian fashion, Mother Jones told women that they held the keys to America's future, that nurturing their families would advance humanity by producing the generations of the future. For many English and American suffragettes, the moral superiority of women was an argument for the vote, and Mother Jones supported suffrage in these early years, though it was never a prominent theme in her speeches. But by the time of the Colorado coal war, she had moved to vocal opposition. Ironically, Mother Jones most strongly rejected woman suffrage just as the drive for a constitutional amendment became a crusade, eventually garnering the support of mainstream politicians like Woodrow Wilson and Theodore Roosevelt.[7]

At the simplest level, Mother Jones no longer believed that the act of voting was so important. She now argued that suffrage was a diversion, that working women must concentrate on the economic struggle. Other radicals also denied the importance of woman suffrage. The anarchist Emma Goldman, for example, called it a fetish of bourgeois society and argued that the power of capitalism to crush freedom was so overwhelming that the right to vote was all but worthless. At her most extreme, Mother Jones agreed; the ballot box gave the appearance of freedom when in fact corporations, not politicians, wielded the real power. In June 1913, even before the horrors of Ludlow, she told *The New York Times* in a much-quoted passage, "I am not a suffragist. In no sense of the word am I in sympathy with woman's suffrage. In a long life of study of these questions I have learned that women are out of place in political work. There already is a great responsibility upon women's shoulders—that of rearing rising generations." She charged that women's neglect of motherhood filled the juvenile courts and reform schools. Besides, women were "unfitted" for the ballot; a mother's task, the most beautiful of tasks, was raising her children. She concluded, "Solve the industrial problem and the men will earn enough so that women can remain home."[8]

There was something willfully contrary in all of this. Mother Jones ignored those single women who chose to support themselves; she failed to acknowledge that many families needed women's wages; she slighted the fact that work was a crucial source of autonomy for many women who did not wish to be dependent on men. Still, there was a truth to her position. The women for whom Mother Jones presumed to speak were not choosing between home and middle-class careers. For her people, jobs usually meant under-pay and overwork and, worse, the necessity of having two meager incomes to make ends meet. In Mother Jones's view, working-class wives and daughters had become a cheap source of labor, ripe for exploitation. Such women rarely rose above bottle washer, spindle tender, seam stitcher, or maid, positions that paid little, took women away from their families, and gave them no security. Given this situation, there was logic in articulating the old ideal of women in the home, where mothers were the center of nurturance and the molders of the next generation. Her ideas about masculinity were equally traditional: men were breadwinners, and they compromised their masculinity when they failed to support their families by supporting their union. She believed with some legitimacy that the choice for working-class families was between unionized husbands making good wages and couples or even whole families working at debased jobs for a pittance.[9]

After her break with the Socialist Party, Mother Jones argued more strongly than ever that in a class-based society, economic relationships mattered more than political ones. She never abandoned electoral politics altogether, and she continued to speak out for particular candidates. She also acknowledged that third parties like the Populists and Socialists could be "most powerful weapons." But money, she added, "prostitutes them all." Ironically, then, even as she staked out a culturally conservative position for old-fashioned motherhood, she also moved closer to the radical view that ballots gave only an illusion of democracy. Real power grew from worker organizations, not from choosing between candidates, most of whom became tools of capital anyway.[10]

Ideology aside, there was a personal dimension to all of this. Mother Jones had always gravitated toward men more than women. In one sense, this was not unusual. It is something of a commonplace that the likes of Jane Addams, founder of Chicago's Hull House settlement, and Florence Kelley, who headed the National Consumers' League, spoke more of their fathers than their mothers in writing about their upbringings. Addams and Kelley helped create a public sphere for women in social service work, but it was their fathers—both very successful men—who first made them aware of the world of affairs. Mother Jones was a working-class version of such women. We do, after all, learn something about her father and his work in her autobiography; her mother is not even mentioned.[11]

Unlike these women, however, Mother Jones continued to be male-centered. She spent much more time with men than with women. The labor leaders she worked with were all male, and she organized relatively few women. Even her closest female correspondents, Emma Powderly and Caroline Lloyd, she knew only because of previous friendships with Terence Powderly and Henry Demarest Lloyd. Moreover, Mother Jones's friends noted that she was very quick to criticize women and sometimes was downright hostile to them. One has to wonder, too, about the coincidence of her advocating a traditional wifely role, her hostility to "career" women, and the death of her own family. Her sense of loss and even guilt may have influenced her calls for mothers to nurture stable families.[12]

Mother Jones made her position clear at a dinner given for her by five hundred prominent women—writers, artists, suffragists, philanthropists—in New York City, just after her release from the Huerfano County jail. Introduced as "the biggest woman in the world," she shocked her audience by inveighing against suffrage, adding that although Colorado women could vote, they harmed the miners' cause by supporting pro-business politicians. The real field for women was the industrial one: "I have no vote," she declared, "and I've raised hell all over this country." She spoke for almost two hours, concluding, "Never mind if you are not lady-like, you are woman-like. God almighty made the woman and the Rockefeller gang of thieves made the ladies."[13]

But what did this mean? On the one hand, Mother Jones rejected female conformity to male ideals of refinement. Women were independent; ladies accommodated themselves to genteel or romantic conventions. But beyond this insight, she was very vague. Her oft-repeated call to organize women along industrial lines was a dead end, since unions enrolled workers, not family members. She also rejected the efforts of those middle-class women who organized alongside their working-class sisters in groups like the Women's Trade Union League, because she seemed to believe that such efforts defined solidarity along lines of gender more than class. This left no options besides a life like that of Mother Jones—a pilgrimage of selfless devotion to the family of labor.[14]

Mother Jones was not entirely wrong to characterize as elitist the wives of industrialists and the middle-class career women who could not understand the needs, aspirations, and ways of working people. To her, women involved in Prohibition and Christian charities were insufferably patronizing. But her blanket disapproval also led her to brush off reformers who brought real change to the world, women like Addams, whose settlement house on Halsted Street aided many working-class families, and Kelley, who more than anyone else made family welfare the business of government. Nor was Mother Jones interested in women's reproductive freedom, so she slighted the work of Margaret Sanger, who before World War I identified birth control as an important tool for working women to gain control of their lives. By insisting narrowly on class solidarity through labor unions, Mother Jones ignored, even denigrated, the work of important women who opened other fronts in the battle for justice.[15]

The limits of her class-based vision are especially clear in a 1915 article she wrote for *Miners' Magazine* called "Fashionable Society Scorned." Mother Jones described calling on Mrs. J. Borden Harriman at the exclusive Colony Club in New York City. Harriman was a wealthy woman, a philanthropist and reformer who had served with the Commission on Industrial Relations. On first encountering her, Mother Jones lampooned Harriman as patronizing and naive. But now she was a bit more sympathetic; not only had Harriman been sensitive to the miners' plight during the Colorado hearings, but she had called Mother Jones "the most significant woman in America." Mother Jones described the parade of "fashionable women" who passed through the club, women who posed and strutted because they had nothing to occupy their minds. When she said "the Rockefeller gang of thieves made the ladies," she meant those who lived to please their husbands and show off their wealth.[16]

Such ladies were guilty of great cruelty, for "the idle rich woman who parades her finery before the hungry and poverty-stricken is a modern inquisitor turning the thumb screws of envy and despair into the very vitals of those who are in reality her sisters." Women's mission was the development of human hearts and minds, but the fashionable set betrayed the "high ideals of womanhood." Mother Jones recalled watching a society lady ask an exhausted shop girl to get down several heavy boxes; when the goods were laid out, she glanced at them and declared that she did not care to buy anything. Such thoughtlessness, such casual cruelty, Mother Jones noted, would cease when "every woman grasps the idea that every other woman is her sister."[17]

Yet many women did grasp that idea. Organizations like the Women's Trade Union League contained wellborn women who walked picket lines, got themselves arrested and even beaten. Mother Jones never gave credit to such women, though they fulfilled her own ideal of sisterhood between the shop girl and the rich woman. Perhaps it was Mother Jones's towering ambition that made her ungenerous toward those whom she perceived as rivals. She was not wrong to fear losing the limelight. America had little room, after all, for talented, aspiring women. And perhaps, too, her insecurities came from her own class and immigrant background. America had even less room for women who were not Protestant, native-born, and young.[18]

Although Mother Jones was sometimes muddled at best, retrograde at worst, she remained a hero to countless progressive and radical women. And that was because her words finally mattered less than her deeds. In a culture that still preferred women to be frail and ineffectual, she had nothing but raw courage. In an era that discouraged women from speaking up, her voice rose loud and clear. She put her body on the line. Mother Jones might have been uncharitable toward other activist women, she might have clung to an antiquated nineteenth-century view of separate spheres and virtuous republican motherhood, but, by God, she was no lady, she was a woman.[19]

She understood that poverty was a woman's issue. When insufficient money came into a household, it was women who dealt with making sure there was food on the table, clothes on the children, a roof over their heads. The unit of production and consumption for working-class people was the family, and women ran those households. No one in

America dramatized better than Mother Jones the ways in which class and family life were interwoven.[20]

Many times as she stepped up to the podium, she remarked that there never was a man who could stop a woman from talking. Her words played on an old stereotype—women are gabby, gossipy, garrulous—but Mother Jones used this old canard to describe something much different from women's supposed obsession with the minutiae of private life. She said, in effect, we will express our opinions, men will not intimidate us, even from jail we will be heard. She overturned gender conventions by insisting that women speak out on public issues. She articulated for them the faith that men were powerless to stop those who upheld moral standards, who revealed a vision of justice, who would change the world with their words.[21]

"There Will Come Another John Brown"

Mother Jones's ideas changed as she aged, but in important respects, the world changed even more. Her work coincided with Progressive Era innovations—the Department of Labor, the Commission on Industrial Relations, the Clayton Act—that gave unions new respectability. The labor movement itself changed too. Increasingly, AFL-style trade unionists had the upper hand. Solidarity became less about ideological opposition to American capitalism, more a tool for building unions that fed off capitalist success. The organizational revolution that transformed business and government into hierarchical bureaucracies also altered unions; corporate capitalism begat corporate unionism. Organizing meant labor seeking its place at the bargaining table rather than fundamental social restructuring and economic change. Of course, radical, class-based challenges to big capital and big labor continued. But trade unionism more than democratic revolution, bureaucratic rationality rather than the old-time religion of solidarity, was winning the day. In her later years, Mother Jones's almost mystical faith in the family of labor, of brothers and sisters standing shoulder to shoulder to fight the good fight sounded a bit anachronistic.[22]

By 1919, the era that began in hope—the era of Bellamy's *Looking*

10. The poet Carl Sandburg wrote, "He had no mother but Mother Jones / Crying from a jail window in Trinidad / 'All I want is room enough to stand / And shake my fist at the enemies of the human race.'" Photograph from the *International Socialist Review*, December 1915 (Courtesy Newberry Library)

Backward, the Populist Party, the *Appeal to Reason*, the IWW, and the Socialist Party—was coming to an end. In part, the mainstream political parties stole the radicals' thunder by enacting moderate reform, such as child-labor legislation, the federal Pure Food and Drug Act, trust-busting, and other forms of government regulation. But equally important was sheer political repression. World War I and the Russian Revolution eventually brought a wave of reaction—killings, beatings, deportations, immigrant bashing, radical hounding, and union busting—as ugly as any America had ever witnessed. Before the Red Scare, however, militant labor burst forth a final time.[23]

Even as she approached eighty, Mother Jones's pace did not slacken. During July and August 1915, for example, she and James Lord toured the Midwest to stir up support for Colorado UMW leaders, many of whom stood accused of murder. She held audiences spellbound, sometimes for two hours or more. Every day for months it was a new town, a new audience, and a new speech. During one month in 1916, for example, trains carried her to Denver, Phoenix, Los Angeles, Chicago, Washington, Atlanta, and points in between. "It was nine o'clock Friday night when I got into Coffeyville, Kans.," she wrote to her friend John Walker. "When I got on the platform I was still tired, John, but nevertheless I delivered the goods, and I had a packed audience from beginning to end." Responsive crowds energized her, kept her rising each morning and catching the train for her next engagement.[24]

Mother Jones's rhetoric grew sharpest when she spoke among the faithful, as she did at the Labor Temple in Pittsburg, Kansas, in 1915. Apparently, she had gotten over some of her deference to John D. Rockefeller, Jr. She called him an "insulting rat" for refusing to negotiate with the President and declared that he should have been brought back to Washington in handcuffs. She quoted a minister who had said that Rockefeller senior (Mother Jones called him "Oily John") was the "greatest man" America ever produced:

> There is no doubt but that he is the greatest murderer the nation had ever produced; no question about it, the greatest thief; there is no question on earth about that. . . . He can't be equaled in crime; he has murdered, shot, starved, sent to an untimely grave men, women and children by the thousands that I know, and if that is your modern version of Christianity, may God Almighty save me from getting any of it into my system.

She went on to say that the leaders of giant corporations had not great brains but "wolf brains," "snake brains," "rat brains."[25]

But she grew impatient with their victims too and goaded her lis-

teners: "Because we are cowards they make us build jails and penitentiaries, and pay wardens and guards, and they put us in them. . . . We
put rags on our women, and we decorate their women with all the finery of the nation." She told mothers that they were to blame for Ludlow, for had they been vigilant, the burglars would not have dared to
"roast our children to death." Such attacks were a call not to cynicism
but to arms: "I agree with Mr. [Clarence] Darrow that the ballot will
not bring us anything. . . . Tie up every industry and for every working
man they kill, you kill one of them. . . . Buy guns, yes. And I will borrow
money or steal it to buy guns for my boys."[26]

Mother Jones continued to expand her mission. In February 1915,
she roused New York's Ladies' Waist and Dress Makers, who were on
the verge of a strike: "I have been up against armed mercenaries in labor troubles all over the country," she told them, "but this old woman
with a hatpin has scared them." Later that same year, she dispatched a
telegram to Secretary of Labor William Wilson from Chicago regarding a massive strike led by the Amalgamated Clothing Workers of
America: "Send at once to investigate clothing strike. It is fierce. Girls
getting eight cents an hour as slaves. —Mother." She spoke before
large crowds of Jewish, Italian, Polish, and Lithuanian women, urging
them on in their resistance to their bosses. Despite police beatings and
countless arrests, the Chicago garment workers won a major victory, including higher pay, a shorter workweek, and union recognition. But
Mother Jones had already moved on. She ended the year organizing in
the Youngstown, Ohio, steel strike: "When I saw the horrible condition
of those slaves of the steel mills, when I saw the shacks they lived in,
when I saw them up against those furnaces for twelve hours a day, when
I saw them going home weary and broken, I thought, 'Some day, not in
the far distant future there will come another John Brown and he will
tear this nation from end to end if this thing does not stop.' "[27]

Politics crept into her speeches in 1916. At the annual Labor Day
picnic in Evansville, Indiana, for example, she declared her socialist beliefs but endorsed Woodrow Wilson for reelection, saying, "Socialism is
a long way off; I want something right now!" Although Wilson was
slightly more accommodating to labor than his Republican predeces-
sors, his administration represented not a break with the past but a

softening of government's pro-business position. Mother Jones's endorsement of him was one more rebuke to the Socialist Party and another sign of her weakness for the attentions of powerful men. Like John Mitchell and young Rockefeller, Woodrow Wilson flattered her by listening to her, and once again, she flattered herself that she was educating one of her "boys."[28]

In 1917, she adopted streetcar workers as her special project. Working ten hours a day, often seven days a week, for under fifty dollars per month, employees of the Bloomington and Normal Railway in Bloomington, Illinois, secretly organized a local of the Amalgamated Association of Street and Electric Railway Employees in April. When the company refused to negotiate, they walked off the job. The strike was a stalemate until John Walker, then head of the Illinois Federation of Labor, brought Mother Jones to town on July 5. No record remains of her speech, but the next day, headlines in Bloomington's *Daily Pantagraph* read, SOLDIERS GUARD THE CITY; BLOOMINGTON IS SCENE OF WILD STRIKE RIOTS; TROUBLE STARTED FOLLOWING A LABOR MEETING ADDRESSED BY "MOTHER" JONES. After she finished her talk, hundreds of workers surrounded the streetcars, threatened strikebreakers when they refused to quit, and shut down the system. Next, the workers marched to the powerhouse, confronted the sheriff, mayor, and chief of police, who gave in and turned off the power. When the strike threatened to spread to men on other lines, management recognized the union, motormen and conductors received a substantial raise, and powerhouse workers got the eight-hour day. "It was a grand settlement," John Walker wrote Mother Jones, and he added that her influence was the single most important reason that the men won.[29]

She moved her organizing to Westchester County, New York, in early October. There, streetcar workers called a strike when the company insisted on a yellow-dog contract, then tried to bring in a company union. With the introduction of strikebreakers, the walkout spread throughout the New York metropolitan area. In a situation already marked by bloodshed, Mother Jones gave a speech in New York City implying that violence sometimes succeeded as a strike weapon. Rioting broke out anew, and a *New York Times* headline on page 1 blamed her: CAR RIOT STARTED BY "MOTHER" JONES; WOMEN RELATIVES OF

STRIKERS HEED AGED AGITATOR'S PLEA TO "RAISE HELL." According to the *Times*, her words inflamed the wives and mothers of striking car men: "You ought to be out raising hell. . . . This is the fighting age. Put on your fighting clothes. . . . You are too sentimental."[30]

As the women left the hall, a streetcar came rumbling toward them. They left their children on the sidewalk and attacked the vehicle with their fists, then with paving stones. They broke every window of the car and fought police, who clubbed and arrested them. An editorial in the next day's *Times* lashed out at Mother Jones: This "notorious apostle of violence" poured new fury on an audience of "dupes." The lesson was clear: "Direct incitements to disorder, violence, and crime must be squelched. You never know into what morbid or crazed brain the gospel of the preacher of force may fall." Mother Jones's right to free speech, the editorial concluded, ended with incitement to riot.[31]

Clearly, Mother Jones knew how to pique emotions. But only if one believed in the *Times*'s simplistic concept of cause and effect—evil ideas arouse dupes to frenzy—could one say that she provoked the trouble. Rioting had occurred before and after her appearance in New York City, and the single most immediate cause was the introduction of strikebreakers. Indeed, on the same day that the *Times* denounced Mother Jones, a well-buried story exonerated her. It stated that the police commissioner's office had just released a report, based on an eyewitness account, declaring that "the speaker said nothing of an inflammatory nature."[32]

In addition to her union work, Mother Jones became more involved in defending arrested labor activists. At the end of 1915, she received a long letter from Thomas J. Mooney of San Francisco, an ironworker and union organizer. Mooney asked her to help raise funds for the new International Workers Defense League, a group dedicated to aiding labor leaders arrested during strikes and lockouts. Mooney told her that the league was conceived in the same spirit "which has won for you the respect of the labor movement of the entire world." Just eight months after Mother Jones agreed to lend her voice, Mooney was arrested along with two other union leaders when a bomb exploded in downtown San Francisco during a Preparedness Day parade, killing ten people. Local business leaders from United Railroads (whose shops

Mooney had recently organized) and Pacific Gas and Electric Company (the employer of the prosecution's key witness) openly advocated framing militants like Mooney by linking them with the explosion. Mooney again appealed to Mother Jones: "The last time I wrote you I was asking your aid to help dig some other fellow out of the Bosses' Bastille. . . . This time it is to try to enlist your support . . . to the end that I, my wife and three others may again walk in free air, to fight in labor's ranks once more."[33]

As the Mooney drama unfolded, it became clear that perjured testimony was the prosecution's main weapon. By the time the court sentenced Mooney to death, Mother Jones and other radicals had persuaded AFL leaders to drop their caution and to recognize that the Mooney case represented a new front in the anti-union, open-shop war. Mother Jones spoke on Mooney's behalf wherever she went. Through her efforts and those of many other labor leaders, the governor of California commuted Mooney's death sentence to life in prison in April 1918. Until she died, Mother Jones never ceased working for Mooney's release, which finally came in 1939.[34]

One thing Mother Jones did not do in these years was return to the Socialist Party. "Not until the workers everywhere shall become politically conscious," she wrote, "not until they shall seize power of the state and wield it in the interests of the working class, will there be any hope of working-class emancipation." Yet she was too disaffected, the break with the Party too deep, for a reconciliation. "One of these days," she wrote one Party stalwart, "we are going to clean house and we will have a real revolutionary socialist movement and we will see that neither lawyers nor sky pilots are running our affairs."

Anger at the Party brought not only self-righteousness but also her tendency to play fast and loose with the facts. For example, early in 1917, she published a letter in *The New York Call* which asserted that she never asked the Socialists for help while in prison, that she always eschewed the aid of lawyers during her legal troubles, and that she never endorsed Woodrow Wilson for President, all untrue. But she was never one to let details stand in the way of a rhetorical point, that being who was most authentically radical: "I have rendered greater service to the Socialist philosophy than the highly-paid star orator, who in some instances receives a hundred dollars a lecture." She concluded, with typical hyperbole, "My life has not been, nor will it be, spent in the parlors of tea parties . . . but in the trenches, with my boys, facing the machine guns. And I expect to close my eyes in these battles."[35]

Because she insisted that the road to social transformation must be traveled with the community of the oppressed, her contempt knew no bounds when it came to anyone who professed radical ideals yet refused to give up bourgeois comforts. More than ever she insisted that only men and women who knew the life of hard work and oppression could change the world. Thus, she wrote to Fred Suytor of Barre, Vermont, that the Party called itself a working man's movement yet had little use for working men. But better times were on the way: "There will arise a movement, with a clear philosophy of the class struggle, and no leeches will be allowed to live off of it. The working people on the whole are becoming more educated; more conscious of their position; more democratic in their ideas." Laborers educating laborers; workers freeing each other; producers of goods, not phrases, leading the movement—these were her true, albeit vague, goals for politics.[36]

Aging did not diminish her tendency to live almost entirely in the public realm, and to disdain a permanent home or a fixed circle of friends. She was closest to like-minded activists, and though her personal letters occasionally contained statements of love and affection, they mainly carried news from the movement. To Edward Crough, for example, with whom she organized copper smelters in Arizona, she wrote about union elections, slammed their mutual enemies, and then asked him to forward her mail to Ed Nockles, secretary of the Chicago Federation of Labor, with whom she stayed when in that city. She added, "I shall always think of you, Ed with the affection of a mother, because you were so kind to me and were so loyal and true to the cause." She signed off, "My love to all at your home . . . and tell the leeches they can go to hell."[37]

Mother Jones's politics remained radically democratic; leaders were not to be trusted. But her insisting on the family of labor and the religion of solidarity played into the dilemma that always plagued American radical movements: How could a fragmented left function in an increasingly bureaucratized society? How could it keep up the utopian spirit in a country run by enormous institutions that were impervious to yearnings for community? In the early days of the movement, Mother Jones often said, no one looked to get paid; leaders were just glad to spread the word. There was lots of cheap nostalgia in such statements, much self-promotion, but a kernel of truth too. The greatest single difference between labor leaders before and after 1900 was that the earlier group did not generally serve in office for long; they began as workers, organized for a while, then returned to their shops and mills. But the new age was one of labor bureaucrats, of men who became professional leaders of large institutions. They had no intention of picking up their tools again; they were full-time managers. Mother Jones deeply mistrusted their cravings for respectability and security, for in such desires, she believed, rested the seeds of betrayal. The world had indeed changed. The hopes of leftists that blossomed in the late nineteenth and early twentieth centuries, their prophetic dreams and utopian yearnings, were smothered from inside the movement as much as crushed from without. But not yet, not entirely.[38]

The Great War

For Mother Jones, the United Mine Workers remained the guiding light of the labor movement. It retained a radical core, and it was the largest industrial union in the country, with 400,000 members on the eve of World War I. But the UMW's success was also potentially its failing. Ever since the days of John Mitchell, the tensions were apparent: the righteousness of the radicals versus the need to keep all factions in line; the desire for union democracy as opposed to the efficiency of a more centralized administration; the utopian impulse to oppose capitalism's single-minded quest for profits against the harsh realities of limited resources and determined enemies. Moreover, the old schism deepened between the leftists, who sought worker control in industry, and business unionists, who merely wanted capitalists to cut them in. Beyond these divisions were growing problems of union corruption, tensions between the districts and the national office, and a burden of debt and recrimination following the Colorado coal war.[39]

In the midst of her peripatetic speech making, Mother Jones settled into some sustained organizing in West Virginia beginning in the spring of 1917 and lasting through much of 1918. Old age had not diminished the controversy that surrounded her. According to one legend, a mine guard tossed leaflets from a railroad car that repeated the prostitution charges against Mother Jones. When the train got to the town of Matewan, a group of miners chased him down. A local doctor later received an anonymous tip saying where the guard's beaten and castrated body could be found.[40]

Yet these were relatively good times for miners. World War I spurred demand, and American entry into the conflict in 1917 made coal, along with many other commodities, doubly valuable. In order to keep the supply of military goods flowing, the federal government regulated wages and prices, banned strikes in major industries, but protected unions in exchange. The UMW took advantage of this situation with a powerful new organizing drive. In West Virginia, wages rose, though prices and profits soared even higher. Restive miners saw this as a golden opportunity for union recognition, higher pay, and better conditions; the rank and file staked out a more militant position than the national officers. By spring 1917, wildcat strikes had begun to plague the industry, operators petitioned state and local governments to stop them, and national UMW officers were unable to control many of the locals.[41]

Mother Jones was in the thick of it. She was quite willing to flaunt the no-strike clause imposed by the Fuel Administration to regulate the wartime economy. Governor John J. Cornwell of West Virginia wrote to Secretary of Labor William Wilson on June 16, 1917, "[W]hat is worrying me is that the extraordinary organizing activities of the United Mine Workers in certain coal fields in southern West Virginia, coupled with numerous speeches by 'Mother' Jones, of a rather incendiary character, are tending to create a condition of unrest." Two weeks later, Cornwell telegrammed Wilson, "WILL YOU NOT PREVAIL UPON NATIONAL OFFICERS OF UNITED MINE WORKERS TO REMOVE MOTHER JONES FROM THIS STATE AGITATION PRODUCING STRIKES AND TYING UP COAL PRODUCTION."[42]

Mother Jones's militancy pushed the limits of UMW policies. Still, the leadership wanted her in the field because she was their best speaker. Her opponents testified to her effectiveness. On July 13, Congressman Adam Littlepage of West Virginia sent a letter to Attorney General Thomas Gregory. Littlepage claimed that illegal strikes broke out wherever Mother Jones spoke, often accompanied by riots, bloodshed, and destruction of property. The congressman included several affidavits testifying to the danger of her words. Her speech in Beckley was "calculated to poison the minds of the ignorant, and breed contempt for decency, law and order." In Raleigh, her talk was full of abuse and slang, oaths and cursing, as she told the men if the operators "don't give you what you want take your guns and fight for it until you do get it." In Mabscott, she said she would not ask the miners to defend Manhattan Island if the Germans attacked it, because "Manhattan Island is owned and controlled by the rich bugs and it's up to them to protect it." Gregory saw no grounds for action.[43]

A month later, the attorney general received another complaint. The head of the New River Association, a coal operators' trade group, declared that Mother Jones's speech in Thayer, West Virginia, was full of "incendiarism and I-W-W-ism," and he pointed out that "hundreds of thousands of tons of coal production have been lost as a result of petty strikes that follow her appearances." Her speech was, in fact, quite pugnacious. If the operators kept abusing her boys, she said, "they would not need to send soldiers to France to fight the Kaiser, for they'd have a war at home." She added that the Russian Revolution overthrew three hundred years of oppression in a single stroke, and concluded that Jesus had no bosses, so her boys better not either. Once again, upon reading the account of her speech, the attorney general's office responded that Mother Jones had broken no federal laws.[44]

Despite accusations that she undermined the war effort, she actually supported the war. Most Americans on the left initially opposed U.S. intervention, but by the time Woodrow Wilson asked Congress for a declaration of war in 1917, many had changed their minds. The contrast between Mother Jones and Eugene Debs is instructive. For Debs, the war was imperialism, pure and simple, a battle among powerful states for territory and markets. Even as socialists overseas and radicals at home gave in to rampant nationalism, Debs declared, "I am not a capitalist soldier; I am a proletarian revolutionist. I am opposed to every war but one; I am for . . . the world wide war of the social revolution." Debs, aging and sick in 1917, rallied American leftists to the antiwar cause. Amid the hysteria whipped up by the Wilson administration, he was arrested for sedition in June 1918 and convicted the following April, after the war ended. He served two and a half years in a federal prison in Atlanta, ran for President a fifth time in 1920, and garnered almost a million votes from his jail cell. Warren Harding commuted his sentence on Christmas Day, 1921.[45]

Mother Jones was surely appalled by the arrest of Debs and that of countless other leftists, but no record of her protest remains. She supported Wilson's reelection in 1916, partly because of his labor policies, partly because he was the peace candidate. In her 1916 speech to the UMW convention, Mother Jones condemned the war as an atrocity against children, and she even suggested that several forceful women— she must have had in mind the delegation from the Woman's Peace Party that Jane Addams led to The Hague—could end the madness. She added that if European men wanted to fight, that was their business, but Americans should stay out. She no doubt agreed with Debs that it was an imperialist war for profit, a boondoggle for the rich.[46]

Once war was declared, however, hysteria against America's enemies swept the country, encouraged by businessmen, journalists, and government officials. The hyper-patriotism, the hounding of German Americans, the shutting down of radical publications like the *Appeal to Reason* and *The Masses,* all testified to the growing attack on dissent. But wartime protection of organized labor by the Wilson administration created a golden opportunity. Despite radical and conservative unionists' suspicions of government, despite labor's long-held inclination to concentrate on the workplace rather than electoral politics, this situation seemed too good to be true. Mother Jones, like countless other labor leaders, swallowed her doubts, endorsed militarization, and encouraged men to work hard to defeat Germany. "If we are going to have freedom for the workers," she told the UMW convention in Indianapolis on January 17, 1918, "we have got to stand behind the nation in this fight to the last man. . . . I was as much opposed to war as anyone in the nation, but when we get into a fight I am one of those who intend to clean hell out of the other fellow, and we have got to clean the kaiser up." Just a year after America's entry into the war, things had changed so dramatically in Charleston, West Virginia, where Mother Jones had been court-martialed just five years before, that she rode at the head of a mile-long "Win the War" parade with the mayor and county sheriff by her side.[47]

She spoke of the Kaiser with the same words she reserved for American titans of industry: "I don't mean the German people . . . , I mean the grafter, the burglar, the thief, the murderer." She told the UMW convention that democracy abroad meant democracy at home; workers must fight German Kaisers and American ones, such as the Supreme Court justices who had recently overturned the federal Child Labor Act. She invoked America's revolutionary fathers: "Let us make one grand body of men in America that stands loyally for the flag. You must understand that the men who watered the clay for seven long years with their blood and blistered feet, weary backs and throbbing heads, they did it in order to hand down to you the noblest emblem ever handed down during all the generations of men as an evidence of their belief in social justice and industrial freedom." She all but placed herself among the heroes of 1776, then hammered home the bond between patriotism, the American Revolution, and the labor movement: "Every star in that flag was bought with the blood of men who believed in freedom, industrial freedom, particularly. Now it is up to us to carry on the work. Organize, organize, organize."[48]

Here was working-class patriotism at its sharpest, uniting the flag, the war, and labor militancy. She told of one West Virginia soldier who said before leaving for the front, "Mother, keep up the union until we come back and then we will all be one." She urged the men to stand together, and when the fight across the waters was over, "if we have any kaisers at home . . . we will have the guns and our boys will be drilled. We will do business then and we will not ask to borrow money to buy guns. We will have the guns Uncle Sam paid for and we will use them on the pirates and put a stop to slavery."[49]

The war gave the UMW a new chance to organize in West Virginia, and the union made the most of it. Under the Lever Act, the federal government enforced the miners' right to collective bargaining in exchange for a no-strike pledge. With aggressive local leaders operating under federal protection, the union had come to dominate West Virginia's northern fields by war's end, and had organized much of the south. More, patriotic pleas from leaders in business and government emphasized the centrality of workers' efforts for winning the war. The miners gained a new awareness of their own importance. They bought bonds, labored extra hours, and believed they helped win the war.[50]

But these exhilarating times did not last. When the war ended, the federal government quickly relinquished its role as labor's protector, and management, squeezed by declining demand, and having the luxury of a growing army of unemployed workers, did its best to roll back labor's gains. Moreover, all the problems left over since the Colorado coal wars came flooding back to the UMW. The old squabbles for power, personal recriminations, and rifts between militants and moderates—all lay just hidden from view until the war ended.[51]

Mother Jones had been playing peacemaker within the UMW since Ludlow. When the union held its national convention at the beginning of 1916, four hundred men faced felony indictments, the union was deep in debt, and the air thick with anger. Adolph Germer and Duncan MacDonald of District 12 (Illinois), which had loaned the national office large sums of money, called for an investigation of the union's finances, a slap in the face to President John White, Vice President Frank Hayes, and Secretary-Treasurer William Green. Although she was not a scheduled speaker, Mother Jones took the podium. "Now boys," she said, "let Mother talk to you, and let's put a stop to this thing." She described the old days in Chicago when she and other unionists had to meet in the back rooms of saloons. She joked with the men, reminded them how hard the past four years had been for everyone, then called on Germer and MacDonald to come forward and shake hands with White, Hayes, and Green. They did, and the resolution for an investigation was defeated. For a moment, Mother Jones had charmed her boys, kept the family together.[52]

Nothing had changed fundamentally, however, and the old angers soon led to a new insurgency. With District 15 president John Lawson and secretary Edward Doyle leading the way, many of the Rocky Mountain miners formed the Independent Union of Mine Workers and broke with the UMW. Mother Jones wrote to her friend Doyle about "burying the hatchet" and "coming back into the family," and she argued that divisions only weakened labor. Doyle responded with a long and heartfelt letter, filled with love for his old friend but nonetheless firmly rejecting her advice. The centralization of power in the national office appalled Doyle. He charged the leadership with corruption and fraud, and he accused the national officers of being more interested in their own jobs than in the miners. The big test for the UMW, Doyle observed, was around the corner, for with the war nearly over, management already was preparing to attack the union movement. "Will the members seize the occasion to rise and clean house, then make their stand, or will they blindly trust to luck and be the losers?" Doyle did not answer his own question.[53]

Doyle overestimated Mother Jones's complacency. Actually, she felt trapped between faith in a radically democratic union movement and the need to close ranks. Even as she tried to mollify Doyle's fears, she echoed them to John Walker, the Illinois Socialist who ran for president of the UMW against John White late in 1916. Walker was convinced that White stole the election from him, and he wrote Mother Jones that "nobody can expect the ordinary working man to have any respect for a known public thief." She liked the UMW leaders no better than Walker, and she complained to him about the settlement that Vice President Frank Hayes and "Johnie Lewis" had worked out for the New River miners of West Virginia. Lewis, President White's representative at the conference, especially alarmed her. She mocked his self-importance, referred to him as "the general Jesus of the movement" and "an empty piece of human slime," and added, "If the organization ever gets into the hands of this fellow that is the end of the miners." She was speaking of John Llewellyn Lewis, who would serve as president of the UMW from 1920 through 1960, the man who organized the Congress of Industrial Organizations during the Great Depression.[54]

Lewis was exactly the sort of labor leader she most loathed—he had never won an election on his own, was far removed from the workers, and craved the trappings of respectability. He was a classic example of what she called a "pie counter hunter," lining up to get his fill, a modern-day John Mitchell but far more ruthless and corrupt. She predicted difficult times for the labor movement. "I look for the most despotic system of industrial slavery after the war the world has ever known," she wrote Walker, and she feared that the UMW leadership was not up to the challenge. "I get so disgusted sometimes," she concluded, "that I feel like giving up the whole field, and going away off some where." A year later, she wrote him, "John this organization is in the hands of the mine owners. . . . I am sick at heart about the poor Devils that are betrayed. This [is] the rottenest age." She even confided to Terence Powderly, "Going over the country as I do, if a revolution started tomorrow I don't know where they would get a leader."[55]

Yet she would not let her fears overwhelm her hopes. In the very same letter to Powderly, Mother Jones described triumphant rallies in which local politicians greeted her with open arms. In Peoria, Illinois, she declared, "We are living today in the greatest age the world has ever passed through in human history. The whole world is ablaze with revolt." She told her listeners that she went to the library to look up the word "Bolsheviki" and discovered that it meant people taking over industry, taking what was rightfully theirs, and she concluded, "If that is the definition, then I am a Bolsheviki, rule by majority." Someday, she speculated, judges would be required to labor in mines and mills before they sat in judgment of workers. Great changes were on the way: "The page is turned. . . . A new civilization is coming; the pendulum is swinging as it has never swung before." With great hopes and deep fears, then, she turned her efforts to organizing steel.[56]

Steel Strike

American leftists might have resisted World War I, but it demonstrated how well nationalization of industry could work. The federal government effectively ran railroad, telephone, and telegraph companies, while regulating prices and production throughout the economy. War reinvigorated labor—unions organized new trades, and workers shared in wartime prosperity. During 1917 and 1918, 1 million people joined the AFL; total membership had swelled to 3.5 million workers by war's end. An unprecedented four million workers participated in more than thirty-five hundred strikes during the war. With profits high, and the War Labor Board encouraging cooperation, many businesses accepted worker pleas for the eight-hour day, higher wages, even union recognition. Laborites believed that the postwar world would include the minimum wage, government ownership of utilities, equal rights for working women, and a labor party. Not just in America but overseas, worker activism, inspired in part by the Russian Revolution, broke out everywhere.[57]

The rising tide of protest was met by a rising tide of repression, including court injunctions, police violence, and vigilante killings. In Bisbee, Arizona, in 1917, for example, sheriff's deputies deported twelve hundred strikers; in Butte, Montana, six masked men lynched IWW organizer Frank Little. The government's zeal to prosecute the war encouraged intolerance. The Espionage Act of 1917 and the Sedition Act of 1918 silenced critics. Dozens of presses were shut down (especially foreign-language ones) and hundreds of dissidents arrested under these laws. Far more subtly, the flood of pro-war propaganda streaming out of the government's Committee on Public Information fostered a climate of fear. The journalist George Creel, who wrote sympathetically about Colorado miners during the 1914 strike, now headed this agency, which distributed millions of pro-war pamphlets, put seventy-five thousand "four-minute men" on the streets giving speeches about loyalty, and goaded neighbors to spy on each other. The watchword was "100% Americanism"—patriotism became intolerance for all things foreign or radical. New agencies like the Military Intelligence Division of the War Department and the Bureau of Investigation (forerunner of the Federal Bureau of Investigation) censored even the most innocent communiqués, such as Mother Jones's telegram to Ed Nockles urging the Chicago Federation of Labor to lobby for a court system free of corporate influence.[58]

Neither labor militancy nor the crackdown on it ended with the war. On the contrary, the tensions crested in 1919. Eighty-two years old, Mother Jones was energized by the outburst of militancy and by businessmen's aggressive counterattack. Besides working for the miners, she held meetings for cigar makers and for shoe workers; she campaigned to have the U.S. attorney general investigate West Virginia's

Sissonville Prison Camp, where conditions allegedly were akin to slavery; and she worked for the release of imprisoned union men. Most dramatically, she threw herself into the great steel strike of 1919.[59]

In the early 1890s, the Amalgamated Association of Iron, Steel, and Tin Workers of North America was one of the strongest trade unions in the country, with nearly twenty-five thousand members, two-thirds of the eligible workers in the industry. But steelmaking was changing. Mechanization of new plants obliterated much of the skill on which craft-union power depended. In 1892, Andrew Carnegie, whose Carnegie Steel Company dominated the industry, provoked a strike against his Homestead, Pennsylvania, plant, confident that non-union mills in Braddock and Duquesne would produce enough steel to break the strike. Henry Clay Frick, who managed Homestead for Carnegie, tried to bring strikebreakers in; the union took up arms to keep them out; sixteen died in the bloody gunfight between steelworkers and Pinkerton detectives on July 6, 1892. The men of the Amalgamated won the battle but lost the war. Violence became an excuse for the governor to send in state troops, who re-opened the plant and ran it with non-union labor. When the Homestead strike collapsed, so did the iron and steelworkers union.[60]

A merger folding Carnegie Steel into the United States Steel Corporation in 1900 under the financial leadership of J. P. Morgan began a new epoch for the industry, and indeed for much of American business. Although the old era of cutthroat competition was not entirely over, the new goal now was to avoid destructive price wars. Judge Elbert H. Gary, the manager of United States Steel, cajoled or browbeat other steel men into uniform prices. Industry leaders felt some responsibility for their workers, and they certainly wished to avoid looking like labor's enemies; but above all else, Morgan, Gary, and the rest sought to keep unions out. Like other businessmen, they advocated the open shop, which neatly blended the ideal of freedom with management control. Indeed, led by the National Association of Manufacturers, the open shop became the battle cry of America's basic industries, especially after World War I.[61]

Work in steel was hard and dangerous. One-third of the men labored seven days a week; three-quarters of them worked twelve-hour shifts (including the notorious twenty-four-hour day every two weeks when night and day shifts were reversed). The men faced hellish heat and fearsome risk of death and dismemberment. Yet after the Homestead strike, workers showed little interest in organizing. Management disciplined them with yellow-dog contracts, tight surveillance by Pinkerton guards, and blacklists. Steel communities in Gary, Indiana, South Chicago, and Youngstown, Ohio, often resembled coal towns—the companies dominated municipal government, controlled local commerce, and built company housing. Above all, ethnic differences divided the workforce. The unskilled men tended to be recent immigrants. Earning less than two dollars a day, Poles and Serbs, Italians and Slovaks worked toward returning to Europe, buying land, and reestablishing households. Union leaders, usually native-born, tended to ignore them, partly out of prejudice, partly because they believed that sojourners were uninterested in the union.[62]

But the war changed everything. Many of the immigrants had been in America for over a generation; some even had sons who followed them into the mills. Longevity brought small but significant rewards, such as higher pay and easier tasks. Moreover, the war ravaged much of the Old World, so America had become home for these immigrant families, and their futures lay in the mills. Finally, steelworkers had the same wartime experience as miners. The rhetoric of democracy, the boom in profits and productivity, the tight labor market, and federal protection of unions, all made organized labor ready for an assault on steel.[63]

Union's first foray into mass-production industries during the war came when John Fitzpatrick, the head of the powerful Chicago Federation of Labor and a friend of Mother Jones's, spearheaded a drive to organize the meat packers. Fitzpatrick's second in command was William Z. Foster, formerly a member of the IWW but now committed to working within the trade-union movement. They won a major victory in March 1918, when a federal arbitrator granted packers the eight-hour day. Now Fitzpatrick and Foster moved that the CFL initiate a drive to organize steel, and they quickly gained the blessings of the AFL—but only if they worked within the craft-union structure. An umbrella organization was formed, the National Committee for Organiz-

ing Iron and Steel, which tried to hold two dozen separate unions together. Machinists, boilermakers, blacksmiths, and electrical workers
unions all participated, but the key was the old Amalgamated Association of Iron, Steel, and Tin Workers as well as the International Union
of Mine, Mill, and Smelter Workers (formerly the Western Federation
of Miners), which together housed most of the unskilled workers. Foster led the organizing drive.[64]

The National Committee for Organizing Iron and Steel made deep
inroads into steel before the end of the war. In February 1919, acting
UMW president John L. Lewis asked Mother Jones to go to Pittsburgh
and represent the Mine Workers in the coalition, probably to get her
out of his way. Given the divisive politics in the UMW, Mother Jones
obliged him without complaining. Addressing a gathering in Pittsburgh, she noted that the mayor of McKeesport refused to allow union
meetings, and she declared, "You men should be ashamed of yourselves to stand back and allow a little parasite and hireling of the
United States Steel Corporation to tell you whether or not you shall
hold a meeting. Don't ask him—go up 10,000 strong and he will give
you all the halls you want." She told the workers that they were the
ones with the brains and the capitalists could not manufacture a thing
without them. She even imagined for them Gary or Rockefeller dying
and going to heaven, where God turned him out: "Away with you, scab-
bing, blood-sucking, murderous, high-class hold-up man."[65]

Union organizers had some success gaining new members in
Chicago-area mills but not in western Pennsylvania. As federal protection for collective bargaining ended and a recession settled over the
American economy, the steel owners' commitment to the open shop
returned with a vengeance. Steel companies initiated new welfare programs and company unions, often modeled on those of Rockefeller's
Colorado Fuel and Iron. More often, they simply broke up meetings
and arrested organizers. With the war to "make the world safe for
democracy" just ending, the union focused on freedom of speech as
the key issue. Even open shops, after all, included the right to join a
union, so organized labor charged the companies with violating the
rights of American citizens. The union sent in "flying squadrons" of
speakers, who would either have their say or garner sympathy when
they were arrested.[66]

In late August, Mother Jones addressed the employees of Southside Iron and Steel in Homestead. She was arrested along with two other organizers for speaking without a permit. An angry group of steelworkers followed her to prison and only when she came out and told them to go home was trouble averted. As she told it in her autobiography, when the judge asked her if she had a permit to speak, she replied, yes, one issued by Patrick Henry, Thomas Jefferson, and John Adams. Still, the crackdown on civil liberties slowed the union's efforts.[67]

As in the coal industry, the rank and file was often ahead of the leadership. Judge Gary and other steel men refused to meet with union representatives, and it became clear to Foster that the National Committee for Organizing Iron and Steel must call a strike or lose its momentum. The union sought the right to collective bargaining above all other demands, but management refused to have anything to do with the union. Labor also asked for the eight-hour day, one day off each week, abolition of the twenty-four-hour shift, double rates of pay for overtime, a dues checkoff, and a substantial wage increase. Finally, the men fought for abolition of company unions. When the organizing committee called the strike for September 22, management believed that most men would remain in the mills.[68]

Over 250,000 workers walked out, far more than expected, enough to shut down many of the plants and slow production to a trickle in others. Mary Heaton Vorse—socialist, feminist, and labor journalist—met Mother Jones while covering the steel strike, and the two hit it off: "I was one of the few women other than workers' wives whom Mother could stand," Vorse recalled. Perhaps the old woman took a liking to this middle-class suffragist because she had been friends with Vorse's husband, Joe O'Brien. Mother Jones would go down to Vorse's room in the late afternoon and renew "her fascinating endless monologue," or she would burst in and shout, " 'Mary O'Brien, throw your things in your bag and come with me to Steubenville,' or 'I'm going up the [Monongahela] river to speak to the miners, come along.' "[69]

Once the strike started, Vorse recalled, Mother Jones seemed to be everywhere:

> During her absence from Pittsburgh one could hear of
> her being in Joliet or in the Calumet basin. She had

greater intimacy with the workers than any one else in America. . . . She is the only American woman that thousands of workers have ever spoken to. She goes about surrounded with the protecting love of young men whose names she does not know. She goes up and down the country and with her walks the memory of the long fight of the working people of America.

Vorse added that Mother Jones had a special rapport with those who knew no English: "The hall was full of men who could not understand her words. What difference does it make what words she used? They understood her anger. Her defiance and her fearlessness they understood too."[70]

The old woman worked with the vigor of one half her age. We do not have a complete record of her activities, but we know that she made several speeches along the southern rim of Lake Michigan in late October. The Military Intelligence agent who recorded her Chicago address on October 22 characterized it as "the foulest and most profane that can be imagined"; it "fairly teemed with ultra-radical suggestions." She opened by inviting the spies sent by business and government to come to the front: "You can't hear back there, and I don't want you to miss anything when you repeat it to your bosses." She declared herself a radical and said anyone who was not one had no business in America. Gary and Morgan stole the country, and only the workers could get it back. More, her boys must use guns if the other side started shooting—"if you should kill a rat, you are doing something everybody approves of." It was time for soldiers to put their uniforms back on and "clean out the Kaisers like Gary and Morgan."[71]

In Gary, Indiana, the next day, she told a crowd of twelve hundred steelworkers and their families that they must take their town back from "the damned gang of robbers":

Our Kaisers sit up and smoke seventy-five cent cigars and have lackeys with knee pants bring them champagne while you starve, while you grow old at forty, stoking their furnaces. You pull in your belts while they banquet. They have stomachs two miles long and two miles wide and you fill them. Our Kaisers have stomachs of steel and hearts of steel and tears of steel.

If Judge Gary believed that twelve-hour shifts were right, she thundered, let him go into the mills and work. Then she turned to the unprecedented profits the war generated and declared they had been extracted from the lives of workers:

> The war—your war—has made the steel lords richer than the emperors of old Rome. And their profits are not from steel alone but from your bodies. . . . Your children play in the muck of mud puddles while the children of the Forty Thieves take their French and dancing lessons, and have their fingernails manicured!

She was nearly ninety now, she reminded her listeners, but she had learned that freedom and defiance flowed together: "You can arrest me, but I'll be free. I can raise more hell in jail than out." She added, "If Bolshevist is what I understand it to be, then I'm a Bolshevist from the bottom of my feet to the top of my head."[72]

Mother Jones despised the conservatism of the craft unions that Foster tried to hold together. She recalled that after she spoke one time, a worker passed out leaflets calling for an end to America's post-Revolution blockade of Russia (the United States and other nations not only cut off trade, creating a dearth of food and medicine for thousands of people, but also secretly sent troops to topple the Communist government). When a union organizer stopped the man doing the leafleting, Mother Jones intervened. The organizer explained that the leaflets would give credence to the claim, propagated by the union's enemies, that the steel strike had been fomented by Moscow. He elicited a torrent of Mother Jones's wrath: "Women and children blockaded and starving! Men women and children dying for lack of hospital necessities! This strike will not be won by turning a deaf ear to suffering wherever it occurs." Nonetheless, the aims of the strike and goals of the union remained highly contentious. Those who shunned even the appearance of radicalism, who correctly saw that *any* union activity would be tarred with the brush of bolshevism, worked in uneasy alliance with the likes of Mother Jones.[73]

The strike wore on, and it became apparent that management's resources far outstripped the unions'. The assault on civil liberties continued—local governments censored mail and broke up meetings, and newspapers fed the public stories about Russian revolutionaries leading the labor movement. The day-to-day grind of the strike weighed heaviest on the workers. Mother Jones described sitting in the tiny home of one steel family as three strikers played cards, babies crawled along the floor, and clothes dried above their heads. The mother of the house described how everyone feared the guards and so stayed indoors:

> The worst thing about this strike, Mother, is having the men folks all home all the time. There's no place for them to go. . . . It's fierce, Mother, with the boarders all home. When the men are working, half of them are sleeping and the other half are in the mills. And I can hang my clothes out in the yard. Now I daren't. The guards make us stay in. It's hell, Mother, with the men home all day and the clothes hanging around too. And the kids are frightened. The guards chase them in the house.

Yet this woman, so unnerved by the strike, would not back down. When Mother Jones asked if the men might give up and go back to work, the woman replied, "My man go back, I kill him!"[74]

But they were forced to return after four months. "Back to the mills trudged the men," Mother Jones remembered, "accepting the terms of the despot, Gary; accepting hours that made them old, old men at forty; that threw them on the scrap heap, along with the slag from the mills." Management's power broke the strike—twenty-two workers died in the struggle—but labor's divisions made it easier. The multitude of craft unions proved unwieldy. Moreover, ethnic and racial tensions were readily manipulated, especially as the companies brought in increasing numbers of black strikebreakers. Above all, anti-radical hysteria, including charges of communist subversion, destroyed union leaders' credibility. Management exploited old stereotypes of bomb-throwing aliens, of blood-drenched fanatics, of anti-American revolutionaries. A new witch-hunt was under way.[75]

Red Scare

Mother Jones's boast of being a Bolshevik was naive, but she hurled her defiance at what quickly became the nation's most terrifying Red Scare. The very word revived old nightmares of the Paris Commune, of the Haymarket riot, of workers uniting in an orgy of blood against the owners of property. The conformity born of war mutated into an ugly assault on American civil liberties. Subversives, reds, radicals were everywhere, if the newspapers were to be believed.[76]

Conservative fears of a revolution spreading from Russia to Europe, then America, seemed far-fetched, but many radicals, too, believed that what began in 1917 might sweep these shores in coming years. At war's end, uprisings in Central Europe were put down only with force, while troops from Western countries, including the United States, attempted to overthrow the Soviet government in Russia. America had its own taste of Armageddon. In 1919 alone, almost one-fifth of American workers went on strike, a figure that has never been surpassed, and total union membership rose to unprecedented heights. The entire city of Seattle shut down in a general strike, the Boston police force walked out, coal miners threatened to quit work as winter came on, and workers everywhere were in revolt. Much more disturbing, in the spring several bombs were planted at the homes of prominent Americans, including Attorney General A. Mitchell Palmer, Justice Oliver Wendell Holmes, Jr., Secretary of Labor William Wilson, John D. Rockefeller, and J. P. Morgan.[77]

The bombs failed to detonate, but they still had an explosive impact. Suddenly, fears of subversion seemed credible. Conservatives seized the moment; the Red Scare became a highly effective way of attacking unions and radical organizations. Through the lens of the Red Scare, the steel strike looked more like a Bolshevik coup than a mere trade-union action. The size of the walkout, the militancy of the men, the violent outbreaks that the press reported with such bias frightened many Americans, even though the strike's goals were explicitly about wages, hours, and collective bargaining. Had William Z. Foster not been a Wobbly and co-author of the fiery tract *Syndicalism?* Did John Fitzpatrick not speak of nationalizing basic industries? Had Mother Jones not called herself a Bolshevik? It was easy for journalists and the public relations experts to paint the strike with a red brush, especially since most of the participants were immigrants. "The foreign element," declared *The New York Times*, was "steeped in the doctrines of the class struggle and social overthrow, ignorant and easily misled."[78]

In the red glare of 1919, not just the steel strike but every progressive cause looked like revolution. Vigilante groups, often led by veterans, trashed the offices of socialists and beat laborites in the streets, while police arrested the victims. Before long, the American Legion began shooting and lynching IWW members in Washington State, labor strife in Chicago fed one of the ugliest race riots in American history, and the Justice Department illegally deported thousands of foreign-born activists. As the 1920s began, the old utopian hopes—for social transformation, for worker dignity, for democracy in the workplace—all faded rapidly.[79]

And Mother Jones was feeling her age. Rheumatism and other maladies plagued her, and many of her speeches were not as sharp as before. Perhaps poor stenography accounts for some of the rambling, but by 1919, her orations sometimes bordered on incoherence, and her ideas seemed lost in words that meandered on and on.[80]

Not the martyr's immolation but old age for Mother Jones. So it was with horror and fascination that she contemplated the death of Fannie Sellins. Before the war, Sellins organized garment workers in St. Louis, then miners in West Virginia. A judge once warned her "not to emulate Mother Jones," which is precisely what Sellins did. In 1919, she joined the steel strike and organized towns along the Allegheny River, gaining the undying hatred of the owners. Then on August 26, while trying to stop company gunmen from beating an old steelworker, she was bludgeoned and shot to death. Although her killers were known, the crime went unpunished.[81]

Mother Jones saw in Sellins a glimpse of her own mortality. Mary Heaton Vorse described finding the old woman staring at a picture of Sellins one day. "I often wonder it wasn't me they got," Mother Jones mused. "Whenever I look at the picture of her I wonder it's not me lying on the ground." Mixed with outrage at the brutal act and empathy for Sellins and her family must have been yearning in one who so often played the martyr's role. Mother Jones had expected a martyr's death, courted it, half wished for it. But Fannie Sellins was the martyr of the steel strike, and Mother Jones now contemplated something much worse than a heroic death in a noble cause. Hers would be a lingering final decade in which illness took her strength, the forces of reaction ravaged the American left, and internecine battles divided labor. Worst of all, people began to forget Mother Jones.[82]

★ 10 ★

The Last Decade

In January 1921, Mother Jones traveled to Mexico with Fred Mooney, secretary of UMW District 17, West Virginia. Mooney described their approach to Mexico City: "When I looked out, there was a string of taxi cabs blocking the railroad tracks. About 40 strikers from a jewelry factory had motored out to meet 'Madre Yones.' . . . They threw crimson carnations and blue violets around Mother until only her head and shoulders could be seen." Mexicans actually called her Madre Juanita, but her arrival was indeed a triumph.[1]

She was there to address the third conference of the Pan-American Federation of Labor. The group was a new one, created to forge stronger bonds between Western Hemisphere unions. Mother Jones came as an honored guest of the Mexican government. Her work on behalf of the *revoltosos*, her talks with the martyred President Francisco Madero in 1911, her praise for Pancho Villa, all made her a very visible American supporter of the Mexican Revolution. Antonio Villarreal, one of the *revoltosos* whom she helped free from an American prison, was now Secretary of Agriculture under the new reform government of Álvaro Obregón, who pledged to carry out a strongly pro-labor agenda. A villa with servants and a car and driver were put at her disposal, and she attended receptions given by President Obregón and by the American ambassador.[2]

Mother Jones probably made Samuel Gompers, head of the American delegation, a little nervous. She told a reporter for *El Heraldo* that Mexico "is the only country in the world where real liberty may be enjoyed." She praised the Russian Revolution, and added that American capitalists were quaking in their scab-made shoes. She spent much of her time with leading Mexican Socialists, including Roberto Haberman, an American émigré, Felipe Carrillo Puerto, an agrarian leader from the Yucatán and follower of Emiliano Zapata, and Luis Morones, Mexico's minister of industry.[3]

Mother Jones was one of the featured speakers at the conference. She called the convention "the greatest event in history," because it marked a new level of international solidarity (but also, one suspects, because she was an honored guest). She stressed unity: "It is a great age; it is a great time to live in. Some people call us Bolsheviks, some call us I.W.W.'s, some call us Reds. Well, what of it! If we are Red, then Jefferson was Red, and a whole lot of those people who turned the world upside down were Red." Only "the soul of unrest" and "the spirit of dissent" mattered. But her friends must have been concerned, maybe saddened, as they listened. The sharp wit, the telling stories, the over-the-top style were missing. Now when she mentioned her imminent demise—"My days are closing in"—there was a disturbing ring of truth.[4]

Despite Mother Jones's extravagant claims for the importance of the Mexico City conference, the Pan-American Federation proved a disappointment. Members voted to condemn the American invasions of the Dominican Republic and Nicaragua; they also denounced the persecution of U.S. radicals under the Espionage Act. But many Latin American countries failed to participate at all, and the presence of Samuel Gompers and other AFL leaders made the Federation seem a showcase for American business unionism. Indeed, the U.S. government backed the proceedings, hoping that the PAFL would encourage craft rather than industrial unions in Mexico, and thereby facilitate the orderly expansion of markets between the two countries. Participants backed important reforms like the eight-hour day and an end to child labor, but the conservatives always held sway. The organization survived only a decade.[5]

Still, the conference was a high moment in Mother Jones's life. It affirmed her status as an elder of the labor movement with an international reputation. Perhaps because she felt her influence in the United States slipping away, the accolades of Mexico City flattered her, and she returned home in mid-April 1921 with thoughts of emigrating to Mexico. Later that spring, when she made another visit, Mexican officials rolled out the red carpet once again. Roberto Haberman, the founder of the Federación de Trabajadores de México, wrote her, "General Villarreal has a house ready for you, and a prettier place cannot be imagined. Also servants, and an automobile."[6]

She toured widely, even went to the Yucatán for a Socialist convention in the industrial city of Orizaba. When John Fitzpatrick and Ed Nockles of the Chicago Federation of Labor wrote on May 1 to wish her a happy birthday, her return letter painted Mexico in the brightest colors. She described the ceremonies in Orizaba: "It was the most remarkable meeting I addressed in years. . . . The town was thoroughly organized, and the spirit they possessed was an inspiration. One got new hope for the future." A union band played, there were no police, and the event occurred in the workers' own municipal building. Most remarkable of all, a flag representing the Haymarket martyrs of 1886 was carried in alongside the Mexican national flag. "Everyone of you would have been put in jail for the next ten years if that occurred in Chicago," she wrote, but in Orizaba, "the tribute paid to that banner as it entered the hall was the most remarkable demonstration I had witnessed in all my years in the industrial conflict."[7]

It was an absurdly romanticized vision, one that grew at least in part out of a need to feel that her decades of work would not be washed away. "After all," she wrote Fitzpatrick and Nockles, "one's life is not in vain when they witness the beautiful conception of industrial freedom that is taking possession of the souls of the workers." As America slipped into the retrograde 1920s, as reactionaries smashed the radical dreams of the previous three decades, Mother Jones found momentary comfort in Mexico. During her last decade, she vacillated between hope and despair. It was a sign not only of a world gone sour but of her own aging and, with it, a need to take stock of her life.[8]

Her gaudy image of Mexico had faded by the end of her stay. She described how this fledgling social democracy was threatened by a cadre of communist "freaks" who "want to rule and dictate," and she feared the day when "those fanatics should ever get to the helm." Equally daunting was a right-wing Christian reaction against the left, for it threatened Mexico with religious zealotry. She wrote John Walker that a whole congregation in Morelia, whipped to a frenzy by some "sky pilot's" sermon, stoned the offices of a socialist newspaper. Meanwhile, the "oil pirates"—American firms, Rockefeller's Standard Oil prime among them—continued bleeding the country. At the end of May, just before returning home, she concluded a letter to Walker by saying that "things are not just as bright here as I would like to see them," and she added that illness plagued her: "I have not been well John . . . ; I have had rheumatism so much, and it is kind of playing on me."[9]

"On to Mingo"

Mother Jones's last decade began with her on the road as usual, and not just in Mexico. In February 1920, she shared a stage with Jane Addams and John Fitzpatrick as ten thousand people attended the "All Chicago Liberty Demonstration Protesting against Raids, Deportations, and Other Infringements of American Civil Liberties." In March, she spoke before San Francisco's striking shipyard workers. That same month, she had the distinction of being one of several dozen radicals—including Eugene Debs, Big Bill Haywood, "Nicholas Lenine," John Reed, Karl Marx, Tom Mooney, and Leon Trotsky—whose names and photographs appeared on a memo circulated within the War Department. By April, she had made headquarters at the UMW Building in Charleston, West Virginia, where a new round of strikes was just heating up and where she described herself as "still at the front, fighting the battle of the workers."[10]

But all was not well. One reason she left Chicago for California during the winter of 1920 was to ease an attack of rheumatism, the disease that progressively crippled her over the next decade. Her letters reveal a recurring pattern of illness. "I took sick on the train going to Washington," she wrote John Walker in June 1920, and so she canceled her speaking engagement in southern Illinois. A month later, she wrote him, "My strength is failing, John, I don't feel able to do the work I did. . . . I put in some very strenuous years for the last ten years, it has not been easy sailing for me." A series of unnamed maladies plagued her, often sending her to friends' homes or to the hospital. Aside from the trips to California, which grew longer and more frequent with rheumatism's advancing pain, she spent decreasing numbers of days on the road, more with friends in Washington and Chicago.[11]

For someone who boasted that her home was like her shoes, going with her wherever she went, her declining vigor and growing immobility must have been terribly frightening, made worse by never knowing when the pain and paralysis would strike. The kindness of friends helped her through. Terence Powderly wrote her in April 1921, "I ask you to always bear in mind that there is only one Mother Jones. I doubt if the world has seen her like before and while I hope for the future, [I] sadly feel the world will not see her like again. Be careful then of her health, remember that the covering of the soul you carry is frail, that time has not dealt too kindly with it and every precaution of yours should be taken to guard it carefully and well." When she became gravely ill in September 1922, Powderly and his wife, Emma, took her in and nursed her back to health. Newspapers across the country reported her condition, and letters poured in from friends, from union locals, and from people she had never met. Over the next five years, Mother Jones spent so much time at the Powderlys' house that she began referring to it as "home." But she never quite found peace in rest, always wishing to be out organizing.[12]

A disturbing disjointedness reappeared in some of her speeches and letters. A fine address, such as the one she gave on June 20, 1920, in Williamson, West Virginia—in the heart of the violent coal counties bordering Kentucky—was followed days later by speeches with many of the same themes and stories, but now told cryptically, almost incoherently. And as Mother Jones grew weaker, her adversaries grew stronger. The early 1920s were lean times for the American left. Postwar repression continued, and, equally important, the economy cooled, resulting in rising unemployment.[13]

Mother Jones remained upbeat in her speeches, but her letters revealed growing pessimism. To John Walker, she wrote that over 130,000 Americans were incarcerated, that this was a powerful indictment of American society, that sometimes she got so discouraged she just wanted to give up the fight for justice. To the journalist Ryan Walker she noted the grim news that the New York legislature expelled five duly elected state representatives for being members of the Socialist Party: "If they can do [that], . . . then farewell to Liberty in America, there is very little of it left anyhow." To Theodore Debs, she wrote of her pain at his brother Eugene's incarceration in Atlanta under the Sedition Act, and at Christmas, she futilely begged Woodrow Wilson for Debs's pardon and release. She spent more and more of her time writing, petitioning, pleading for the release of political prisoners.[14]

As always, nothing perked up Mother Jones more than a good fight, and a big one was brewing in West Virginia. At the end of World War I, three-quarters of a million men mined coal in America, and over half of them belonged to the United Mine Workers. Demand for coal dropped precipitously with the end of the war, falling prices made organizing much more difficult, and rich new coal lands in southern West Virginia threatened the union in the old fields. The owners of these thick veins of coal intended to keep the UMW out. In Logan County, operators kept Sheriff Don Chafin in power, and he ran a brutal regime of terror against union organizers. But the UMW was equally determined to win this new territory. Beginning with the early efforts in 1902 and culminating with the drives of World War I, the union had organized roughly sixty thousand miners in the Kanawha, New River, and Fairmont fields. The UMW now had a real chance to capture the entire state, and West Virginia was the key to organizing the whole American coal-mining industry.[15]

Wildcat strikes rolled across the region in 1919. District 17 president Frank Keeney and secretary Fred Mooney asked the men to honor their contracts, but they disciplined no one who walked out. Nothing, however, matched the raw violence and abrogation of constitutional liberties in Logan, Mingo, and McDowell Counties or the reaction of the miners to the attack on their rights. The union sent in organizers and formed new locals; guards escalated the violence to stop the drive; miners armed themselves once again. In the spring of

1920, Keeney asked the operators for a collective bargaining agreement. They refused, locked out and evicted union miners, paid bonuses to non-union men, and brought in more guards. The union officially called a strike, and the cycle of burnings, explosions, ambushes, beatings, and killings accelerated.[16]

On May 19, 1920, thirteen Baldwin-Felts guards, led by Albert and Lee Felts, two of the three brothers who ran the company, went to the town of Matewan to evict families. Sheriff Sid Hatfield (a former miner and UMW member), Mayor Cabell C. Testerman, and several armed miners confronted the detectives and questioned their right to carry out the evictions. Words grew heated; guns were drawn. It remains unclear who fired first, but when the shooting ended, eleven had perished, including both Felts brothers, five detectives, Mayor Testerman, and two miners. During the next year, West Virginia governors John J. Cornwell then Ephraim Morgan declared martial law three times, and twice the U.S. infantry took over for the inadequate state troops. This would be West Virginia's bloodiest time yet.[17]

Mother Jones traveled through the southern counties in 1920–1921, though her role seems to have been confined to occasional speech making. John L. Lewis kept her on the UMW payroll, but their relationship was strained. He demanded complete loyalty from his subordinates, something she refused to give those she respected, much less men she reviled. Moreover, Lewis did not like having women on the staff. Mother Jones privately mocked him, especially for his overbearing manner and naked ambition. Many of her friends, John Walker prime among them, lost jobs to the Lewis juggernaut, and she barely contained her anger at his autocratic rule. When Lewis called off a national coal strike scheduled for November 1919 under pressure from the federal government, it merely confirmed her opinion that he was spineless and out for himself.[18]

Mother Jones could still rise to the occasion for a big speech. In the town of Williamson, in the heart of Mingo County, she told her listeners that World War I profiteering created one new millionaire for every three thousand dead Americans; she fulminated against the recent deportations of five thousand dissidents under the Sedition Act; she observed that the labor movement was rising all over the world—in

Portugal, in Ireland, in Central Europe, even in England, where dock-workers refused to load munitions to fight the Bolsheviks in the East. Unionism, she declared, was Americanism: "Before I would be a lap-dog for those steel robbers . . . I would stand like an American under the flag as the revolutionists did before." She rejected the renewed racism that was sweeping the nation and its labor unions, told the men that divisions between black and white miners merely played into the operators' hands, and warned journalists not to stir such dissensions. Above all, she showed the old fire: "I want to say to the robbers of Logan that Mother Jones is going in. . . . We are going to clean up West Virginia. We are going to put her on the map. . . . I am not going to take any guns. I am going in there with the American flag; that is my banner, and no rotten robber or gunman can meddle with me, because I will just raise Hell with him."[19]

Mother Jones stayed mostly in Charleston, West Virginia, from mid-1920 through the fall of 1921. Ill health slowed her down, "but the boys are good to me," she reported to Walker. "They don't overwork me, the fact of the matter is they let me come and go as I want to." Perhaps the boys failed to work her very hard because they were just as happy without her. Indeed, a few letters went out from UMW locals asking the national office to remove Mother Jones. The reasons are not entirely clear. Bitter feelings still lingered from her efforts to discourage dissension within the union in 1916; clearly she was no longer so reliable as a speaker and organizer; one letter even accused her of doing Governor Morgan's bidding, and, as we shall see, there is some evidence that this was true.[20]

An accusation also emerged that Mother Jones was being paid by the coal operators. Although the charge proved false, the Bureau of Investigation took it seriously enough to make inquiries. Union leaders often were accused of treachery by the operators and by their rivals inside organized labor. The evidence offered in this case was that Mother Jones seemed to have a lot of spending money (of course, the union gave her cash for expenses) and that sometimes she was so militant she must have been trying to get union activities blocked by court injunctions (others accused her of aiding the operators by being too cautious). Her rhetoric *was* inconsistent, partly out of ambivalence over this particular strike, partly because her mind was not as well focused as in earlier years.[21]

After a year of threats, shootings, and martial law, the tensions came to a crisis. As many as 90 percent of Mingo County's miners were UMW members. The operators brought in trainloads of strikebreakers, along with more guards for protection; snipers shot at them. When state police were sent in to keep the mines open, UMW men shot them too. And then on August 1, 1921, more than a year after Matewan, Sid Hatfield was ambushed and assassinated by Baldwin-Felts guards as he walked up the steps of the McDowell County Courthouse. Rage boiled over in the mining camps. Hatfield was a local hero, and his murder symbolized the operators' arrogance.[22]

A week after Hatfield's murder, Mother Jones led a thousand miners to Charleston to petition Governor Morgan for a settlement; he refused. Next, the state supreme court upheld the legality of martial law and declined to release jailed UMW officials. Meanwhile, stories of new atrocities by the guards and deputies leaked out of Logan and Mingo. On August 20, armed miners began pouring into a town called Marmet on Lens Creek, about ten miles south of Charleston. Thousands gathered, a "citizens army," some of them wearing their uniforms from the Great War. They declared they would march through Logan County, hang Don Chafin, move into Mingo County, end martial law, and free their imprisoned brothers. Five to seven thousand men—the total reached perhaps fifteen to twenty thousand a few days later—assembled to hear their leaders on August 24. Mother Jones addressed them at the height of their fury.[23]

She had mostly taken a militant tone in the weeks before Hatfield's death, but since that event, her words had grown more moderate. There is no extant copy of her speech at Marmet. In the days before the men gathered, she had visited Mingo County, observed martial law there, and spoken to some of the imprisoned miners. Maybe she feared a bloodbath, feared that her boys would be decimated by superior forces, especially since the U.S. Army surely would intervene. We know that she corresponded with Governor Morgan, who tried to convince her that turning back the miners was the only way of avoiding massive bloodshed. Apparently, he persuaded her. To the miners' astonishment on August 24, she told them they could not win, urged moderation, implored them to go home. More, she said that she had just received a telegram from Warren Harding. "I request," she quoted the President, "that you abandon your purpose and return to your homes, and I assure you that my good offices will be used to forever eliminate the gunman system from the state of West Virginia."[24]

District leaders Keeney and Mooney were incredulous. They asked to see the telegram; Mother Jones refused. They suggested it was fake; she told them to go to hell. The miners were confused, their leadership divided. Many prepared to return home. Keeney and Mooney drove to Charleston, called the White House, and came back with the news: Warren Harding's secretary said that the President had sent no message to Mother Jones. Keeney issued a statement calling the telegram bogus and denying reports that the miners had voted to return home. Indeed, within a day or two, seven or eight thousand men were marching toward Logan County with the password "On to Mingo." Words like "sellout" and "traitor" crossed men's lips as they marched.[25]

Over the next few days, the miners were joined by thousands more men. They commandeered food and supplies and even hijacked trains on their way to Mingo. Union locals shipped guns and ammunition. The Secretary of War dispatched to the scene General Harry Bandholz, who warned the local UMW leadership to turn back the march or be prosecuted for treason. They followed his orders, and some of the men began to withdraw. But when word came that Chafin had attacked and killed a group of UMW men, the miners moved in force again toward Logan, where they engaged Chafin's army in the largest battle on American soil since the Civil War.[26]

The Battle of Blair Mountain, as it is known in Appalachian lore, lasted for three days at the end of August. Thousands of armed men fought a continuous campaign, much of it guerrilla-style in thick summer vegetation. The defenders had machine guns; their command was unified; they dropped homemade bombs from airplanes. The miners' equipment was less sophisticated, their ranks disorganized, but they had at least twice as many men. Behind the lines, women cooked meals, nursed the wounded, brought up supplies. The number of casualties is unknown, but one witness claimed that a million rounds of ammunition were fired. Fighting raged until September 1, when President Harding issued a proclamation ordering all insurgents to cease fire and retire to their homes. The miners were unwilling to fight against American troops, so when the Army finally arrived—the Eighty-eighth Light Bombing Squadron, a chemical warfare unit, and two thousand infantrymen armed with trench mortars—they quietly surrendered their weapons and went home.[27]

The UMW men more than held their own, but the Battle of Blair Mountain was a crushing defeat for the union. Fighting now in the courts, the mine owners tarred the union with the brush of treason. In Boone County, where the march originated, the grand jury indicted over three hundred individuals; in Logan County, the number reached nine hundred, and the charges included insurrection and murder. The operators supplied legal assistance to prosecutors, who made sure all of the leaders were arrested. Eventually, most of the charges were dismissed, but the legal battles did not end until 1924 and not before union treasuries were drained and morale sucked dry. By the end of the 1920s, non-union coal from the southern counties had virtually driven the UMW from West Virginia.[28]

What do we make of Mother Jones's role in these events? She never explained herself. Her autobiography is silent and her private correspondence says little of substance. The simplest interpretation is that she feared the miners were walking into a trap, that they could not win this fight, that marching against state and federal troops would be seen as treason. It was a perfectly reasonable position. By encouraging the men to go home, she only did what Mooney and Keeney were forced to do two days later. Perhaps she was thinking back thirty years to Eugene Debs's arrest during the Pullman strike, when his American Railway Union resisted the federal government and was crushed as a result. Moreover, her behavior was consistent; she had often talked the militant line before, pushed it as far as she dared for strategic purposes, then backed down. If that was the case now, she read the situation accurately: armed miners could not win a battle against the U.S. Army, but trying, they surely would destroy their union. Viewed this way, her shock at Keeney's and Mooney's "betrayal" made sense; insurrection was suicide, the march must be turned back.[29]

But it was not that simple. The fake telegram was deeply condescending to the miners. Coming from someone whose lifework was educating and empowering workers, this cheap ruse was offensive in its presumption that Mother Jones's "boys" could be so easily manipulated. Worse, it proceeded from the arrogant conceit that "Mother knows best," that distorting the truth was acceptable because she alone was wise enough to guide the movement. As *Mother* Jones, she felt justified in imposing a parent's will on her children. The tension between industrial democracy and family authority was clear; her goal was the former, but she took her influence, her very identity from the latter.[30]

Family authority betrayed her in another way. Mother Jones had always been attracted to powerful men. She engaged in a sort of game with them, matching their authority against her own venerable motherhood. Thus, as a woman, she gained a rough and temporary equality with men like Terence Powderly, John Mitchell, even John D. Rockefeller by making them into surrogate sons. Her persona commanded respect, but she never fully escaped her dependency on such men. She needed them around to challenge, persuade, and manipulate in order to assert her influence, for they were the ones with the power. She enjoyed that power, though always in indirect and unacknowledged ways, and because of this, her attitudes toward such men often were volatile. Governor Morgan was no friend of the UMW, yet Mother Jones convinced herself that he was labor's man. As with young Rockefeller, she probably thought she was manipulating him, when clearly it worked the other way around. Five days after the fake telegram, as miners and troops fought pitched battles, she wrote Morgan a one-line telegram: "Can [I] be of any assistance in restoring order?" to which he responded, "Situation still tense May have to call on you Certainly appreciate your offer of assistance." These telegrams were not public knowledge in 1921; if they had been, miners might well have spoken even more pointedly about treason and betrayal.[31]

After the strike was crushed, Mother Jones condemned the district leaders as inexperienced and not up to the job. To William Green, secretary-treasurer of the UMW, she wrote, "If the right man had been placed in charge of Mingo at the beginning of that strike, it could have been settled, and the hatred that has developed would not show its hand." (Perhaps she wanted to say "the right woman" but could not.)

No doubt she felt that Keeney and the others walked into the opera-tors' trap. And given how completely the UMW had been devastated in West Virginia by the end of the decade, she might have been right. Mother Jones was deeply humiliated when Mooney and Keeney chal-lenged her, then proved her a liar. The episode contributed to her becoming very sick, almost mortally ill, during the next year. To Gover-nor Morgan, with whom she subsequently developed a friendship, she wrote at the end of 1921, "I have not been well Governor ever since I left. That shock was so sever[e] that I had a nervou[s] breakdown from it and a severe attack of rheumatism, and I have been here [with John Walker in Springfield, Illinois] under the care of a specialist physician for the last four weeks."[32]

Despite her humiliation, she worked to get arrested miners freed from prison. She played her old games with Morgan, writing him with motherly discernment that youthful hotheadedness brought the state to the brink of war: "Those young fellows, void of any experience in the great industrial conflicts, were carried away thinking they could change the world over night. They will not be able to change it with guns and bullets. It has got to be done through practical, fundamental, patriotic education." A few months later, Morgan wrote her that nearly all of those indicted in the Logan insurrection had been let go, and she urged him to pardon the remaining few.[33]

During their correspondence, Mother Jones hinted that it had been Morgan's idea all along for her to tell the miners to turn back in Au-gust 1921: "Governor, I owe you a debt of gratitude that I don't think I can ever compensate you for. If you had not sent me down to stop that day I would have been the victim of it all. . . . I have put up with more insults for the sake of the poor wretches that they might see a brighter day for their children." Was the Harding telegram Morgan's idea? She never said definitively. It was the height of self-delusion on Mother Jones's part to think that Morgan was the miners' friend, yet because they were mixed up in this together, to that delusion she clung: "In the twenty four years that I have been going in and out of West Virginia you are the one man I could approach for the sake of the poor helpless man who had been exploited and robbed. . . . I shall clear you before the world and for those who are going to come after us. . . . You saved me from destruction." Clear him before the world? Saved her from destruction? Whatever Mother Jones meant, she no longer felt welcome in West Virginia; she returned only once.[34]

By late 1922, Mother Jones had constructed her own history of the insurrection, and everything was Mooney's and Keeney's fault. She wrote John Walker that their treatment—their betrayal—almost destroyed her: "They are dirty and treacherous a group of Vultures as could be found They would cut the throat of Jesus Christ to save themselves." Her next few sentences were almost incoherent with rage:

> Keeney gave me my Death blow I saved the lives of thousands of men Those Lap Dogs of Al Hamilton [an operator whom she and Walker suspected of paying off UMW officials in West Virginia] left nothing undone to crucify me Look at what they did to poor Howtt You know I helped to build up West Va I waded creeks to get meeting I faced machine guns I spent months in Military Prisson I was carried 84 miles in the night taken in to the Federal Court . . . Lewis never did that

She was quite ill when she wrote this letter. Still, her inability to structure, let alone punctuate, it and her confusion of people and issues—Alexander Howatt, Keeney, Lewis, Hamilton, the strikes of 1902, 1913, and 1921—testify to her hurt and to her tenuous grip on reality.[35]

Underneath it all was the fear that her work building the union in West Virginia was unraveling and, worse, that her reputation was ruined. "I am sick at heart, I am broken down," she wrote William Green six months after the false telegram. She reached her nadir physically in the summer of 1922, spent a month near death at the Powderlys' house, then finally pulled through. But she was never quite the same.[36]

By mid-1923, Mother Jones had regained enough strength for a bit of activism. In July, she addressed the Farmer-Labor Party, an organization that saw itself as a successor to the nearly defunct Socialist Party. Despite her skepticism about politics, she was impressed with recent social changes in Russia and Mexico. In the United States, even little improvements mattered, like getting judges appointed who would not cripple strikes with injunctions. She attended the Party convention in Chicago knowing that the bloc led by William Z. Foster was communist. Indeed, she voted against a resolution to expel the radicals and remained seated when her old friend John Fitzpatrick staged a walkout to protest the presence of those who would not disavow violent revolution. Mother Jones spoke up boldly for the new Party and insisted that everyone be allowed to participate, because "too long has labor been subservient to the old betrayers, politicians and crooked labor leaders." She told the delegates that unity would allow them to clean up corruption and return to the spirit of America's revolutionary fathers: "The producer, not the meek, shall inherit the earth," she declared. "Not today perhaps, nor tomorrow, but over the rim of the years my old eyes can see the coming of another day." That day, however, would be postponed one more time; within a year, the Farmer-Labor Party dissolved into warring factions.[37]

She could not sustain her commitment anyway. On top of illness, her alienation from the UMW leadership, and the state of American politics, money became a problem. Cut off from her small UMW salary, she grew anxious over finances, and she wrote William Green about it in October 1922. He allowed her to preserve her dignity: she sent a "bill"; he dipped into union coffers and sent her a check. Several times they repeated the exchange. She was dependent now in ways she never had been before. The new Internal Revenue Service questioned why she did not pay tax on more than two thousand dollars earned from the UMW in 1921 (the last year she was retained as an organizer). John Walker paid her taxes and fines—$72.50. She berated him in a letter, asking why the government harassed an elderly widow. Had she not lived on a fraction of her small stipend, used most of it for union expenses, and given away the rest to those in need? Why did the IRS not tax Rockefeller for the food she ate while confined to his bull pen in Colorado? Walker placated her.[38]

After the war, Mother Jones's speeches often employed the metaphor of a man in a tower who can see lightning long before those on the ground know a storm is coming. She meant, of course, that experience allowed her to see further and deeper than others into the great social issues. But whatever magisterial view she might have once possessed, she was more cut off than she had ever been, and few paid attention to her. For thirty years, she had thrust herself into the midst of events, and now she was an outsider. It was time to turn inward and think about what her life had meant, time to tell her story, shape its meaning, and keep it alive for future generations.[39]

The Autobiography of Mother Jones

Father William Richard Harris passed away in Toronto on March 5, 1923, after a short bout with the flu. The obituary on the front page of the *Globe* praised his accomplishments as an orator and scholar. Born in Ireland, educated in the Toronto separate schools during the 1850s, he studied for the priesthood and was ordained in 1870. Father Harris held a series of administrative and pastoral positions over the next thirty years, rising to dean of the diocese of St. Catherine's. He also traveled through North and South America, Spain and Portugal, and with these experiences, wrote book after book on the Catholic Church in early Canada, on the archaeology of ancient North American civilizations, and on foreign lands and peoples—twelve books in all, widely reviewed, making him one of the most prolific writers in English-speaking Canada. The *Globe* concluded that Harris was among the best-known clerics in Ontario.[40]

Yet he was a very private individual. "Harris seldom spoke about his family or himself," one of his biographers observed. "If the conversation turned on these topics he avoided a direct answer and in a humorous way made it clear that the subject should be changed." Still, a bit of private history crept into his books. In *The Catholic Church in the Niagara Peninsula*, Harris wrote of the Great Hunger in Ireland and of the coffin ships and fever sheds of 1847: "Only an inspired writer may record the sufferings of the unhappy people when the dread scourge of ship-fever rioted among them. He alone may tell of the crushed hopes and ruined prospects of the full grown man, of the sorrows of the delicate Irish mother." Harris himself was newly born when his father and elder brother left Ireland for Canada, was but a lad when he crossed the Atlantic with his mother and sisters a few years later.[41]

Harris's first biographer mentioned rumors that the reverend was brother to Mary Harris Jones, but given her autobiography's claim that her family emigrated in 1835, he rejected the possibility. The next chronicler of Harris's life decided that they were half brother and sister. Of course William and Mary were full siblings. She was nine years older than he, and no doubt had spent considerable time taking care of him in Cork and Toronto. Yet as adults, they ignored each other. Mother Jones mentioned William briefly in newspaper interviews at the turn of the century, noted that he wanted her to live with him in Toronto, but added that she rejected his offer in favor of a life of activism. After that, she stopped talking about him. There is no record of correspondence between them, and apparently neither spoke of the other. What kept them apart? Was it his devotion to the faith and her scoffing at it? Maybe her life as an independent woman, or perhaps her radical politics, offended him. Whatever the cause, their estrangement was deep; William's last will and testament named a sister and niece but not Mary Jones.[42]

William and Mary had much in common: both made their living with words, each was tremendously ambitious, they achieved far more in life than promised by their humble origins, wanderlust struck them both, and they had no desire to discuss their upbringings. William Harris was barely cold in the ground when Mary Jones began work on her life story in the spring of 1923. No flood of intimate memories followed his death. He is not mentioned in the *Autobiography*, but then neither is any other member of her family, except in passing. She wrote, after all, an autobiography of *Mother* Jones, not Mary Jones.[43]

The idea of Mother Jones's writing a book had been around for years. In 1910, *Miners' Magazine* reported that she was gathering materials, and added, "A history of the labor movement penned by 'Mother' Jones will be a volume that will be treasured by countless thousands of men and women." Just before the war, she asked Clarence Darrow for help writing her life story, and in 1922, she wrote John Walker, "I am picking up notes to write my book and I want you to help me a little." She became ill a few months later, but when she recovered, she told Walker that Darrow was after her to write her story and that she would do it, "for I cannot do anything else." She needed to keep the memory of Mother Jones alive, to tell the version of her life she wanted remembered. The spring and summer of 1923 found her ensconced in Chicago at the home of Ed Nockles, secretary of the Chicago Federation of Labor. "I am working away—I can't work very fast—the boys are good to me here," she reported to Terence Powderly.[44]

We can only speculate on how the *Autobiography* was written. Having no permanent home, Mother Jones could not have saved many letters or newspaper clippings from which to work, but she already knew most of the stories she wanted to tell, for they had long been set pieces in her speeches. Initially, Nockles served as secretary for the work, but soon Mary Field Parton (née Mary Field), a journalist who had penned a very flattering piece on Mother Jones for *Everybody's Magazine*, assumed the role of editor. As a young woman, Parton had been a supporter of Eugene Debs, worked in a Chicago settlement house, become Darrow's friend and mistress, and through Darrow she met Mother Jones. (She recalled of the notoriously parsimonious Darrow, "Once when I was worried about Mother Jones . . . he pulled a wad of rumpled money out of his pocket and told me to buy her some woolen underwear. It came to almost $100.")[45]

"Writing" the *Autobiography* consisted of Mother Jones telling stories while Parton transcribed them. This is evident from the frequent misspellings of proper nouns—War John instead of Wardjon, M. F. Langdon for Emma F. Langdon, Roughner rather than Ruffner. Since such errors remained in the book, it is unlikely that Mother Jones ever read the manuscript, though it may have been read back to her for corrections. Parton must have edited fairly heavily since the *Autobiography* often departs from the grammar and diction of Mother Jones's speeches. The language is cleaned up, and most swearing expunged. Parton seems to have accepted the order of events Mother Jones gave her, and since the old woman was never very good with dates, several errors of chronology appear. There are also long passages that seem to come straight from newspaper stories, particularly from *The New York Times*, which was indexed and available in Chicago libraries. Reports from government committees that investigated the mine wars also were consulted. With her advanced age and fragile health, Mother Jones found the work quite taxing. "I am getting so D—— tired writing this book," she wrote Emma Powderly; "This work I am not used to but I am nearing the end." Even after she finished, around August 1923, it must have taken Parton several months to edit the final draft, since the book did not appear until two years later.[46]

The Autobiography of Mother Jones was published by Charles H. Kerr and Company of Chicago, the largest English-language distributor of labor and radical works, though still a very small publisher by commercial standards. A Socialist and supporter of organized labor since the 1890s, Kerr published the International Socialist Review—long considered the voice of the Party's left wing—in which some of Mother Jones's early essays appeared, as well as works by Eugene Debs, Jack London, Big Bill Haywood, Elizabeth Gurley Flynn, Clarence Darrow, and Carl Sandburg. Kerr had the Autobiography typeset by John F. Higgins, himself a Socialist and keeper of a union shop. Higgins printed 4,500 copies and delivered them to Kerr in August 1925. Mother Jones got 250 copies in lieu of payment (not an uncommon arrangement for small presses), and Kerr shipped 125 copies to newspapers and magazines for review. Parton received five hundred dollars out of the Garland Fund, which was established to aid progressive causes; if the book sold well, Kerr would return the money to the fund.[47]

Clarence Darrow wrote a brief introduction to the first edition. Mother Jones is no philosopher, he tells us; activism is her forte. Her life evokes the heroes of the antislavery campaign: "Mother Jones is the Wendell Phillips of the labor movement. . . . She has the power of moving masses of men by her strong, living speech and action. She has likewise his disregard for personal safety." Or again, "like [John] Brown, she has a singleness of purpose, a personal fearlessness and a contempt for established wrongs." Also like these immortals, she is uncompromising; she sees right and wrong as clear-cut, which is precisely the origin of her restless courage.[48]

The Autobiography of Mother Jones is not a memoir in the sense of revealing a person in the act of becoming; there is no unfolding of character here, no revelation of intimacies. Nor is it an apologia, an acknowledgment of shortfalls, or a plea for exoneration. Mother Jones did not, for example, deny the Polly Pry charges; she did not mention them at all. On these pages, she has no interior life; the world of affairs is everything, interpersonal relationships all but nonexistent.[49]

The book is a long polemic, its goal to fire the faithful and convert nonbelievers. It reprises Mother Jones's career, but it does so to emphasize the triumph of good over evil, which is to say, victory through solidarity for the family of labor. With an episodic structure and highly quotable style, it places Mother Jones at the center of social protest—organizing, cajoling, berating, triumphing. Sometimes the text reads like religious testimony, bearing witness to the extirpation of evil through faith; other times, it more resembles a melodrama of class oppression and resistance. There are defeats on these pages but no defeatism. "Pray for the dead, and fight like hell for the living"—activism itself, regardless of outcome, is a victory.[50]

At the most superficial level, the *Autobiography* is a series of stories—the march of the Coaldale women, the house arrest in Pratt, West Virginia, the defeat of the steelworkers in 1919. The brief cameo appearances of Mary Harris and Mary Jones at the beginning set the stage. These matter-of-fact sketches of her as daughter, wife, mother, widow, teacher, seamstress, even nurse for the sick, establish her authority as a woman. She presents herself as someone people can identify with, a worker, an immigrant, an American—everywoman. Emphasizing her age and experience also licenses her to speak; her long life gave her venerability, and from venerability came authority.[51]

The *Autobiography* at times reads like an adventure story, a plot-driven action drama with a woman at the center of the excitement: "Late that night, a group of miners gathered about a mile from town between the boulders. We could not see one another's faces in the darkness. By the light of an old lantern I gave them the [union] pledge." The lesson, of course, is that heroism is available to all. The *Autobiography* also contains elements of another popular American genre, the success story. The lack of introspection, the main character's luck, pluck, and hard work, her victories over adversity, all give the *Autobiography* a strange kinship to those tales of triumph in business and politics that were meant to fire Americans with virtuous ambition. Of course, Mother Jones turned the genre on its head—the hero here is a woman, she is not particularly humble, and she defines success in working-class, not bourgeois, terms. But above all, the *Autobiography* is a morality play, the story of a mother's fight against the exploitation of her children. It is an emotional book, continually outraged, occasionally overwrought. Emotion authenticated motherhood, and motherhood made the emotions genuine.[52]

Although the book borrows heavily from Mother Jones's public appearances, it is not merely stump speeches set in type. Its goals were to convert workers to organized labor and to justify beliefs to those who might not understand. Mother Jones addressed middle-class as well as working-class readers: "My class, the working class, is exploited, driven, fought back with the weapons of starvation." Such words were intended less for believers than for skeptics. Miners know what they do for a living; they would not describe themselves with such sentimentality as men "who crawl through dark, choking crevices with only a bit of lamp on their caps to light their silent way; whose backs are bent with toil, whose very bones ache, whose happiness is sleep, and whose peace is death." In story after story, Mother Jones explains her life and, through it, a whole world of work and exploitation—of the realities of class—to readers who, she assumes, do not know much about such things. To reach the middle class, her language (hers and Parton's) shifts from the vernacular to the sentimental; profanity is expunged, colloquialism cleaned up, and the tone elevated. The old anger is still there but also much more pity than usually crept into her speeches.[53]

In line with this shift in language, the *Autobiography* often depicts workers as hapless, uncertain what to do without Mother's intervention. In her most self-absorbed moments, Mother Jones saw things that way, but she was usually more clear eyed, and her career was built on the belief that workers could empower themselves and change their own lives. Some of the book's patronizing tone grew out of her need to claim a legacy by inflating her own accomplishments. One suspects too that Parton—whose reporting on Mother Jones following the Ludlow Massacre was worshipful and romantic—engendered this attitude.[54]

The book hits the old themes of patriotism and religion especially hard. George Washington's name is invoked four times, Abraham Lincoln's five. Mother Jones argues that militant labor organizing itself is patriotic, because patriotism and dissent go hand in hand. Worker solidarity reinforces republican selflessness; strikes for better conditions improve the nation by raising the standard of living and fostering democracy. Fenians, *revoltosos*, and Russian revolutionaries rightly use the United States as a safe haven to foment rebellion abroad, because America is the cradle of liberty.[55]

Even more than patriotism, the *Autobiography* is infused with religious imagery: "We camped in the open fields and held meetings on the road sides and in barns, preaching the gospel of unionism"; labor, Mother Jones feared, would be forced to "bear the cross for others' sins"; capitalists "crucified" child laborers. She even describes organizing a local in a darkened church, and she compares company spies and union turncoats to Judas Iscariot, selling out their brothers for a handful of silver. The dramas of religion and of social struggle were one: " 'I think the strike is lost, Mother,' said an old miner whose son had been killed. 'Lost! Not until your souls are lost!' said I."[56]

The characters striding the *Autobiography*'s stage are mostly one-dimensional—craven capitalists, cowardly governors, selfless union men, corrupt labor bosses. Proclamations of Mother Jones's own heroism get more than a little tiring, but we must remember that her voice comes to us from a time when *publicly* assertive women were still unusual. The Mother Jones persona—that self-assured "I"—is quite remarkable, especially coming from a working-class woman.[57]

Still, her desire for the spotlight precluded her giving much attention to others. The *Autobiography* fails to mention prominent women in labor or politics, much as Mother Jones failed to acknowledge them throughout her career. Kate Richards O'Hare, Elizabeth Gurley Flynn, Jane Addams, Florence Kelley, Emma Goldman, Margaret Sanger are never mentioned. Mother Jones's tendency to scorn all middle-class reformers and philanthropists accounts for her ignoring some women, but, finally, in her desire to give herself the longest pedigree, she failed even to acknowledge others as co-workers in the cause.[58]

There are other important omissions. Although the *Autobiography* does not mask her radicalism, it fails to mention her presence at the founding of the Industrial Workers of the World, perhaps because of how vilified they had become in 1920s America. Moreover, she attacks the Socialist Party in these pages as hopelessly bourgeois, but she never mentions that she spent years working for them. Nor does she reveal that the United Mine Workers paid her for her efforts. And she says nothing about the humiliating Harding telegram.[59]

Mother Jones's failure to mention John L. Lewis is also striking. Maybe she wished to avoid stirring disunity, but the very last chapter of the book, "Progress in Spite of Leaders," reads like a buildup to an assault on Lewis. She describes the selflessness of the early union men—Powderly, Martin Irons, and others—then observes that too many modern leaders have wandered from the path blazed by these pioneers: "Never in the early days of the labor struggle would you find leaders wining and dining with the aristocracy; nor did their wives strut about like diamond-bedecked peacocks; nor were they attended by humiliated, cringing colored servants." Having set Lewis up, however, she ignores him and launches into a harangue against the deceased John Mitchell, who serves as a surrogate for all other enemies.[60]

Perhaps her diatribes against careerist officials expressed her secret feeling that she could have run a giant union, done it better than the men under whom she served. After all, she watched countless mediocre, even incompetent, individuals assume leadership positions while she, as a woman, was never allowed to rise in the hierarchy. But her criticism was not just personal. Her evaluations of labor leaders held real insight, for she recognized the early signs of a fundamental flaw in the labor movement, a tumor that metastasized after she passed away. Many unions grew not only bureaucratic but corrupt; worse, centralized power threatened union democracy. Mother Jones disagreed with those like Lewis who believed that bureaucratization was essential to union success, that worker participation and education were secondary goals. Once again, she harked back to the old days of the Knights of Labor, for she still insisted that citizen-workers were labor's source of strength, that men too concerned with power ultimately menaced the union movement. The fundamental tenet of her faith was belief in industrial democracy, in workers' shaping their own futures.[61]

With all of its blindnesses, then, there is still something magnificent about *The Autobiography of Mother Jones*. Despite its self-righteous posturing, shortages of candor, lack of generosity toward others, and appalling dearth of self-awareness, it has keen social insight at its core. In the midst of the 1920s obsession with success, Mother Jones wrote with stark honesty of poverty, injustice, violence: "I told the great audience that packed the hall that when their coal glowed red in their fires, it was the blood of the workers, of men who went down into the black holes to dig it, of women who suffered and endured. . . . 'You are being warmed and made comfortable with human blood!' "[62]

The Autobiography of Mother Jones is a deeply flawed yet powerful book. It made social class palpable for a culture trying to deny its existence. It spoke of solidarity crossing barriers of race, gender, and ethnicity. Above all, it expressed Mother Jones's faith that working people would find justice. Crudely, imperfectly, but with a strong voice, she told of the excluded, remembered their suffering, and offered hope for their redemption.[63]

The Final Years

In a letter to the editor of *The Nation* in 1922, George P. West nominated Mother Jones for that magazine's list of the twelve greatest American women: "She has preached the stamina and self-reliance of the old-time America," West declared. "Her shrewdness and wisdom and courage and sincerity have impressed Presidents and Governors. . . . Love and tenderness are as warm in her as her courage. . . . She is loved and venerated in ten thousand humble homes." West concluded that Mother Jones's life was a national epic, and it was shameful that America's "tradition of cheap gentility" kept her story from being told. But even if her story was told, who would listen?[64]

When the *Autobiography* finally appeared in print, Mother Jones was not pleased. She commented to John Walker that she planned to retain an attorney and go to Chicago. "I don't trust that Charles Kerr," she told Walker. "The book is not printed as I wrote it anyway, and I have never been satisfied with it." It is unclear what displeased her. Maybe she felt that Parton—cutting and pasting stories, smoothing the prose, transforming idiomatic oral legends into writing—prettified the book. Perhaps she misunderstood the agreement with Kerr and assumed she would be paid a royalty. Maybe she did not believe the sales figures and assumed that he had exploited her hard work. Certainly pride must have made her incredulous that sales were so poor.[65]

The Autobiography of Mother Jones was a commercial failure. Fewer than two thousand copies were sold the first year, and fifteen hundred sets of sheets remained unbound, waiting for demand to catch up with supply. It never did. Reviews were scant, and not until the 1970s did a second edition appear. Except among militant devotees of the labor movement, Mother Jones's name was rapidly being forgotten.[66]

Her letters to friends resumed the litany of physical woes, especially the crippling effects of rheumatism. She also acknowledged how much she depended on others now for daily care and a roof over her head. "It looks as if I will not get well again," she confided to John Walker in 1924. And later, "O John I . . . cannot hold a pen in my fingers They are crippled." She made her last strike appearance in Chicago in 1924, returning to her old trade to rally dressmakers, hundreds of whom were arrested and blacklisted during an ill-fated four-month-long walk-out. She also visited labor's martyrs in prison, including Thomas J. Mooney, Matthew Schmidt, and J. P. MacNamara in California, wrote to governors on their behalf, even proposed that the proceeds from her autobiography be used to help her boys.[67]

She dealt too now with the deaths of old friends. "Well John," she wrote Walker, "the one faithfull friend I had for the last 45 years has passed away Terence V. Powderly he fought my battles for years he faced all the Slanders and boldly Deffended me." On top of her own maladies and the deaths of others, she witnessed the erosion of all she had worked for. "There is a peculiar apathy in the labor movement to day, unknown in its history," she mused. She wrote with alarm about another organization stealing some of labor's thunder: "They have a hard time in Colorado. . . . The Ku Klux control the whole state now. . . . I am afraid they are going to create a great deal of trouble before they are done away with." Such observations grew less common as her letters became shorter and more cryptic, and her political sympathies veered wildly now. Having championed the left wing of the Farmer-Labor Party in 1923, she endorsed Calvin Coolidge for President in 1924, apparently because his opponent supported the operators in the West Virginia strikes. She also backed conservative senator William Borah from Idaho, because of his loyalty to her during the troubles on Paint and Cabin Creeks.[68]

When Mother Jones was not with Emma Powderly in Washington, she found companionship on her trips to California. She stayed with well-off friends, like the philanthropist Catherine Yarnell, who invited Mother Jones to live with her and wrote her checks for a few hundred dollars now and again. Mother Jones described one "glorious" dinner party in Los Angeles at which she was the center of attention. Everyone there "had an open mind and advanced ideas," and a professor even asked if he might bring his students by to hear her stories about the labor movement. Yet neither friends nor California's lovely weather kept her sadness at bay. "This day is just like a June day," she wrote Emma Powderly from Pasadena during the winter of 1926, "and this evening is like a spring evening." But there was no excitement, not even a band "to beat the last dirge for some poor person who is to be laid away."[69]

By 1927, her health had become too fragile for train rides to the coast. Slowing down allowed Mother Jones to cultivate friendships that her earlier frenetic life precluded, and this especially included Emma. Old-timers from the labor movement dropped by the house often, and though seeing them did not restore her health, "still," she observed, "it does away with the blues." More, the Powderly household was an extended family of children and grandchildren, aunts and uncles, the sort of Irish American household Mother Jones had not known for decades, a comforting surrogate family.[70]

Late in 1928, John Walker sent Mother Jones a check for one thousand dollars, money she originally loaned him for his daughter's education and to purchase a home. She wrote Walker that he relieved her of much worry: "I was limited to three dollars and hardly knew what to do." Of course, her daily needs were met at Emma's home, but still she told Walker that before his letter arrived, she did not know "whether to ask William Green [who had become president of the AFL in 1924] to help me or to apply to the poor house," and she added, "You know I do not like to sponge off any one or live like a pauper." Walker apologized for not returning the money sooner, and added, "I feel that I owe you and all the folks that have lived like you, for everything that I have in this world that is worth having, and as long as I have a dollar you will be welcome to it. . . . It will be just repaying, in a small measure, the obligations we are all under to you."[71]

It was a lovely testament to their friendship, but in fact Mother Jones was not so poor. Legal papers indicate that she had more than six thousand dollars, half of it in cash, plus bonds and a few shares of stock. Since she had lived in others' households for several years now, she probably had been banking the money that friends like Green and Yarnell sent. Shortly before she died, she transferred guardianship of her assets from Emma Powderly to Ed Nockles and John Fitzpatrick of the Chicago Federation of Labor for donation to needy families.[72]

As the end neared, Mother Jones made plans for her own funeral. Back in 1923, just after finishing work on her autobiography, she gave a speech, one of her last, at the Virden Day celebration in Mount Olive, Illinois: "When the last call comes for me . . . will the miners see that I get a resting place in the same clay that shelters the miners who gave up their lives on the hills of Virden? . . . They are responsible for Illinois being the best organized labor state in America."[73]

It was at Mount Olive that the United Mine Workers won the victory that allowed them to organize the Central Competitive Field. Back in 1898, most operators were ready to accept a union contract, but the owners in Virden held out. They tried to bring in scabs from Alabama, blacks who were not informed of the strike. On October 12, when their train pulled into Virden, armed miners shot it out with the guards on board. In the ten-minute battle, forty-seven union men were shot, seven mortally; four of nine wounded detectives died. None of the would-be strikebreakers was hit, but the train never unloaded its cargo at Virden, and the coal company was forced to settle the strike. It was this final battle in the fight to organize the Central Competitive Field that made the UMW the most powerful union in America.[74]

Union workers began commemorating Miners Day on October 12, 1899, in Mount Olive, and every year thousands of families came into town for a parade, music, and speeches. In the Union Miners Cemetery lay the four men from that small Illinois village who fell in the battle of Virden. It was (and is) the only union-owned burial place in America, opened by UMW Local 728 in 1898, when other cemeteries refused to accept the union's dead. Here the martyrs fell; here the union buried its own; here the UMW became America's first great industrial union. And here Mother Jones chose as her final resting place.[75]

Even as she grew more frail—and perhaps because her end was near—she received a stream of visitors at the Powderly home, union officials, workers, politicians, friends. Among these were Walter and Lillie May Burgess, who had known Mother Jones since 1905. When Mother Jones felt up to it, the Burgesses took her to their truck farm in Hyattsville, Maryland, for visits. By 1929, it had become difficult for Emma Powderly, herself an old woman now, to care for her aging visitor, so in May of that year, Mother Jones moved in with the Burgesses. The stream of well-wishers now flowed to Hyattsville. When not catching up on union matters, Mother Jones enjoyed the country air, riding into town for an ice cream cone, chatting with the local parish priest, or lying on the sofa and listening to the Burgesses' neighbor play Irish tunes on the piano. She also gave occasional interviews. She told the newspaper *Labor* that if she could only walk, she would still be out organizing workers. In *The Washington Times*, she offered verbal support to the striking textile workers of North Carolina. The *Washington Evening Star* reported her remarks that Prohibition was an invasion of personal liberty and that she drank whiskey herself under orders from her doctor. She added that she intended to live fifteen more years.[76]

Mother Jones was ninety-two years old on her hundredth birthday. She began thinking about a party at least two and a half years in advance, knowing that it would put her in the spotlight for a final time. She wrote Nockles and Fitzpatrick at the end of 1927 that she hoped to come to Chicago to celebrate the event. But as May 1, 1930, drew closer, it became clear that her health would not permit the trip. Instead, the Burgesses began preparing for a party in their home. A funeral seemed more likely than a birthday when pneumonia struck Mother Jones down in February, but she rallied. Ten days before May Day, *The New York Times* reported that eighty years of industrial battles—as always, the press followed her lead in exaggerating her life story—had left her "a frail shell." Still, "that amazing voice leaps out, eloquent and cutting, to lash what she terms the 'foes' of labor."[77]

Three days before the party, the Baltimore *Sun* devoted the lead story of its Sunday magazine to the old warrior and included a large drawing of her. The article measured just how far legend and life diverged. She was there at Ludlow when the machine guns were turned on the women and children, "and she made her voice rise above the din and smoke . . . until the rich man in lower Broadway heard it." Rockefeller speedily remedied conditions in his mines, and the two became fast friends. She worked for the old *Appeal to Reason,* "but when it became radical and took on a Socialistic and even anarchistic taint, she turned on it with an almost unbelievable fury." Now "night and morning she prays for Mooney's freedom," and should that prayer be granted, "she is willing to call it a day, the battle over, the victory won." Her apotheosis was complete. Prayerful, anti-radical, a friend of Rockefeller's, she had been declawed, defanged, domesticated.[78]

But she was no sweet old lady yet. On the day of her party, when Lillie May Burgess tried to pin a corsage on her, Mother Jones snapped, "Hell, I never have worn those and I don't want to now." When she took a drink of water and someone reminded her that she used to drink beer, she cursed "those old fools" who forced Prohibition on the country. Union bakers made an enormous cake, decorated with one hundred candles. Local fire departments provided bunting to decorate the Burgess home, and the Soldiers Home Band played tune after tune. Although she was bedridden most of the time now, Mother Jones walked down the stairs, assisted by her hosts, and took a seat in the back yard. Hundreds of well-wishers arrived, telegrams poured in all day and all night, and a delegation of one hundred unemployed men, led by Dan O'Brien, the "Hobo King" and a veteran of Coxey's Army, paid their respects. Workers, labor leaders, politicians, and friends all came to celebrate—and to say goodbye.[79]

She exchanged telegrams—pleasant, heartfelt messages—with young Rockefeller. She called him a "damned good sport" for sending his best wishes, since she had "licked him many times." But she recalled for reporters that Rockefeller had her incarcerated, and she added, "Yes, I forgive them . . . but I don't forget." She also breathed a bit of her old fire for the newsreel cameras: "America was not built on dollars but on the blood of men who gave their lives for your benefit. Power lies in the hands of labor to retain American liberty, but labor has not yet learned how to use that power. A wonderful power is in the hands of women, too, but they don't know how to use it. Capitalists sidetrack the women into clubs and make ladies of them. Nobody wants a lady, they want women." She had long uttered such words, but here in 1930, with the labor movement sputtering and Mother Jones enfeebled, they seemed antiquated, even a bit sad.[80]

Mother Jones was delighted with her party, but it was her last public appearance. She returned to her room after the festivities and mostly remained there until the end of her life six months later. More than once she weakened, then rallied, but each setback took its toll. A few admirers were let in to discuss politics, labor issues, and, above all, the deepening depression, already worse than any in memory. Journalists came by for interviews or to check on her condition. In July, she dictated birthday greetings to John D. Rockefeller, Sr.: "Congratulations on the arrival of your ninety-first birthday. Thank God we have some men in the world yet as good as you." But she told reporters, "I wouldn't trade what I've done for what he's done. I've done the best I could to make the world a better place for poor, hard-working people." As her last public act, she sent one thousand dollars to John Walker for the United Mine Workers Reorganized, a group led by Illinois miners to oust John L. Lewis from his UMW presidency. Her goal, she said, was to help "defend the miners against leaders who are thinking more of themselves than they are of my boys."[81]

As summer gave way to autumn, Mother Jones's health broke down completely. A local priest administered extreme unction and the Blessed Sacrament. Finally, on November 30, 1930, Mother Jones passed away. The Certificate of Death gave senility as the cause of her demise. Her physician put it more bluntly: she just wore out.[82]

Two days after her death, a high requiem Mass was celebrated at St. Gabriel's Church in Washington. In the audience sat working men and women, the Secretary of Labor, union presidents, the unemployed, and countless friends of Mother Jones. "Her zeal and earnestness in behalf of the poor will be a pleasant memory long after her body is gone," intoned Father William Sweeney. Mother Jones would have bristled; Sweeney's words made her seem just another charitable old woman, not the fiery organizer who led angry workers in their quest for justice. But he was merely following a trend that reduced the militant warrior to an old saint, that hid the angry matriarch of laboring families behind the sweet grandmother. The Mother Jones persona had always contained that danger.[83]

After Mass, a special railroad car took her body to St. Louis and, from there, to Mount Olive, following the route of Lincoln's funeral sixty-five years earlier. Thirty-five hundred people lived in Mount Olive, but four or five times that number pressed into the depot when the train arrived on Thursday night. Survivors of the Virden Massacre carried her coffin to the Odd Fellows Temple, where it lay in state until Sunday. Mine families and union supporters by the thousands filed past the casket, past the mounds of flowers and the union banners.[84]

On Sunday, her admirers crowded Mount Olive's Ascension Church, but only about three hundred of them made it inside. Loudspeakers carried the eulogy, delivered by Father John Maguire, a veteran of the 1919 steel strike and president of St. Viator's College in Bourbonnais, Illinois, to the thousands standing outside. Thousands more of Mother Jones's admirers heard the service over WCFL, the radio station of the Chicago Federation of Labor. "My Dear friends," Maguire declared,

> today in gorgeous mahogany furnished and carefully guarded offices in distant capitals wealthy mine owners and capitalists are breathing sighs of relief. Today upon the plains of Illinois, the hillsides and valleys of Pennsylvania and West Virginia, in California, Colorado and British Columbia, strong men and toil worn women are weeping tears of bitter grief. The reasons . . . are the same. Mother Jones is dead.[85]

Maguire recounted her heroic deeds, her life of work and struggle. "She had a small frail body," he said, "but she had a great and indomitable spirit. She was relatively uneducated but she had a flaming tongue. She was poor, but she had a great blazing love for the poor, the down-trodden, and the oppressed. She was without influence but she had a mother's heart, great enough to embrace the weak and defenseless babes of the world." To her eloquence, courage, and love Maguire might have added towering ambition for herself and her people. Only with singular ambition could an old Irish widow so impress herself on the nation and help build a movement that challenged America's culture of capitalist individualism with a culture of solidarity for working families. Towering ambition, and a remarkable flare for the dramatic.[86]

The men and women who attended Mother Jones's funeral remembered her passion, but a convenient amnesia had settled like fog over their countrymen. During the 1920s, several large corporations embraced welfare capitalism, company unions, and "industrial democracy," ideas popularized by Rockefeller after Ludlow. With labor unions in retreat, many workers gave corporate paternalism a try. Mother Jones's obituaries blunted memories of America's radical tradition and effaced the vision of the militant old warrior. Papers like *The New York*

11. The funeral of Mother Jones in Mount Olive, Illinois. Pictures of the Virden martyrs line the wall, and a wreath from the Chicago Federation of Labor rests above her casket (Courtesy State Historical Society of Wisconsin)

Times and the *Chicago Tribune* simply ran an Associated Press story that declared she opposed socialism, the IWW, and bolshevism, that she "stood for years by the principles of the American Federation of Labor." The story added that she had a "distinct aversion" to woman suffrage but failed to note that she organized women in bold and militant protest. Even *The Nation* described her as "unqualifiedly averse to socialism." Indeed, the press in general embraced this apostle of working-class militance by domesticating her: "She was never one of the hot and heedless radicals who would burn down the barn to get rid of the rats," *The Duluth Herald* declared. "She lived to win the respect and admiration of all who recognized her truth and sincerity," wrote the *Youngstown Daily Vindicator*. "She had been called a 'menace' in the old days . . . but she lived to know the admiration of those against whom she had battled," said the *Albany Evening News*. Old age and death had rendered Mother Jones less fearsome; her enemies might love her now that she no longer threatened them. It was hard to imagine that anyone had ever thought of her as the most dangerous woman in America.[87]

Epilogue: "Mother Jones Is Not Forgotten"

Memories of Mother Jones still nurtured rebellion even after her death. In the summer of 1932, in the very depths of the Great Depression, United Mine Workers president John L. Lewis agreed to a contract that so angered many Illinois miners, they walked off their jobs. The men gathered in Mount Olive, formed a caravan fifteen thousand strong, and headed downstate to organize their brothers. They clashed not only with police but with UMW stalwarts, and soon the rebels formed a new organization, the Progressive Mine Workers of America.[1]

PMWA leaders declared that they acted in the spirit of Mother Jones and that one of their first orders of business was to place a proper marker over her grave. They challenged the UMW in court and won the right to build the memorial. By 1936, PMWA locals and their women's auxiliaries had raised over sixteen thousand dollars for the project. Workers donated their labor and erected eighty tons of Minnesota pink granite, with bronze statues of two miners flanking a twenty-foot shaft featuring a bas-relief of Mother Jones at its center. At the dedication on Miners Day, October 11, 1936, fifty thousand people came to Mount Olive for a parade, tributes to Mother Jones, and denunciations of John L. Lewis and his "fascist" United Mine Workers. Thereafter, the annual gathering in Mount Olive became known as "Mother Jones Day."[2]

Her memory survived in folklore. Just three months after her passing, a young singer named Gene Autry recorded a song called "The Death of Mother Jones":

> *The world today's in mourning*
> *O'er the death of Mother Jones;*
> *Gloom and sorrow hover*
> *Around the miners' homes.*
> *This grand old champion of labor*
> *Was known in every land;*
> *She fought for right and justice*
> *She took a noble stand.*

The tune was elegiac, and the style understated. It was not a commercially successful song, and certainly the lyrics were too hackneyed to capture the old woman's singularity.[3]

Although it quickly went out of print, "The Death of Mother Jones" did not die out altogether, not in the mountains, for it took on a life of its own in oral tradition. No one knows who wrote the song, but local singers in the mine country kept it alive, and even schoolchildren learned the lyrics. Two years after Mother Jones's passing, one teacher recalled:

> The great moment for the class comes when, a hundred
> strong, students and teachers, grizzled miners with their
> tired wives, nursing babies at their breasts, and children
> of all sizes stand under the trees with dusk coming on
> singing "The Death of Mother Jones," and "Solidarity For-
> ever." It is a ragged crowd, inarticulate and downtrodden,
> but for the moment there is an exaltation that fills the
> spirit of all who participate in the gathering.

Years later, another mountain song boldly declared, "Mother Jones is not forgotten."[4]

Legends embellishing her fearlessness also kept her memory alive in the mine country. James Farrance told of seeing her in Monongah,

West Virginia, during an organizing drive: "She came down Pike Street in a buggy and horse. Two company thugs grabbed the horse by the bridle and told her to turn around and get back down the road. She wore a gingham apron, and she reached under it and pulled out a .38 special pistol and told them to turn her horse loose, and they sure did. . . . She wasn't afraid of the devil."[5]

Women of West Virginia remembered her remarkable courage with special fondness. Grace Jackson described Mother Jones leading a march in Leewood on Cabin Creek in 1912. When armed guards confronted the marchers with a cannon, Mother Jones cussed them and dared them to shoot. "She didn't care nothing for Christian language," Jackson concluded, "because she loved the people, and hated them operators. . . . Oh, she was a female Robin Hood if ever there was." Mandy Porter recalled seeing Mother Jones in a restaurant in Mingo County, surrounded by gun-toting men. Despite the threat of violence everywhere, she still rode through the coalfields and made her speeches. Monia Baumgartner remembered bullets whizzing past Mother Jones as she spoke, but the old woman finished her talk, then admonished young Monia, "Now don't you get scared."[6]

Although Mother Jones lived on in the folklore of the mine country, elsewhere her memory faded quickly. Her name rarely found its way into the news after her death. She had backed the losing side in the UMW, so as John L. Lewis's star rose, her memory was relegated to the shadows. Moreover, when the Communist Party emerged as America's dominant leftist organization, many labor leaders became staunchly anti-radical, and they found ideas like hers embarrassing if not dangerous. Mother Jones would have been an ideal candidate for canonization in the popular front, that broad Communist-led coalition of progressive organizations and ideas of the late 1930s which extolled a wide range of American heroes. But twenty years had passed since her last big organizing drive, and memories of her had grown dim. Except in the mine country, she was all but forgotten in mid-century America, with its spasms of witch-hunting that evoked the dark days of Haymarket and the Red Scare.[7]

Then came the 1960s and their aftermath, when Mother Jones gained new life as an icon of revolt. Her legend grew most prominent in the southern mountains, where a tide of labor militance and community organizing was on the rise. In a 1970 issue of *People's Appalachia*, a leftist newsletter, Keith Dix offered a brief synopsis of her life, quoted Clarence Darrow's belief that she was "the most forceful and picturesque figure in the American labor movement," and argued that her memory was spreading to young people who sought social change. As if to prove Dix's point, a popular pamphlet, "The Thoughts of Mother Jones," published in 1971, excerpted some of her most epigrammatic lines. In 1972, a long front-page article in *The New York Times* titled "Ideal of Unity Stirs Appalachian Poor" declared that whereas images of movie stars stared down from walls across America, "here in a storefront office in Appalachia, the pop poster features Mother Jones."[8]

Beyond the old mining country, her name reemerged during the folk-song revival on new recordings of "The Death of Mother Jones" and other songs. The Charles Kerr Company finally issued a second edition of *The Autobiography of Mother Jones* in 1972, and two years later, the journalist Dale Fetherling published the first and only book-length biography of her. In 1976, *Mother Jones* magazine appeared, featuring an editorial announcement that included an artist's sketch, a romanticized description of her life, and a promise of muckraking journalism in the Progressive Era tradition. Union newspapers began to run features about her, though these emphasized her colorful character more than her radical ideas. Even daily papers on occasion retraced her steps, quoted her speeches, and marveled at how much relations between labor and management had improved since her day. Books for young adults appeared, too, as well as stage adaptations of her life; she even appeared in a novel. As women's history developed into an important field within the historical profession, Mother Jones received at least brief mention in several works. Finally, Edward Steel and Philip Foner brought out substantial editions of her letters and speeches, and Kerr published yet another edition of her autobiography.[9]

Her old fire rekindled again in the late 1980s when Pittston Coal Company's harsh policies led to a bitter strike in Appalachia. In the midst of the struggle, forty women, all miners and UMW members, occupied the company's offices for thirty hours. They talked about

Mother Jones during their sit-in, and one of their leaders recalled, "If somebody would say 'I'm tired,' we would say: 'Mother Jones, there was times she would be tired. . . . If we've got to go to jail and pull time, we will. Mother Jones did.' " When police arrested the women, they identified themselves simply as the "Daughters of Mother Jones."[10]

Mother Jones had found her way back to the fringes of American memory. The U.S. Labor Department inducted her into its "Labor Hall of Fame" in 1992, alongside Samuel Gompers and John L. Lewis. The state of Pennsylvania erected a statue of her on Penn Square in downtown Philadelphia, commemorating the march of the mill children, and the governor even proclaimed May 1, 1993, "Mother Jones Day." A special 1997 issue of *Life* magazine, "Celebrating Our Heroes," named her one of the twenty-five "most heroic Americans ever." (She was not, however, heroic enough to deserve much text, just a few lines on how, after the death of her family, "she hit the road and spent the rest of her hundred-year life traveling with her Crusaders from mine to mill.") At the end of the 1990s, *Irish America* magazine gave her a prominent place among "The Greatest Irish-Americans of the Century." As the millennium ended, her name was well enough known that *The New York Times* called an organizer of computer workers "The Mother Jones of Silicon Valley."[11]

Her memory, then, has enjoyed a modest reawakening. But largely forgotten still is the old radical, preaching her sermons of solidarity to working families. She is more an elf of good causes now, a twinkly-eyed grandmother, than the embattled champion of American workers.

What is Mother Jones's legacy? In a narrow sense, her accomplishments were limited. She lost more industrial battles than she won, and the United Mine Workers failed to organize the entire coal industry. Moreover, her belief in women's inherent nurturing qualities blinded her to a whole range of emerging issues, including women's right to equality in political, social, and economic life. She never even found a way of expressing the injustice of less-than-competent men serving as high union officials while she, with her intelligence, ability, and ambition, was kept out. Her bent toward the practical rather than the theoretical sometimes made her evasive about means and ends and about articulating a long-term vision of the future. By the time she died, many unions had rejected their democratic heritage, labor's power had declined steeply, and leftists had been hounded into silence. Equally important, many workers prospered modestly in the consumer society that emerged in the 1920s, and they were not so interested in old struggles and dreams.

Yet there is much more to tell. Mother Jones constructed an amazing life of courage and commitment. At a time when American labor was riven by racism and nativism, she sought, though imperfectly, to bring black and immigrant workers into the fold. For her, solidarity was not just a union slogan but a culture, a way of life, one that rejected America's worship of individualism and embraced instead the community of labor.

If Mother Jones advocated that women tend to their homes, she did so out of a belief that family was the bedrock of working-class life. This was how most laboring people saw it, too, for given their harsh economic circumstances, men, women, and children knew that they must depend on one another for survival. In place of the untrammeled rule of the marketplace, she substituted her metaphor of the family of labor, which assumed that all change must be directed toward creating humane communities. As *Mother* Jones, she invoked wrenching images of blood stolen, bodies mangled, and youth exploited to dramatize the injustice of poverty in America. Above all, she gave people hope and told them that their aspirations for change were in the best traditions of patriotism and religion. Hundreds of thousands of American workers fought for and received better wages and working conditions during her years of activism, and they embraced a renewed ideal of democratic citizenship.

The way Mother Jones lived her life was breathtaking. She tailored her appearance to match every sentimental notion about mothers. Then she subverted the very idea of genteel womanhood on which such stereotypes were based with her vituperative, profane, electric speeches. Women—especially old women—were not supposed to have opinions about politics and economics; they were not supposed to travel alone; they were too delicate for controversy. Yet there she was, haranguing workers, berating politicians, attacking the "pirates," and telling women to take to the streets, all under the cover of sacred motherhood. Before the business of public relations even existed, she organized events that garnered tremendous publicity. By creating Mother Jones, she manufactured her own image, getting maximum exposure for her cause.

Mother Jones began with nineteenth-century ideological tools—the concept of Irish exile, Catholicism's renewed cult of Mary, antislavery doctrine, producer ideology, republicanism, separate spheres for men and women, the idealization of motherhood—and reshaped them for twentieth-century battles. It was her lived experience of class—in Cork, Toronto, Memphis, and Chicago—that gave her insight into the suffering of working families. And it was her insistence on speaking for the poor, not as an outsider but as one of them, that made her so beloved. She was their Jeremiah, decrying injustice and calling its perpetrators to account. More, she was Mother Mary, interceding on their behalf.

And who was she to do all of this? A common woman whose early years yielded toil and tragedy and whose old age promised nothing but obscurity. She was expected to go silently through life, for she was a mere worker in a country that worshipped success, an immigrant in a nativist land, a woman in a male-dominated society, and an elderly person in a nation that cherished youth. Hers was a voice that Americans were not supposed to hear. That was her final legacy—out of nothing but courage, passion, and commitment, she created a unique voice, a prophetic voice, and raised it in the cause of renewing America's democratic promise.

List of Archives

ARCAT, Archives of the Roman Catholic Archdiocese of Toronto, Toronto, Canada

CHS, Chicago Historical Society, Manuscripts, Chicago

ColHS, Colorado Historical Society Archives, Denver

ColSA, Colorado State Archives, Denver

CUA, Catholic University of America, Mother Jones Collection, Archives Department, Washington, D.C.

DPL, Denver Public Library, Western History Collection

HL, Huntington Library, San Marino, California

INA, Irish National Archives, Dublin, Ireland

ISHL, Illinois State Historical Library Archives, Springfield

LC, Library of Congress, Washington, D.C.

NARA, National Archives and Records Administration, Washington, D.C.

NL, Newberry Library, Special Collections, Chicago

PAO, Provincial Archives of Ontario, Toronto, Canada

SCPL, Shelby County Public Library, Memphis, Tennessee

SHSW, State Historical Society of Wisconsin, Madison

UCB, University of Colorado, Boulder, Library, Archives and Special Collections

USHA, Utah State Historical Archives, Salt Lake City

WSU, Wayne State University, Walter P. Reuther Library of Labor and Urban Affairs, Detroit, Michigan

WVaU, West Virginia University Library, West Virginia and Regional History Collection, Morgantown

Notes

1. Mary Harris

1. Mother Jones, *The Autobiography of Mother Jones*, ed. Mary Field Parton (Chicago: Charles H. Kerr and Company, 1925), p. 11. The first chapter of the *Autobiography* covers the years 1830–1880, pp. 11–16.
2. For a discussion of the *Autobiography*, see Chapter 10.
3. The literature on biography is enormous, but see Linda Wagner-Martin, *Telling Women's Lives: The New Biography* (New Brunswick, N.J.: Rutgers University Press, 1994); Jill Kerr Conway, *When Memory Speaks: Reflections on Autobiography* (New York: Knopf, 1998); Leon Edel, *Writing Lives: Principia Biographica* (New York: Norton, 1984); Mary Rhiel and David Suchoff, eds., *The Seductions of Biography* (New York: Routledge, 1996); Richard Holmes, *Footsteps: Adventures of a Romantic Biographer* (New York: Viking, 1985); Carolyn G. Heilbrun, *Writing a Woman's Life* (New York: Norton, 1988); William Zinsser, ed., *Extraordinary Lives: The Art and Craft of American Biography* (Boston: Houghton Mifflin, 1986); Samuel H. Baron and Carl Pletsch, eds., *Introspection in Biography: The Biographer's Quest for Self-Awareness* (Hillsdale, N.J.: Analytic Press, 1985); Ira Bruce Nadel, *Biography: Fiction, Fact, and Form* (New York: St. Martin's Press, 1984); Paul Murray Kendall, *The Art of Biography* (New York: Norton, 1985); Sara Alpern et al., eds., *The Challenge of Feminist Biography: Writing the Lives of Modern American Women* (Urbana: University of Illinois Press, 1992).
4. Alice Kessler-Harris, "Gender Ideology in Historical Reconstruction: A Case Study from the 1930s," *Gender and History* 1 (Spring 1989), pp. 31–49, argues that the idea of separate spheres applied more to middle-class than working-class families.
5. In addition to Mother Jones, *Autobiography*, see "About Mother Jones," *Wilkes-*

Barre Record, March 30, 1901; letter from Rolla G. G. Onyon, *Washington Evening Star,* January 13, 1930; unnamed newspaper, September 9, 1904, all in CUA, 7/2.5; "Mother Jones," *Appeal to Reason,* November 17, 1900, reprinted in *Miners' Magazine,* November 1900, pp. 27–30, originally from New York *World.*

6. It is impossible to trace the ancestry of Richard Harris or Ellen Cotter with any certainty because their names were so common. The parish records of St. Mary's Cathedral in Cork city have a Richard Harris, son of William Harris and Mary White, baptized on September 7, 1802 (Mary and William also had a son, John, baptized four years earlier). That date agrees well with the Richard Harris of the Canadian census, and the parents' names of William and Mary reappear for Richard's children. Ellen Cotter was an even more common name, and lacking additional information (a baptismal date, a middle name), it is impossible to know for sure which one in Cork or Inchigeelagh was Mary Harris's mother. Inchigeelagh is described in J. Windele, *Historical and Descriptive Notices of the City of Cork* (Cork: Bradford and Company, 1849), pp. 280–81. Inchigeelagh Parish was mapped in remarkable detail in the Ordinance Townland Survey of Ireland, sheets 80–82, in the early 1840s. See also Bruno O'Donoghue, *Parish Histories and Place Names of West Cork* (Tralee: Kerryman Ltd., 1991).

7. In Ireland, baptism usually followed a day or two after birth. In addition to my own digging, I have relied on the reports of two professional genealogists; the first, by Nora Hickey of Cork Family History, Kinsale, County Cork, done in July 1995, was based largely on the records compiled in Albert Eugene Casey, *O'Kief, Coshe Mang, Slieve Lougher, and Upper Blackwater in Ireland* (Birmingham, Ala.: Knocknagree Historical Fund, 1952). The other report, labeled "0.798, Harris, M. O'C.," came from the Genealogical Office, Dublin Castle, Dublin, and was based on parish records from the city of Cork. Unfortunately, no manuscript census returns for Cork prior to the twentieth century have survived, and civil registrations of birth, marriages, and deaths did not begin until 1864. Much information is also to be found in the International Genealogical Index, 1993 ed., British Isles, under Harris and Cotter.

8. Windele, *Historical and Descriptive Notices,* pp. 278–80.

9. The quote is from Windele, *Historical and Descriptive Notices,* pp. 278–80. Windele says that the eastern townlands were owned by an English company that manufactured swords and by one Jasper Pyne, Esq. Inchigeelagh is also described in W. Maziere Brady, *Clerical and Parochial Records of Cork, Cloyne, and Ross,* vol. 1 (London: Longman, 1864), pp. 122–23.

10. Griffith's *Primary Valuation of Ireland* lists twenty-eight Cotter and two Harris households in Inchigeelagh. None was a large holding, and nearly all were rented, not owned; see Richard John Griffith, *Valuation of Tenements, County of Cork, Part of the Barony of West Muskerry, in the Union of Dunmanway, Parish of Inchigeelagh* (Dublin, 1852). On the dairy trade, see David Dickson, "Butter Comes to Market: The Origins of Commercial Dairying in Country Cork," in Patrick O'Flanagan and Cornelius G. Buttimer, eds., *Cork: History and Society*

(Dublin: Geography Publications, 1993), pp. 368–82; and William O'Sullivan, *The Economic History of Cork City from the Earliest Times to the Act of Union* (Dublin and Cork: Cork University Press, 1937), pp. 255–75.

11. Kerby Miller, *Emigrants and Exiles: Ireland and the Irish Exodus to North America* (New York: Oxford University Press, 1985), pp. 26–29; Gearóid Ó Tuathaigh, *Ireland before the Famine, 1798–1848* (Dublin: Gill and Macmillan, 1990), pp. 5–7. For a description of larger farms, see Reverend Horatio Townsend, *Statistical Survey of the County of Cork* (Dublin: Graisberry and Campbell, 1810), pp. 651–54. Townsend noted that Irish women assisted in field labor, hay making, binding corn, picking stones, planting the family patch, and digging potatoes.

12. Ó Tuathaigh, *Ireland before the Famine*, p. 108; Cecil Woodham-Smith, *The Great Hunger: Ireland, 1845–1849* (London: Penguin, 1962), pp. 31–36.

13. William J. Smyth, "Social, Economic, and Landscape Transformations in County Cork from the Mid-Eighteenth to the Mid-Nineteenth Centuries," in O'Flanagan and Buttimer, eds., *Cork*, pp. 655–98; Miller, *Emigrants and Exiles*, pp. 26–27.

14. G.D.H. Cole and M. Cole, eds., *Rural Rides by William Cobbett*, vol. 3 (London: Peter Davies, 1930), pp. 898–99, quoted in Patrick O'Flanagan, "Three Hundred Years of Urban Life: Villages and Towns in County Cork c. 1600–1901," in O'Flanagan and Buttimer, eds., *Cork*, p. 439; Ó Tuathaigh, *Ireland before the Famine*, p. 148.

15. Miller, *Emigrants and Exiles*, pp. 21–25, 30–35; Ó Tuathaigh, *Ireland before the Famine*, pp. 129–55. The best work on the rural economy of Cork before the famine is James S. Donnelly, Jr., *The Land and the People of Nineteenth-Century Cork* (London: Routledge and Kegan Paul, 1975), pp. 16–59. During the 1830s and 1840s, about three-quarters of county Cork's rural population was landless, and according to a parliamentary commission of 1835, three million Irish lived "subject every year to the chances of absolute destitution."

16. Miller, *Emigrants and Exiles*, pp. 41–44; Ó Tuathaigh, *Ireland before the Famine*, pp. 146–48.

17. For a survey of Irish culture before the famine, see Kevin Whelan, "Pre- and Post-famine Landscape Change," in Cathal Póirtéir, ed., *The Great Irish Famine* (Dublin: Mercier Press, 1995), pp. 19–33. For a description of Gougane Barra, see Townsend, *Statistical Survey of the County of Cork*, pp. 643–46.

18. The traveler William Wilde is quoted in Whelan, "Pre- and Post-famine Landscape Change," pp. 31–32; also see Cornelius G. Buttimer, "Gaelic Literature and Contemporary Life in Cork, 1700–1840," in O'Flanagan and Buttimer, eds., *Cork*, pp. 585–653. For a survey of the uses of language, see Ó Tuathaigh, *Ireland before the Famine*, pp. 146–51. Windele, *Historical and Descriptive Notices*, pp. 283–84, greatly exaggerates the persistence of the Irish language in Inchigeelagh when he declares that English was hardly known there as of 1849.

19. Miller, *Emigrants and Exiles*, p. 70; Buttimer, "Gaelic Literature," pp. 585, 604–12; Ó Tuathaigh, *Ireland before the Famine*, pp. 151–56.

20. St. Mary's was a very small, densely populated parish. Padraig Ó Maidín, "Mother Jones Labor Agitator," *Irish Weekly Examiner*, November 11, 1976, p. 18; Maura Murphy, "The Working Classes of Nineteenth Century Cork," *Cork Historical and Archaeological Society Journal* 80 (1980), pp. 26–27. Nine thousand children received free education each day in Catholic institutions; Cork city schools are listed in Windele, *Historical and Descriptive Notices*, pp. 132–34.

21. A. M. Fahy, "Place and Class in Cork," in O'Flanagan and Buttimer, eds., *Cork*, pp. 793–96; M. Cronin, "Work and Workers in Cork City and County, 1800–1900," in O'Flanagan and Buttimer, eds., *Cork*, pp. 721–29; Maura Murphy, "The Economic and Social Structure of Nineteenth Century Cork," in David Harkness and Mary O'Dowd, eds., *The Town in Ireland* (Belfast: Appletree Press, 1981), pp. 125–54; Murphy, "Working Classes," pp. 26–29; Windele, *Historical and Descriptive Notices*, pp. 116–19; John B. O'Brien, "Population, Politics, and Society in Cork, 1780–1900," in O'Flanagan and Buttimer, eds., *Cork*, pp. 699–707, 713–17.

22. Miller, *Emigrants and Exiles*, pp. 65–66; O'Brien, "Population, Politics, and Society," pp. 713–17; Murphy, "Economic and Social Structure," pp. 144–45, 151–54; Murphy, "Working Classes," pp. 41–45.

23. O'Brien, "Population, Politics, and Society," pp. 710–17; Cronin, "Work and Workers," pp. 725–32; Murphy, "Economic and Social Structure," pp. 140–54. On the burning of St. Mary's, see Murray Nicolson, "William O'Grady and the Catholic Church in Toronto prior to the Irish Famine," in Mark George McGowan and Brian P. Clarke, eds., *Catholics at the "Gathering Place": Historical Essays on the Archdiocese of Toronto, 1841–1991* (Toronto: Canadian Catholic Historical Association, 1993), p. 25.

24. Miller, *Emigrants and Exiles*, pp. 61–67, 82–84, 92–101; Samuel Clark and James S. Donnelly, *Irish Peasants: Violence and Political Unrest* (Madison: University of Wisconsin Press, 1983), pp. 64–66.

25. Miller, *Emigrants and Exiles*, pp. 82–84, 92–101; Clark and Donnelly, *Irish Peasants*, pp. 104–36.

26. Peter O'Leary, "The Battle of Keimaneigh," *Camann Staire Bheal Athan Ghaorthaidh* 2 (1993), pp. 13–15; Peter O'Leary, "Cath Cheim an Fhia: Its Place in the Rockite Campaign," *Journal of the Cork Historical and Archaeological Society* 97 (1992), pp. 97–103.

27. O'Leary, "Battle of Keimaneigh," pp. 13–15; O'Leary, "Cath Cheim an Fhia," pp. 97–103.

28. My thanks to Peter O'Leary and Joe Creedon of Inchigeelagh for discussing these and other events with me on a lovely Sunday, July 30, 1995. When I went across the street from Creedon's Hotel to photocopy some articles Peter O'Leary offered, the old gentleman who helped me recalled learning the ballad of the Battle of Keimaneigh when he was a schoolboy. Later that afternoon, Joe Creedon sang a few stanzas with his fine tenor voice. O'Leary, "Battle of Keimaneigh," pp. 13–15; O'Leary, "Cath Cheim an Fhia," pp. 97–103. The

song, incidentally, was written by Máire Buidhe Ó Laoghaire, whose son participated in the fighting.

29. Garrett Cotter is mentioned in the County Cork Gaol Register, Department of Justice, Prisons, 1/8/2, entry 113 in 1822, INA. The letter from Magistrate John Savage was addressed to the Lord Lieutenant General of Ireland and is located in the State of the Country Papers, 2345/46, January 31, 1822, INA. For an incident that occurred the night after Savage's report, again involving a mysterious leader, perhaps the very same Cotter, see State of the Country Papers, 2343/3, letter dated February 1, 1822, from Major Carter to the chief secretary, Dublin.

30. On her stories about her father, see Ó Maidín, "Mother Jones Labor Agitator," p. 18. In searching for Harrises and Cotters, I carefully examined the following sources at the Irish National Archives: the State of the Country Papers, Cork City and County Gaol Registries, Convict Reference Books, the Registered Papers Index of the Chief Secretary's Office, Prisoners Petitions, and the Rebellion Papers. I would especially like to thank archivist Tom Quinlan and historian Michelle O'Neil for helping me in my search. It is impossible to disprove Mother Jones's contention that her father was involved in resistance, but if Richard Harris was a rebel, his name failed to show up in any of the major collections or registers in the Irish National Archives between 1830 and 1850.

31. Janet Nolan, *Ourselves Alone: Women's Emigration from Ireland, 1885–1920* (Lexington: University Press of Kentucky, 1989), pp. 23–25; Ó Tuathaigh, *Ireland before the Famine*, pp. 203–7; James S. Donnelly, Jr., *The Land and the People of Nineteenth-Century Cork* (London: Routledge and Kegan Paul, 1975), pp. 73–75.

32. Donnelly, *Land and People of Cork*, pp. 100–20; Miller, *Emigrants and Exiles*, pp. 280–90.

33. Miller, *Emigrants and Exiles*, pp. 286–91. James S. Donnelly, "Mass Eviction and the Great Famine"; Peter Gray, "Ideology and the Famine," Christine Kinealy, "The Role of the Poor Law during the Famine," and Mary E. Daly, "The Operations of Famine Relief, 1845–1847," all in Póirtéir, ed., *Great Irish Famine*, pp. 86–134, 155–73; R. Dudley Edwards and T. Desmond Williams, eds., *The Great Famine: Studies in Irish History* (Dublin: New York University Press, 1956), pp. 209–59.

34. Quotes from Ó Tuathaigh, *Ireland before the Famine*, p. 207; Donnelly, *Land and People of Cork*, pp. 86–91, 120–31; Miller, *Emigrants and Exiles*, pp. 284–85. Epidemics more than simple starvation killed the weakened victims; see Laurence M. Geary, "Famine, Fever, and the Bloody Flux," in Póirtéir, ed., *Great Irish Famine*, pp. 74–85; Sir William P. MacArthur, "Medical History of the Famine," in Edwards and Williams, eds., *Great Famine*, pp. 263–315.

35. Woodham-Smith, *The Great Hunger*, pp. 131, 159, 168, 186; Donnelly, *Land and People of Cork*, pp. 86–91.

36. Miller, *Emigrants and Exiles*, pp. 280–344; Ó Tuathaig, *Ireland before the Famine*, p. 206; Woodham-Smith, *The Great Hunger*, ch. 11; Nolan, *Ourselves Alone*, p. 24;

Donnelly, *Land and People of Cork*, pp. 120–31. An excellent overview is provided by Oliver MacDonagh, "Irish Emigration to the United States of America and the British Colonies during the Famine," in Edwards and Williams, eds., *Great Famine*, pp. 319–88.

37. Donnelly, *Land and People of Cork*, pp. 120–31.
38. Miller, *Emigrants and Exiles*, pp. 556–68.
39. Donnelly, "Mass Eviction," pp. 172–73; David Fitzpatrick, "Flight from Famine," in Póirtéir, ed., *Great Irish Famine*, p. 181. On working women in Cork, most of whom were employed in manufacturing or as domestics, see Murphy, "Economic and Social Structure," pp. 127–28.
40. Mother Jones, *Autobiography*, p. 11.
41. Journalists in the early twentieth century gave many versions of her story. They repeated that her father was an Irish patriot forced to flee his country; Mary's birth year was given variously between the late 1830s and early 1840s; some had her migrate with her father at age three; their point of disembarkation was variously given as Provincetown, Ottawa, Toronto, or Vermont; some said she attended convent schools rather than public schools; one said she taught in New England as well as Canada; a couple mentioned that her brother became a prominent priest in Canada. *Appeal to Reason*, November 17, 1900, from New York *World*; *Miners' Magazine*, November 1900, p. 28, from New York *World*; *Denver Republican*, August 11, 1901, p. 13; *Wilkes-Barre Record*, March 30, 1901; unspecified newspaper, story datelined New York, September 9, 1904; all in CUA, 7/3.4.
42. Federal Census of 1850, Vermont, Chittenden County, vol. 4, p. 295.
43. Eighteen forty-seven was the only year in which the numbers immigrating to British North America almost equaled those to the United States. One hundred thousand Irish landed in Canada in 1847, three to four times the average of later famine years; after 1847, the yearly total to the United States approached and even exceeded 200,000. Edwards and Williams, eds., *Great Famine*, pp. 368–76, 388.
44. Edwards and Williams, eds., *Great Famine*, pp. 362–66; Donald MacKay, *Flight from Famine: The Coming of the Irish to Canada* (Toronto: McClelland and Stewart, 1990), pp. 243–59; Terry Coleman, *Passage to America: A History of Emigrants from Great Britain and Ireland to America in the Mid-Nineteenth Century* (London: Hutchinson of London, 1972), pp. 128–54; Carl Frederick Wittke, *The Irish in America* (Baton Rouge: Louisiana State University Press, 1956), pp. 15–17.
45. The passenger, Steven Devere, is quoted in MacKay, *Flight from Famine*, pp. 266–78. On the voyage across, see Coleman, *Passage to America*, pp. 100–27; Miller, *Emigrants and Exiles*, pp. 291–92.
46. Edwards and Williams, eds., *Great Famine*, pp. 368–73; Miller, *Emigrants and Exiles*, pp. 315–16; MacKay, *Flight from Famine*, pp. 268–71.
47. Edwards and Williams, eds., *Great Famine*, pp. 371–73; Miller, *Emigrants and Exiles*, pp. 315–16. MacKay, *Flight from Famine*, pp. 272–94, is filled with descriptions of the voyage and arrival.

48. Miller, *Emigrants and Exiles*, pp. 317–18. According to Wittke, *Irish in America*, p. 51, immigrants sent home about $65 million, an amazing amount of money given that most laborers earned around a dollar a day. Also see Lawrence J. McCaffrey, *The Irish Diaspora in America* (Bloomington: Indiana University Press, 1976), p. 62.

49. Catherine and Ellen Harris were listed in the half-yearly returns of the separate schools for the unified wards of St. Andrews and St. George, January–June 1855, in Provincial Records of Ontario, record group 2, series F, 3F, box 1, PAO. On St. Mary's School, see *St. Mary's Hundred Birthdays, 1852–1952* (Toronto: St. Mary's Parish, 1952), p. 23, ARCAT. The career of William Harris is traced in Michael Power, "An Introduction to the Life and Work of Dean Harris, 1847–1923," in McGowan and Clarke, eds., *Catholics at the "Gathering Place,"* pp. 119–35, and in Robert J. Scollard, "Reverend William Richard Harris, 1846–1923," *Proceedings of the Forty-first Canadian Catholic Historical Association* (1974), pp. 65–80. Note that Harris's two biographers do not agree on the date of his birth. On school attendance, see Michael B. Katz, "Who Went to School?" in Michael B. Katz and Paul H. Mattingly, eds., *Education and Social Change: Themes from Ontario's Past* (New York: New York University Press, 1975), pp. 276–84.

50. Canadian Census, 1861, City of Toronto, Upper Canada, St. Patrick's Ward, District 4, reel C-1109, no. 84, p. 870, PAO. The census taker recorded Mary's name as Maria. Average household size in the west of Ireland before the famine, incidentally, was over six persons; Nolan, *Ourselves Alone*, p. 16.

51. Canadian Census, 1861, City of Toronto, Upper Canada, St. Patrick's Ward, District 4, reel C-1109, no. 84, p. 870, PAO; City of Toronto, Assessment Roll for the Ward of St. Patrick, 1861, reel GS6114, no. 1290, p. 61, and 1869, reel GS6154, no. 1589, pp. 75–76, PAO. Harris was listed as a milkman rather than a laborer beginning with the 1866 Toronto City Directory, so clearly the family was involved in dairying earlier than the tax rolls indicate. As of 1869, the total value of personal property in the Harris household was estimated by the assessor to be $150.

52. Thomas Hutchinson, comp., *Hutchinson's Toronto Directory, 1862–1863* (Toronto: Lovell and Gibson, 1863), p. 144; Brian P. Clarke, *Piety and Nationalism: Lay Voluntary Associations and the Creation of an Irish-Catholic Community in Toronto, 1850–1895* (Montreal: McGill-Queen's University Press, 1993), pp. 19–30.

53. Clarke, *Piety and Nationalism*, pp. 19–30.

54. See, for example, Charlotte Erikson, ed., *Emigration from Europe, 1815–1914* (London: Adam and Charles Black, 1976), pp. 9–13.

55. The Toronto context of these changes is nicely discussed in Gregory S. Kealey, "Toronto's Industrial Revolution, 1850–1892," in Michael S. Cross and Gregory S. Kealey, eds., *Canada's Age of Industry, 1849–1896* (Toronto: McClelland and Stewart, 1982), pp. 17–61; Michael Katz has contributed two important studies focused on Canada, *The People of Hamilton, Canada West: Family and Class in a*

Mid-Nineteenth-Century Town (Cambridge, Mass.: Harvard University Press, 1975), and, with Michael J. Doucet and Mark J. Stern, *The Social Organization of Early Industrial Capitalism* (Cambridge, Mass.: Harvard University Press, 1982). See also Bryan D. Palmer, *Working-Class Experience: Rethinking the History of Canadian Labour, 1800–1991* (Toronto: McClelland and Stewart, 1992), pp. 81–83. The list of works on this great transformation is endless, but some of the most prominent ones include Eric Hobsbawm, *The Age of Revolutions, 1789–1848* (London: Phoenix Press, 1962); Edward P. Thompson, *The Making of the English Working Class* (London: Penguin, 1991); Herbert Gutman, *Work, Culture, and Society in Industrializing America* (New York: Knopf, 1977); Sean Wilentz, *Chants Democratic: New York City and the Rise of the American Working Class* (New York: Oxford University Press, 1984).

56. Palmer, *Working-Class Experience*, pp. 87–89, 98–102 (quote unattributed in Palmer, p. 88). On the relative health and high pay of working-class immigrants, see William Forbes Adams, *Ireland and Irish Emigration to the New World* (New Haven, Conn.: Yale University Press, 1932), pp. 340–42. Gordon Darroch and Lee Soltow, *Property and Inequality in Victorian Ontario: Structural Patterns and Cultural Communities in the 1871 Census* (Toronto: University of Toronto Press, 1994), argue that the 1871 Ontario census reveals a pattern of widespread small property holding throughout the province. Also see Wittke, "The Irish in the Labor Movement," in *Irish in America*, ch. 20; Gregory S. Kealey, *Toronto Workers Respond to Industrial Capitalism, 1867–1892* (Toronto: University of Toronto Press, 1980), pp. 3–9, 18–22; Frederick H. Armstrong, *City in the Making: Progress, People, and Perils in Victorian Toronto* (Toronto: Dundurn Press, 1988), pp. 49–57, 251–54; G.P.deT. Glazebrook, *The Story of Toronto* (Toronto: University of Toronto Press, 1971), pp. 95–113.

57. Peter Goheen, *Victorian Toronto, 1850–1900: Pattern and Process of Growth* (Chicago: University of Chicago Department of Geography Research Paper No. 127, 1970), pp. 54–57, 78, 141–54; Gregory S. Kealey, "The Orange Order in Toronto: Religious Riot and the Working Class," in Gregory S. Kealey and Peter Warrian, eds., *Essays in Canadian Working Class History* (Toronto: McClelland and Stewart, 1976), pp. 13–40; MacKay, *Flight from Famine*, pp. 307, 325–26; Miller, *Emigrants and Exiles*, pp. 315, 322–25; Clarke, *Piety and Nationalism*, pp. 14–17, 42–44, 154–55.

58. MacKay, *Flight from Famine*, pp. 332–34; Miller, *Emigrants and Exiles*, pp. 322–28; Clarke, *Piety and Nationalism*, pp. 153–67, from which the *Globe*, September 6, 1855, August 7, 1857, February 13, 1856, is quoted.

59. This is the central thesis of Miller's magisterial *Emigrants and Exiles*, esp. pp. 102–30, 312–13, 556–68; also see Kerby Miller, "Paddy's Paradox: Emigration to America in Irish Imagination and Rhetoric," in Dirk Hoerder and Horst Rossler, eds., *Distant Magnets: Expectations and Realities in the Immigrant Experience, 1840–1930* (New York: Holmes and Meier, 1993), pp. 264–93; and Nolan, *Ourselves Alone*, pp. 27–28.

60. On Irish nationalism in America, see Lawrence J. McCaffrey, *Textures of Irish*

America (Syracuse, N.Y.: Syracuse University Press, 1992), pp. 133–51; Miller, *Emigrants and Exiles*, pp. 335–44; Wittke, *Irish in America*, pp. 150–60.

61. Emmet Larkin, "The Devotional Revolution in Ireland, 1850–1875," *American Historical Review* 77, no. 3 (June 1972), pp. 625–52; Miller, *Emigrants and Exiles*, pp. 331–34.

62. Clarke, *Piety and Nationalism*, pp. 5–11, 31–32, 152–67; also see Brian P. Clarke, "Lay Nationalism in Victorian Toronto," in McGowan and Clarke, eds., *Catholics at the "Gathering Place,"* pp. 43–48.

63. Clarke, *Piety and Nationalism*, pp. 62–74, 78–89.

64. Ibid., pp. 66–74.

65. See Jeroslav Pelikan, *Mary through the Centuries: Her Place in the History of Culture* (New Haven, Conn.: Yale University Press, 1996).

66. On pre-famine Irish women, see Nolan, *Ourselves Alone*, pp. 29–36; for women in Canada, see Bettina Bradbury, "The Home as Workplace," in Paul Craven, ed., *Laboring Lives: Work and Workers in Nineteenth-Century Ontario* (Toronto: University of Toronto Press, 1995), pp. 412–76; and Bettina Bradbury, "The Fragmented Family: Family Strategies in the Face of Death, Illness, and Poverty, Montreal, 1860–1891," in Bonnie J. Fox, ed., *Family Patterns, Gender Relations* (Toronto: Oxford University Press, 1993), pp. 87–113.

67. Registration list of students for Toronto Normal School, 1847–1859, record group 2, series H.1, vol. 10, records for the nineteenth and twentieth sessions, PAO. On Irish women and work, see Hasia Diner, *Erin's Daughters in America: Irish Immigrant Women in the Nineteenth Century* (Baltimore: Johns Hopkins University Press, 1983); and Nolan, *Ourselves Alone*, pp. 26–42.

68. These themes are well discussed in Katz and Mattingly, eds., *Education and Social Change*, especially Susan E. Houston, "Politics and Social Change in Upper Canada," pp. 34–46; Peter N. Ross, "The Free School Controversy in Toronto, 1848–1852," pp. 64–65; Haley P. Bamman, "Patterns of School Attendance in Toronto, 1844–1878: Some Spatial Considerations," pp. 217–18.

69. Clarke, *Piety and Nationalism*, pp. 39–41; Bamman, "Patterns of School Attendance," pp. 226–31.

70. Alison Prentice, *The School Promoters: Education and Social Class in Mid-Nineteenth-Century Upper Canada* (Ontario: Oxford University Press, 1999); Alison Prentice, " 'Friendly Atoms in Chemistry': Women and Men at Normal School in Mid-Nineteenth-Century Toronto," in David Keane and Colin Rad, eds., *Old Ontario: Essays in Honour of J.M.S. Careless* (Toronto: Dundurn Press, 1990), pp. 285–317; Donna Varga Heise, "Gender Differentiated Teacher Training: The Toronto Normal School, 1847–1902" (master's thesis, University of Toronto, 1987).

71. Superintendent of Education, *Annual Report of the Normal, Model, Grammar, and Common Schools, in Upper Canada* (Toronto, 1858, 1859; Quebec, 1860); *Toronto Normal School Jubilee Celebration* (Toronto, 1898), pp. 41–47; Prentice, " 'Friendly Atoms,' " pp. 294–311.

72. Superintendent of Education, *Annual Report* (1858, 1859, 1860); Prentice, " 'Friendly Atoms,' " pp. 294–311; Nolan, *Ourselves Alone*, pp. 38–42.

73. Diner, *Erin's Daughters*, pp. 15–17. Diner, pp. 18, 67–69, incidentally, points out that mothers more commonly than fathers were singled out in the memoirs of prominent Irish Americans, so Mother Jones's totally ignoring her mother was unusual.

74. Although *Ourselves Alone* is primarily about the late nineteenth and early twentieth centuries, Nolan demonstrates a pattern of independence among Irish women—in their work lives and migration patterns—that applied to many of the famine immigrants as well.

2. Mary Jones

1. Mother Jones, *The Autobiography of Mother Jones*, ed. Mary Field Parton (Chicago: Charles H. Kerr and Company, 1925), pp. 11–12.

2. Talcott E. Wing, ed., *History of Monroe County, Michigan* (New York: Munsell and Company, 1890), pp. 519–20; Sister M. Rosalita, *No Greater Service: The History of the Congregation of the Sisters, Servants of the Immaculate Heart of Mary, Monroe, Michigan, 1845–1945* (Detroit, Mich.: IHM, 1948), pp. 106–7, 123, 240.

3. Hasia Diner, *Erin's Daughters in America: Irish Immigrant Women in the Nineteenth Century* (Baltimore: Johns Hopkins University Press, 1983), pp. 139–41, 150–51; Janet Nolan, *Ourselves Alone: Women's Emigration from Ireland, 1885–1920* (Lexington: University Press of Kentucky, 1989), pp. 12–13; Mother Jones, *Autobiography*, pp. 11–12; International Genealogical Index, 1993 ed., North America, Marriage, December 1860, Memphis, Shelby County, Tennessee, George E. Jones and Mary Harris. The original source of this IGI information is not given. There is no marriage license record for George and Mary in Bettie B. Davis, comp., *Shelby County Tennessee Marriage Bonds and Licenses, 1850–1865* (Memphis, Tenn.: printed privately by Richard Harris, 1983).

4. Kathleen C. Berkeley, *"Like a Plague of Locusts": From an Antebellum Town to a New South City, Memphis, Tennessee, 1850–1880* (New York: Garland, 1991), p. 16; John H. Ellis, *Yellow Fever and Public Health in the New South* (Lexington: University Press of Kentucky, 1992), pp. 16–19; Gerald M. Capers, *The Biography of a River Town: Memphis, Its Heroic Age* (Chapel Hill: University of North Carolina Press, 1939), pp. 106–8, 134; Robert Alan Sigafoos, *Cotton Row to Beale Street: A Business History of Memphis* (Memphis, Tenn.: Memphis State University Press, 1979), pp. 38–39.

5. For a survey of the rise of Southern cities, see Howard N. Rabinowitz, "Continuity and Change: Southern Urban Development, 1860–1900," in Blaine A. Brownell and David R. Goldfield, eds., *The City in Southern History: The Growth of Urban Civilization in the South* (Port Washington, N.Y.: Kennikat Press, 1977), pp. 92–101; Sigafoos, *Cotton Row to Beale Street*, p. 35. For a more detailed look at the growth of Memphis, see Russell S. Kirby, "Urban Growth and Economic

Change in the Nineteenth Century South: The Hinterland of Memphis, Tennessee, 1830–1900" (Ph.D. diss., University of Wisconsin, 1981). Also see Berkeley, *"Like a Plague,"* pp. 54–55; Ellis, *Yellow Fever,* pp. 15–16.

6. Carl Frederick Wittke, *The Irish in America* (Baton Rouge: Louisiana State University Press, 1956), pp. 24, 32–37; Kerby Miller, *Emigrants and Exiles: Ireland and the Irish Exodus to North America* (New York: Oxford University Press, 1985), pp. 313–22; William M. Stanton, "The Irish of Memphis," *West Tennessee Historical Society Papers* 6 (1952), pp. 87–118; Sterling Tracey, "The Immigrant Population of Memphis," *West Tennessee Historical Society Papers* 4 (1950), pp. 72–82.

7. Berkeley, *"Like a Plague,"* pp. 32–33; Capers, *Biography of a River Town,* pp. 106–7, 111, 115–17; Ellis, *Yellow Fever,* pp. 19–22.

8. Lee N. Newcomer, "The Battle of Memphis, 1862," *West Tennessee Historical Society Papers* 12 (1958), pp. 41–57; Berkeley, *"Like a Plague,"* pp. 74–75; Capers, *Biography of a River Town,* pp. 136–38; Charles W. Crawford, *Yesterday's Memphis* (Miami, Fla.: E. A. Seemann, 1976), pp. 29–36.

9. Deegee Lester, "The Memphis Riots of 1866," *Eire-Ireland* 30, no. 3 (Fall 1995), pp. 59–66; Capers, *Biography of a River Town,* p. 164; Berkeley, *"Like a Plague,"* p. 107; Sigafoos, *Cotton Row to Beale Street,* p. 50. Also see David R. Roediger, *The Wages of Whiteness: Race and the Making of the American Working Class* (New York: Verso, 1991).

10. Lester, "The Memphis Riots," pp. 60–69, gives the best account of the rioting. For eyewitness testimony, see U.S. House of Representatives, Report of the Select Committee, *Memphis Riots and Massacres* (Washington, D.C.: Government Printing Office, 1866). For an account sympathetic to the white South, see Jack D. L. Holmes, "The Effects of the Memphis Race Riot of 1866," in *West Tennessee Historical Society Papers* 12 (1958), pp. 58–79. Also see Berkeley, *"Like a Plague,"* pp. 124–25; Capers, *Biography of a River Town,* pp. 177–79, 183; Crawford, *Yesterday's Memphis,* pp. 36–39; Sigafoos, *Cotton Row to Beale Street,* pp. 39, 45–47; Shields McIlwaine, *Memphis Down in Dixie* (New York: Dutton, 1948), pp. 149–55. The accounts by Capers and McIlwaine, incidentally, are tinged with stereotypical depictions of African Americans.

11. Jones is listed in the Memphis City Directory, 1865, p. 88, and Memphis City Directory, 1866, p. 66, both in SCPL; Diner, *Erin's Daughters,* pp. 96–101; Jonathan Grossman, *William Sylvis, Pioneer of American Labor* (New York: Columbia University Press, 1945), pp. 22–44. On Irish community structure, see Berkeley, *"Like a Plague,"* pp. 138–39.

12. Memphis Directory, 1865, pp. 88, 150; Memphis Directory, 1866, p. 56, both in SCPL; Grossman, *William Sylvis,* pp. 22–44; Berkeley, *"Like a Plague,"* p. 55.

13. Grossman, *William Sylvis,* pp. 45–80; David Montgomery, *Beyond Equality: Labor and the Radical Republicans, 1862–1872* (Urbana: University of Illinois Press, 1972), pp. 202–3, 228–29, 444–47. Also on Sylvis, see David Montgomery, "William H. Sylvis and the Search for Working Class Citizenship," in Melvyn Dubofsky and Warren Van Tine, eds., *Labor Leaders in America* (Urbana: Uni-

versity of Illinois Press, 1987); James C. Sylvis, *The Life, Speeches, Labors, and Essays of William H. Sylvis* (Philadelphia: Green, Remsen, and Haffelfinger, 1872).

14. Grossman, *William Sylvis*, pp. 78–80, 84–87, 122–31.

15. In a few newspaper stories published around 1900, Mary Jones mentioned that her husband's membership in the Iron Molders Union had a major impact on her. See especially *Boston Herald*, September 11, 1904, pp. 1, 3, in CUA.

16. Grossman, *William Sylvis*, pp. 84–151; Montgomery, *Beyond Equality*, pp. 176–85, 229. Also see Charlotte Todes, *William H. Sylvis and the National Labor Union* (New York: International Publishers, 1992).

17. Most Irish women gave up their jobs when they married; Diner, *Erin's Daughters*, pp. 54–55. The children's names are listed under births to George E. Jones and Mary Harris, International Genealogical Index, 1993 ed., North America; it is unclear how the IGI got these names and dates. I have found no manuscript sources recording the presence of the Jones children in Memphis or Shelby County, with one exception—the parish registry for St. Mary's Church for January 27, 1867, has an entry for the youngest child, Mary Jones (Marriam in the Latinate spelling of the register), born to Mary Frances Jones and George Jones on January 18, 1867. Samuel Tighe is listed as godfather, Mary Murphy as godmother; the Reverend Cornelius Thoma presided at the event. My thanks to Cheryl Williams and Father Maury Smith of St. Mary's for their help unearthing this information. St. Mary's Parish was established in 1860, but the church building was not dedicated until 1870, and the parish register is quite incomplete—some of 1862 is missing, all of 1863, and most of 1864, so it is possible that more Jones children were baptized there. The only other Catholic church in Memphis when the Jones family lived there was St. Peter's, and the Joneses do not appear in that parish registry. The history of St. Mary's is contained in Brother Joel William McGraw, F.S.C., Reverend Milton J. Guthrie, and Mrs. Josephine King, *Between the Rivers: The Catholic Heritage of West Tennessee* (Memphis, Tenn.: Catholic Diocese of Memphis, 1996), pp. 15–17.

18. Memphis Directory, 1865, p. 150, in SCPL; Ellis, *Yellow Fever*, pp. 26–29; Capers, *Biography of a River Town*, pp. 187–89; McGraw, Guthrie, and King, *Between the Rivers*, pp. 16–17. St. Mary's Parish when the Joneses lived in the neighborhood was a mixture of Germans and Irish, with an Italian immigrant as pastor.

19. Grossman, *William Sylvis*, pp. 166–88. The monthly reports of "subordinate unions" (locals) carried in the *Iron Molders' International Journal* 4 (1867) indicated that trade was dull throughout the year in Memphis and that by October there were only twenty-one members left in the local since many had been suspended for not paying dues.

20. Ellis, *Yellow Fever*, pp. 30–32; Khaled J. Bloom, *The Mississippi Valley's Great Yellow Fever Epidemic of 1878* (Baton Rouge: Louisiana State University Press, 1993), pp. 2–3, 22, 30–31; Jo Ann Carrigan, "Yellow Fever: Scourge of the South," in Todd Savitt and James Harvey Young, eds., *Disease and Distinctiveness in the American South* (Knoxville: University of Tennessee Press, 1988), pp. 55–64.

21. Memphis *Appeal*, September 7, 1867, p. 1, September 8, 1867, p. 4; Patricia La-Pointe, "The Disrupted Years: Memphis City Hospitals, 1860–1867," *West Tennessee Historical Society Papers* 37 (December 1983), pp. 27–28; Bloom, *Great Yellow Fever Epidemic*, pp. 10–11, 39; Capers, *Biography of a River Town*, pp. 188–92; Carrigan, "Yellow Fever," p. 64; Ellis, *Yellow Fever*, pp. 30–32. J. M. Keating, *A History of the Yellow Fever Epidemic of 1878* (Memphis, Tenn.: Howard Association, 1879), pp. 134–35, guesses at a death toll in 1867 of about 250, certainly an underestimate. In 1878, by contrast, 17,000 cases resulted in 5,000 deaths.

22. Bloom, *Great Yellow Fever Epidemic*, pp. 5–9.

23. Ibid.; Dale Fetherling, *Mother Jones: The Miners' Angel* (Carbondale: Southern Illinois University Press, 1974), p. 4. The long quote describes a patient in the 1878 epidemic and is taken from John F. Cochran, "Observations on Yellow Fever at Bartlett, Tenn.," *Richmond and Louisville Medical Journal* 27 (1879), p. 13, quoted in Bloom, *Great Yellow Fever Epidemic*, pp. 8–9. For precautions against the disease, see "To Yellow Fever Patients," *Memphis Daily Appeal*, October 17, 1867, p. 4. Memphis newspapers were filled with information, advice, even lectures on the history and progress of the disease. Jubilation greeted the winter season, which generally ended yellow fever epidemics. "The frost, the frost, the beautiful frost . . ." began a front-page story in *The Daily Memphis Avalanche* on November 1, 1867, under the title "Heavy Frost—Disease Disappearing."

24. Mother Jones, *Autobiography*, p. 12. The Register of Shelby County Death Records, 1848–1901, file 10938, p. 208, SCPL, lists George Jones as a white male, aged thirty-two, who died on October 13, 1867. Different versions of the death of Mary Jones's family were told over the years. Sometimes it was said George Jones was a miner; the number of her children was variously given as between one and four. *The Wilkes-Barre Record*, March 30, 1901, in CUA, 7/2.5, for example, told how her whole family died within a month but gave yellow fever as the cause of George's death and diphtheria as the killer of her four children. An unidentified article dated September 9, 1904, in CUA, 7/3.4, claimed that the Joneses had two children.

25. Shelby County Death Records do not mention any of the Jones children, nor is the family listed in the Canale Funeral Home records, in SCPL, which did most of the Catholic funerals in Memphis. Records for St. Peter's and Calvary cemeteries are very fragmentary, and St. Mary's Parish did not keep death records between August 1866 and December 1868. Given her remark in the *Autobiography* that the dead "were buried at night quickly and without ceremony," it is possible that the family was interred in a potter's field.

26. *Iron Molders' International Journal* 4, no. 9 (October 1867), p. 165.

27. Mother Jones, *Autobiography*, p. 12. The epidemic ended in early December, so for two months or so, Mary Jones did volunteer work, probably with the Howard Association, a recently formed organization dedicated to helping victims of such disasters.

28. Mother Jones, *Autobiography*, pp. 12–13.

29. Ibid., p. 13.

30. Ibid., pp. 12–13; *Edwards' Chicago Directory, 1871* (Chicago: R. Edwards, 1871).

31. Diner, *Erin's Daughters*, pp. 70–75; Miller, *Emigrants and Exiles*, pp. 318–19. On Chicago as the fulcrum for economic development in the nation's interior, see William Cronon's outstanding *Nature's Metropolis: Chicago and the Great West* (New York: Norton, 1991). Also see Harold M. Mayer and Richard C. Wade, *Chicago: Growth of a Metropolis* (Chicago: University of Chicago Press, 1969); Bessie Louise Pierce, *A History of Chicago*, 3 vols. (Chicago: University of Chicago Press, 1937–1957); Donald L. Miller, *City of the Century: The Epic of Chicago and the Making of America* (New York: Simon and Schuster, 1996).

32. Karen Sawislak, *Smoldering City: Chicagoans and the Great Fire, 1871–1874* (Chicago: University of Chicago Press, 1995), pp. 8–14. On Chicago's ethnic diversity, see Melvin G. Holli and Peter d'Alroy Jones, eds., *Ethnic Chicago* (Grand Rapids, Mich.: Eerdmans Publishing, 1981); for daily life in the city, see Perry Duis, *Challenging Chicago: Coping with Everyday Life, 1837–1920* (Urbana: University of Illinois Press, 1998); on the Chicago Irish, see Lawrence J. McCaffrey et al., *The Irish in Chicago* (Urbana: University of Illinois Press, 1987); for development of Chicago society, see Robin Einhorn, *Property Rules: Political Economy in Chicago, 1833–1872* (Chicago: University of Chicago Press, 1991); on Chicago neighborhoods, see Dominic Pacyga and Ellen Skerrett, *Chicago: City of Neighborhoods* (Chicago: Loyola University Press, 1986).

33. The sources on the great fire are numerous, but two very fine recent works are Carl Smith, *Urban Disorder and the Shape of Belief: The Great Chicago Fire, the Haymarket Bomb, and the Model Town of Pullman* (Chicago: University of Chicago Press, 1995), part 1; and Sawislak, *Smoldering City*. Also see Miller, *City of the Century*, pp. 143–71; David Lowe, ed., *The Great Chicago Fire* (New York: Dover, 1979); Ross Miller, *American Apocalypse: The Great Fire and the Myth of Chicago* (Chicago: University of Chicago Press, 1990).

34. Mother Jones, *Autobiography*, pp. 13–14.

35. Sawislak, *Smoldering City*, pp. 44–47, 90–100; Smith, *Urban Disorder*, pp. 34–63.

36. Sawislak, *Smoldering City*, pp. 203–7, 215–16, 262–63.

37. Mother Jones, *Autobiography*, pp. 13–14.

38. Terence Powderly, *The Path I Trod: The Autobiography of Terence V. Powderly*, ed. Harry J. Carman, Henry David, and Paul Guthrie (New York: Columbia University Press, 1940), p. 45; Fetherling, *Mother Jones*, pp. 10–11; Craig Phelan, *Grand Master Workman: Terence Powderly and the Knights of Labor* (Westport, Conn.: Greenwood Press, 2000), pp. 154–56; Leon Fink, *Workingmen's Democracy: The Knights of Labor and American Politics* (Urbana: University of Illinois Press, 1983), pp. 3–15.

39. Mother Jones, *Autobiography*, pp. 14–23.

40. Events leading up to the railroad strike of 1877 and the strike itself are nicely described in Herbert Gutman et al., *Who Built America? Working People and the*

Nation's Economy, Politics, Culture, and Society, vol. 1 (New York: Pantheon Books, 1989), pp. 545–58; "Reverend Henry Ward Beecher Condemns the Strike," *New York Times*, July 23, 1877.

41. Paul Avrich, *The Haymarket Tragedy* (Princeton, N.J.: Princeton University Press, 1984), pp. 15–25, gives an exceptional description of these events. Also see Eric L. Hirsch, *Urban Revolt: Ethnic Politics in the Nineteenth-Century Chicago Labor Movement* (Berkeley: University of California Press, 1990), pp. 20–23; Smith, *Urban Disorder*, pp. 101–11.

42. See especially Philip Foner, *The Great Labor Uprising of 1877* (New York: Monad Press, 1977); Richard Schneirov, "Chicago's Great Upheaval of 1877," *Chicago History* 9 (Spring 1980), pp. 3–17; Robert V. Bruce, *1877: Year of Violence* (Chicago: Quadrangle Books, 1970), pp. 237–53; Jeremy Brecher, *Strike* (Boston: South End Press, 1997); David O. Stowell, *Streets, Railroads, and the Great Strike of 1877* (Chicago: University of Chicago Press, 1999).

43. Mother Jones, *Autobiography*, pp. 14–16. Eugene Debs found the strike threatening to his concept of working-class citizenship and manhood, which in turn were rooted in his faith in a harmony of interests between capital and labor. Only later, after becoming a Socialist, did he claim that he had supported the strike. See Nick Salvatore, *Eugene Debs: Citizen and Socialist* (Urbana: University of Illinois Press, 1982), pp. 32–38.

44. Hirsch, *Urban Revolt*, pp. 23–31.

45. Brecher, *Strike*, pp. 9–22; Foner, *Great Labor Uprising*, pp. 203–30; Schneirov, "Chicago's Great Upheaval of 1877," pp. 3–17; Bruce, *1877*, pp. 237–53.

46. Avrich, *Haymarket Tragedy*, pp. 26–38; Smith, *Urban Disorder*, pp. 101–11.

47. Mother Jones, *Autobiography*, pp. 17–23; Avrich, *Haymarket Tragedy*, pp. 39–79, 87–89. On the Knights of Labor, see Kim Voss, *The Making of American Exceptionalism* (Ithaca, N.Y.: Cornell University Press, 1993).

48. Avrich, *Haymarket Tragedy*, pp. 89–98, 160–77; Hirsch, *Urban Revolt*, p. xiv; also see Bruce C. Nelson, *Beyond the Martyrs: A Social History of Chicago's Anarchists, 1870–1900* (New Brunswick, N.J.: Rutgers University Press, 1988); Henry David, *A History of the Haymarket Affair: A Study in the American Social-Revolutionary and Labor Movements* (New York: Farrar and Rinehart, 1936); David Roediger and Franklin Rosemont, eds., *The Haymarket Scrapbook* (Chicago: Charles Kerr Co., 1986).

49. Avrich, *Haymarket Tragedy*, pp. 181–87; *Chicago Mail*, May 1, 1886, is quoted in Avrich, p. 187. Also see David, *History of Haymarket*, pp. 157–97.

50. Avrich, *Haymarket Tragedy*, pp. 197–214.

51. Ibid., pp. 215–24; David, *History of Haymarket*, pp. 206–35.

52. Hirsch, *Urban Revolt*, pp. 73–80. Also see Voss, *American Exceptionalism*, pp. 231–49.

53. Mother Jones, *Autobiography*, pp. 18–22.

54. Ibid., pp. 22–23.

55. There is a hint that Mary Jones might have spent time in Toronto after her fa-

ther passed away. A Maria Jones showed up in the Toronto City Directory for 1869. On Europe and San Francisco, see "About Mother Jones," *Wilkes-Barre Record*, March 30, 1901, from *Scranton Republican*; Dorothy Adams, "Through West Virginia with Mother Jones," *Denver Republican*, August 11, 1901, p. 13; *Boston Herald*, September 11, 1904, pp. 1, 3. The *Boston Herald* story said she spent five years in San Francisco. Some accounts of her California years claimed that she got to know and work for Mrs. George Pullman, the wife of the millionaire manufacturer of railroad cars, and that the two women developed great respect for each other despite their class differences. San Francisco's Working-Men's Party, including its leader, Dennis Kearney, was heavily Irish, and it became far more concerned with anti-Chinese nativism than with socialism.

56. Hirsch, *Urban Revolt*, pp. 127–41; Miller, *Emigrants and Exiles*, pp. 332–44; Lawrence J. McCaffrey, *Textures of Irish America* (Syracuse, N.Y.: Syracuse University Press, 1992), pp. 140–51; Michael F. Funchion, "Irish Chicago: Church, Homeland, Politics, and Class—the Shaping of an Ethnic Group, 1870–1900," in Holli and Jones, eds., *Ethnic Chicago*, pp. 9–22, 25–29. Matthew Frye Jacobson argues for a bond between immigrant nationalism and labor organizing in *Special Sorrows: Irish-, Polish-, and Yiddish-American Nationalism and the Diasporic Imagination* (Cambridge, Mass.: Harvard University Press, 1995).

57. We know from some of her early-twentieth-century correspondence that Mary Jones worked with the Chicago Socialist Thomas J. Morgan in the 1890s trying to elect candidates to local office. See Edward M. Steel, ed., *The Correspondence of Mother Jones* (Pittsburgh, Pa.: University of Pittsburgh Press, 1985), p. xxiv.

58. Mother Jones, *Autobiography*, pp. 11–23.

59. The mutability of identity is a central theme of Chicago-based fiction; see Carl Smith, *Chicago and the American Literary Imagination, 1880–1920* (Chicago: University of Chicago Press, 1984).

60. Cronon, *Nature's Metropolis*, pp. 97–259. On daily life in the city, see Duis, *Challenging Chicago*.

3. Mother Jones

1. *Chicago Evening Journal*, June 21, 1897, p. 1, in Annals of Labor and Industry, CHS; Fred Thompson, "Notes on 'The Most Dangerous Woman in America,' " in Mother Jones, *The Autobiography of Mother Jones*, ed. Mary Field Parton (Chicago: Charles H. Kerr and Company, 1990), p. 260; Nick Salvatore, *Eugene Debs: Citizen and Socialist* (Urbana: University of Illinois Press, 1982), pp. 163–69.

2. Dorothy Adams, "Through West Virginia with Mother Jones," *Denver Republican*, August 11, 1901, p. 13; *National Labor Tribune*, August 26, 1897, quoted in *Pittsburgh Press*, January 20, 1974, in CUA; Thompson, "Notes," p. 261.

3. There are no extant speeches, letters, or writings of Mary Jones before 1900. Just as the persona Mother Jones appeared rather suddenly, so too does the evidence of her life. For the biographer, her papers are rather scant. Roughly two hundred letters (both to and from her) survive, as well as about three dozen full speeches and a dozen or so short essays. Edward M. Steel edited critical editions of her work, and my research indicates that he found all but a few items. See his *The Speeches and Writings of Mother Jones* (Pittsburgh, Pa.: University of Pittsburgh Press, 1988), and *The Correspondence of Mother Jones* (Pittsburgh, Pa.: University of Pittsburgh Press, 1985). Philip Foner got most of the same material, as well as a few other items, in his *Mother Jones Speaks* (New York: Monad Press, 1983). Beyond these materials, there is Mother Jones's *Autobiography*, the correspondence and memoirs of those whom she knew, much newspaper and magazine coverage of her life, and lots of manuscript materials scattered in various archives and historical societies. For the sake of availability to readers, I refer to Steel's critical editions of her letters, speeches, and writings wherever possible.

4. *Locomotive Firemen's Magazine* 9 (September 1885), p. 547.

5. On Mrs. Jones, see *Railroad Brakemen's Journal* 4 (July 1887), p. 298.

6. On the world of late-nineteenth-century labor, see Salvatore, *Eugene Debs*, pp. 23–82; Melvyn Dubofsky, *Industrialism and the American Worker, 1865–1920* (New York: Harlan Davidson, 1985), pp. 29–71; Bruce Laurie, *Artisans into Workers* (New York: Hill and Wang, 1989), pp. 113–75; Alice Kessler-Harris, *Out to Work: A History of Wage-Earning Women in the United States* (New York: Oxford University Press, 1982), pp. 75–179; David Montgomery, *The Fall of the House of Labor: The Workplace, the State, and American Labor Activism, 1865–1925* (New York: Cambridge University Press, 1987), pp. 9–170; Leon Fink, *Workingmen's Democracy: The Knights of Labor and American Politics* (Urbana: University of Illinois Press, 1983).

7. See, for example, *Railroad Brakemen's Journal* 4 (August 1887), p. 378.

8. Ladies Department, *Railroad Brakemen's Journal* 4 (December 1887), p. 548.

9. "The Dream" appeared in *Railroad Brakemen's Journal* 4 (August 1887), pp. 356–57. On the culture of the song poems, see Clark Halker, *For Democracy, Workers, and God: Labor Song Poems and Labor Protest, 1865–1895* (Urbana: University of Illinois Press, 1991), pp. 36–39, 170–72. My thanks to Clark Halker for telling me about the first Mother Jones.

10. Salvatore, *Eugene Debs*, pp. 88–177.

11. Halker, *For Democracy*, pp. 192–94, 205–9.

12. For a fine discussion of the relationship between the AFL and the Knights of Labor, see Craig Phelan, *Grand Master Workman: Terence Powderly and the Knights of Labor* (Westport, Conn.: Greenwood Press, 2000), pp. 241–48.

13. Salvatore, *Eugene Debs*, pp. 88–177. The changes in work and culture during this era have been the subject of many works, but particularly helpful are David Montgomery, *Workers' Control in America* (New York: Cambridge University

Press, 1979); Montgomery, *Fall of the House of Labor*; Dubofsky, *Industrialism and the American Worker*; Laurie, *Artisans into Workers*; and Herbert Gutman, *Work, Culture, and Society in Industrializing America* (New York: Knopf, 1977).

14. On producer ideology, see Fink, *Workingmen's Democracy*, pp. 3–17; Salvatore, *Eugene Debs*, pp. 23–82; Kim Voss, *The Making of American Exceptionalism* (Ithaca, N.Y.: Cornell University Press, 1993), pp. 72–101.

15. Adams, "Through West Virginia," p. 13.

16. Carlos A. Schwantes, *Coxey's Army: An American Odyssey* (Lincoln: University of Nebraska Press, 1985), pp. 13–16, 129.

17. In addition to Edward Bellamy, *Looking Backward*, and Henry Demarest Lloyd, *Wealth against Commonwealth*, see John Thomas's excellent commentary on these and related works, *Alternative America: Henry George, Edward Bellamy, Henry Demarest Lloyd, and the Adversary Tradition* (Cambridge, Mass.: Harvard University Press, 1983). Bellamy, incidentally, imagined his utopia without class conflict; the good sense of everybody, not a struggle for power, leads to socialism in *Looking Backward*.

18. Schwantes, *Coxey's Army*, pp. 34–132.

19. *Wilkes-Barre Record*, March 30, 1901, from *Scranton Republican*, Mother Jones Papers, CUA.

20. Schwantes, *Coxey's Army*, pp. 261–71. The movement of the army was covered in *The Kansas City Star*, June 10–18, 1894.

21. *Chicago Tribune*, April 24, 1894, p. 5, in Annals of Labor and Industry, CHS; Robert David Ward and William Warren Rogers, *Labor Revolt in Alabama: The Great Strike of 1894* (University: University of Alabama Press, 1965), esp. pp. 104–7. The apparent solidarity of black and white miners was always fragile and fraught with contradictions; see Daniel Letwin, *The Challenge of Interracial Unionism: Alabama Coal Miners, 1878–1921* (Chapel Hill: University of North Carolina Press, 1998); Alex Lichtenstein, "Racial Conflict and Racial Solidarity in the Alabama Coal Strike of 1894: New Evidence for the Gutman-Hill Debate," *Labor History* 36 (Winter 1995), pp. 63–76.

22. Salvatore, *Eugene Debs*, pp. 88–146; Ward and Rogers, *Labor Revolt*, pp. 104–7.

23. Ward and Rogers, *Labor Revolt*, pp. 104–7; Mother Jones, *Autobiography*, pp. 115–19.

24. Mother Jones, *Autobiography*, pp. 115–17; Thompson, "Notes," p. 260; Ward and Rogers, *Labor Revolt*, pp. 18–23, 63–74, 92–93, 104–13; Debs quoted in the *Appeal to Reason*, May 24, 1913, p. 4.

25. Salvatore, *Eugene Debs*, pp. 147–77.

26. Steel, introduction to *Correspondence*, pp. xxiv–xxv. Mother Jones also claimed that she witnessed the battle between Pinkerton detectives and striking steelworkers at Homestead, Pennsylvania, in 1892; her story lacks details. On populism, see Lawrence Goodwyn, *Democratic Promise: The Populist Moment in America* (New York: Oxford University Press, 1976).

27. Mother Jones to Caroline Lloyd, April 27, 1913, in Steel, ed., *Correspondence*, p.

111; Howard H. Quint, *The Forging of American Socialism: Origins of the Modern Movement* (Columbia: University of South Carolina Press, 1953), pp. 210–46; Goodwyn, *Democratic Promise*, pp. 470–514.

28. Elliott Shore, *Talkin' Socialism: J. A. Wayland and the Role of the Press in American Radicalism, 1890–1912* (Lawrence: University Press of Kansas, 1988), pp. 7–31. Still a useful work is Donald Drew Egbert and Stow Persons, eds., *Socialism and American Life*, 2 vols. (Princeton, N.J.: Princeton University Press, 1952).

29. Quint, *Forging of American Socialism*, pp. 175–81. On western radicalism, see David Brundage, *The Making of Western Labor Radicalism* (Champaign: University of Illinois Press, 1994).

30. Shore, *Talkin' Socialism*, pp. 29–35.

31. Ibid., pp. 58–73. Mother Jones recalled thirty years later in the *Autobiography*, p. 28, her belief that individuals jockeying for power would tear the colony apart. Besides, utopian communities usually had religious foundations, and by the late 1890s, she had come to believe that the labor movement must be its own religion.

32. Mother Jones, *Autobiography*, pp. 28–29; Shore, *Talkin' Socialism*, pp. 75–93. According to Wayland's biographer, Mother Jones's account of the *Appeal to Reason*'s beginning is the only one that survives.

33. Jack London cited in John Graham, ed., *"Yours for the Revolution": The "Appeal to Reason," 1895–1922* (Lincoln: University of Nebraska Press, 1990), pp. ix, 8–12; Dale Fetherling, *Mother Jones: The Miners' Angel* (Carbondale: Southern Illinois University Press, 1974), p. 24; Shore, *Talkin' Socialism*, pp. 75–93.

34. Mother Jones to Walter Wayland, November 15, 1918, in Steel, ed., *Correspondence*, p. 184; *Appeal to Reason*, March 17, 1900, p. 1; Fetherling, *Mother Jones*, p. 24; Mother Jones, *Autobiography*, p. 29.

35. Fetherling, *Mother Jones*, pp. 21–24; Shore, *Talkin' Socialism*, pp. 34–54, 141; Salvatore, *Eugene Debs*, pp. 88–177.

36. Priscilla Long, *Where the Sun Never Shines: A History of America's Bloody Coal Industry* (New York: Paragon House, 1989), pp. 19, 55, 57, 117; David A. Corbin, *Life, Work, and Rebellion in the Coal Fields: The Southern West Virginia Miners, 1880–1922* (Urbana: University of Illinois Press, 1981), pp. 4–5.

37. Ronald Eller, *Miners, Millhands, and Mountaineers: Industrialization of the Appalachian South, 1880–1930* (Knoxville: University of Tennessee Press, 1982), pp. 39–85. Also see Duane Lockard, *Coal: A Memoir and Critique* (Charlottesville: University Press of Virginia, 1998).

38. Long, *Sun Never Shines*, pp. 36–42.

39. Eller, *Miners, Millhands, and Mountaineers*, pp. 128–60; Long, *Sun Never Shines*, pp. 97, 106–10, 120–25.

40. Long, *Sun Never Shines*, pp. 66–67, makes this case for the western miners; Corbin, *Life, Work, and Rebellion*, pp. 38–40, on the other hand, argues for much more autonomy and skill retention in West Virginia. On the transformation of mining, see Keith Dix, *What's a Coal Miner to Do? The Mechanization of Coal Mining* (Pittsburgh, Pa.: University of Pittsburgh Press, 1988).

41. Corbin, *Life, Work, and Rebellion*, pp. 77–79; Long, *Sun Never Shines*, pp. 125–32; Eller, *Miners, Millhands, and Mountaineers*, pp. 46–48, 165–75. On the impact of ethnic diversity, see Stephen Brier, " 'The Most Persistent Unionists': Class Formation and Class Conflict in the Coal Fields, and the Emergence of Interracial and Interethnic Unionism, 1880–1904" (Ph.D. diss., University of California, Los Angeles, 1992).

42. Corbin, *Life, Work, and Rebellion*, pp. 61–79; Long, *Sun Never Shines*, pp. 126–28.

43. Long, *Sun Never Shines*, pp. 128–39.

44. Corbin, *Life, Work, and Rebellion*, pp. 10, 16–17, 29–30; Long, *Sun Never Shines*, pp. 43–51; Harold Aurand, *From the Molly Maguires to the United Mine Workers: The Social Ecology of an Industrial Union, 1869–1897* (Philadelphia: Temple University Press, 1971), pp. 39–43, 145–54; Maier B. Fox, *United We Stand: The United Mine Workers of America* (Washington, D.C.: United Mine Workers, 1990), pp. 196–210.

45. Eller, *Miners, Millhands, and Mountaineers*, pp. 31–32, 125–26, 232–33, 237; Long, *Sun Never Shines*, pp. 42–43, 72–73; Corbin, *Life, Work, and Rebellion*, pp. 15–16, 33–35, 92–93.

46. Crandall A. Shiffett, *Coal Towns: Life, Work, and Culture in Company Towns* (Knoxville: University of Tennessee Press, 1991), pp. 33–66, 145–98; Long, *Sun Never Shines*, pp. 78–83; Corbin, *Life, Work, and Rebellion*, pp. 61–76, 119, 134–36; Eller, *Miners, Millhands, and Mountaineers*, pp. 182–98; Aurand, *From the Molly Maguires*, pp. 20–32.

47. Kevin Kenny, *Making Sense of the Molly Maguires* (New York: Oxford University Press, 1998); Wayne G. Broehl, *The Molly Maguires* (Cambridge, Mass.: Harvard University Press, 1965); Long, *Sun Never Shines*, pp. 97–115; Aurand, *From the Molly Maguires*, pp. 96–114.

48. Aurand, *From the Molly Maguires*, pp. 115–32; Fox *United We Stand*, pp. 12–49; Long, *Sun Never Shines*, pp. 141–45. Also see Fink, *Workingmen's Democracy*, pp. 3–17, and Voss, *Making of American Exceptionalism*, pp. 72–101.

49. Long, *Sun Never Shines*, pp. 148–51; Aurand, *From the Molly Maguires*, pp. 115–32; Fox, *United We Stand*, pp. 12–49. Also see Perry K. Blatz, *Democratic Miners: Work and Labor Relations in the Anthracite Coal Industry* (Albany: SUNY Press, 1994), ch. 2.

50. Corbin, *Life, Work, and Rebellion*, pp. 61–79, argues persuasively that the solidarity of West Virginia miners largely transcended race and ethnicity. Steven Brier, "Interracial Organizing in the West Virginia Coal Industry," in Gary Fink and Merl Reed, eds., *Essays in Southern Labor History* (Westport, Conn.: Greenwood Press, 1977), pp. 18–43, agrees, but Long, *Sun Never Shines*, pp. 151–65, is much less sanguine. Their differences echo a much larger controversy within labor history on the relationship between race and class, and the role of racism in the formation of identity. This lively debate is discussed with great clarity by Eric Arnesen, "Up from Exclusion: Black and White Workers, Race, and the State of Labor History," *Reviews in American History* 26, no. 1 (March 1998), pp.

146–74. The poles of the debate were initially established by Herbert G. Gutman, "The Negro and the United Mine Workers of America: The Career and Letters of Richard L. Davis and Something of Their Meaning, 1890–1900," in Julius Jacobson, ed., *The Negro and the American Labor Movement* (Garden City, N.Y.: Anchor Books, 1968), pp. 49–127; Herbert Hill, "Myth-Making as Labor History: Herbert Gutman and the United Mine Workers of America," *International Journal of Politics, Culture, and Society* 2 (Winter 1988), pp. 132–200; Herbert Hill, "The Importance of Race in American Labor History," *International Journal of Politics, Culture, and Society* 9 (1995), pp. 317–43; and various authors, "Labor, Race, and the Gutman Thesis: Responses to Herbert Hill," *International Journal of Politics, Culture, and Society* 2 (Spring 1989), pp. 361–403. The status of black miners is also discussed in Joe William Trotter, Jr., *Coal, Class, and Color: Blacks in Southern West Virginia, 1915–1932* (Urbana: University of Illinois Press, 1995); Ronald Lewis, *Black Coal Miners in America: Race, Class, and Community Conflict, 1780–1980* (Lexington: University Press of Kentucky, 1987). Although Mother Jones emphasized solidarity across racial lines, she never seems to have explicitly spoken out against discrimination in the union hierarchy. She also endorsed the UMW position on restricting Chinese immigration. And on at least one occasion, she opened a speech with a "darky" joke, a type of joke that was very popular in this era.

51. Fox, *United We Stand*, pp. 52–101; John H. M. Laslett, ed., *The United Mine Workers of America: A Model of Industrial Solidarity?* (University Park: Pennsylvania State University Press, 1996).

52. John Brophy, *A Miner's Life* (Madison: University of Wisconsin Press, 1964), pp. 74–75.

53. Ibid.

54. In 1901, her first full year as an international organizer, the UMW paid Mary Jones $1,577.87, about two-thirds of this as salary, one-third for expenses, though the line between them was not very clear. Hers was one of the higher salaries within the union hierarchy and about half that of President John Mitchell. Twenty years later, the UMW paid her $4,529.76 in salary and expenses. See *Minutes of the Thirteenth Annual Convention of the United Mine Workers of America* (Indianapolis, 1902), p. 71; *Proceedings of the Twenty-eighth Annual Convention of the United Mine Workers of America* (Indianapolis, 1921), vol. 1, p. 279.

55. Because its papers have been in such disarray, there are surprisingly few histories of the UMW, but see Fox, *United We Stand*.

56. Long, *Sun Never Shines*, pp. 154–57; Fox, *United We Stand*, pp. 82–101.

57. Unfortunately, all we have are these brief descriptions of her efforts. Quoted in Lois McLean, "Mother Jones . . . The Miners' Striking Spirit," *Pittsburgh Press*, January 20, 1974, p. 6; Thompson, "Notes," pp. 260–61; Long, *Sun Never Shines*, pp. 154–57.

58. John H. M. Laslett, "British Immigrant Colliers and the Origins and Early De-

velopment of the UMWA, 1870–1912," in Laslett, ed., *United Mine Workers*, pp. 39–40; Frank Julian Warne, *The Coal-Mine Workers: A Study in Labor Organizations* (New York: Longmans, Green, and Co., 1905), pp. 55–95; McLean, "Mother Jones . . . ," p. 6; Thompson, "Notes," pp. 260–61; Long, *Sun Never Shines*, pp. 154–57.

59. Isaac Cohen, "Monopoly, Competition, and Collective Bargaining: Pennsylvania and South Wales Compared," in Laslett, ed., *United Mine Workers*, pp. 395–408; Perry K. Blatz, "Workplace Militancy and Unionization: The UMWA and the Anthracite Miners, 1890–1912," in Laslett, ed., *United Mine Workers*, pp. 59–61. The authoritative work on anthracite, originally published at the turn of the century, is Robert J. Cornell, *The Anthracite Coal Strike of 1902* (New York: Russell and Russell, 1971); it is succeeded by Blatz, *Democratic Miners*.

60. Michael Novak, *The Guns of Lattimer* (New York: Basic Books, 1977); Cohen, "Monopoly," pp. 411–12; Blatz, "Workplace Militancy," pp. 62–63; Fox, *United We Stand*, pp. 84–86.

61. Blatz, "Workplace Militancy," pp. 68–71; Victor R. Greene, *The Slavic Community on Strike: Immigrant Labor in Pennsylvania Anthracite* (Notre Dame, Ind.: University of Notre Dame Press, 1968), pp. 129–50.

62. Greene, *Slavic Community*, pp. 129–50; Blatz, "Workplace Militancy," pp. 57, 68–71; Long, *Sun Never Shines*, pp. 154–59; Brier, "Interracial Organizing," pp. 18–43. For a sampling of how these issues were discussed in contemporary journals of opinion, see J. G. Brooks, "An Impression of the Anthracite Coal Troubles," *Yale Review*, August 27, 1897, pp. 306–11; "The Coal Miners' Strike," *Gunton's Magazine*, October 1900, pp. 316–23; "Triumph of Arbitration," *Gunton's Magazine*, November 1902, pp. 369–79.

63. Frank Julian Warne, "Organized Labor in the Anthracite Coal Fields," *Outlook*, May 24, 1902, pp. 273–75; Cohen, "Monopoly," pp. 413–16; Cornell, *Anthracite Coal Strike*, pp. 60–94.

64. On Mitchell, see Elsie Gluck, *John Mitchell, Miner: Labor's Bargain with the Gilded Age* (New York: John Day, 1929); and Craig Phelan, *Divided Loyalties: The Public and Private Life of Labor Leader John Mitchell* (Albany: State University of New York Press, 1994). Mitchell is quoted in Warne, *Coal-Mine Workers*, pp. 20–21.

65. Mother Jones, *Autobiography*, pp. 30–34; Fetherling, *Mother Jones*, pp. 37–38; Judith Elaine Mikeal, "Mother Mary Jones: The Labor Movement's Impious Joan of Arc" (master's thesis, University of North Carolina, 1965), pp. 12–14.

66. Mother Jones, *Autobiography*, pp. 35–36; *New York Times*, September 21, 1900, p. 6; Fetherling, *Mother Jones*, pp. 40–41.

67. Mother Jones, *Autobiography*, pp. 36–37.

68. Ibid., pp. 36–38; Irwin M. Marcus, "Labor Discontent in Tioga County, Pennsylvania, 1865–1905," *Labor History* (Summer 1973). Mother Jones also told the story about William Wilson in 1901 in her first speech at a UMW annual convention, in Steel, ed., *Speeches and Writings*, January 25, 1901, p. 8.

69. Mother Jones, *Autobiography*, pp. 38–39; Katherine A. Harvey, *The Best-Dressed*

Miners: Life and Labor in the Maryland Coal Region, 1835–1910 (Ithaca, N.Y.: Cornell University Press, 1969), pp. 313–16; "A Tribute to Mother Jones," *Appeal to Reason*, June 30, 1900, p. 3, reprinted from the New York *World*. For a description of the tribute in Blossburg, see "Mother Jones," *Appeal to Reason*, March 17, 1900, p. 1.

70. For the buildup to this strike, see Sister John Francis Raffaele, "Mary Harris Jones and the United Mine Workers of America" (master's thesis, Catholic University of America, 1964), pp. 14–20; Cornell, *Anthracite Coal Strike*, pp. 39–41; Thompson, "Notes," pp. 262–65; Mother Jones, *Autobiography*, p. 89; Fox, *United We Stand*, pp. 89–101.

71. Mother Jones, *Autobiography*, pp. 89–90. Did this incident with the priest really take place? It is impossible to say.

72. Ibid., pp. 85–86.

73. Ibid., pp. 92–93.

74. William Mailly, " 'Mother' Jones," *Socialist Spirit* 1, no. 12 (August 1902), pp. 23–25; Mikeal, "Mother Mary Jones," pp. 14–16; John Mitchell to Mother Jones, November 30, 1900, and Jones to Mitchell, December 3, 1900, in Steel, ed., *Correspondence*, pp. 3–5. These letters are the first bits of her correspondence to have survived.

75. Mother Jones, *Autobiography*, pp. 84–93; Thompson, "Notes," pp. 262–65. Mother Jones also told of these episodes, though not always with identical details, in U.S. Senate Commission on Industrial Relations, *Final Report and Testimony*, 64th Cong., 1st sess., 1916, S. Doc. 215, vol. 11, pp. 10619–22. Also see Raffaele, "Mary Harris Jones," pp. 26–39.

76. Thompson, "Notes," p. 264; Mikeal, "Mother Mary Jones," p. 16; Cornell, *Anthracite Coal Strike*, pp. 47–48.

77. Robert Wiebe, "The Anthracite Strike of 1902: A Record of Confusion," *Mississippi Valley Historical Review* 48, no. 2 (September 1961), p. 229; Thompson, "Notes," pp. 264–65; Cornell, *Anthracite Coal Strike*, pp. 95–122; Blatz, *Democratic Miners*, ch. 6; Mikeal, "Mother Mary Jones," pp. 17–21; *United Mine Workers Journal*, March 20, 1901, p. 7, July 4, 1901, p. 10.

78. Thompson, "Notes," pp. 264–65; Wiebe, "Anthracite Strike of 1902," p. 229; Cornell, *Anthracite Coal Strike*, pp. 95–122; Mother Jones, speech at UMW convention, Indianapolis, July 19, 1902, fifth session, in Steel, *Speeches and Writings*, pp. 16–21.

79. Wiebe, "Anthracite Strike of 1902," pp. 229–51, tells the story of ending the strike very well; also see Warne, *Coal-Mine Workers*, pp. 124–52; Fox, *United We Stand*, pp. 89–101.

80. As early as August 21, *The New York Times* reported rising prices and scarce supplies of anthracite in Chicago. Cohen, "Monopoly," pp. 412–16; Thompson, "Notes," pp. 265–66; Cornell, *Anthracite Coal Strike*, pp. 143–259; Wiebe, "Anthracite Strike of 1902," pp. 229–51; Warne, *Coal-Mine Workers*, pp. 124–52.

81. Gluck, *John Mitchell*, chs. 6 and 7; Fetherling, *Mother Jones*, pp. 44–47.

82. Gluck, *John Mitchell*, chs. 6 and 7, esp. pp. 132, 155, is particularly good on these conflicts, though she is partial to Mitchell; Fetherling, *Mother Jones*, pp. 44–47, on the other hand, is very critical of Mother Jones's militant stance, and he attributes her intransigence to her jealousy of young Mitchell. Also see Mother Jones, *Autobiography*, pp. 59–60.

83. Gluck, *John Mitchell*, pp. 156–78; Warne, *Coal-Mine Workers*, pp. 20–24; Fetherling, *Mother Jones*, pp. 42–43; and especially, Craig Phelan, "John Mitchell and the Politics of the Trade Agreement, 1898–1917," in Laslett, ed., *United Mine Workers of America*, pp. 72–103.

4. "There Comes the Star of Hope"

1. Mother Jones, speech at UMW convention, Indianapolis, January 25, 1901, in Edward M. Steel, ed., *The Speeches and Writings of Mother Jones* (Pittsburgh, Pa.: University of Pittsburgh Press, 1988), pp. 3–4.

2. Ibid., pp. 4–8, 10–11.

3. Ibid., pp. 4–6.

4. Ibid., pp. 6–8.

5. Ibid., pp. 10–11. See the essays in Ava Baron, ed., *Work Engendered: Toward a New History of American Labor* (Ithaca, N.Y.: Cornell University Press, 1991), especially Nancy Hewitt, "The Voice of Virile Labor," pp. 142–67.

6. Mother Jones, speech, January 25, 1901, in Steel, ed., *Speeches and Writings*, pp. 11–14. On the family metaphor in a different labor context, see Jacquelyn Dowd Hall et al., *Like a Family: The Making of a Southern Cotton Mill World* (Chapel Hill: University of North Carolina Press, 1987).

7. Mother Jones, speech, January 25, 1901, in Steel, ed., *Speeches and Writings*, p. 10. Robert Wiebe, "The Anthracite Strike of 1902: A Record of Confusion," *Mississippi Valley Historical Review* 48, no. 2 (September 1961), pp. 231, 239–40, tells this story particularly well.

8. David A. Corbin, *Life, Work, and Rebellion in the Coal Fields: The Southern West Virginia Miners, 1880–1922* (Urbana: University of Illinois Press, 1981), pp. 1–8; Altina Waller, *Feud: Hatfields, McCoys, and Social Change in Appalachia, 1860–1900* (Chapel Hill: University of North Carolina Press, 1988). Also see Duane Lockard, *Coal: A Memoir and Critique* (Charlottesville: University Press of Virginia, 1998).

9. Corbin, *Life, Work, and Rebellion*, pp. 8–10; Dale Fetherling, *Mother Jones: The Miners' Angel* (Carbondale: Southern Illinois University Press, 1974), pp. 25–26.

10. Corbin, *Life, Work, and Rebellion*, pp. 10–18.

11. Fetherling, *Mother Jones*, pp. 26–27; Corbin, *Life, Work, and Rebellion*, pp. 8–18.

12. Fetherling, *Mother Jones*, pp. 26–27; Judith Elaine Mikeal, "Mother Mary Jones: The Labor Movement's Impious Joan of Arc" (master's thesis, University of North Carolina, 1965), pp. 46–47. Mother Jones discusses West Virginia in *The*

Autobiography of Mother Jones, ed. Mary Field Parton (Chicago: Charles H. Kerr and Company, 1925), chs. 6, 7, 9.

13. Mikeal, "Mother Mary Jones," pp. 47, 54–55; Edward M. Steel, "Mother Jones in the Fairmont Field, 1902," *Journal of American History* 57, no. 2 (September 1970), pp. 290–92; Sister John Francis Raffaele, "Mary Harris Jones and the United Mine Workers of America" (master's thesis, Catholic University of America, 1964), pp. 40–45; "Mine Workers Here," *United Mine Workers Journal*, January 23, 1902, p. 1. Also see *United Mine Workers Journal*, June 6, 1901, p. 7, and December 27, 1900, p. 1; Maier B. Fox, *United We Stand: The United Mine Workers of America, 1890–1990* (Washington, D.C.: United Mine Workers of America, 1990), pp. 50–66.

14. George Scott in *United Mine Workers Journal*, December 23, 1900, p. 1. Mother Jones to John Mitchell, July 31, 1901; Mitchell to Jones, August 3, 1901; Jones to Mitchell, October 20, 1901, all in Edward M. Steel, ed., *The Correspondence of Mother Jones* (Pittsburgh, Pa.: University of Pittsburgh Press, 1985), pp. 10–12, 15–16.

15. Fred Mooney, *Struggle in the Coal Fields: The Autobiography of Fred Mooney* (Morgantown: West Virginia University Library, 1967), pp. 20–21; *United Mine Workers Journal*, April 10, 1902, pp. 3, 6, and May 1, 1902, p. 7; Mother Jones to John Mitchell, May 6, 1902, in Steel, ed., *Correspondence*, pp. 29–30. Also see *United Mine Workers Journal*, March 6, 1902, p. 7, and March 13, 1902, p. 8.

16. Mother Jones to William B. Wilson, November 15, 1901, Mother Jones to John Mitchell, December 2, 1901, Jones to Mitchell, May 6, 1902, all in Steel, ed., *Correspondence*, pp. 16–17, 29–30.

17. See Mother Jones to John Mitchell, May 6, 1902; Jones to Mitchell, February 2, 1902; Mother Jones to William Wilson, February 19, 1902; Jones to Mitchell, February 27, 1902; Jones to Mitchell, May 6, 1902; all in Steel, ed., *Correspondence*, pp. 29, 20, 21–23, 30.

18. Mother Jones to John Mitchell, May 6, 1902; Jones to Mitchell, February 7, 1902; Mother Jones to William Wilson, February 19, 1902; Jones to Mitchell, February 27, 1902; Jones to Mitchell, May 6, 1902, all in Steel, ed., *Correspondence*, pp. 20–23, 29–30.

19. Mother Jones, speech at UMW convention, Indianapolis, July 19, 1902, in Steel, ed., *Speeches and Writings*, pp. 16–21.

20. Steel, "Mother Jones in the Fairmont Field," pp. 292–94; Mikeal, "Mother Mary Jones," pp. 52–53; Fetherling, *Mother Jones*, pp. 30–31; Lois McLean, "Mother Jones in West Virginia," in Ken Sullivan, ed., *The Goldenseal Book of the West Virginia Mine Wars* (Charleston, W.Va.: Pictorial Histories Publishing Co., 1991), pp. 4–5. McLean has done pioneering research on Mother Jones and plans to publish a biography of her.

21. John Mitchell to Mother Jones, May 10, 1902, in Steel, ed., *Correspondence*, p. 32; Mother Jones, *Autobiography*, pp. 42–44; Mother Jones, speech at UMW convention, July 19, 1902, in Steel, ed., *Speeches and Writings*, pp. 17–18. In a letter

to John Mitchell dated June 23, 1902, Mother Jones said she expected that the "old czar of West Virginia"—Judge John J. Jackson—would sentence her to prison. She also criticized two of her fellow organizers for abandoning her and Poggiani when the thugs attacked; Jones to Mitchell, June 23, 1902, in Steel, ed., *Correspondence*, p. 33.

22. Steel, "Mother Jones in the Fairmont Field," pp. 294–97; *United Mine Workers Journal*, June 26, 1902, p. 3, July 3, 1902, p. 1. Mother Jones, *Autobiography*, p. 49, quotes her just before her arrest. According to the Parkersburg *Daily Morning News*, June 21, 1905, she ended her speech by urging the miners "not to work, not to drink, to avoid all lawlessness and to stick together and continue to 'agitate' "; see also July 25, 1905, both reprinted in Philip Foner, ed., *Mother Jones Speaks* (New York: Monad Press, 1983), pp. 78–82. While under arrest, she was interviewed in the *Parkersburg Sentinel*, June 21, 1902, reprinted in Foner, ed., *Mother Jones Speaks*, pp. 481–83.

23. Mother Jones, speech at UMW convention, Indianapolis, July 19, 1902, in Steel, ed., *Speeches and Writings*, pp. 16–21; *Chronicle*, July 27, 1902, quoted in Foner, ed., *Mother Jones Speaks*, pp. 92–93.

24. *Guarantee Trust Co. of New York* v. *Haggerty et al.*, United States Circuit Court, N.D. West Virginia, July 24, 1902, *Federal Reporter*, vol. 116, pp. 516–17; Fetherling, *Mother Jones*, p. 33; Steel, "Mother Jones in the Fairmont Field," pp. 299–301. Mother Jones wrote in the *Autobiography*, p. 51, "The prosecuting attorney jumped to his feet and shaking his finger at me, he said, 'Your honor, there is the most dangerous woman in the country today. She called your honor a scab. But I will recommend mercy of the court if she will consent to leave the state and never return.' "

25. Steel, "Mother Jones in the Fairmont Field," pp. 300–1; Mikeal, "Mother Mary Jones," pp. 54–55; *Guarantee Trust* v. *Haggerty*, *Federal Reporter*, pp. 518–19; Fetherling, *Mother Jones*, pp. 33–34. For an account that was very favorable to Judge Jackson, see Walter Wellman, *Fairmont Coal Region: A Treatise* (n.p., n.d.), a compilation of Wellman's articles originally published in *The Chicago Record-Herald*, WVaU.

26. Steel, "Mother Jones in the Fairmont Field," pp. 300–1; Mikeal, "Mother Mary Jones," pp. 54–55; Fetherling, *Mother Jones*, pp. 33–34. Mother Jones, *Autobiography*, pp. 49–52, later retracted the charge she made that Judge Jackson had "scabbed on his father"; U.S. Senate Commission on Industrial Relations, *Final Report and Testimony*, 64th Cong., 1st sess., 1916, S. Doc. 215, vol. 11, pp. 10622–23.

27. Steel, "Mother Jones in the Fairmont Field," pp. 304–7. Steel is very convincing on Fleming's role: "With practiced ease he moved from countinghouse to courtroom to capitol. He needed no guide to fit into and make use of the institutions of his native state. The courtroom where he fought to preserve his interests was a familiar environment, and law a pliable medium for justifying and confirming his economic manipulations."

28. McLean, "Mother Jones in West Virginia," pp. 4–6; "From Mother Jones," *Appeal to Reason*, November 1, 1902, p. 4, an open letter dated October 5, 1902.

29. The best treatment of these incidents, including the Stanaford Mountain tragedy is McLean, "Mother Jones in West Virginia," pp. 4–7; also see Fred Thompson, "Notes on 'The Most Dangerous Woman in America,' " in Mother Jones, *The Autobiography of Mother Jones*, ed. Mary Field Parton (Chicago: Charles Kerr Co., 1990 ed.), pp. 265–67. Mother Jones told the story in her testimony before the Commission on Industrial Relations, *Final Report and Testimony*, pp. 10623–24, and in *Autobiography*, pp. 67–70.

30. For examples, see Mother Jones, "A Picture of American Freedom in West Virginia," *International Socialist Review* 2 (1901–1902), pp. 177–79; Mother Jones, "The Coal Miners of the Old Dominion," *International Socialist Review* 2 (1901–1902), pp. 575–78, reprinted in *Appeal to Reason*, March 15, 1902, p. 2; "Mother Jones Fiery," *Toledo Bee*, March 25, 1903, CUA, 7/3.1; Mother Jones to Henry Demarest Lloyd, April 19, 1903, in Steel, ed., *Correspondence*, pp. 44–45.

31. *United Mine Workers Journal*, February 5, 1903, p. 2.

32. Ibid., July 17, 1902, p. 3. For another good example of her invoking this theme, see *United Mine Workers Journal*, September 18, 1902, p. 7.

33. *Boston Herald*, September 11, 1904, p. 3.

34. Priscilla Long, *Where the Sun Never Shines: A History of America's Bloody Coal Industry* (New York: Paragon House, 1989), pp. 190–94; George G. Suggs, Jr., "The Colorado Coal Miners' Strike, 1903–1904," *Journal of the West* 12, no. 1 (January 1973), pp. 36–37; Fox, *United We Stand*, pp. 66–74.

35. George S. McGovern and Leonard F. Guttridge, *The Great Coalfield War* (Boulder: University Press of Colorado, 1996), pp. 22–24; Long, *Sun Never Shines*, pp. 205–11; Suggs, "Coal Miners' Strike," p. 37. On labor conditions for the miners, see report of Committee to Investigate Conditions in Relation to Coal Strike in the State of Colorado, February 26, 1901, MS, Roche Papers, 6–1, Department of Archives, UCB. A 1901 investigation by the Colorado legislature also noted the remarkable profitability of the mines; see Winifred Bannerman MS, "Running Story—Insert: '1901 Legislative Investigation,' " pp. 1–12, DPL, a verbatim transcript of the legislative report.

36. Long, *Sun Never Shines*, pp. 202–5, 214–16; Fetherling, *Mother Jones*, pp. 60–68. For an account of the WFM in Colorado early in the twentieth century, see George G. Suggs, Jr., *Colorado's War on Militant Unionism* (Norman: University of Oklahoma Press, 1991), pp. 15–28. Also see Sharon Reitman, "Class Formation and Union Politics: The Western Federation of Miners and the United Mine Workers, 1880–1910" (Ph.D. diss., University of Michigan, 1991); David Brundage, *The Making of Western Labor Radicalism: Denver's Organized Workers, 1878–1905* (Urbana: University of Illinois Press, 1994). Emma F. Langdon, *The Cripple Creek Strike* (Denver, Colo.: Great Western Publishing, 1904), gives a favorable account of the WFM in Colorado, and she includes the story of the coal strike on pp. 260–66. The casual anti-Chinese sentiment within the union

was revealed by the organizer Duncan MacDonald. He noted several Chinese restaurants in the town of Rock Springs and declared he would leave town before he ate Chinese food; the next day he discovered that the cook at the hotel where he had been eating was "a very robust Chinaman"; Duncan MacDonald, MS autobiography, p. 23, in the MacDonald Collection, ISHL. On unions and Asian workers, see Chris Friday, "Asian American Labor History and Historical Interpretation," *Labor History* 35 (Fall 1994), pp. 524–45. On the Chinese, see Alexander Saxton, *The Indispensable Enemy: Labor and the Anti-Chinese Movement in California* (Berkeley: University of California Press, 1971).

37. Suggs, "Coal Miners' Strike," pp. 39–42; Long, *Sun Never Shines*, pp. 218–20; Mikeal, "Mother Mary Jones," pp. 92–93; Bannerman, "Running Story," pp. 7–9; MacDonald, MS autobiography, pp. 20–21.

38. Long, *Sun Never Shines*, pp. 211–14, 218–20; Suggs, "Coal Miners' Strike," pp. 39–42; Mikeal, "Mother Mary Jones," pp. 92–93; Bannerman, "Running Story," pp. 7–9; McGovern and Guttridge, *Great Coalfield War*, pp. 6–18, 30–35.

39. Fetherling, *Mother Jones*, pp. 58–60; Suggs, *Colorado's War*, pp. 84–117; Suggs, "Coal Miners' Strike," pp. 38–39; Bannerman, "Running Story," pp. 7–9; Long, *Sun Never Shines*, pp. 217–20. For the rise of labor in the West, see Brundage, *Western Labor Radicalism*.

40. Mikeal, "Mother Mary Jones," pp. 92–94; Long, *Sun Never Shines*, pp. 220–24; Suggs, "Coal Miners' Strike," p. 43.

41. "Friendly Chat with Mother Jones," *Denver Republican*, August 16, 1903, p. 7.

42. Mother Jones, *Autobiography*, p. 95; Long, *Sun Never Shines*, p. 221. Commission on Industrial Relations, *Final Report and Testimony*, p. 10624, written ten years before the *Autobiography*, does have Mother Jones going west to see if the desire for a strike was deep enough, but she did not go as a peddler. Also see "Mother Jones May Come to Colorado," *Denver Republican*, October 18, 1903, n.p.; "Labor's Joan of Arc in This City," *Denver Times*, October 19, 1903, p. 1, both clippings from the DPL clipping file under "Mother Jones." "Great Power of Mother Jones," *Denver Post*, reprinted in *United Mine Workers Journal*, October 29, 1903, p. 7. Two weeks before the strike, it was reported that Mother Jones bore John Mitchell's instructions to District 15; see "That Coal Strike," *Colorado Springs Gazette*, October 28, 1903, p. 1, and "Mother Jones Returns to Colorado Miners," *Denver Republican*, October 29, 1903, n.p., from DPL clipping file.

43. Mother Jones to William B. Wilson, October 29, 1903, in Steel, ed., *Correspondence*, pp. 48–49; "Failure of the Coal Strike," *Denver Republican*, November 14, 1903, p. 6; "Worse Than in the East," *United Mine Workers Journal*, November 18, 1903, p. 1. In her April 1904 letter to Wilson, Mother Jones complained that too many of the organizers discussed the affairs of the union with the press, and she added, "I have learned that men are as big mouthed as women and are just as empty brained." The organizer Duncan MacDonald traveled with her in Colorado: "For a number of years I had known 'Mother Jones.' She was the best organizer on the staff and a wonderful rabble-rouser. She was absolutely

fearless and didn't hesitate in going to places that so many of the rocking chair artists were afraid to tackle. Perhaps her sex was a safeguard, but she made an appeal to miners where ever she went, and I was one of her special admirers. When the Colorado strike began she was with us as she had been in every contest the miners had for many years." MacDonald added he was especially proud to speak at the unveiling of her monument at the Union Miners Cemetery in 1932; see MacDonald, MS autobiography, p. 34.

44. McGovern and Guttridge, *Great Coalfield War*, pp. 45–56; Long, *Sun Never Shines*, pp. 228–29; Mikeal, "Mother Mary Jones," pp. 92–96; Fetherling, *Mother Jones*, pp. 60–62.

45. Mother Jones, *Autobiography*, pp. 98–99.

46. Mother Jones, speech, reprinted in *Denver Post*, November 22, 1903, in DPL; also see *Autobiography*, pp. 99–100.

47. Mother Jones's speech reprinted in *Denver Post*, November 22, 1903, in DPL; *Autobiography*, pp. 99–100; Long, *Sun Never Shines*, p. 229; Mikeal, "Mother Mary Jones," pp. 94–96. See also Stephen Brier, " 'The Most Persistent Unionists': Class Formation and Class Conflict in the Coal Fields, 1880–1904" (Ph.D. diss., University of California, Los Angeles, 1992).

48. *Denver Post*, November 22, 1903, in DPL; Thompson, "Notes," pp. 269–70; Long, *Sun Never Shines*, pp. 228–30.

49. "Ouray Miners' Union Denounces the Post," *Denver Times*, December 30, 1902, p. 2; "Clever Denver Woman to Start a New Magazine, to Be Called 'The Polly Pry,' " *Denver Republican*, February 30, 1903, n.p.; both in Biography Clippings File, Mrs. Leonel Ross O'Bryan, DPL.

50. "Clever Denver Woman, to Start a New Magazine," *Denver Republican*, February 30, 1903, n.p.; "Polly Pry Did Not Just Report the News; She *Made* It," *Smithsonian*, January 1991, pp. 48–56; "Out West," *Denver Post*, December 9, 1984, n.p.; *Polly Pry*, December 26, 1903, pp. 1–5; all in Biography Clippings File, Mrs. Leonel Ross O'Bryan, DPL.

51. *Polly Pry*, January 2, 1904, p. 2, and January 9, 1904, p. 5.

52. Thompson, "Notes," p. 270; Fetherling, *Mother Jones*, pp. 135–38; Long, *Sun Never Shines*, p. 233. Even in private correspondence, Mother Jones never categorically denied the *Polly Pry* charges. The closest she came was in a letter to UMW secretary William Wilson almost two years after the allegations: "No matter the filthy minds may say whose own mothers were rotton to the core. I know that you . . . believe me still a woman *pure and true*." Two days later, Wilson responded, "You can rest assured that no amount of slander will ever reduce my high opinion of your goodness." See Mother Jones to William Wilson, October 4, 1904, Wilson to Jones, October 6, 1904, both in Steel, ed., *Correspondence*, pp. 55, 56. On the demographics of prostitution in nineteenth-century New York, see Timothy J. Gilfoyle's outstanding *City of Eros: New York City, Prostitution, and the Commercialization of Sex, 1790–1920* (New York: Norton, 1992), esp. ch. 3.

53. Gilfoyle, *City of Eros*, ch. 3. My thanks to Clark Secrest of the Colorado Histori-

cal Society for sharing his expertise on the history of Denver's demimonde. The establishments of Jennie Rogers and Minnie Hall were listed in the *Denver Red Book* (1892), ColHS, a compendium of brothels and gambling dens for sporting men. Fred Mazzulla and Jo Mazzulla, "Brass Checks and Red Lights" (n.p., n.d.), ColHS, list Julia C. Bullette, on whose tombstone in Virginia City appeared the words "Angel to Miners." Sanborn Perris Insurance Maps for Denver, vol. 2 (New York, 1890), label nearly all the housing just above the 2000 block on Market Street as "female boarding." A "Mrs. Mary Jones" is listed in both the 1885 and the 1890 Denver City Directories, in the former at 609 Glenarm, in the latter at 1865 Grand Avenue; of course the name was so common that there is no way of knowing if this is the future Mother Jones (although *Polly Pry* claimed that Jones called herself Harris). Also see Ballinger and Richards *Denver City Directory* for 1893, listing Mary Jones the dressmaker at 315 Twenty-third Street. See also MacDonald, MS autobiography, pp. 34–36.

54. Fetherling, *Mother Jones*, p. 137; Thompson, "Notes," p. 270; McGovern and Guttridge, *Great Coalfield War*, pp. 47–48; Long, *Sun Never Shines*, pp. 233, 370, nn. 93, 94. For an example of organizers being charged with promiscuity, see Jacquelyn Dowd Hall, "Private Eyes, Public Women: Images of Class and Sex in the Urban South, Atlanta, Georgia, 1913–1915," in Baron, ed., *Work Engendered*, pp. 243–72.

55. Upton Sinclair, *The Brass Check: A Study of American Journalism* (Pasadena, Calif.: privately published by the author, 1920), pp. 180–81, argued that the *Polly Pry* story was an example of how corporations corrupted American journalism. On James McParland (who had changed his name from McParlan), see J. Anthony Lukas, *Big Trouble: A Murder in a Small Western Town Sets Off a Struggle for the Soul of America* (New York: Simon and Schuster, 1997), pp. 176–95.

56. See, for example, "Correspondence," *Miners' Magazine*, January 21, 1904, pp. 11–12, in which a letter to the editor, written by a WFM member, charged that the Citizens' Alliance bribed *Polly Pry*'s editor, who was too cowardly to make charges that could be tested in a court of law. Mother Jones could not have been a Denver madam, the letter argued, because after the death of her Welsh coal-miner husband, she worked in the breakers of Pennsylvania's anthracite region, where she became a great advocate for organized labor.

57. For an example of the divisions among the miners, see "The Coal Strike," *Appeal to Reason*, January 30, 1904, p. 2. Mother Jones repeated her praise for Italian miners in a speech she gave before the New York City Central Federated Union, August 7, 1904, from *New York Times*, August 8, 1908, reprinted in Foner, ed., *Mother Jones Speaks*, pp. 109–10.

58. Long, *Sun Never Shines*, pp. 226–28, 234–38; Commission on Industrial Relations, *Final Report and Testimony*, pp. 10624–25; Suggs, "Coal Miners' Strike," pp. 44–51; Mother Jones, *Autobiography*, pp. 94–113; Langdon, *Cripple Creek Strike*, pp. 267–69, 105–13; Bannerman, "Running Story," pp. 10–17; MacDonald MS autobiography, pp. 27–34. Union miners claimed that the $200,000

used to pay for martial law came out of their paychecks; see "Our Money," box 26716.16, "Las Animas Strike, March 1904," Governor James H. Peabody Collection, ColSA. Also see "General Orders #2" from Zeph T. Hill, commander of the First Provisional Battalion, National Guard of Colorado, Las Animas County, March 23, 1904, in box 26716.16, "Las Animas Strike," Governor James H. Peabody Collection, ColSA.

59. Mother Jones, *Autobiography*, pp. 101–7; Commission on Industrial Relations, *Final Report and Testimony*, pp. 10625–27; Long, *Sun Never Shines*, pp. 234–36; McGovern and Guttridge, *Great Coalfield War*, pp. 48–49; Mikeal, "Mother Mary Jones," p. 97. Commander Zeph Hill explicitly asked Governor Peabody for permission to deport the "disturbing element" from the strike district rather than allow civil authorities to prosecute them; see Hill to Governor James Peabody, March 25, 1904, in box 26716.16, "Las Animas Strike," Governor James H. Peabody Collection, ColSA. The day before they were deported, Wardjon and Mother Jones were overheard by spies in Santa Clara; Wardjon urged violence against scabs and anyone who attacked the strikers; Mother Jones advised against it. See "JTK, Denver 3/25/04," in box 26716.16, "Las Animas Strike," Governor James H. Peabody Collection, ColSA. Before she was quarantined in Utah, according to one account, Mother Jones was forced to hide under a bed in the home of Paul Passetto near Helper, Utah. Passetto and his family gave shelter to union people, and Mother Jones was being pursued by three mine guards, including the notorious "Gunplay" Maxwell; see S. V. Litizzette's biographical sketch of Caterina Passetto Bottino, June 8, 1977, MS A2319, USHA.

60. "Expression from Mother Jones," in Langdon, *Cripple Creek Strike*, pp. 271–74.

61. Randall and Mitchell quoted in UMW, *Proceedings of the 16th Annual Convention*, 1905, pp. 177–228; Long, *Sun Never Shines*, pp. 239–41; Fetherling, *Mother Jones*, pp. 68–69; Elsie Gluck, *John Mitchell, Miner: Labor's Bargain with the Gilded Age* (New York: John Day, 1929), pp. 173–78. Also see Craig Phelan, *Divided Loyalties: The Public and Private Life of Labor Leader John Mitchell* (Albany: State University of New York Press, 1994).

62. UMW, *Proceedings*, 1905, pp. 177–228; Long, *Sun Never Shines*, pp. 239–41; Fetherling, *Mother Jones*, pp. 68–69; Gluck, *John Mitchell*, pp. 173–78.

63. Mother Jones, *Autobiography*, pp. 100–1.

64. Mother Jones to John H. Walker, January 4, 1905, in Steel, ed., *Correspondence*, pp. 52–53.

65. William Mailly to Mother Jones, April 15, 1903, in Steel, ed., *Correspondence*, pp. 43–44. Mailly's letter makes clear Mother Jones's frustrations with other organizers.

66. The UMW sent dozens of organizers into Colorado, but the *Appeal to Reason*, for example, referred to how Mother Jones organized the southern field, as if she had done it herself. See "The Coal Strike," *Appeal to Reason*, January 30, 1904, p. 2.

5. The Children's Crusade

1. Dorothy Adams, "Through West Virginia with Mother Jones," *Denver Republican*, August 11, 1901, p. 13, originally printed in *New York Herald*; it was reprinted, for example, as " 'Mother Jones' in the Coal Mines," *United Mine Workers Journal*, October 3, 1901, p. 2.

2. Adams, "Through West Virginia," p. 13.

3. William Mailly, " 'Mother' Jones," *Socialist Spirit* 1, no. 12 (August 1902), pp. 19–25.

4. *United Mine Workers Journal*, July 3, 1903, p. 2, quoting from *The Indianapolis News; United Mine Workers Journal*, April 25, 1901, p. 4; *Appeal to Reason*, June 30, 1900, p. 3, reprinted from the New York *World*.

5. *Boston Herald*, September 11, 1904, pp. 1, 3.

6. Adams, "Through West Virginia," p. 13; " 'Mother Jones' in the Coal Mines," *United Mine Workers Journal*, October 3, 1901, p. 2.

7. *National Labor Tribune*, August 26, 1897, quoted in *Pittsburgh Press*, January 20, 1974, CUA; "Mary Jones—the Life Story of the Mother of the Strikers," *Miners' Magazine*, September 1900, pp. 27–30, reprinted in *Appeal to Reason*, November 17, 1900, p. 2, originally from the New York *World*; Mailly, " 'Mother' Jones," pp. 19–25.

8. *United Mine Workers Journal*, April 25, 1901, p. 4. See also "Mother Jones Fiery," *Toledo Bee*, March 25, 1903, CUA, 7/3.1. *Appeal to Reason*, February 16, 1901, p. 4; *Appeal to Reason*, March 15, 1902, p. 2, from the *International Socialist Review*.

9. "Mary Jones," *Miners' Magazine*, September 1900, pp. 27–30.

10. *Boston Herald*, September 11, 1904, pp. 1, 3.

11. Agnes Burns Wieck Collection, box 2, file 22, pp. 171–73, WSU. Wieck wrote her reminiscences around 1922; they were incorporated into David Thoreau Wieck's recollections of his mother, *Woman from Spillertown: A Memoir of Agnes Burns Wieck* (Carbondale: Southern Illinois University Press, 1992), pp. 11–17.

12. *Boston Herald*, September 11, 1904, pp. 1, 3.

13. Ibid.

14. "Mother Jones, Martyr," *Appeal to Reason*, January 3, 1903, p. 3; letter from Ben Davis, Montgomery, West Virginia, April 24, 1902, to *United Mine Workers Journal*, May 1, 1902, p. 7.

15. " 'Mother Jones' in Colorado," *Miners' Magazine*, October 29, 1903, p. 5.

16. William James, *The Varieties of Religious Experience* (London: Longmans, 1928), pp. 367–69.

17. Dorothy Adams, "Little Strikers: Blighted Childhood of Tiny Girl Mill Hands," *Appeal to Reason*, February 8, 1902, p. 3, originally published in *The New York Herald*.

18. Mother Jones had previously written on the horrors of child labor in the textile industry: Mother Jones, "Civilization in Southern Mills," *International Socialist Review* 1 (March 1901), pp. 539–41, reprinted in *Appeal to Reason*, March 16, 1901, p. 2.

19. John Spargo, *The Bitter Cry of the Children* (New York: Macmillan, 1906), pp. 142–47; Viviana A. Zelizer, *Pricing the Priceless Child: The Changing Social Value of Children* (New York: Basic Books, 1985), pp. 56–64; Robert Bremner, ed., *Children and Youth in America: A Documentary History*, vol. 2 (Cambridge, Mass.: Harvard University Press, 1971), p. 601.

20. Steven Mintz and Susan Kellog, *Domestic Revolutions: A Social History of American Family Life* (New York: Free Press, 1988), pp. 90–95, 103; David Nasaw, *Children of the City, at Work and at Play* (Garden City, N.Y.: Anchor Press/Doubleday, 1985), pp. 38–47; Zelizer, *Priceless Child*, pp. 58–59, 68–70; Elliott J. Gorn, ed., *The McGuffey Readers: Selections from the 1879 Edition* (Boston: Bedford Books, 1998), p. 19.

21. Mintz and Kellog, *Domestic Revolutions*, pp. 90–95; Nasaw, *Children of the City*, pp. 38–47; Zelizer, *Priceless Child*, pp. 58–59, 68–70.

22. Jeremy P. Felt, *Hostages of Fortune: Child Labor Reform in New York State* (Syracuse, N.Y.: Syracuse University Press, 1965), pp. 17–36; Walter I. Trattner, *Crusade for the Children: A History of the National Child Labor Committee and Child Labor Reform in America* (Chicago: Quadrangle Books, 1970); Jacquelyn Dowd Hall et al., *Like a Family: The Making of a Southern Cotton Mill World* (Chapel Hill: University of North Carolina Press, 1987), pp. 52–65; Elizabeth H. Davidson, *Child Labor Legislation in the Southern Textile States* (Chapel Hill: University of North Carolina Press, 1939), pp. 1–17. On mill work as a family affair, see Allen Tullos, *Habits of Industry: White Culture and the Transformation of the Carolina Piedmont* (Chapel Hill: University of North Carolina Press, 1989).

23. The literature on the Progressive Era is enormous, but see Nell Irvin Painter, *Standing at Armageddon: The United States, 1877–1919* (New York: Norton, 1987); Robert Wiebe, *The Search for Order, 1877–1920* (New York: Hill and Wang, 1967); Samuel P. Hays, *The Response to Industrialism, 1885–1914* (Chicago: University of Chicago Press, 1957); Alan Dawley, *Struggles for Justice: Social Responsibility and the Liberal State* (Cambridge, Mass.: Belknap Press of Harvard University Press, 1991); Richard Hofstadter, *The Age of Reform* (New York: Knopf, 1955); James Weinstein, *The Corporate Ideal in the Liberal State* (Boston: Beacon Press, 1968); Martin J. Sklar, *The Corporate Reconstruction of American Capitalism, 1890–1916* (Cambridge, U.K.: Cambridge University Press, 1988); Gabriel Kolko, *The Triumph of Conservatism* (New York: Free Press, 1963); Olivier Zunz, *Making America Corporate, 1870–1920* (Chicago: University of Chicago Press, 1990).

24. Felt, *Hostages of Fortune*, chs. 3 and 4; Nasaw, *Children of the City*, pp. 44–47; Bremner, *Children and Youth*, pp. 602–3. On the creation of the concept of adolescence as a special stage of human development, see Joseph Kett, *Rites of Passage: Adolescence in America* (New York: Basic Books, 1977).

25. Felt, *Hostages of Fortune*, chs. 3 and 4; Nasaw, *Children of the City*, pp. 44–47; Bremner, *Children and Youth*, pp. 602–3; C. K. McFarland, "Crusade for Child Laborers: 'Mother' Jones and the March of the Mill Children," *Pennsylvania History* 38, no. 3 (July 1971), p. 283; Davidson, *Child Labor Legislation*, details

these changes in four Southern states, but for a summary, see ch. 14. On Florence Kelley, see Kathryn Kish Sklar, *Florence Kelley and the Nation's Work* (New Haven, Conn.: Yale University Press, 1995), pp. 140–61, 239–52.

26. Zelizer, *Priceless Child*, pp. 70–72. On the complexities of union workers confronting young laborers, see Ava Baron, "An 'Other' Side of Gender Antagonism at Work," in Baron, ed., *Work Engendered: Toward a New History of American Labor* (Ithaca, N.Y.: Cornell University Press, 1991), pp. 47–69.

27. Mother Jones, "Civilization in Southern Mills," pp. 539–41.

28. Ibid., p. 541.

29. Mother Jones, "The Coal Miners of the Old Dominion," *International Socialist Review* 2 (1901–1902), pp. 575–78. The essays in the *International Socialist Review* read like heavily edited versions of Mother Jones's speeches. Certain stories and tropes, such as references to the poodles of the rich and to feckless preachers, appear in both. However, these articles laid on the socialist message more heavily than Mother Jones did in her speeches; I suspect that the *ISR* editors added phrases like "I shudder for the nation" and "the dawning of the new day of socialism."

30. Mother Jones, speech at UMW convention, Indianapolis, January 25, 1901, in Edward M. Steel, ed., *The Speeches and Writings of Mother Jones* (Pittsburgh, Pa.: University of Pittsburgh Press, 1988), pp. 4–5. There was plenty of muckraking journalism on child labor in the early years of the twentieth century. For example, see Lillian W. Betts, "The Coal Strike, I—the Families of the Miners," *Outlook*, October 13, 1900, pp. 412–16; Peter Roberts, "Child Labor in Eastern Pennsylvania," *Outlook*, December 17, 1904, pp. 982–85; Leonora Beck Ellis, "Child Operatives in Southern Mills," *Independent*, October 26, 1901, pp. 2637–47; Leonora Beck Ellis, "Educating Southern Factory Children," *Gunton's Magazine*, May 1903, pp. 459–70; B. O. Flowers, "The Cry of the Children," *Arena*, July 1902, pp. 305–17; Reverend Jesse Armon Baldwin, "Evils of Southern Factory Life," *Gunton's Magazine*, April 1902, pp. 326–37; Kellogg Durland, "Child Labor in Pennsylvania," *Outlook*, May 9, 1903, pp. 124–27; Francis H. Nichols, "Children of the Coal Shadow," *McClure's Magazine*, November 1902, pp. 435–55.

31. Mother Jones, speech at UMW convention, January 25, 1901, in Steel, ed., *Speeches and Writings*, pp. 4–5; Max Hayes, "The World of Labor," *International Socialist Review* 1 (June 1901), p. 816.

32. Helen Collier Camp, "Mother Jones and the Children's Crusade" (master's thesis, Columbia University, 1970), pp. 1–8; Russell E. Smith, "The March of the Mill Children," *Social Science Review* 41 (September 1967), p. 300; Mother Jones, *Autobiography of Mother Jones*, ed. Mary Field Parton (Chicago: Charles H. Kerr and Company, 1925), pp. 71–72; Dale Fetherling, *Mother Jones: The Miners' Angel* (Carbondale: Southern Illinois University Press, 1974), pp. 48–49.

33. Mother Jones discussed the event in *Autobiography*, pp. 72–83; also see Camp, "Mother Jones and the Children's Crusade," pp. 8–9; McFarland, "Crusade for Child Laborers," pp. 284–86.

34. Camp, "Mother Jones and the Children's Crusade," pp. 8–9; Mother Jones, *Autobiography*, pp. 72–73; McFarland, "Crusade for Child Laborers," pp. 284–86.

35. Camp, "Mother Jones and the Children's Crusade," pp. 1, 10; Smith, "March of the Mill Children," pp. 300–1; Fetherling, *Mother Jones*, p. 50; Spargo, *Bitter Cry*, p. 151; *New York Times*, July 8, 1903, p. 5. One eleven-year-old told John Spargo, a Socialist who marched with the group, that she had worked every single day for two years.

36. Camp, "Mother Jones and the Children's Crusade," pp. 1–22; Smith, "March of the Mill Children," pp. 301–2; Mother Jones, *Autobiography*, pp. 74–77; *New York Times*, July 10, 1903, p. 1, July 12, 1903, p. 1; *Miners' Magazine*, August 27, 1903, p. 3.

37. Mother Jones, *Autobiography*, pp. 75–77.

38. McFarland, "Crusade for Child Laborers," pp. 287–91; Camp, "Mother Jones and the Children's Crusade," pp. 12–25; Smith, "March of the Mill Children," pp. 301–2; Fetherling, *Mother Jones*, pp. 50–51; Carol Ann Downing makes this point about the evolving goals of the march in "An Examination of Rhetorical Strategies Utilized by Mary Harris 'Mother' Jones within the Context of the Agitative Rhetoric Model Developed by John Waite Bowers and Donovan J. Ochs" (Ph.D. diss., Ohio University, 1985), pp. 202–3; *New York Times*, July 14, 1903, p. 2. Downing is particularly good at tracing press reaction to the march.

39. *New York Times*, July 11, 1903, p. 1; Camp, "Mother Jones and the Children's Crusade," pp. 14–22; Fetherling, *Mother Jones*, pp. 50–51; McFarland, "Crusade for Child Laborers," pp. 289–91; Downing, "Rhetorical Strategies," pp. 190–210.

40. Downing, "Rhetorical Strategies," pp. 202–10, 291–93. Camp and others describe the children's crusade as though going to Sagamore Hill was part of the plan from the beginning. Mother Jones did tell the Philadelphia *North American* on July 7, 1903, the day the march began, "I am going to show President Roosevelt the poor little things on which the boasted commercial greatness of our country is built." The idea of going to Sagamore Hill perhaps occurred before the march began, but it did not become a goal until about a week after the marchers started their journey.

41. Mother Jones to Theodore Roosevelt, July 15, 1903, from the Philadelphia *North American*, July 31, 1903, reprinted in Philip Foner, ed., *Mother Jones Speaks* (New York: Monad Press, 1983), pp. 555–56; McFarland, "Crusade for Child Laborers," pp. 292–93. Several newspapers castigated Mother Jones and her followers for threatening to "storm the President," as the *Trenton Times* put it.

42. Camp, "Mother Jones and the Children's Crusade," pp. 23–26; Fetherling, *Mother Jones*, p. 53; McFarland, "Crusade for Child Laborers," p. 294; *New York Times*, July 20, 1903, p. 10, July 24, 1903, p. 5.

43. McFarland, "Crusade for Child Laborers," pp. 293–95; Downing, "Rhetorical Strategies," pp. 210–12; Camp, "Mother Jones and the Children's Crusade," pp. 26–30; Fetherling, *Mother Jones*, pp. 54–55; *New York Times*, July 24, 1903, p. 5; Mother Jones, *Autobiography*, pp. 77–79.

44. *New York Times*, July 27, 1903, p. 10; Fetherling, *Mother Jones*, pp. 54–55; Camp, "Mother Jones and the Children's Crusade," pp. 30–32; Downing, "Rhetorical Strategies," pp. 221–23; Mother Jones, *Autobiography*, pp. 79–82.

45. *New York Times*, July 27, 1903, p. 10; Camp, "Mother Jones and the Children's Crusade," pp. 30–31; Downing, "Rhetorical Strategies," pp. 212–13; Fetherling, *Mother Jones*, pp. 54–55; Mother Jones, *Autobiography*, pp. 80–81.

46. Camp, "Mother Jones and the Children's Crusade," pp. 32–36; McFarland, "Crusade for Child Laborers," pp. 295–96; Downing, "Rhetorical Strategies," pp. 216–18; Fetherling, *Mother Jones*, pp. 55–56.

47. Mother Jones to Theodore Roosevelt, July 30, 1903, in Foner, ed., *Mother Jones Speaks*, pp. 554–56.

48. Camp, "Mother Jones and the Children's Crusade," pp. 32–36; McFarland, "Crusade for Child Laborers," pp. 295–96; Downing, "Rhetorical Strategies," pp. 216–18; Fetherling, *Mother Jones*, pp. 55–56.

49. *Miners' Magazine*, September 24, 1903, p. 5; Camp, "Mother Jones and the Children's Crusade," pp. 38–40.

50. Mother Jones, "The Strike in Scranton," *St. Louis Labor*, April 13, 1901, in Steel, ed., *Speeches and Writings*, p. 268.

51. On the Carbondale strike, see Bonnie Stepenoff, "Keeping It in the Family: Mother Jones and the Pennsylvania Silk Strike, 1900–1901," *Labor History* 38, no. 4 (Fall 1997), pp. 432–49, which argues, "as fathers and brothers of the silk workers, UMWA members took control of the strike, although strikers protested that miners knew nothing about the silk industry. As a mother figure within the union, Jones reinforced the desire of fathers to support and protect their daughters. Jones and the miners kept the silk strike firmly within the UMWA family. By defining the silk workers' protest as a children's strike, Jones turned attention from issues of wages and working conditions to issues of parental responsibility and control—again keeping it in the family" (p. 449). Stepenoff elaborates her ideas further in *Their Fathers' Daughters: Silk Mill Workers in Northeastern Pennsylvania* (Selinsgrove, Pa.: Susquehanna University Press, 1999). Also see Mother Jones, speech at UMW convention, January 25, 1901, in Steel, ed., *Speeches and Writings*, pp. 6, 13.

52. *United Mine Workers Journal*, August 6, 1903, p. 1; Fetherling, *Mother Jones*, pp. 56–57; Downing, "Rhetorical Strategies," pp. 219–24; Camp, "Mother Jones and the Children's Crusade," pp. 38–42; McFarland, "Crusade for Child Laborers," pp. 295–96.

53. Robert Willard McAhren, "Making the Nation Safe for Childhood: A History of the Movement for Federal Regulation of Child Labor, 1900–1938" (Ph.D. diss., University of Texas, Austin, 1967); Viviana A. Zelizer, "From Child Labor to Child Work: Changing Cultural Conceptions of Children's Economic Roles, 1870s–1930s," in Peter A. Coclanis and Stuart Bruchey, eds., *Ideas, Ideologies, and Social Movements: The United States Experience since 1800* (Columbia: University of South Carolina Press, 1999), pp. 98–101; John Clayton Drew, "Child La-

bor and Child Welfare: The Origins and Uneven Development of the American Welfare State" (Ph.D. diss. University of Michigan, 1987); Trattner, *Crusade for the Children.*

54. Camp, "Mother Jones and the Children's Crusade," pp. 35–36, 41–42; McFarland, "Crusade for Child Laborers," p. 296. Mother Jones's efforts were echoed a decade later during the great strike of 1912 in Lawrence, Massachusetts, which had its own children's crusade.

6. "Faithfully Yours for the Revolution"

1. Kate Richards O'Hare, "How I Became a Socialist Agitator," *Socialist Woman,* October 10, 1908, p. 5; Elizabeth Gurley Flynn, *The Rebel Girl: An Autobiography, My First Life, 1906–1926* (New York: International Publishers, 1973), pp. 88–90.
2. Edward M. Steel, ed., *The Speeches and Writings of Mother Jones* (Pittsburgh, Pa.: University of Pittsburgh Press, 1988), pp. xxvi–xxvii. Mother Jones appears ten times in *The New York Times Index* before 1905, vanishes for eight years until 1913, then reemerges in dozens of stories during the mine wars in West Virginia and Colorado.
3. Steel, ed., *Speeches and Writings,* p. xxvii.
4. For works on the Progressive Era, see Chapter 5, note 23.
5. On the history of socialism, see James R. Green, *Grass-roots Socialism: Radical Movements in the Southwest, 1895–1943* (Baton Rouge: Louisiana State University Press, 1978); James Weinstein, *The Decline of Socialism in America, 1912–1925* (New York: Monthly Review Press, 1967); John H. M. Laslett, *Labor and the Left: A Study of Socialist and Radical Influences in the American Labor Movement, 1881–1924* (New York: Basic Books, 1970); John H. M. Laslett and Seymour Martin Lipset, eds., *Failure of a Dream? Essays in the History of American Socialism* (Garden City, N.Y.: Anchor Press, 1974); William M. Dick, *Labor and Socialism in America: The Gompers Era* (Port Washington, N.Y.: Kennikat Press, 1972); Mari Jo Buhle, *Women and American Socialism, 1870–1920* (Urbana: University of Illinois Press, 1981), Donald Drew Egbert and Stow Persons, eds., *Socialism and American Life,* 2 vols. (Princeton, N.J.: Princeton University Press, 1952); Howard H. Quint, *The Forging of American Socialism: Origins of the Modern Movement* (Columbia: University of South Carolina Press, 1953); David A. Shannon, *The Socialist Party of America: A History* (Chicago: Quadrangle Books, 1967).
6. In addition to the sources cited in note 5, see Nick Salvatore, *Eugene Debs: Citizen and Socialist* (Urbana: University of Illinois Press, 1982), pp. 181–261; Melvyn Dubofsky, *Industrialism and the American Worker* (Arlington Heights, Ill.: A.H.M. Publishing, 1975), pp. 14–16; Steel, ed., *Speeches and Writings,* p. xxiv.
7. James Creelman, "America's Trouble-Makers," *Pearson's Magazine,* July 1908, pp. 3–28. Creelman had worked as a correspondent for the *New York Herald* and the New York *World.*

8. *New York Times*, August 8, 1904, p. 14; Eugene V. Debs to Mother Jones, in James Robert Constantine, ed., *The Letters of Eugene V. Debs*, vol. 1 (Urbana: University of Illinois Press, 1990), p. 156; Eugene V. Debs, *Unionism and Socialism*, reprinted in Arthur M. Schlesinger, Jr., ed., *Writings and Speeches of Eugene V. Debs* (New York: Hermitage Press, 1948), pp. 95–125. Debs wrote to Mother Jones on January 28, 1901, "I am trying to build up a little book business out of which to make a living so that I shall not have to accept anything from any sources for any service I may render the cause. I feel confident you can help me a little and at the same time help yourself as well as the movement"; see Edward M. Steel, ed., *The Correspondence of Mother Jones* (Pittsburgh, Pa.: University of Pittsburgh Press, 1985), pp. 6–7. She also sold cheap editions of *Merrie England*, a popular socialist tract written by the Englishman Robert Blatchford, and often she carried other pamphlets that she gave away or sold.

9. Mother Jones, "Civilization in Southern Mills," *International Socialist Review* 1 (March 1901), p. 541; *Washington Post*, February 17, 1903, CUA, 7/3.2. Dale Fetherling, *Mother Jones: The Miners' Angel* (Carbondale: Southern Illinois University Press, 1974), esp. pp. 149–54, questions Mother Jones's commitment to socialism, but I believe he overdraws his case. Certainly, she was not particularly interested in doctrine or ideology, she sometimes broke ranks to support mainstream politicians, and occasionally her words veered toward anarcho-syndicalism. Nonetheless, Mother Jones's fundamental social ideas, which she maintained until her death, are best described as socialist. Philip Foner, ed., *Mother Jones Speaks* (New York: Monad Press, 1983), argues strongly for the consistency of Mother Jones's socialist beliefs in his introduction.

10. Mother Jones to Jack London, September 19, 1905, November 2, 1905, May 17, 1906, box 334 (71–73), JL15620–22, Jack London Collection, HL.

11. Steel, ed., *Speeches and Writings*, p. xiii; *New York Times*, April 15, 1905, p. 7.

12. *Miners' Magazine*, July 6, 1905, p. 7. As she described her efforts in a letter to William Wilson: "We are permeating them with clear conception of their class interest, trying to put the Spirit [of] Solidarity in them." See Mother Jones to William B. Wilson, May 9, 1905, in Steel, ed., *Correspondence*, pp. 53–54.

13. *Miners' Magazine*, July 6, 1905, p. 8; also see *Miners' Magazine*, May 4, 1905, p. 8, for a similar speech in Calumet, Michigan, among striking copper miners.

14. *Miners' Magazine*, July 5, 1906, p. 3; October 10, 1907, p. 4; April 9, 1908, p. 4; September 23, 1909, p. 6.

15. Mother Jones to Mrs. Potter Palmer, January 12, 1907, in *Miners' Magazine*, January 24, 1907, reprinted in Steel, ed., *Correspondence*, pp. 61–62.

16. Mary Heaton Vorse, *A Footnote to Folly* (New York: Farrar and Rinehart, 1935), pp. 287–88, claimed that Mother Jones simply did not trust anyone but those of the working class.

17. Steel, ed., *Correspondence*, pp. xvi–xviii; Mother Jones, *Autobiography of Mother Jones*, ed. Mary Field Parton (Chicago: Charles H. Kerr and Company, 1925), p. 242.

18. Melvyn Dubofsky, *We Shall Be All: A History of the Industrial Workers of the World* (Chicago: Quadrangle Books, 1969), pp. 57–87; Sister John Francis Raffaele, "Mary Harris Jones and the United Mine Workers of America" (master's thesis, Catholic University of America, 1964), pp. 33–35. The IWW manifesto was printed in *Miners' Magazine*, January 26, 1905, pp. 4–5. *Miners' Magazine*, July 6, 1905, also reported the proceedings of the June convention. *The Outlook*, which was not sympathetic to the WFM or the IWW, ran a series of articles on them during 1906 and 1907; see especially May 19, 1906, pp. 125–33, and July 7, 1906, pp. 551–55. Other materials can be found in box 1, IWW Collection, WSU.

19. Fetherling, *Mother Jones*, pp. 70–73; "Remarks at the First Convention of the Industrial Workers of the World," Chicago, June 27–July 8, 1905, in Steel, ed., *Speeches and Writings*, pp. 22–23, quoted from Franklin Rosemont, Joyce Kornbluh, and Fred Thompson, eds., *Rebel Voices: An IWW Anthology* (Ann Arbor: University of Michigan Press, 1968), pp. 12–13. On the IWW, also see Dubofsky, *We Shall Be All*, and *Proceedings of the First Convention of the Industrial Workers of the World* (New York: Labor News Company, 1905).

20. Mother Jones's name was the first of the twenty-six signers on the IWW manifesto. On her role in the founding of the IWW, see "Remarks at the First Convention of the Industrial Workers of the World," in Steel, ed., *Speeches and Writings*, pp. 22–23; Fetherling, *Mother Jones*, pp. 70–73.

21. The fullest telling of the case is J. Anthony Lukas, *Big Trouble: A Murder in a Small Western Town Sets Off a Struggle for the Soul of America* (New York: Simon and Schuster, 1997), pp. 15–200. Also see Dubofsky, *We Shall Be All*, pp. 96–98. Note that McParlan changed the spelling of his name to McParland shortly after the Molly Maguire case in 1877.

22. Lukas, *Big Trouble*, pp. 201–510; Dubofsky, *We Shall Be All*, pp. 98–102. The *Appeal to Reason* gave the trial extensive coverage with headlines such as DESTRUCTION OF FEDERATION PURPOSE OF CONSPIRACY and PINKERTON CRIMES LAID BARE; see, for example, April 14, 1906, p. 2.

23. Mother Jones to Terence Powderly, May 9, 1906; Mother Jones to the Socialists of Massachusetts (an open letter, originally published in the *Appeal to Reason*, August 18, 1906); Jones to Powderly, May 24, 1907, all in Steel, ed., *Correspondence*, pp. 58, 60, 63–64; Lukas, *Big Trouble*, pp. 329, 461; Fetherling, *Mother Jones*, pp. 73–76; Mother Jones, "The Dawning of a New Era," *Appeal to Reason*, February 23, 1907, reprinted in Steel, ed., *Speeches and Writings*, pp. 276–78.

24. Lukas, *Big Trouble*, chs. 11–14; Mother Jones devoted four pages to the trial in the *Autobiography*, pp. 132–35.

25. Lukas, *Big Trouble*, ch. 14.

26. William Dirk Raat, *Revoltosos: Mexico's Rebels in the United States, 1903–1923* (College Station: Texas A&M University Press, 1981), pp. 13–18. Also see Ward S. Albro, *Always a Rebel: Ricardo Flores Magón and the Mexican Revolution* (Fort Worth: Texas Christian University Press, 1992).

27. Raat, *Revoltosos*, pp. 19–43.

28. Ibid., pp. 43–46; Fetherling, *Mother Jones*, pp. 79–82.

29. Manuel Sarabia told his story in "How I Was Kidnapped," *International Socialist Review* 9, no. 11 (May 1909), pp. 853–62. The *International Socialist Review* gave considerable space to the Mexican Revolution, especially in a series of articles by John Murray in 1909 and John Kenneth Turner in 1910, including excerpts from Turner's book *Barbarous Mexico*, published that same year by the Chicago socialist press Charles Kerr and Company. The indictments are from the National Archives, Southwest Branch, *United States of America* v. *R. Flores Magón, Antonio I. Villarreal, Librado Rivera, and Manuel Sarabia*, in the District Court of the Second Judicial District of the Territory of Arizona, December 28, 1907. Mother Jones told a sketchy version of this story in the *Autobiography*, pp. 136–44.

30. See Mother Jones, "Testimony before the Committee on Rules, House of Representatives, on H. J. Res. 201, Providing for a Joint Committee to Investigate Alleged Persecutions of Mexican Citizens by the Government of Mexico, Washington, D.C., June 14, 1910," in Philip Foner, ed., *Mother Jones Speaks* (New York: Monad Press, 1983), pp. 370–72; Fetherling, *Mother Jones*, pp. 79–81; Judith Elaine Mikeal, "Mother Mary Jones: The Labor Movement's Impious Joan of Arc" (master's thesis, University of North Carolina, 1965), pp. 38–41; Raat, *Revoltosos*, pp. 47–48.

31. Mother Jones, speech at UMW convention, Indianapolis, January 27, 1909, in Steel, ed., *Speeches and Writings*, pp. 27–31.

32. Ibid.

33. Ibid., pp. 24, 27–31; Flynn, *Rebel Girl*, p. 88. Mother Jones had another bout with illness not long after she gave this speech, in the spring of 1909; see Eugene V. Debs to Adolph Germer, April 5, 1909, in Constantine, ed., *Letters of Eugene V. Debs*, vol. 1, p. 303.

34. Mother Jones, "To the Socialists and Trade Unionists of America," *Appeal to Reason*, February 20, 1909, and *Miners' Magazine*, February 25, 1909, pp. 6–7, in Steel, ed., *Correspondence*, pp. 67–69. For Mother Jones's participation in these cases, see Raffaele, "Mary Harris Jones," pp. 38–41; Fetherling, *Mother Jones*, pp. 79–82; Raat, *Revoltosos*, pp. 48–49.

35. Mother Jones, "Oh! Ye Lovers of Liberty!" *Appeal to Reason*, January 23, 1909, in Steel, ed., *Speeches and Writings*, pp. 285–87. The U.S. Supreme Court in 1857 ruled that the slave Dred Scott must be returned to bondage.

36. Mother Jones to Gottlieb Hoehn, June 17, 1909; Mother Jones to William Howard Taft, December 2, 1909, both in Steel, ed., *Correspondence*, pp. 69–70, 73–74; Mother Jones, "Testimony before the Committee on Rules," in Foner, ed., *Mother Jones Speaks*, pp. 372–73; Mother Jones, *Autobiography*, pp. 142–43. Declared *Miners' Magazine*, July 1, 1909, p. 3, of her intercession with Taft, "This heroic woman has been tireless in her efforts, and if earnestness, sincerity, logic, and eloquence have any influence upon the chief magistrate of the

nation, he will certainly feel impressed with the fact that the cases of the Mexicans deserve his most serious consideration."

37. Mother Jones, "Mexico and Murder," *Appeal to Reason*, October 23, 1909, in Steel, ed., *Speeches and Writings*, pp. 288–89; Mother Jones, "The Tyranny of Mexico," *New York Call*, December 13, 1909, speech delivered at People's Forum, Hart's Hall, Brooklyn, New York, December 12, 1909, in Foner, ed., *Mother Jones Speaks*, pp. 138–39.

38. Mother Jones, "Testimony before the Committee on Rules," in Foner, ed., *Mother Jones Speaks*, pp. 370–74. She continued to lobby for the release of the *revoltosos*. In "A Sacred Call to Action," she wrote, "Some humane congressmen have introduced a bill of inquiry asking the attorney general to explain why as revolutionists these men are held. I beg you in the name of freedom to flood Congress with letters demanding that this investigation be pushed through Congress." See *St. Louis Labor*, April 16, 1910, in Steel, ed., *Speeches and Writings*, p. 203.

39. Letter of *revoltosos* to Mother Jones, November 31, 1909, in Steel, ed., *Correspondence*, pp. 72–73.

40. Foner, ed., *Mother Jones Speaks*, pp. 121–22, 132–35, 584–86; Mother Jones to Manuel Calero, October 25, 1911; Mother Jones to Ricardo Flores Magón, November 4, 1911, both in Steel, ed., *Correspondence*, pp. 97–100, 100–1; Fetherling, *Mother Jones*, pp. 81–82; Raat, *Revoltosos*, pp. 58–60.

41. Eugene Debs felt less optimistic about Madero; see his "The Crisis in Mexico," *International Socialist Review* 12 (July 1911), pp. 22–24. A few years after Madero's assassination in 1911, Pancho Villa raided American border towns and became an outlaw in the eyes of the U.S. government, but Mother Jones declared that America could use half a dozen Pancho Villas. On Americans' response to Villa, see Friedrich Katz, *The Life and Times of Pancho Villa* (Stanford, Calif.: Stanford University Press, 1998), pp. 309–30.

42. Fetherling, *Mother Jones*, pp. 78–79, 82–83.

43. Steel, ed., *Correspondence*, pp. xxvii–xxviii; *United Mine Workers Journal*, April 7, 1910, p. 2; Nancy Woloch, *Women and the American Experience* (New York: Knopf, 1984), pp. 212, 237–38; Mother Jones, "Girl Slaves of the Milwaukee Brewers," *United Mine Workers Journal*, April 7, 1910, p. 2. On the shirtwaist strike, see William Mailly, "The Working Girls' Strike," *Independent*, September 2, 1909, pp. 1416–20; and *Outlook*, December 11, 1909, pp. 799–801.

44. Mother Jones, "Mother Jones' Plea for Babies," in *United Mine Workers Journal*, October 27, 1910, p. 2. Also see Mother Jones, "Girl Slaves of the Milwaukee Brewers," p. 2; Mother Jones, "Governor Comer's Alabama Cotton Mills," *United Mine Workers Journal*, November 12, 1908, p. 5; "Mother Jones Gives Out Story," *United Mine Workers Journal*, October 8, 1908, p. 6; "Mother Jones' Latest Visit to the Anthracite Fields," *United Mine Workers Journal*, November 24, 1910, p. 7.

45. Mother Jones to Thomas J. Morgan, July 20, 1909, August 1, 1910, March 12,

1911; "Statement of Mother Jones," May 12, 1910; all in Steel, ed., *Correspondence*, pp. 71–72, 77–78, 92–93, 75–76. Morgan's papers are in Special Collections, University of Illinois, Champaign, and Special Collections, University of Chicago (box 1, files 3–7, are particularly helpful for this episode).

46. "Affidavit of Mother Jones," January 31, 1911, in Steel, ed., *Correspondence*, pp. 87–90. Morgan's newspaper, *The Provoker*, carried the story of Mother Jones's charges against Barnes.

47. Mother Jones to Thomas J. Morgan, September 9, 1910, October 14, 1910, December 16, 1910; all in Steel, ed., *Correspondence*, pp. 80–81, 81–82, 82–83.

48. Fetherling, *Mother Jones*, pp. 149–51; "Affidavit of Mother Jones" and Mother Jones to Thomas J. Morgan, February 11, 1911, both in Steel, ed., *Correspondence*, pp. 87–90, 91–92. The whole ugly incident received an airing in the pages of *Miners' Magazine*. Fifty years later, Ralph Korngold repeated Berger's charges in a 1963 letter to Adolph and Vivian Germer; Adolph Germer responded to Ralph and Piri Korngold on February 16, 1963, Correspondence, Korngold Collection, NL. After Barnes was forced to resign, Mother Jones referred to the executive board as "that whole bunch of blood-sucking grafters" and told Thomas Morgan, "I think the Socialists of this Country owe me a debt of gratitude for the exposures." See Jones to Morgan, August 8, 1911, in Steel, ed., *Correspondence*, pp. 96–97.

49. George H. Goebel to Eugene V. Debs, August 11, 1912; Debs to Goebel, August 13, 1912; Eugene V. Debs to John Spargo, July 12, 1912; Debs to Goebel, July 29, 1912; Eugene V. Debs to James M. Reilly, August 7, 1912; all in Constantine, ed., *Letters of Eugene V. Debs*, vol. 1, pp. 537–38, 543–48, 494–99, 516–19, 529–33. Also see Eugene V. Debs, "Mother Jones," *Appeal to Reason*, November 23, 1907, reprinted in Arthur Schlesinger, Jr., ed., *Writings and Speeches of Eugene V. Debs* (New York: Hermitage Press, 1948), pp. 285–86.

50. Mother Jones to Thomas J. Morgan, December 16, 1910, in Steel, ed., *Correspondence*, pp. 82–83.

51. Mother Jones to Thomas J. Morgan, December 25, 1910, in Steel, ed., *Correspondence*, pp. 83–84. During the Pennsylvania strike in early 1911, Mother Jones stayed in the town of Greensburg at the home of Peter and Catherine Conroy, a mining family. "I am very lonesome after my room and all of you— particularly after little Joe," she wrote after she left. (Young Joe worked as a messenger for Mother Jones, carrying bail money to the sheriff for jailed miners.) But once again, her mission took her away from domestic comforts. From Denver, she wrote and asked the Conroys to "do up all my things" and send them to Chicago. See Mother Jones to Catherine M. Conroy, February 5, 1911, in Steel, ed., *Correspondence*, pp. 90–91.

52. The strike against Gould was a particularly low moment for the Knights of Labor; see Craig Phelan, *Grand Master Workman: Terence Powderly and the Knights of Labor* (Westport, Conn.: Greenwood Press, 2000), pp. 178–85; and Leon Fink, *Workingmen's Democracy: The Knights of Labor and American Politics* (Urbana: University of Illinois Press, 1983), pp. 119–20.

53. Mother Jones to Terence V. Powderly, May 24, 1907, in Steel, ed., *Correspondence*, p. 63; Mother Jones, "The Grave of Martin Irons," *Appeal to Reason*, May 11, 1907, in Steel, ed., *Speeches and Writings*, pp. 279–80; Mother Jones, speech at UMW convention, Indianapolis, January 29, 1916, in Steel, ed., *Speeches and Writings*, pp. 183–84; Mother Jones, speech at UMW convention, Indianapolis, September 17, 1919, in Steel, ed., *Speeches and Writings*, pp. 208–9. Powderly tells the story of Martin Irons in his *The Path I Trod: The Autobiography of Terence V. Powderly*, ed. Harry J. Carman, Henry David, and Paul Guthrie (New York: Columbia University Press, 1940), pp. 114–39. Also see Martin Irons, "My Experiences in the Labor Movement," *Lippincott's Monthly Magazine*, June 1886, pp. 618–27.

7. "Medieval West Virginia"

1. Mother Jones, *The Autobiography of Mother Jones*, ed. Mary Field Parton (Chicago: Charles H. Kerr and Company, 1925), p. 235.
2. Ronald Eller, *Miners, Millhands, and Mountaineers: Industrialization of the Appalachian South, 1880–1930* (Knoxville: University of Tennessee Press, 1982), pp. 128–29; David A. Corbin, *Life, Work, and Rebellion in the Coal Fields: The Southern West Virginia Miners, 1880–1922* (Urbana: University of Illinois Press, 1981), pp. 4–5.
3. Eller, *Miners, Millhands, and Mountaineers*, pp. 134, 138, 153, 178–82.
4. Ibid., pp. 165–75, 193–94, 197–98; Corbin, *Life, Work, and Rebellion*, pp. 8–10; Maier B. Fox, *United We Stand: The United Mine Workers of America, 1890–1990* (Washington, D.C.: United Mine Workers, 1990), pp. 146–47.
5. Eller, *Miners, Millhands, and Mountaineers*, pp. 210–19; Corbin, *Life, Work, and Rebellion*, pp. 10–18; Fox, *United We Stand*, p. 147.
6. Corbin, *Life, Work, and Rebellion*, pp. 25–52. For an intertwining of history and memory, see Duane Lockard, *Coal: A Memoir and Critique* (Charlottesville: University Press of Virginia, 1998).
7. Corbin, *Life, Work, and Rebellion*, pp. 61–79, 110–11, 146–69; the miner-preacher is quoted on p. 159.
8. Fox, *United We Stand*, pp. 147–48.
9. Corbin, *Life, Work, and Rebellion*, pp. 110–11.
10. Howard B. Lee describes the mines as independently owned, but John Alexander Williams, looking a bit more carefully, found most independent operations to be in fact controlled by eastern interests, thus his invoking of the concept of the "colonial" economy. See Howard B. Lee, *Bloodletting in Appalachia* (Morgantown: West Virginia University Press, 1969), pp. 15–18; John Alexander Williams, *West Virginia: A Bicentennial History* (New York: Norton, 1976), pp. 148–57. Also see Fox, *United We Stand*, pp. 147–48.
11. Sister John Francis Raffaele, "Mary Harris Jones and the United Mine Workers of America" (master's thesis, Catholic University of America, 1964), pp. 46–47;

Corbin, *Life, Work, and Rebellion,* pp. 87–89; Edward M. Steel, *The Court-Martial of Mother Jones* (Lexington: University Press of Kentucky, 1995), pp. 3–5, 71–73; Lee, *Bloodletting,* pp. 15–25; Lawrence R. Lynch, "The West Virginia Coal Strike," *Political Science Quarterly* 29, no. 4 (December 1914), pp. 629, 641–42. A useful summary of events during the year beginning April 1912 is Walter B. Palmer, "An Account of the Strike of Bituminous Miners in the Kanawha Valley of West Virginia, April 1912 to March 1913," MS in General Records of the Labor Department, Chief Clerk's Files, record group 174, box 23, file 16/13, Coal Fields, West Virginia, NARA.

12. Mother Jones, speech at UMW convention, Columbus, Ohio, January 21, 1911, in Edward M. Steel, ed., *The Speeches and Writings of Mother Jones* (Pittsburgh, Pa.: University of Pittsburgh Press, 1988), pp. 44–55; Dale Fetherling, *Mother Jones: The Miners' Angel* (Carbondale: Southern Illinois University Press, 1974), pp. 85–86; Judith Elaine Mikeal, "Mother Mary Jones: The Labor Movement's Impious Joan of Arc" (master's thesis, University of North Carolina, 1965), pp. 41–44.

13. Mother Jones, *Autobiography,* pp. 148–49; Lynch, "West Virginia Coal Strike," pp. 634–35; Fetherling, *Mother Jones,* pp. 86–87; U.S. Senate Commission on Industrial Relations, *Final Report and Testimony,* 64th Cong., 1st sess., 1916, S. Doc. 215, vol. II, pp. 10627–28.

14. *Charleston Daily Gazette,* June 11, 1912, reprinted in *International Socialist Review,* March 13, 1913, pp. 648–49, and in Philip Foner, ed., *Mother Jones Speaks* (New York: Monad Press, 1983), pp. 491–92; Steel, *Court-Martial,* pp. 8–10.

15. Lee, *Bloodletting,* pp. 26–27. Lee declares in a footnote, "In 1925, the late Jess Sullivan, secretary of the West Virginia Coal Operators Association, loaned me a transcribed copy of this speech by Mother Jones. These excerpts were taken from it." The UMW leadership in 1912 was coming more into line with Mother Jones's progressive views; see manuscript essay titled "The Mine Workers," p. 2, box 9, "Staunton Mining" folder, Archives of Labor and Urban Affairs, Edward Wieck Collection, WSU.

16. The originals of Mother Jones's speeches are available in manuscript at WVaU, "West Virginia Mining Investigation Committee," pp. 1–151. They are conveniently reprinted in Steel, ed., *Speeches and Writings,* pp. 56–117; but see especially Mother Jones's speech in Charleston, West Virginia, August 1, 1912, p. 59, and September 6, 1912, p. 112. Also see Fetherling, *Mother Jones,* pp. 85–87, and Mikeal, "Mother Mary Jones," pp. 59–61. According to Daniel J. O'Regan's report to the Senate Committee on Education and Labor investigating the disturbances, reliable sources said that Mother Jones told the miners to "drive the guards out of the county"; see "Paint and Cabin Creek, West Virginia, August 5, 1914," Commission on Industrial Relations Records, 1912–1915, record group 174, box 17, file 392, NARA. Local West Virginia newspapers gave a strong—sometimes overheated—sense of the confrontations; for examples, see "Troops Respond to Call for Aid," Huntington *Herald-Dispatch,* July 28, 1912,

p. 1; "Strikers Threaten to Kill the Mine Guards," *Wheeling Intelligencer,* August 16, 1912, p. 1; "Charleston to Be 'Invaded' Again by Miners En Masse," *Charleston Gazette,* September 15, 1912, p. 1.

17. "West Virginia Mining Investigation Committee," pp. 1–20, 53–77, 89–116, 130–44, 148–51, in Steel, ed., *Speeches and Writings,* pp. 56–118. The quote is from her speech in Charleston, West Virginia, August 1, 1912, p. 64. Also see her speeches in Montgomery, West Virginia, August 4, 1912; Charleston, August 15, 1912; Montgomery, August 4, 1912; Charleston, August 1, 1912; all in Steel, ed., *Speeches and Writings,* pp. 60, 64, 71, 77, 95, 86, 68.

18. Mother Jones, speeches in Charleston, West Virginia, August 1, 1912, and August 15, 1912, both in Steel, ed., *Speeches and Writings,* pp. 65, 92.

19. Mother Jones, speech in Montgomery, West Virginia, August 4, 1912, in Steel, ed., *Speeches and Writings,* pp. 73–74, 81, 83. On workers and Christianity, see Herbert Gutman's classic essay "Protestantism and the American Labor Movement: The Christian Spirit in the Gilded Age," in *Work, Culture, and Society in Industrializing America* (New York: Knopf, 1977), pp. 79–117.

20. Mother Jones, speech in Charleston, West Virginia, August 15, 1912, in Steel, ed., *Speeches and Writings,* pp. 96, 100.

21. Mother Jones, speeches in Montgomery, West Virginia, August 4, 1912; and in Charleston, West Virginia, August 15, 1912, September 6, 1912, September 21, 1912; all in Steel, ed., *Speeches and Writings,* pp. 81, 89, 91, 109, 107, 116.

22. Mother Jones, speeches in Charleston, August 1, 1912; Morgantown, August 4, 1912; Charleston, August 1, 1913; all in Steel, ed., *Speeches and Writings,* pp. 69, 78, 80, 62.

23. Mother Jones, speeches in Charleston, August 1, 1912; Montgomery, August 4, 1912; Charleston, August 15, 1912; all in Steel, ed., *Speeches and Writings,* pp. 59–61, 65–66, 76, 85, 96, 102, 114.

24. Mother Jones, speeches in Charleston, West Virginia, August 1, 1912, and September 6, 1912, both in Steel, ed., *Speeches and Writings,* pp. 59–61, 65, 114.

25. "Our Strike in West Virginia," *United Mine Workers Journal,* September 26, 1912, p. 1; Mother Jones, speech in Charleston, August 15, 1912, in Steel, ed., *Speeches and Writings,* p. 104; Corbin, *Life, Work, and Rebellion,* pp. 93–95; "Strikers' Wives Are Now Incited," *Wheeling Register,* November 2, 1912, p. 1.

26. Mother Jones, speech in Charleston, September 6, 1912, in Steel, ed., *Speeches and Writings,* p. 112.

27. Mother Jones, speeches in Charleston, September 6, 1912, and September 21, 1912; both in Steel, ed., *Speeches and Writings,* pp. 112, 116. Mother Jones always described supplicants using the same formulaic language—"For God's sake, Mother, come up and do something for us."

28. Ralph Chaplin, *Wobbly: The Rough and Tumble Story of an American Radical* (Chicago: University of Chicago Press, 1948), p. 120; Lynch, "West Virginia Coal Strike," p. 645; Fred Mooney, *Struggle in the Coal Fields: The Autobiography of Fred Mooney* (Montgomery: West Virginia University Library, 1967), p. 20.

29. "3,000 More Go Out on Strike," *United Mine Workers Journal*, August 15, 1912, p. 3; Mother Jones, *Autobiography*, pp. 154–56.

30. Mother Jones, *Autobiography*, pp. 154–56; Commission on Industrial Relations, *Final Report and Testimony*, p. 10628; Mother Jones, speech at District 14 UMW convention, Pittsburg, Kansas, April 30, 1914, in Steel, ed., *Speeches and Writings*, pp. 147–48; Mikeal, "Mother Mary Jones," pp. 62–64; Steel, *Court-Martial*, pp. 5–6. The UMW did not supervise Mother Jones very closely in these years. Though she was paid by the national organization once again, starting in 1911, and would remain on the payroll for a decade, she denied that anyone told her what to do. District 17 president Tom Cairnes disavowed responsibility for her; he said that she neither was employed by nor represented District 17 (which was technically true, since she worked for the national office). The purpose of such disclaimers was to limit legal liability. But ten years after the Cabin Creek strike, Mother Jones indicated that she had been in close touch with national UMW president John White, that she had even gone to Indianapolis to consult with him, and that she communicated with district leaders as well. See "West Virginia Mining Investigation Committee," testimony of Tom Cairnes, vol. 4, pp. 601–19, in WVaU; Edward M. Steel, ed., *The Correspondence of Mother Jones* (Pittsburgh, Pa.: University of Pittsburgh Press, 1985), pp. 9–10.

31. Harold E. West, "Civil War in the West Virginia Coal Mines," *Survey*, April 5, 1913, p. 50; "West Virginia Mining Investigation Committee," vol. 7, pp. 1229–31, 1380–83, 1438–42, vol. 5, pp. 971–72, WVaU; Mikeal, "Mother Mary Jones," pp. 64, 65, 68; Raffaele, "Mary Harris Jones," p. 47; Fetherling, *Mother Jones*, pp. 88–89; David A. Corbin, ed., *The West Virginia Mine Wars: An Anthology* (Charleston, W.Va.: Appalachian Editions, 1997), pp. 50–52. Coal operator W. P. Tams, Jr., when asked about Mother Jones, said, "Oh, she was a terrible old thing. She was an old battle axe." See oral interview with Major W. P. Tams, Jr., manuscript collection 2584, WVaU. After the strike was over, the operators summarized their position for the Senate Committee on Education and Labor in a preliminary statement, a printed copy of which is available in CUA, 7/2.11. Operators and guards repeated the charge over and over again that Mother Jones—using vulgar, inflammatory, and profane language—unleashed the lawlessness and intimidation that caused contented men to strike; see *Congressional Investigation of Conditions in the Paint Creek District, West Virginia*, part 2, testimony of James Clagett, pp. 1176–77, Ira F. Davis, pp. 1298–302, J. E. Staton, pp. 1565–69, R. H. Anderson, pp. 1586–88, J. H. Mayfield, pp. 1619–21. On her profanity, see testimony of S. P. Richmond, pp. 1190–91, and C. C. Woods, pp. 1179–81.

32. Even Fetherling, who often questions Mother Jones's aims and motives, never questions her effectiveness among the miners. On American civil religion, see, for example, Russell E. Richey and Donald G. Jones, *American Civil Religion* (New York: Harper & Row, 1974).

33. "The Strike in West Virginia," *United Mine Workers Journal*, August 29, 1912,

p. 3; Mikeal, "Mother Mary Jones," pp. 64–65; Commission on Industrial Relations, *Final Report and Testimony*, pp. 10628–29; Steel, *Court-Martial*, p. 8; Fetherling, *Mother Jones*, pp. 89–90.

34. Mother Jones, *Autobiography*, pp. 157–58; Commission on Industrial Relations, *Final Report and Testimony*, p. 10628; Fetherling, *Mother Jones*, pp. 89–94; Steel, *Court-Martial*, pp. 11–13. According to Mayfield's testimony, Mother Jones claimed that the "hot heads" followed her toward the town of Red Warrior, that about a third of the 150 men were armed, that they made some threatening gestures but dispersed when asked to do so. "West Virginia Mining Investigation Committee," testimony of J. H. Mayfield, guard, vol. 6, pp. 1158–61, and C. A. Cabell, manager Carbon Coal Co., vol. 5, pp. 9770–71.

35. Raffaele, "Mary Harris Jones," pp. 49–50; Fetherling, *Mother Jones*, pp. 90–94; Steel, *Court-Martial*, pp. 11–13; "Our Strike in West Virginia," *United Mine Workers Journal*, September 12, 1912, p. 1; "Mother Jones Thrills Thousands," *United Mine Workers Journal*, September 26, 1912, p. 2. In the November 1912 elections, Kanawha County voted in the entire Socialist slate, a measure of how radicalized the area had become.

36. Steel, *Court-Martial*, pp. 10–11; Raffaele, "Mary Harris Jones," pp. 50–52; "Notify Militia to Be Ready at Moment's Notice," *Huntington Advertiser*, November 4, 1912, p. 1; "Mine Workers to Hold Meeting," *United Mine Workers Journal*, November 21, 1912, p. 1; "Weekly News Letter from West Virginia," *United Mine Workers Journal*, January 23, 1913, p. 2; "Affidavit from Escaping Peons of Cabin Creek," *United Mine Workers Journal*, February 13, 1913, p. 8.

37. "Guerilla War Opens," *Fairmont West Virginian*, November 13, 1912, p. 1; "Three Hundred Miners Open Fire on Train Yesterday," *Charleston Gazette*, November 15, 1912, p. 1; *Report of the West Virginia Mining Investigation Commission* (Charleston, W.Va.: Tribune Printing Co., 1912), pp. 1–12, in WVaU; Raffaele, "Mary Harris Jones," pp. 50–52; Mikeal, "Mother Mary Jones," pp. 68–70; Fetherling, *Mother Jones*, pp. 94–95; Steel, *Court-Martial*, pp. 7–8, 12–13; "Our Strike in West Virginia," *United Mine Workers Journal*, January 2, 1913, p. 1. Mother Jones referred privately to Bishop Donahue as the "Wheeling Sky-Pilot." She wrote to Terence Powderly, "How a man in his position could display such a lack of knowledge of the economic struggle, is more than I know. He has very little grasp of the affair in West Virginia, and cares less. He was fed and entertained by the exploiters of labor." See Jones to Powderly, September 20, 1913, in Steel, ed., *Correspondence*, p. 119. Before the congressional investigating committee, Bishop Donahue accused Mother Jones of making speeches that encouraged violence, including the shooting of mine guards and operators; see *Conditions in the Paint Creek District*, vol. 2, pp. 1716–18.

38. Steel, *Court-Martial*, pp. 14–17; Fetherling, *Mother Jones*, pp. 95–96; Mikeal, "Mother Mary Jones," pp. 71–73; Raffaele, "Mary Harris Jones," pp. 53–54; "Our Strike in West Virginia," *United Mine Workers Journal*, February 20, 1913, p. 1. Much of the story is in dispute—Quinn Morton insisted that the Bull

Moose Special was fired on first; a mine guard who was on the train, Lee Calvin, was certain that the miners did not initiate the shooting; see Corbin, *West Virginia Mine Wars*, pp. 35–46. The story of Sesco Estep's murder is well told in Lois McLean, "Blood Flows on the Creeks," in Ken Sullivan, ed., *The Goldenseal Book of the West Virginia Mine Wars* (Charleston, W.Va.: Pictorial Histories Publishing Co., 1991), pp. 25–28; also see Ralph Chaplin interview, box 112, file 7, pp. 7687–90, IWW Collection, WSU.

39. Steel, *Court-Martial*, pp. 14–17; Fetherling, *Mother Jones*, pp. 95–96; Mikeal, "Mother Mary Jones," pp. 71–73; Raffaele, "Mary Harris Jones," pp. 53–54.

40. Steel, *Court-Martial*, pp. 20–24, 100; Mikeal, "Mother Mary Jones," pp. 73–75; Fetherling, *Mother Jones*, pp. 95–96; "Our Strike in West Virginia," *United Mine Workers Journal*, March 13, 1913, p. 1; "Our Strike in West Virginia," *United Mine Workers Journal*, March 6, 1913, p. 1. Three years after the trial, Mother Jones claimed that she told the governor: "I want to tell the governor of the State that he can chain me to that tree outside there and he can get his dogs of war to riddle this body with bullets, but I will not surrender my constitutional rights to him. I happen to be one of the women who tramped the highways where the blood of the revolutionists watered it that I might have a trial by jury." See Commission on Industrial Relations, *Final Report and Testimony*, p. 10630. Only one West Virginia Supreme Court justice dissented from the state's decision to impose martial law; Ira E. Robinson's argument was reprinted by the union in a pamphlet called "Three Great Protests against Trial of Civilians by Military Commissions" (Charleston, W.Va.: Kanawha Citizen Print, 1913), pp. 3–26.

41. Steel, *Court-Martial*, pp. 20–25.

42. For testimony against her in the trial, see Steel, *Court-Martial*, pp. 46–50, 155–57, 185, 209–12, 246–56, 274–77.

43. T. H. Huddy, superintendent of the Boomer Coal and Coke Company, testified that Mother Jones used abusive language toward mine managers, questioned why the superintendents lived in larger homes than the miners, and asked why the bosses' wives did not do their own washing and cleaning instead of hiring the wives and daughters of the coal camps. Huddy added that Mother Jones accused Governor Glasscock of weakness and inefficiency, made disparaging remarks about the clergy, told the miners to keep their guns, and declared, "The coal in these hills is rightfully yours, and if these operators don't give you what you want, go after it and get it." See Steel, *Court-Martial*, p. 252.

44. Steel, *Court-Martial*, pp. 33–39, 55–57; Fetherling, *Mother Jones*, pp. 95–96; " 'Mother Jones' Defiant," *New York Times*, March 11, 1913, p. 1. Although many people were aghast at the arrests in West Virginia, not until March did anything like a campaign to secure the prisoners' release get moving. As late as April—two months after her arrest—UMW president John P. White sent a telegram to Secretary of Labor William Wilson pointing out that Mother Jones and others had been arrested outside martial-law territory and transported to the military district, a dangerous precedent for constitutional rights. See White

to Wilson, April 8, 1913, Department of Labor, Chief Clerk's File, 1907–1942, record group 174, box 23, file 16/13, "Coalfields—West Virginia," NARA.

45. Mrs. Fremont Older, "Answering a Question," *Collier's*, April 19, 1913, pp. 26, 28. Older also covered the trial for *The Independent*; see "The Last Day of the Paint Creek Court Martial," May 5, 1913. "Our Strike in West Virginia," *United Mine Workers Journal*, March 20, 1913, p. 1; "Some Day," *Miners' Magazine*, May 15, 1913, p. 5.

46. A few of her letters from prison were edited and published in the radical press, especially the *Appeal to Reason*, which campaigned aggressively for her release. Fetherling, *Mother Jones*, pp. 98–99; Mother Jones to Senator William E. Borah, February 20, 1913; Mother Jones to Caroline Lloyd, March 17, 1913; Jones to Lloyd, April 4, 1913, all in Steel, ed., *Correspondence*, pp. 107–10. In other letters, she contrasted her own suffering to that of her enemies in the movement, especially some Socialists, whom she accused of being most concerned with their own comfort; for example, see Mother Jones to Maude Walker, April 27, 1913, in Steel, ed., *Correspondence*, pp. 112–13. To Terence Powderly she complained that William Wilson had failed to help her get out of confinement (in fact, Wilson made prodigious efforts to have her freed); see Jones to Powderly, May 1, 1913, in Steel, ed., *Correspondence*, pp. 113–14.

47. Quote from Debs to Claude G. Bowers, May 10, 1913; also see Debs to John M. Work, April 4, 1913; Debs to Fred Warren, April 25, 1913, p. 20, Debs to Bowers, May 3, 1913; all in James Robert Constantine, ed., *The Letters of Eugene V. Debs*, vol. 2 (Urbana: University of Illinois Press, 1990), pp. 26, 14–15, 20, 23. Eugene Debs, "To the Rescue of Mother Jones," *Appeal to Reason*, May 3, 1913; Eugene Debs, "Mother Jones: An Appreciation," *Appeal to Reason*, May 24, 1913, p. 4; Eugene Debs, "Arrest of Mother Jones," *United Mine Workers Journal*, February 27, 1913, p. 1; Fetherling, *Mother Jones*, p. 98.

48. T. J. Llewellyn to William Wilson, March 20, 1913; Margaret R. Duvall to William B. Wilson, March 13, 1913; A. Van Tassel to Woodrow Wilson, May 2, 1913, all in General Records of the Department of Labor, 1907–1942, Chief Clerk's File, record group 174, box 24, file 16/13, "Conditions of Coal Fields in West Virginia," NARA.

49. J. A. Bradley, "Mother Jones," *United Mine Workers Journal*, May 10, 1913, p. 3. For further examples of the protests, see petition from an unnamed group, Siskiyou, Oregon, to Woodrow Wilson, May 4, 1913; resolution from National Women's Trade Union League of America to William Wilson, September 1, 1913; Florence Kelley to Congressman William Kent, April 26, 1913, all in General Records of the Department of Labor, 1907–1942, Chief Clerk's File, record group 174, box 13, file 16/13, NARA. Boxes 23 and 24 of record group 174 contain hundreds of letters and petitions for Mother Jones's release; many of the letters were written on stationery from small businesses and professions by the proprietors.

50. M. Michelson penned "Feudalism and Civil War in the United States of Amer-

ica, Now" for the May 1913 issue of *Everybody's Magazine*. The opening sentences said it all: "There is now being waged in West Virginia a civil war, a real war. It is a war against feudalism, in which five thousand armed coal-miners are opposed by the entire military organization of the state." The article featured descriptions and photographs of Mother Jones, depicting her as fiercely dedicated, beloved by her boys, determined to break the hold of despotism. For a similar treatment, see West, "Civil War," pp. 37–50.

51. Corbin, *Life, Work, and Rebellion*, pp. 95–99; Steel, *Court-Martial*, pp. 59, 74. Much later in life, former governor Hatfield told of visiting the strike zone immediately after he assumed office. He carried his medical doctor's bag and found Mother Jones to be quite sick and feverish; he ordered her to a hospital until she recovered. It's a touching story, but there is not a shred of evidence to corroborate it. See Steel, *Court-Martial*, p. 57.

52. Corbin, *Life, Work, and Rebellion*, pp. 97–99; Steel, *Court-Martial*, pp. 58–61; Raffaele, "Mary Harris Jones," pp. 56–57; Foner, ed., *Mother Jones Speaks*, pp. 218–19; W. H. Thompson, "How a Victory Was Turned into a 'Settlement' in West Virginia," *International Socialist Review* 14, no. 1 (July 1913), pp. 12–17.

53. Thompson, "How a Victory Was Turned into a 'Settlement,'" pp. 12–17; Corbin, *Life, Work, and Rebellion*, pp. 97–99; Steel, *Court-Martial*, pp. 58–61.

54. Raffaele, "Mary Harris Jones," pp. 57–59; Fetherling; *Mother Jones*, pp. 99–102; Mother Jones to Senator Kern, May 4, 1913, in Steel, ed., *Correspondence*, pp. 114–15; U.S. Senate, *Investigation of Conditions in Paint Creek District, West Virginia*, 63rd Cong., 1st sess., May 26, 1913, Calendar 37, Rept. 52, pp. 1–2, in serial 6511, CIS.

55. *New York Times*, May 19, 1913, p. 2.

56. Corbin, *Life, Work, and Rebellion*, pp. 97–101; Steel, *Court-Martial*, pp. 59–61; Raffaele, "Mary Harris Jones," pp. 57–63; Lynch, "West Virginia Coal Strike," pp. 640–41; Mikeal, "Mother Mary Jones," p. 82. For a useful summary of the investigation, see "Digest of Report on Investigation of Paint Creek Coal Fields of West Virginia," no. 9, 1914, General Records of the Department of Labor, Commission on Industrial Relations, record group 174, box 17, file 93, NARA. Although the testimony taken by the Senate subcommittee between June and October 1913 amounted to 2,291 pages, the committee's conclusions were vague and evasive, since a working settlement was in effect. Yet amid the verbiage, the committee did recognize the brutality of the guards, the relentless spying, the inability of miners to purchase their own homes or even be buried where they chose, and above all the determination of the operators to keep out the union as fundamental causes of the troubles; U.S. Senate, *Investigation of Paint Creek Coal Fields of West Virginia*, 63rd Cong., 2nd sess., March 9, 1914, Rept. 321, serial 6511. Mother Jones described her confinement and release in an open letter to Senator Kern in the pages of the *United Mine Workers Journal*, May 15, 1913, p. 7. Eugene Debs wondered aloud to his friend and fellow Socialist Adolph Germer why Mother Jones, along with the Socialists John Brown

and Charles Boswell, who were also arrested, failed to testify before the Senate subcommittee. Germer wrote back that, whatever their acts, they were not West Virginians, lending credence to the operators' claims that outside agitators caused all the problems, so it was best that they keep a low profile. See Debs to Germer, June 19, 1913, and Germer to Debs, July 8, 1913, both in U.S. MSS 125, box 1, file 2, Adolph Germer Collection, SHSW.

57. Corbin, *Life, Work, and Rebellion*, pp. 87–105, is particularly strong on how the strike was about far more than mere bread-and-butter issues, on how miners and their leaders saw it in deeply ideological terms.

58. All quoted in *Miners' Magazine*, April 10, 1913, p. 4; September 26, 1912, p. 1; May 8, 1913, p. 7.

59. "Mother Jones, 81, Leads Labor War in West Virginia," *Brooklyn Daily Eagle*, June 1, 1913, in CUA, reprinted in Foner, ed., *Mother Jones Speaks*, pp. 492–500. "One of the most striking things to me," she says, "is the gradual dying out of the American type. In fifty years the changes in type have been almost beyond belief. The Japs are not the only orientals to be feared. The Hindus will some day be a serious menace. They are coming in large numbers now, although little has been said about them." Certainly anti-Asian animosity was on the rise again, especially in California, and it extended past the Chinese to Japanese and Indian workers. Mother Jones had always sought to include all workers in her organizing, but like other unionists, she feared the importation of strikebreakers. The phrase "dying out of the American type" echoes the renewed racism of these years. Back in 1902, she had written of an operator who sent someone to keep an eye on her, "he sent a niger to watch me." And in her autobiography, she referred to the "lick-spittle Jews" who sold out Christ. She clearly was not without prejudice. But these are the only examples of such language in the surviving record. If Mother Jones was not immune to bigotry, still the dominant theme of her life and work was inclusion, not exclusion. Beyond that, she probably never thought about racism and inequality as problems, which of course they were in the coal towns and in the union hierarchy. See Mother Jones to John Mitchell, May 6, 1902, in Steel, ed., *Correspondence*, p. 31; Mother Jones, *Autobiography*, p. 219.

60. " 'Mother' Jones, Mild-Mannered, Talks Sociology," *New York Times*, June 1, 1913, sec. 5, p. 4, excerpts reprinted in *Current Opinion*, July 1913, pp. 19–20.

61. " 'Mother' Jones, Mild-Mannered, Talks Sociology," sec. 5, p. 4.

62. Ibid.

63. Ibid. For a fine discussion of women organizers in the South, see Mary Frederickson, "Heroines and Girl Strikers: Gender Issues and Organized Labor in the Twentieth-Century South," in Robert Zieger, ed., *Organized Labor in the Twentieth-Century South* (Knoxville: University of Tennessee Press, 1991), pp. 84–112.

8. The Colorado Coal War

1. " 'Mother' Jones, Mild-Mannered, Talks Sociology," *New York Times,* June 1, 1913, sec. 5, p. 4. Priscilla Long, "The 1913–1914 Colorado Fuel and Iron Strike, with Reflections on the Causes of Coal Strike Violence," in John H. M. Laslett, ed., *The United Mine Workers of America: A Model of Industrial Solidarity?* (University Park: Pennsylvania State University Press, 1996), pp. 345–70, refutes that violence during the Colorado coal strike grew out of UMW policy, the miners' culture, or Mother Jones's incendiarism. Long demonstrates that the charges of Mother Jones inciting violence were constantly exaggerated by management.

2. Kate Richards O'Hare, "Mother Jones of the Revolution," *Miners' Magazine,* September 18, 1913, pp. 8–9, reprinted from *National Rip-Saw,* which O'Hare edited.

3. See Warren Van Tine, *The Making of the Labor Bureaucrat: Union Leadership in the United States, 1870–1920* (Amberst: University of Massachusetts Press, 1973).

4. On conditions in Colorado, see George S. McGovern and Leonard F. Guttridge, *The Great Coalfield War* (Boulder: University Press of Colorado, 1996), pp. 71–95; C. J. Stowell, "Report on the Situation in the Coal Fields of Colorado," March 19, 1914, Commission on Industrial Relations, Strikes and Lockouts, record group 174, box 16, file 162, pp. 3–6, NARA; M. McCuster, "McCuster Report on the Colorado Coal Mine Situation," February 1915, record group 174, box 16, file 259, pp. 1–26, NARA; Edward M. Steel, ed., *The Correspondence of Mother Jones* (Pittsburgh, Pa.: University of Pittsburgh Press, 1985), pp. xxxi–xxxiii. For an anecdotal account of the life of John C. Osgood, owner of Victor Fuel Company, see Sylvia Ruland, *The Lion of Redstone* (Boulder, Colo.: Johnson Books, 1981). Before going to Colorado Mother Jones went to Michigan. On the copper strike there, see Arthur W. Thurner, *Rebels on the Range: The Michigan Copper Miners' Strike of 1913–1914* (Lake Linden, Mich.: John H. Forster Press, 1984), and for Mother Jones's role, see Dale Fetherling, *Mother Jones: The Miners' Angel* (Carbondale: Southern Illinois University Press), pp. 140–41.

5. Priscilla Long, *Where the Sun Never Shines: A History of America's Bloody Coal Industry* (New York: Paragon House, 1989), pp. 242–47, 258–59; McGovern and Guttridge, *Great Coalfield War,* pp. 63–68; Maier B. Fox, *United We Stand: The United Mine Workers of America, 1890–1990* (Washington, D.C.: United Mine Workers, 1990), pp. 152–53.

6. Long, *Sun Never Shines,* pp. 248–58; Fox, *United We Stand,* pp. 153–56. Barron Beshoar, *Out of the Depths: The Story of John R. Lawson, a Labor Leader* (Denver, Colo.: Golden Ball Press, 1980), pp. 32–34, claimed that when sixteen union leaders were arrested for violating an injunction, Mother Jones worked out a deal in which they would be released in exchange for a public apology. According to Beshoar, executive board member John Lawson and President John

White forbade the deal, insisting that the men had nothing to apologize for. It should be pointed out that Beshoar is not always a reliable source.

7. Long, *Sun Never Shines*, pp. 258–61. For a fascinating glimpse into industrial espionage, see the reports that have survived from the Globe Inspection Company, April and May 1910, in box 6, file 6, Roche Papers, UCB. Inspector "D-85" in Trinidad, Colorado, for example, recommended that miners be granted a wage increase in order to head off growing union sentiment in the southern field; case AAI, April 8, 1910. Most of the reports track the comings and goings of union sympathizers and organizers.

8. Fetherling, *Mother Jones*, pp. 109–12; Long, *Sun Never Shines*, pp. 258–65. For the upbeat tone of union officials on the eve of the strike, see, for example, Adolph Germer to John P. White, September 2, 1913, U.S. MSS 125, box 1, file 2, Adolph Germer Papers, SHSW.

9. Bowers letter quoted in McGovern and Guttridge, *Great Coalfield War*, p. 98; Long, *Sun Never Shines*, pp. 264–69. On employment agencies, see, for example, Paul J. Paulsen (who was a UMW board member) to AF of L, November 25, 1913, film 8505, reel 144, frame 441, AFL Papers, Samuel Gompers Era, Department of Mining Records, 1911–1915, LC.

10. "Enthusiastic Meetings Prior to Convention," *United Mine Workers Journal*, September 25, 1913, p. 2; Mother Jones to Terence Powderly, September 20, 1913, in Steel, ed., *Correspondence*, p. 119; Edward M. Steel, ed., *The Speeches and Writings of Mother Jones* (Pittsburgh, Pa.: University of Pittsburgh Press, 1988), pp. 123–24; Fetherling, *Mother Jones*, pp. 113–14; Long, *Sun Never Shines*, pp. 264–69. Beshoar, *Out of the Depths*, p. 58, quotes a paragraph of this speech but certainly takes liberties with it. Incidentally, Mother Jones ended her letter to Powderly, "I am always yours, not for the revolution, but in it."

11. Mother Jones, speech at District 15 convention, Trinidad, Colorado, September 16, 1913, in Steel, ed., *Speeches and Writings*, pp. 121, 123–28. In a brief aside before her speech, she urged the men to boycott Pells beer, since the Brewery Workers Union was on strike against the company: "Be sure you don't touch the Pells Brewery Beer; if you drink it you will be full of scabs, so I warn each and all if you do get beer get union beer, get beer that is made by men working under decent conditions, and don't patronize those places, if you get hold of any fellow who does, hammer him good."

12. Mother Jones, speech at District 15 convention, Trinidad, Colorado, September 16, 1913, in Steel, ed., *Speeches and Writings*, pp. 123–28.

13. McGovern and Guttridge, *Great Coalfield War*, pp. 104–8; Beshoar, *Out of the Depths*, pp. 59–64; Long, *Sun Never Shines*, pp. 269–75; Fetherling, *Mother Jones*, pp. 114–15; Stowell, "Report on the Situation," pp. 6–10, 15–22.

14. Stewart's frustrations with Colorado Fuel and Iron's intransigence were expressed in his memos to the Labor Department, October 10, October 21, November 13, 1913, Federal Mediation and Conciliation Service Case Files, record group 280, box 90, file 41-10A, NARA. Along with a long letter to Pres-

ident Wilson defending his company's position, Lamont Bowers included a reprint of the *Polly Pry* accusations, underlining key words and phrases in blue pencil; see McGovern and Guttridge, *Great Coalfield War*, pp. 135–36.

15. McGovern and Guttridge, *Great Coalfield War*, pp. 110–19; Judith Elaine Mikeal, "Mother Mary Jones: The Labor Movement's Impious Joan of Arc" (master's thesis, University of North Carolina, 1965), pp. 107–8; Long, *Sun Never Shines*, pp. 274–79; Fetherling, *Mother Jones*, p. 116.

16. Mikeal, "Mother Mary Jones," pp. 108–9; Beshoar, *Out of the Depths*, p. 65; Fetherling, *Mother Jones*, p. 115; Sister John Francis Raffaele, "Mary Harris Jones and the United Mine Workers of America" (master's thesis, Catholic University of America, 1964), p. 70; U.S. Congress, *Conditions in the Coal Mines of Colorado: Hearings before a Subcommittee of the Committee on Mines and Mining*, 63rd Cong., 2nd sess., 1914, part 11, vol. 3, pp. 2920–23; "Colorado Strike," *United Mine Workers Journal*, October 2, 1913, p. 1; "Mine Guards Precipitate Battle," *United Mine Workers Journal*, October 16, 1913, p. 4; "Our Strike in Colorado," *United Mine Workers Journal*, October 30, 1913, p. 1; "She Fights for Humanity," *Miners' Magazine*, October 30, 1913, pp. 6–7, reprinted in *United Mine Workers Journal*, November 6, 1913, p. 4; Fred Thompson, "Notes on 'The Most Dangerous Woman in America,'" in Mother Jones, *Autobiography of Mother Jones*, ed. Mary Field Parton (Chicago: Charles H. Kerr Company, 1990 ed.), p. 276. Mother Jones told the congressional subcommittee that the governor just happened to show up in town during the children's parade; press coverage makes it clear that the demonstration was planned with his presence in mind.

17. McGovern and Guttridge, *Great Coalfield War*, pp. 125–43; Fox, *United We Stand*, pp. 156–59; Long, *Sun Never Shines*, pp. 280–83; Philip Foner, ed., *Mother Jones Speaks* (New York: Monad Press, 1983), pp. 238–39; Stowell, "Report on the Situation," pp. 10–13; and especially the confidential "Statement of Mr. Don MacGregor; Representative of the United Press," Commission on Industrial Relations Papers, Strikes and Lockouts, record group 174, box 16, file 130, NARA. MacGregor pointed out that the UMW leadership asked the men to cooperate with the National Guard; as relations between the troops and the miners grew increasingly bitter, anger at the union leadership also deepened.

18. Long, *Sun Never Shines*, pp. 280–83; Wilson to Bowers, quoted in McGovern and Guttridge, *Great Coalfield Wars*, p. 147; Ethelbert Stewart to Louis F. Post, November 21, 1913, Federal Mediation and Conciliation Service Case Files, record group 280, box 89, file 41-10, NARA. In the same file, Post wrote a long memo to Woodrow Wilson's assistant Joe Tumulty very critical of Colorado Fuel and Iron policies. For a summary of each side's arguments, see the memos prepared by C. J. Stowell for the Commission on Industrial Relations, "Digest of Brief of the Coal Mining Operators" and "Digest of Brief for the Striking Miners," Commission on Industrial Relations Papers, record group 174, box 16, file 162, NARA.

19. McGovern and Guttridge, *Great Coalfield Wars*, pp. 149–65; William Wilson to Woodrow Wilson, December 10, 1913, Federal Mediation and Conciliation

Service Papers, record group 280, box 89, file 14-10a, part 1, NARA; "Miners Unanimously Refuse to Surrender," *United Mine Workers Journal*, December 11, 1913. Also see the memo from Governor Ammons to Jesse Welborn et al., November 27, 1913, record group 280, box 89, file 41-10, NARA.

20. Frank Hayes to Mother Jones, November 28, 1913, in Steel, ed., *Correspondence*, pp. 120–21; Steel, ed., *Speeches and Writings*, pp. 122–23, 129; Mikeal, "Mother Mary Jones," pp. 109–10; Fetherling, *Mother Jones*, pp. 116–17; Foner, ed., *Mother Jones Speaks*, p. 239; "Miners Unanimously Refuse to Surrender," p. 1; " 'I Wish They'd Slay Me, I'd Win Fight,' Cries Mother Jones," *United Mine Workers Journal*, December 18, 1913, p. 1. For the union list of grievances against the militia, see Federal Mediation and Conciliation Service Case Files, record group 280, box 89, file 41-10, NARA. For more details on the mine operators' importing Mexican workers as strikebreakers (a violation of federal law), see Frank Hayes to William B. Wilson, December 19, 1913, record group 280, box 89, file 14-10a, part 1, NARA.

21. Fetherling, *Mother Jones*, pp. 117–18; Foner, ed., *Mother Jones Speaks*, pp. 239–40; Beshoar, *Out of the Depths*, p. 128; Mikeal, "Mother Mary Jones," pp. 110–13; Raffaele, "Mary Harris Jones," pp. 71–72; Long, *Sun Never Shines*, p. 283; U.S. Congress, *Conditions in the Coal Mines of Colorado*, part 11, vol. 3, pp. 2923–24; Mother Jones, testimony, U.S. Senate Commission on Industrial Relations, *Final Report and Testimony*, 64th Cong., 1st sess., 1916, S. Doc. 215, vol. 11, pp. 10633–34.

22. Fetherling, *Mother Jones*, pp. 117–18; Foner, ed., *Mother Jones Speaks*, pp. 239–40; Mikeal, "Mother Mary Jones," pp. 110–13; Raffaele, "Mary Harris Jones," pp. 71–72; Long, *Sun Never Shines*, p. 283; "Colorado Troops Oust Mother Jones," *New York Times*, January 5, 1914, p. 6; "Mother Jones," *United Mine Workers Journal*, January 8, 1914, pp. 1, 4. On January 6, *The New York Times*, p. 10, noted that union leaders told strikers to arm themselves to resist future deportations; the *Times* also reported that violence was feared if Mother Jones returned to Trinidad. On the union side, President White and Vice President Hayes of the UMW immediately telegraphed Woodrow Wilson to request his intervention to protect constitutional liberties; see Federal Mediation and Conciliation Service, record group 280, box 90, file 41-10a, NARA.

23. Fetherling, *Mother Jones*, pp. 119–20; Mikeal, "Mother Mary Jones," pp. 111–12; Raffaele, "Mary Harris Jones," p. 72; Long, *Sun Never Shines*, pp. 283–84; Mother Jones testimony, Commission on Industrial Relations, *Final Report and Testimony*, vol. 11, p. 10634; "Mother Jones Goes to Trinidad; Is Under Arrest," *Denver Post*, January 12, 1914, p. 4; "Mother Jones Arrested," *New York Times*, January 13, 1914, p. 3; "Mother Jones Re-arrested," *United Mine Workers Journal*, January 15, 1914, p. 1. Chase even wrote a telegram to President Wilson, denying that Mother Jones was held against her will; see Justice Department, Civil Division, record group 60, file 168733a, NARA. She told a slightly different version of her re-arrest in a manuscript in the Mary Harris Jones Collection, folder 2, CHS. According to Charles Newell, editor of *The Denver Express*, who

testified before the Subcommittee on Mines and Mining, Governor Ammons told him that all of the violence in the strike zone "was due to the incendiary teachings of Mother Jones" and that he planned to have her arrested and held incommunicado. "Governor," Newell responded, "don't you know that is exactly what Mother Jones wants? That the minute she is arrested on the order . . . of the governor of this state or any other state, she will immediately talk to the whole country in behalf of the people whom she represents." See U.S. Congress, *Hearings before a Subcommittee of the Committee on Mines and Mining*, 63rd Cong., 2nd sess., 1914, part 1, vol. 1, pp. 298–300, part 2, vol. 3, pp. 2924–27. Newell's testimony, incidentally, was taken on February 9, 1914, before Mother Jones's second incarceration.

24. McGovern and Guttridge, *Great Coalfield Wars*, pp. 170–76; Fetherling, *Mother Jones*, pp. 119–20; Raffaele, "Mary Harris Jones," p. 72; Long, *Sun Never Shines*, pp. 283–85; "To Rescue Mother Jones," *New York Times*, January 17, 1914, p. 1; J.R.B., "Notes and Comments from Colorado Battlefield," *United Mine Workers Journal*, January 22, 1914, p. 1; "Mounted Troopers," *United Mine Workers Journal*, January 29, 1914, p. 7; "Military Authorities Get Delay in Habeas Corpus Suit . . . ," unidentified newspaper, late January 1914, Edward Doyle Scrapbook, DPL; "Miners Ask Federal Strike Inquiry," *New York Times*, January 21, 1914, p. 3; testimony of Walter MacIntosh, in U.S. Congress, *Hearings before Subcommittee on Mines and Mining*, vol. 1, p. 880.

25. Fetherling, *Mother Jones*, pp. 120–24; McGovern and Guttridge, *Great Coalfield War*, pp. 189–90; *United Mine Workers Journal*, February 19, 1914, p. 4; "Mother Jones Dispersed Mob, Witness Swears," and "Our Strike in Colorado," *United Mine Workers Journal*, March 5, 1914, pp. 2, 1; General John Chase, *The Military Occupation of the Coal Strike Zone of Colorado* (Denver, Colo.: Smith-Brooks Printing Co., 1914), pp. 31–32, pam file, UCB; "Mother Jones Turned Loose," *Denver Post*, March 16, 1914, pp. 1, 4; "Mother Jones Freed," *Denver Times*, March 16, 1914, pp. 1, 2; *United Mine Workers Journal*, March 19, 1914, pp. 4, 7; Paul Paulsen, "News Exchange," and "Our Strike in Colorado," *United Mine Workers Journal*, April 2, 1914, pp. 6–7, 1; "Mother Jones Held Prisoner in Dingy Jail," *Rocky Mountain News*, March 24, 1914, p. 1, in Clippings, box J, file Jones, Mary (Mother), DPL. UMW attorney Horace Hawkins made his plea in "In the Supreme Court of the State of Colorado, In Re Mary Jones, Application for Original Writ of Habeas Corpus," CUA, 7/2.11.

26. Mother Jones to Terence Powderly, March 22, 1914, in Steel, ed., *Correspondence*, pp. 122–25.

27. Mother Jones testimony, Commission on Industrial Relations, *Final Report and Testimony*, vol. 11, p. 10636. The union claimed that a young man had earlier contracted rheumatic fever in that same cell.

28. "Mother Jones Smuggles Letter out of Colorado Military Bastille," *United Mine Workers Journal*, April 9, 1914, p. 1 (the letter was widely reprinted—see, for example, *Denver Times*, April 3, 1914, p. 3, *Illustrated Union News*, May 1914, p. 3);

Moses Oppenheimer, "Mother Jones, Incommunicado," *United Mine Workers Journal*, April 2, 1914, p. 2, originally published in *New York Call*. It is found most conveniently in Steel, ed., *Correspondence*, pp. 125–26: Mother Jones to the Public, March 31, 1914.

29. "The Menace of Mother Jones," *Denver Express*, April 22, 1914, in Edward Doyle Scrapbook, DPL; Eugene Debs, "Mother Jones," *United Mine Workers Journal*, March 26, 1914, p. 1; "Colorado Coal Wars," Justice Department, Civil Division, record group 60, file 168733a, NARA; Federal Mediation and Conciliation Service Case Files, record group 280, box 89, file 10a, pp. 41–47, NARA; "A Mass Meeting of the Women of Las Animas," record group 280, box 89, file 41-10, NARA. Declared one newspaper of Mother Jones, "Did one ever see such bravery? Can the history of our nation produce another such martyr? Think what it means when an 82-year-old woman would forsake all—love of life, sunshine, flowers and liberty—that others might have these things! That the tired, depressed, overburdened laboring masses of this state might throw off their burden of serfdom"; unidentified clipping dated March 27, 1914, Edward Doyle Scrapbook, DPL. Many petitions and letters can be found in record group 280, box 89-90, NARA. At a meeting of prominent women held at Cooper Union, New York City, on April 23, 1914, called to protest U.S. intervention in Mexico, the California suffragist Helen Todd declared, "There is only one cause for which I would go to war, and that is for the woman I think the greatest in the world—Mother Jones," and Florence Kelley praised her as an American rebel, "aged, gray haired, and bowed down with years of fighting against the men controlling the country." From *New York Times*, April 23, 1914, and *New York Call*, April 23, 1914, both in Foner, ed., *Mother Jones Speaks*, p. 42.

30. Letter from several miners to Congressman O. A. Stanley, March 19, 1914, Federal Mediation and Conciliation Service Case Files, record group 280, box 89, files 41-10, NARA; Britt Adams to Woodrow Wilson, March 19, 1914, record group 280, box 90, file 41-10b, NARA; Friedrich Katz, *The Life and Times of Pancho Villa* (Stanford, Calif.: Stanford University Press, 1998), pp. 321–22. For poetry celebrating her, see Pease, "The Capture of Mother Jones," *Miners' Advocate*, January 27, 1914; Ralph Chaplin, "Mother Jones," *International Socialist Review* 14 (April 1914), pp. 604–5; Elizabeth Waddell, "The Little Old Woman," *Everybody's Magazine*, April–May 1914, p. 2; Covington Hall, "The Soul of Mother Jones," *Voice of the People*, March 16, 1914, p. 1.

31. McGovern and Guttridge, *Great Coalfield War*, pp. 191–93; Fetherling, *Mother Jones*, pp. 120–24; Mikeal, "Mother Mary Jones," pp. 114–16; Raffaele, "Mary Harris Jones," pp. 75–76; Mother Jones testimony, Commission on Industrial Relations, *Final Report and Testimony*, vol. 11, pp. 10637–40; "Mother Jones Routs Ammons and His Army," *United Mine Workers Journal*, April 23, 1914, pp. 1–2; Chase, *Military Occupation*, pp. 45–47; " 'Mother' Jones Released," *New York Times*, April 24, 1914, p. 1; "Our Strike in Colorado," *United Mine Workers Journal*, April 16, 1914, p. 1; "Mother Jones Freed; Coming Here Tonight," *Denver*

Times, April 16, 1914, p. 5. Chase added, incidentally, that Mother Jones's police record was in the hands of the Pinkerton Detective Agency; his *The Military Occupation of the Coal Strike Zone of Colorado* is remarkable for its relentless skewering of the union. Although Mother Jones made the most of publicity opportunities, privately she expressed gratitude to one of her captors. On July 30, 1914, she wrote to Mrs. Edward Verdeckberg, "Permit me to express my deep appreciation to Colonel Verdeckberg's courtesy and kind treatment to me while I was a military prisoner in the Colorado bastille at Walsenburg. . . . He could have been very unkind and cruel to me, if he so wished, but fortunately even in military uniform I found traits of a well-bred man, which indicates that he came from the training of a real woman." Edward Verdeckberg Collection, scrapbook, p. 163, ColHS.

32. Long, *Sun Never Shines,* pp. 286–90; Raffaele, "Mother Mary Jones," pp. 77–81; McGovern and Guttridge, *Great Coalfield War,* pp. 186–93.

33. Stowell, "Report on the Situation," pp. 13–14; Long, *Sun Never Shines,* pp. 286–90; Raffaele, "Mary Harris Jones," pp. 77–81; "Troops Drive Miners Out," *New York Times,* March 11, 1914, p. 2. The union published a series of pamphlets on the costs of martial law; see "Militarism: What It Costs the Tax Payers," "Militarism in Colorado," and "Military Despotism in Colorado," all printed in 1914 and found in the Roche Papers, 6–9, UCB. For a clergyman's assessment of the strike that was sympathetic to the union's demands, see Reverend Henry A. Atkinson, *The Church and Industrial Warfare* (n.p., 1914), pam file, UCB.

34. McGovern and Guttridge, *Great Coalfield War,* pp. 204–6, 210–12. Also see Jesse Welborn's testimony, June 8, 1914, Lawson Collection, DPL.

35. The battle is best described by McGovern and Guttridge, *Great Coalfield War,* pp. 212–31, and Alvin R. Sunseri, *The Ludlow Massacre: A Study in Misemployment of the National Guard* (n.p.: Salvadore Books, 1972); also see Long, *Sun Never Shines,* pp. 289–93, including the Bowers quote; Fetherling, *Mother Jones,* pp. 125–26; John Reed, "The Colorado War," *Metropolitan* (n.p., n.d.), in record group 280, box 89, file 41-10, NARA. One of the best contemporary accounts comes from the reporter Peter Clark MacFarlane, "The Colorado Strike," *Gay City Bulletin,* October 10, 1914, pp. 237–46. Equally impressive is George West's "Report to the Commission on Industrial Relations," May 15, 1914, pp. 1–20, Department of Labor, Commission on Industrial Relations, record group 174, box 17, file 47, NARA.

36. Long, *Sun Never Shines,* pp. 293–300; McGovern and Guttridge, *Great Coalfield War,* pp. 232–68, 282–90; West, "Report to the Commission on Industrial Relations," pp. 1–5.

37. Long, *Sun Never Shines,* pp. 293–300; McGovern and Guttridge, *Great Coalfield War,* pp. 232–68, 282–90; Fox, *United We Stand,* pp. 161–66; *New York Times,* May 11, 1914, p. 1. For a sample of the response to Ludlow, see Federal Mediation and Conciliation Service Case Files, record group 280, box 90, file 41-10,

NARA, which contains hundreds of letters, petitions, and resolutions. DPL maintains a file of ephemera on Ludlow, including "Statement of the Strike Situation in Colorado" (n.p., May 1914); "Songs of the Ludlow Massacre," reprinted from the *United Mine Workers Journal,* April 15, 1955; Walter H. Fink, "The Ludlow Massacre" (n.p., 1914); "Ludlow" (n.p., 1914); "Militarism in Colorado" (n.p., 1914); "A Plain Statement of Industrial and Political Conditions in Colorado" (n.p., n.d.).

38. U.S. Congress, *Conditions in the Coal Mines of Colorado,* part 11, vol. 3, pp. 2917–40; Raffaele, "Mary Harris Jones," pp. 82–85; "Mother Jones Tells Horrors to Congress," *United Mine Workers Journal,* April 30, 1914, p. 7; also see *United Mine Workers Journal,* May 7, 1914, p. 3. The quote is from the *Rocky Mountain News,* April 27, 1914. Attorney Horace Hawkins and his staff wrote "Conditions in the Coal Mines of Colorado: Brief for the Striking Miners" for the hearings before the Subcommittee on Mines and Mining; it lays out the UMW arguments quite clearly; see the 1914 manuscript version, pam file, UCB.

39. Mother Jones, speech at UMW District 14 convention, Pittsburg, Kansas, April 30, 1914, in Steel, ed., *Speeches and Writings,* pp. 129–32. Coverage of events in Colorado during the weeks following Ludlow was very extensive, despite competing reports of military skirmishes along the Mexican border. In addition to dailies like *The New York Times,* magazines such as *The Independent* and *The Outlook* gave Colorado considerable ink, as did the *International Socialist Review,* for which Carl Sandburg wrote.

40. Mother Jones, speech in Pittsburg, Kansas, April 30, 1914, in Steel, ed., *Speeches and Writings,* pp. 129–32.

41. Ibid., pp. 132–34.

42. Ibid., pp. 134–49.

43. "Revolution Imminent Says Mother Jones," *United Mine Workers Journal,* May 7, 1914, pp. 2–3; Mother Jones, speech in Vancouver, British Columbia, June 10, 1914, in Foner, ed., *Mother Jones Speaks,* pp. 250–57; Mikeal, "Mother Mary Jones," pp. 117–20; Raffaele, "Mary Harris Jones," pp. 82–85; Fetherling, *Mother Jones,* p. 136.

44. Mikeal, "Mother Mary Jones," pp. 117–20; Raffaele, "Mary Harris Jones," pp. 82–85; Beshoar, *Out of the Depths,* p. 212; Fetherling, *Mother Jones,* p. 136; Foner, ed., *Mother Jones Speaks,* pp. 245–50; Mother Jones to Mrs. Edward Keating, July 30, 1914, box 5, file 17, Edward Keating Papers, UCB; *Congressional Record,* June 13, 1914, vol. 51, part 17, p. 638. The *Pueblo Chieftain,* for example, published "History of Mary Harris Jones," on July 28, 1914, which repeated the prostitution charge as if it were fresh news, just revealed in congressional sources. Mother Jones's forays from New York City to Vancouver were covered in the *United Mine Workers Journal.*

45. McGovern and Guttridge, *Great Coalfield War,* pp. 298–305; Long, *Sun Never Shines,* pp. 300–4; Fetherling, *Mother Jones,* pp. 127–29; Mother Jones, speech at

UMW District 15 special convention, Trinidad, Colorado, September 15, 1914, in Steel, ed., *Speeches and Writings*, pp. 150–55, also available as "Proceedings of the Special Convention to Consider President Wilson's Proposition for Settlement of Colorado Coal Strike," in pam file, UCB. Union locals flooded Washington with petitions urging federal action; see Federal Mediation and Conciliation Service Case Files, record group 280, box 90, file 41-10q, NARA. At midyear, a war of words raged among various officials of Colorado's Episcopal Church; see letters to Secretary of Labor William Wilson in record group 280, box 89, file 41-10a, part 2, NARA. In private correspondence to Industrial Relations Commissioner Frank Walsh, investigator George West declared that the operators "become wild men when they begin to discuss the strike. They are a long way from recovering their sanity." See West to Walsh, June 26, 1914, and June 27, 1914, General Records of the Department of Labor, Commission on Industrial Relations Papers, record group 174, box 17, file 47, NARA.

46. Mother Jones to Woodrow Wilson, October 17, 1914, in Federal Mediation and Conciliation Service Case Files, record group 280, box 91, file 41-10t, NARA; "Wilson Considers Closing Colorado Mines; Mother Jones Asks President to Enforce Peace Proposition," *United Mine Workers Journal*, November 5, 1914, p. 1; "Receives 'Mother' Jones" and "Mother Jones at the White House," *New York Times*, October 29, 1914, p. 10; "Mother Jones Flays Oil King," *United Mine Workers Journal*, November 19, 1914, p. 2; "Mother Jones Seeks Mine Peace," *New York Tribune*, November 22, 1914, in CUA, 7/2.7.

47. McGovern and Guttridge, *Great Coalfield War*, pp. 298–305; Long, *Sun Never Shines*, pp. 300–4; Fetherling, *Mother Jones*, pp. 127–29. In a May 14, 1914, memo to Frank Walsh, the investigators John B. Lennon, S. T. Ballard, and George P. West estimated that at least one hundred people had died so far in the strike and stated that no end was in sight; see record group 174, box 16, file 47, NARA. Mother Jones and other union leaders also lobbied cabinet members; see letter from James Lord to Frank Hayes, October 9, 1914, film 8505, reel 144, frames 225–26, American Federation of Labor—The Samuel Gompers Era Collection, LC, taken from AFL Mining Department Records, 1911–1915. Commissioners of the Federal Mediation and Conciliation Service, established just a few years previously, worked very hard to obtain a settlement during these months; these records are in Federal Mediation and Conciliation Service Case Files, record group 280, boxes 89–90, NARA. For a remarkably detailed account of life in the mining camps just after Ludlow, see the letter of the sociologist Daniel McCorkle to Miriam L. Woodberry, August 31, 1914, record group 280, box 91, file 41-10p, NARA. Seth Low, chair of the President's Colorado Coal Commission, wrote to Rockefeller junior on December 31, 1914, warning that thousands of mine families had "barely enough food to support life"; see record group 280, box 92, file 41-10bb, NARA.

48. McGovern and Guttridge, *Great Coalfield War*, pp. 269–81; Long, *Sun Never Shines*, pp. 305–8.

49. For a blistering denunciation of the coal companies after Ludlow, see George Creel; "What the Industrial Commission Discovered," *Pearson's Magazine*, March 1916, pp. 194–202. On Ludlow, the rise of Rockefeller junior, and the new order in Rockefeller family business, see Ron Chernow, *Titan: The Life of John D. Rockefeller Sr.* (New York: Random House, 1998), pp. 570–90.

50. McGovern and Guttridge, *Great Coalfield War*, pp. 325–37, 341–43; Long, *Sun Never Shines*, pp. 317–23.

51. "Report Arraigns Rockefeller Jr.," *New York Times*, March 20, 1915, p. 20; McGovern and Guttridge, *Great Coalfield War*, pp. 325–37, 341–43; Long, *Sun Never Shines*, pp. 317–23. See also the letter of John Lawson, District 15 president, to Secretary William Wilson, December 18, 1914, regarding Rockefeller's involvement with Colorado Fuel and Iron management, in record group 280, file 90-41-10a, part 1, NARA; "Will Colorado Act?" *Labor Clarion*, in CUA, 7/2.7; *New York Times*, May 15, 1915, p. 1. President Wilson's Colorado Coal Commission had great praise for the reforms at Colorado Fuel and Iron; see Seth Low, Charles Mills, and Patrick Gilday, *Report of the Colorado Coal Commission on the Labor Difficulties in the Coal Fields of Colorado during the Years 1914 and 1915*, 64th Cong., 1st sess., 1916, H. Doc. 659, pp. 5–10. George Creel, who would head the Committee on Public Information during World War I, wrote a series of scathing reports on the mine operators in general and Rockefeller in particular; for an example, see New York *World*, January 31, 1915, CUA, 7/3.3. Reverend A. A. Berle, on the other hand, castigated the union leadership: "Nobody can tolerate for a moment the invasion of the State by a group of men who seek, with irresponsible and unlimited funds, to supply arms and ammunition to ignorant men and urge them to commence a bloody assault upon the laws and orderly administration of public affairs"; "The Colorado Mine War," Article 3 from Biblioteca Sacra, October 1914, in UCB.

52. Long, *Sun Never Shines*, pp. 308–17; Fetherling, *Mother Jones*, pp. 124–25. Rockefeller's testimony before the Subcommittee on Mines and Mining is found in U.S. Congress, *Conditions in the Coal Mines of Colorado*, part 10, vol. 3, pp. 2841–916, esp. pp. 2851–53. For a bitter denunciation of Rockefeller's "sincerity," charging him with willful ignorance, see "Amos Pinchot Objects," a letter to the editor of *Harper's Weekly*, November 21, 1914, pp. 499–500. On Mother Jones's testimony, see "Mother Jones before Commission on Industrial Relations," *United Mine Workers Journal*, May 20, 1915, pp. 14–15. For internal memoranda between Welborn, Lee, Rockefeller, and King, exploring the possibilities for the new order, see documents in the Welborn Collection (1218), box 1, files 2–4, ColHS.

53. Long, *Sun Never Shines*, pp. 308–17; McGovern and Guttridge, *Great Coalfield War*, pp. 290–98, 305–11; John Ensor Harr and Peter J. Johnson, *The Rockefeller Century* (New York: Scribner, 1988), pp. 138–40. George Creel, himself one of the founders of modern public relations, refuted the operators' new publicity campaign in an article titled "Poisoners of Public Opinion." He attacked the

distortions and half-truths contained in "The Struggle in Colorado for Industrial Freedom" point by point, and he went out of his way to denounce the
prostitution charges against Mother Jones as "filth"; see *Harper's Weekly*, November 7, 1914, pp. 436–38, and November 14, 1914, pp. 465–66.

54. Chernow, *Titan*, pp. 583–90; Long, *Sun Never Shines*, pp. 308–17; McGovern
and Guttridge, *Great Coalfield War*, pp. 290–98, 305–11; Harr and Johnson,
Rockefeller Century, pp. 138–40; "Lawson Public Protest Meeting," report of a
special meeting of the Chicago Federation of Labor, July 11, 1915, unidentified source, Mary Harris Jones file, CHS; Rockefeller to Jesse Welborn, June 8,
1914, and "Extract from letter of W. L. Mackenzie King, dated August 6, 1914,"
accompanying letter of Rockefeller to Welborn, August 11, 1914, all in Welborn Collection, box 1, file 2, ColHS.

55. On the history of public relations and advertising, see Stuart Ewen, *PR! A Social
History of Hype* (New York: Basic Books, 1996); Edward Bernays, *The Engineering
of Consent* (Norman: University of Oklahoma Press, 1955); William Lyon
Mackenzie King, *Industry and Humanity: A Study of the Principles Underlying
Industrial Reconstruction* (Boston: Houghton Mifflin, 1918); Philip Gold, *Adver-
tising, Politics, and American Culture: From Salesmanship to Therapy* (New York:
Paragon House, 1987); Roland Marchand, *Creating the Corporate Soul: The Rise of
Public Relations and Corporate Imagery in American Big Business* (Berkeley: University of California Press, 1998); Roland Marchand, *Advertising the American
Dream: Making Way for Modernity, 1920–1940* (Berkeley: University of California Press, 1985); T. J. Jackson Lears, *Fables of Abundance: A Cultural History of
Advertising in America* (New York: Basic Books, 1994). In its indictments on August 29, 1914, the Las Animas County grand jury characterized the UMW as a
murderous mob led by outside agitators; see Federal Mediation and Conciliation Service Case Files, record group 280, box 87, file 41-10a, part 3, NARA. In
1927, Colorado congressman George Kindel, who had read the *Polly Pry* articles into the *Congressional Record*, sent a letter to Rockefeller on the letterhead
of the Kindel Bedding Company. Now a private businessman, he reminded
Rockefeller of his past services: "I was the one Congressman who stood by you
during your troubles with the labor skates headed by Mother Jones during the
Ludlow strike. . . . I have this day mailed you under separate cover my speech
exposing Mother Jones, which I think had the effect of putting a damper on
her by informing the world of what a fraud and a she-devil she was." Kindel
also claimed to have gotten freight rates reduced by the Interstate Commerce
Commission on coal shipped from Colorado to Chicago, which allowed Colorado Fuel and Iron to compete in the Great Lakes market. Kindel now asked
Rockefeller for five hundred dollars to support his lobbying efforts to lower
freight rates and thereby bring his mattresses to market more cheaply. See
Kindel to Rockefeller, February 26, 1927, Business Interests Series, C. F. and
I./Colorado Strike, record group 2, box 19, folder 168, Rockefeller Family
Archive, Hyde Park, New York. My thanks to Robin Bachin for this source. On

the unjust indictments of union men, their blacklisting from employment, and their inability to leave Colorado to seek work because of their legal difficulties, see Charles W. Mills (a member of the President's Colorado Coal Commission and himself a coal operator from Pennsylvania) to Secretary of Labor William Wilson, January 18, 1916, in record group 280, box 92, file 41-10bb, NARA.

56. Chernow, *Titan*, pp. 583–90; McGovern and Guttridge, *Great Coalfield War*, pp. 325–37, 341–43; Long, *Sun Never Shines*, pp. 317–23; Fox, *United We Stand*, pp. 235–36.

57. See, for example, Colorado Fuel and Iron Company, *Industrial Bulletin*, July 31, 1918, pp. 3–7; McGovern and Guttridge, *Great Coalfield War*, pp. 325–37, 341–43; Long, *Sun Never Shines*, pp. 317–23. For the controversy over King's plan, see Federal Mediation and Conciliation Service Case Files, record group 280, box 90, file 41-10a, NARA. John A. Fitch, "Two Years of the Rockefeller Plan," *Survey*, October 6, 1917, pp. 14–20, found much to praise at Colorado Fuel and Iron; Chernow, *Titan*, pp. 586–90, is also rather celebratory.

58. Fetherling, *Mother Jones*, pp. 130–33; McGovern and Guttridge, *Great Coalfield War*, pp. 318–20; Foner, ed., *Mother Jones Speaks*, pp. 263–68. For Mother Jones's letter to Rockefeller trying to set up a meeting the previous spring, see Jones to Rockefeller, May 12, 1914, in Steel, ed., *Correspondence*, pp. 127–28; and "Registered Letter Refused," *New York Times*, May 14, 1914, p. 6. Mother Jones and Rockefeller's meeting was widely reported; see, for example, " 'Mother Jones' and Mr. Rockefeller," *Outlook*, February 10, 1915, p. 302; and "Rockefeller Aid Is Mother Jones," January 27, 1915, p. 2, "Labor Wins Over Mr. Rockefeller," January 28, 1915, p. 1, "Foes Meet in Friendly Conversation," January 28, 1915, p. 8 (an unctuous editorial, praising Rockefeller's wisdom and generosity), "Strike Heads See Mr. Rockefeller," January 29, 1915, p. 1, all in *New York Times*. Chernow, *Titan*, pp. 587–88, mentions only the immediate reconciliation.

59. Fetherling, *Mother Jones*, pp. 130–33; McGovern and Guttridge, *Great Coalfield Wars*, pp. 318–20; Foner, ed., *Mother Jones Speaks*, pp. 263–68. Her speech calling for Rockefeller's deeds to follow his pious words was reprinted in *The New York Times*, January 29, 1915, and *New York Call*, January 29, 1915.

60. Mother Jones to James Lord, December 23, 1914, March 23, 1915, and Lord to Jones, April 3, 1915, film 8505, reel 144, frames 245–46, 297–99, 307–8, American Federation of Labor—The Samuel Gompers Era Collection, LC, reprinted in Steel, ed., *Correspondence*, pp. 132–33, 136–40.

61. Mother Jones to John D. Rockefeller, Jr., March 15, 1915, in Steel, ed., *Correspondence*, p. 134.

62. Mother Jones to John D. Rockefeller, Jr., March 15, 1915, in Steel, ed., *Correspondence*, p. 134. On maternalism, see Seth Koven and Sonia Michel, eds., *Mothers of a New World: Maternalist Politics and the Origins of the Welfare State* (New York: Routledge, 1993); Kathleen A. Brown, "The 'Savagely Fathered and Unmothered World' of the Communist Party, USA: Feminism, Maternalism, and

'Mother Bloor,' " *Feminist Studies* 25 (1999), pp. 537–70; Patrick Wilkinson, "The Selfless and the Helpless: Maternalist Origins of the U.S. Welfare State," *Feminist Studies* 25 (1999), pp. 571–99.

63. Rockefeller wrote a note of thanks to "My dear Mrs. Jones," describing his mother as one who considered all men brothers and adding, "She was deeply interested in my meeting with you. I gave her a full account of our pleasant conference, telling her of your fearless devotion to the cause to which you have given so many years of earnest work"; see Rockefeller to Jones, [March 1915], in Steel, ed., *Correspondence*, pp. 138–39. Also see Mother Jones to Walter Watson Stokes, March 17, 1915, in Steel, ed., *Correspondence*, pp. 134–36.

9. "The Walking Wrath of God"

1. Upton Sinclair, *The Coal War* (Boulder: Colorado Associated University Press, 1976), pp. 88–90, 268–69. Sinclair was so outraged at the Colorado coal strike that he wrote two books about it. In *King Coal* (1917), he pleased his publisher with an exciting story that used the coalfields as a backdrop. But Sinclair wished to tell the very specific story of the Colorado strike, so in the sequel, *The Coal War*, he wrote a dramatized history of the events of 1914. He failed to find a publisher for *The Coal War*, and the book did not appear until 1976. Also see "Mother Jones," *United Mine Workers Journal*, January 21, 1915, p. 4.

2. Peter C. Michelson, " 'Mother' Jones," *Delineator* 86 (May 1914), p. 8; "Mother Jones: An Impression," *New Republic*, February 20, 1915, pp. 73–74; Elizabeth Waddell, "The Little Old Woman," and Leonard D. Abbott, "The Incarnation of Labor's Struggle," both in *Everybody's Magazine*, April–May 1914, frontispiece and pp. 5–11.

3. For a fine discussion of Mother Jones's appeal to working-class, especially ethnic, women, see Donna R. Gabbacia, "Mary Harris Jones: Immigrant and Labor Activist," in Ballard C. Campbell, ed., *The Human Tradition in the Gilded Age and Progressive Era* (Wilmington, Del.: Scholarly Resources, 2000), pp. 85–100. Also see Mari Boor Tonn, "The Rhetorical Personae of Mary Harris 'Mother' Jones: Industrial Labor's Maternal Prophet" (Ph.D. diss., University of Kansas, 1987).

4. Mary Field, "She 'Stirreth Up the People,' " *Everybody's Magazine*, April–May 1914, pp. 8–11.

5. Ibid. *Collier's* gave Mother Jones a prominent place in its photo-essay "Props of Labor Propaganda," November 4, 1916, pp. 16–17. Underneath a kindly picture, there is a quote of her saying, "If they want to hang me, let them hang me; but when I'm on the scaffold, I'll cry 'Freedom for the working classes!' "

6. On women and feminism, see Nancy Cott, *The Grounding of Modern Feminism* (New Haven, Conn.: Yale University Press, 1987); William H. Chafe, *The American Woman: Her Changing Social, Economic, and Political Roles, 1920–1970* (New York: Oxford University Press, 1972), Glenna Matthews, *The Rise of Public*

Woman: Woman's Power and Woman's Place in the United States, 1630–1970 (New York: Oxford University Press, 1992).

7. On suffrage, see Aileen S. Kraditor, *The Ideas of the Woman Suffrage Movement, 1890–1920* (New York: Columbia University Press, 1965); Eleanor Flexner, *Century of Struggle: The Woman's Rights Movement in the United States* (Cambridge, Mass.: Belknap Press of Harvard University Press, 1975); Paula Baker, "The Domestication of Politics: Women and American Political Society, 1780–1920," *American Historical Review* 89 (June 1984), pp. 620–47; Ellen Carol DuBois, *Woman Suffrage and Women's Rights* (New York: New York University Press, 1998); Ellen Carol DuBois, *Harriot Stanton Blatch and the Winning of Woman Suffrage* (New Haven, Conn.: Yale University Press, 1997); Anne Benjamin, *A History of the Anti-suffrage Movement in the United States from 1895 to 1920: Women against Equality* (Lewiston, N.Y.: Edwin Mellen Press, 1991); Jane Jerome Camki, *Women against Women: American Anti-suffragism, 1880–1920* (New York: Carlson Publishing, 1994); Margaret Mary Finnegan, *Selling Suffrage: Consumer Culture and Votes for Women* (New York: Columbia University Press, 1999); Susan E. Marshall, *Splintered Sisterhood: Gender and Class in the Campaign against Woman Suffrage* (Madison: University of Wisconsin Press, 1997).

8. " 'Mother' Jones, Mild-Mannered, Talks Sociology," *New York Times,* June 1, 1913, sec. 5, p. 4; Benjamin, *History of the Anti-suffrage Movement,* pp. 140–44; Emma Goldman, "Woman Suffrage," in her *The Traffic in Women and Other Essays on Feminism* (New York: Times Change Press, 1971); Candace Falk, *Love, Anarchy, and Emma Goldman* (New Brunswick, N.J.: Rutgers University Press, 1990), pp. 81–82.

9. The literature on women and work is enormous; for a sampling, see Alice Kessler-Harris, *Out to Work: A History of Wage-Earning Women in the United States* (New York: Oxford University Press, 1982); Alice Kessler-Harris, *A Woman's Wage: Historical Meanings and Social Consequences* (Lexington: University Press of Kentucky, 1990); Jacqueline Jones, *Labor of Love, Labor of Sorrow: Black Women, Work, and Family from Slavery to the Present* (New York: Basic Books, 1985); Leslie Woodcock Tentler, *Wage-Earning Women: Industrial Work and Family Life in the United States, 1900–1930* (New York: Oxford University Press, 1979); Susan Porter Benson, *Counter Cultures: Saleswomen, Managers, and Customers in American Department Stores, 1890–1940* (Urbana: University of Illinois Press, 1988); Sharon Strom Hartman, *Beyond the Typewriter: Gender, Class, and the Origins of Modern American Office Work, 1900–1930* (Urbana: University of Illinois Press, 1992); Lisa M. Fine, *The Souls of the Skyscraper: Female Clerical Workers in Chicago, 1870–1930* (Philadelphia: Temple University Press, 1990); Susan Glenn, *Daughters of the Shtetl: Life and Labor in the Immigrant Generation* (Ithaca, N.Y.: Cornell University Press, 1990); Alice Kessler-Harris, "Where Are the Organized Women Workers?" *Feminist Studies* 3 (Fall 1975), pp. 92–110; Susan Estabrook Kennedy, *If All We Did Was to Weep at Home: A History of White Working-Class Women in America* (Bloomington: Indiana University Press, 1979);

Julie A. Matthaei, *An Economic History of Women in America: Women's Work, the Sexual Division of Labor, and the Development of Capitalism* (New York: Schocken Books, 1982); Lynn Y. Weiner, *From Working Girl to Working Mother: The Female Labor Force in the United States, 1820–1980* (Chapel Hill: University of North Carolina Press, 1985); Mari Jo Buhle, *Women and American Socialism, 1870–1920* (Urbana: University of Illinois Press, 1981); Ruth Milkman, ed., *Women, Work, and Protest: A Century of U.S. Women's Labor History* (Boston: Routledge and Kegan Paul, 1985).

10. Mother Jones, speech in Peoria, Illinois, April 6, 1919, in Edward M. Steel, ed., *The Speeches and Writings of Mother Jones* (Pittsburgh, Pa.: University of Pittsburgh Press, 1988), pp. 194–99.

11. Kathryn Kish Sklar, *Florence Kelley and the Nation's Work: The Rise of Woman's Political Culture, 1830–1900* (New Haven, Conn.: Yale University Press, 1995), pp. 43–49; Jane Addams, *Twenty Years at Hull House* (New York: Macmillan and Co., 1910), pp. 1–42; Mother Jones, *Autobiography,* pp. 11–12.

12. Only about one-tenth of Mother Jones's surviving letters were written to women.

13. "500 Women Cheer for Mother Jones," *New York Times,* May 23, 1914, p. 3; Mother Jones, *Autobiography,* pp. 203–4.

14. See Buhle, *Women and American Socialism;* DuBois, *Harriot Stanton Blatch and the Winning of Woman Suffrage;* Sklar, *Florence Kelley and the Nation's Work.*

15. See Sklar, *Florence Kelley and the Nation's Work;* Allen F. Davis, *American Heroine: The Life and Legend of Jane Addams* (New York: Oxford University Press, 1973); Gioia Diliberto, *A Useful Woman: The Early Life of Jane Addams* (New York: Scribners, 1999); David M. Kennedy, *Birth Control in America: The Career of Margaret Sanger* (New Haven, Conn.: Yale University Press, 1970); Ellen Chesler, *Woman of Valor: Margaret Sanger and the Birth Control Movement in America* (New York: Simon and Schuster, 1992); Annelise Orleck, *Common Sense and a Little Fire* (Chapel Hill: University of North Carolina Press, 1999).

16. Mother Jones, "Fashionable Society Scorned," *Miners' Magazine,* April 1, 1915, pp. 1, 3, in Philip Foner, ed., *Mother Jones Speaks* (New York: Monad Press, 1983), pp. 468–71; Mother Jones, speech at UMW convention, January 21, 1911, in Steel, ed., *Speeches and Writings,* p. 52; Florence Harriman, *From Pinafores to Politics* (New York: Henry Holt and Company, 1923), p. 143.

17. Mother Jones, "Fashionable Society Scorned," pp. 1, 3. In the small collection of Mother Jones's papers at the Chicago Historical Society are two poems about the plight of shop girls:

> *The Wolf of Poverty follows me on*
> *Through the dingy streets of Town*
> *So close beside his shaggy hide*
> *Might almost brush my Gown. . . .*

Reprinted in Foner, ed., *Mother Jones Speaks,* pp. 472–73.

18. On cross-class women's organizing, see, for example, DuBois, "Working Women, Class Relations, and Suffrage Militance," pp. 34–58; Nancy Schrom Dye, *As Equals and as Sisters: Feminism, the Labor Movement, and the Women's Trade Union League of New York* (Columbia: University of Missouri Press, 1980); Meredith Tax, *The Rising of the Women: Feminist Solidarity and Class Conflict, 1880–1917* (New York: Monthly Review Press, 1980); and Rosalyn Fraad Baxandall, *Words on Fire: The Life and Writing of Elizabeth Gurley Flynn* (New Brunswick, N.J.: Rutgers University Press, 1987).

19. For a fine example of a feminist deeply influenced by Mother Jones, see Meridel Le Sueur, "Mother Jones and the Global Family," *In These Times*, February 21, 1990, p. 18, reprinted as the foreword to the 1990 edition of *The Autobiography of Mother Jones*.

20. On low-wage work, see, for example, Matthaei, *Economic History of Women in America*; Jones, *Labor of Love, Labor of Sorrow*; Milkman, ed., *Women, Work, and Protest*; Tentler, *Wage-Earning Women*; Kennedy, *If All We Did Was to Weep at Home*; Weiner, *From Working Girl to Working Mother*.

21. Mother Jones, speech at Peoria, Illinois, April 6, 1919, in Steel, ed., *Speeches and Writings*, p. 195.

22. See David Montgomery, *The Fall of the House of Labor: The Workplace, the State, and American Labor Activism, 1865–1925* (New York: Cambridge University Press, 1987); Irving Bernstein, *The Lean Years: A History of the American Worker, 1920–1933* (Baltimore: Penguin, 1966). The conjunction of business unionism and bureaucratization of unions is the subject of Warren Van Tine's *The Making of the Labor Bureaucrat: Union Leadership in the United States, 1870–1920* (Amherst: University of Massachusetts Press, 1973).

23. On the complexities of the decade following the Progressive Era, see Lynn Dumenil's excellent *The Modern Temper: American Culture and Society in the 1920s* (New York: Hill and Wang, 1995).

24. For Mother Jones's Midwest tour with James Lord, see *United Mine Workers Journal*, July 8–August 26, 1915. Mother Jones's schedule during the period from early June through early July 1916 can be followed in her correspondence, published in Edward M. Steel, ed., *The Correspondence of Mother Jones* (Pittsburgh, Pa.: University of Pittsburgh Press, 1985), pp. 146–54; the quote is from her letter to John Walker, June 30, 1916, p. 151. Her visit to Los Angeles was covered in unidentified newspaper clippings titled "Mother Jones Visits Los Angeles," and Gertrude M. Price, "Mother Jones, Labor's 85-Year-Young 'Joan of Arc' Pays Flying Visit to Los Angeles," CUA, 7/3.5.

25. Mother Jones, speech at public meeting in Pittsburg, Kansas, August 7, 1915, in Steel, ed., *Speeches and Writings*, pp. 156–66.

26. Ibid.

27. *New York Times*, February 7, 1915; Fetherling, *Mother Jones*, p. 142; Mother Jones to William Wilson, October 18, 1915, William Wilson to P. L. Prentiss, October 18, 1915, Prentiss to Wilson, October 19, 1915, "Girls Slaving for 78 Cents a Week," *Washington Times*, October 22, 1915, all in Federal Mediation

and Conciliation Service Case Files, 1913–1948, record group 280, box 8, file 33/121, NARA; Mother Jones, speech at UMW convention, Indianapolis, January 20, 1916, in Steel, ed., *Speeches and Writings*, p. 175. On the Chicago strike, see Young-soo Bae, "Men's Clothing Workers in Chicago, 1871–1929: Ethnicity, Class, and a Labor Union" (Ph.D. diss., Harvard University, 1988), pp. 226–37.

28. "Mother Jones Demands 6-Hour Day; Wants Wilson," unidentified Evansville, Indiana, newspaper, n.d., CUA, 7/2.5; "Labor Leader Scores Hughes; Boosts Wilson," unidentified Davenport, Iowa, newspaper, CUA, 7/2.7; Fetherling, *Mother Jones*, pp. 142–44; "Mother Jones at Evansville," *United Mine Workers Journal*, September 14, 1916; Mother Jones, "Arizona in 1916," unpublished MS in Mother Jones folders, John Fitzpatrick Collection, CHS; Mother Jones to John H. Walker, June 30, 1916, in Steel, ed., *Correspondence*, p. 151. Mother Jones helped organize copper workers in Bisbee, Arizona, where she endorsed George Hunt for governor, arguing that he was a true friend of labor because he refused to allow scabs or gunmen into the strike zone against the Copper Queen Corporation. Later, she wrote Governor Hunt a letter of thanks for the reception she received in Phoenix. She noted that most governors sent her bayonets, not flowers. Still governor in 1927, Hunt showed labor leader Fred Mooney an inscribed photograph of Mother Jones, kept behind a curtain in his office, and declared, "I think she is unquestionably the greatest woman this nation has ever produced." See Jones to Hunt, June 12, 1916, and Hunt to Jones, June 14, 1916, in Steel, ed., *Correspondence*, pp. 147–49; Fetherling, *Mother Jones*, pp. 142–44; Mother Jones, *Autobiography*, pp. 172–77; *Arizona Daily Star*, quoted in Fetherling, *Mother Jones*, p. 143.

29. The story is well told, including excerpts from the local press, in Michael G. Matejka, "Streetcar Strike Won with 'Mother' Jones," *Livingston & McLean Counties Union News*, June 1992, pp. 4–5; John Walker to Mother Jones, July 12, 1917, in Steel, ed., *Correspondence*, pp. 176–77.

30. "Mother Jones Arrives to Speak in Cleveland Square," *El Paso Herald*, August 16, 1916, and " 'Mother' Jones Roasts Militia," *El Paso Herald*, August 17, 1916, both in CUA, 7/2.7, reprinted in Foner, ed., *Mother Jones Speaks*, pp. 284–90; "New Rochelle Also Kills Carmen's Law," *New York Times*, October 5, 1916, p. 5.

31. "New Rochelle Also Kills Carmen's Law," *New York Times*, October 5, 1916, p. 5; "Car Riot Started by Mother Jones," *New York Times*, October 6, 1916, p. 1; "A Visitor," *New York Times*, October 7, 1916, p. 10; "Mother Jones Says She Approves Riot," *New York Times*, October 7, 1916, p. 20; Foner, ed., *Mother Jones Speaks*, pp. 287–89.

32. The *Times* carried the police informant's report in a story with the subtitle "Has No Apology to Offer for Thursday's Outbreak, She Says in Speech." Fetherling, *Mother Jones*, tends to accept any charge that Mother Jones fomented violence, and the New York streetcar strike is a good example of his

gullibility on this point (pp. 147–48). No doubt Mother Jones was very skillful at working a crowd up to the edge of militant action; occasionally she did advocate spilling blood, though usually her words fell short of straightforward incitement to violence. Simply put, when she told miners to arm themselves if the guards shot at them, her opponents heard a call to arms, not a call for group defense.

33. Thomas J. Mooney to Mother Jones, December 15, 1915, Mooney to Jones, November 25, 1916, in Steel, ed., *Correspondence*, pp. 142–45, 162–64. Mother Jones was also active in trying to secure the release of Matthew Schmidt, David Kaplan, and the MacNamara brothers, convicted in the *Los Angeles Times* bombing in 1910. She became friends with Schmidt's sister Katherine, a member of the office employees union who wrote her a long letter suggesting they start a women's movement to free all of labor's political prisoners. See Katherine Schmidt to Mother Jones, October 29, 1916, in Steel, ed., *Correspondence*, pp. 157–60. In 1915, Mother Jones visited the prisoners in San Quentin.

34. Fetherling, *Mother Jones*, pp. 144–47; Mother Jones to Tom Mooney, December 15, 1916, in Steel, ed., *Correspondence*, pp. 169–70; Robert Minor, "The San Francisco Frame-Up," *International Socialist Review* 17 (October 1916), pp. 216–17. Mother Jones to Sara J. Dorr, December 16, 1918; Mother Jones to John Walker, December 18, 1918, and December 28, 1918; all in Steel, ed., *Correspondence*, pp. 185–86, 186–87, 187–88. Mother Jones wrote to Woodrow Wilson's closest adviser, Colonel Edward M. House, to gain the President's attention for a pardon; see Jones to House, December 9, 1916, in Steel, ed., *Correspondence*, pp. 167–68. She also campaigned to have members of the International Association of Bridge and Structural Ironworkers released who were imprisoned for transporting dynamite; see Samuel Graham to Mother Jones, January 2, 1917, in Steel, ed., *Correspondence*, pp. 173–74. On one of her trips to California in 1917 to aid Mooney, she stopped in the town of Taft and spent a week helping organize oil workers.

35. "Mother Jones at Indiana Federation Convention," *United Mine Workers Journal*, October 5, 1916, p. 12; "Run of Mine," *United Mine Workers Journal*, October 19, 1916, p. 5; Marguerite Prevey to Mother Jones, October 26, 1916, and Jones to Prevey, October 31, 1916, in Steel, ed., *Correspondence*, pp. 157, 161–62. Mother Jones, "Arizona in 1916," MS, John Fitzpatrick Papers, CHS; Mother Jones, speech at UMW convention, Indianapolis, January 29, 1916, in Steel, ed., *Speeches and Writings*, p. 180; *New York Call*, January 21, 1917, in Steel, ed., *Correspondence*, pp. 174–76, in response to Meyer's "Time to Clean House," December 17, 1917.

36. Mother Jones to Fred Suytor, December 24, 1915, Aldrich Public Library, Barre, Vermont (my thanks to Robin Bachin for providing me with a copy of this letter). The irony, of course, was that Mother Jones herself was a producer of phrases, her claims to having worked on the night shift and the day shift notwithstanding.

37. Mother Jones to Edward Crough, June 30, 1916, in Steel, ed., *Correspondence*, pp. 149–50.
38. Van Tine, *Making of the Labor Bureaucrat*, pp. 1–31.
39. John L. Lewis's career highlights these conflicts; see Melvyn Dubofsky and Warren Van Tine, *John L. Lewis: A Biography* (New York: Quadrangle Books, 1977), pp. 20–66; Van Tine, *Making of the Labor Bureaucrat*, pp. 57–84; Robert H. Zieger, *John L. Lewis, Labor Leader* (Boston: Twayne Publishers, 1988), pp. 1–2.
40. John L. Spivak, *A Man in His Time* (New York: Horizon Press, 1967), pp. 72–73.
41. See Valerie Jean Conner, *The National War Labor Board: Stability, Social Justice, and the Voluntary State in World War I* (Chapel Hill: University of North Carolina Press, 1983); David A. Corbin, *Life, Work, and Rebellion in the Coal Fields: The Southern West Virginia Miners, 1880–1922* (Urbana: University of Illinois Press, 1981), ch. 7.
42. John J. Cornwell to William Wilson, June 16, 1917, Department of Labor, Chief Clerk's Files, record group 174, box 132, file 121/1, NARA; also see the correspondence in Federal Mediation and Conciliation Service, record group 280, box 19, file 33/390, NARA, esp. Cornwell to Wilson, July 1, 1917.
43. Adam Littlepage to Thomas Gregory, July, 13, 1917, along with affidavits, Department of Justice, record group 60, box 3362, file 16/72, NARA. Mother Jones was accompanied by Lawrence Dwyer, a swaggering organizer known to his friends as "Peggy" because of his wooden leg.
44. U. S. Blake to Attorney General Thomas Gregory, August 22, 1917, including the transcript of mother Jones's speech and the attorney general's response, Department of Justice, record group 60, box 3362, file 16/72, NARA. Mother Jones's tour through West Virginia was also covered by the *United Mine Workers Journal* between April and August 1917. Her reference to the Russian Revolution predated the Bolshevik takeover.
45. Nick Salvatore, *Eugene Debs: Citizen and Socialist* (Urbana: University of Illinois Press, 1982), pp. 280–302.
46. See David Montgomery's discussions of the war and labor in *The Fall of the House of Labor: The Workplace, the State, and American Labor Activism, 1865–1925* (New York: Cambridge University Press, 1987), pp. 330–410; and David Montgomery, *Workers' Control in America* (New York: Cambridge University Press, 1979), pp. 94–108. Wilson looked especially good next to his opponent in the 1916 election, the Republican Charles Evans Hughes, who as a Supreme Court justice had voted against labor in the notorious Danbury Hatters and the Buck's Stove and Range cases.
47. Mother Jones, speech at UMW convention, Indianapolis, January 17, 1918, in Steel, ed., *Speeches and Writings*, pp. 186–87; Nell Irvin Painter, *Standing at Armageddon: The United States, 1877–1919* (New York: Norton, 1987), pp. 318–20; Conner, *National War Labor Board*, pp. 18–67. The *Autobiography* is silent on the Russian Revolution, and Mother Jones said little—besides calling herself a Bol-

shevik—to gauge her reaction to that dramatic event. An unnamed, undated, and unidentified essay, "The Russian Revolution in the United States," can be found in the Mother Jones Collection, CUA. The author, whether Mother Jones or someone else, wrote approvingly of the revolution but was careful to note that each nation must find its own way. Mother Jones's autobiography railed against World War I as a betrayal of workers and democracy; nowhere does she mention that she supported the war.

48. Mother Jones, speech at UMW convention, Indianapolis, January 17, 1918, in Steel, ed., *Speeches and Writings*, pp. 189–90.

49. Mother Jones, speech at UMW convention, January 17, 1918, in Steel, ed., *Speeches and Writings*, pp. 191–92. She also urged citizens to join the home guards in preparation for war's aftermath.

50. Corbin, *Life, Work, and Rebellion*, pp. 176–90. For the UMW during the war, see Maier B. Fox, *United We Stand: The United Mine Workers of America, 1890–1990* (Washington, D.C.: United Mine Workers, 1990), pp. 177–95.

51. Conner, *National War Labor Board*, pp. 158–86; Montgomery, *Fall of the House of Labor*, pp. 370–410.

52. Mother Jones, speech at UMW convention, Indianapolis, January 20, 1916, in Steel, ed., *Speeches and Writings*, pp. 167–70.

53. Only Doyle's half of this correspondence survives; see Edward Doyle to Mother Jones, December 13, 1918, in envelope 5, folder 3, Edward Doyle Papers, DPL.

54. John Walker to Mother Jones, July 19, 1917, and Jones to Walker (no date, but clearly in reply to Walker's July 19 letter), both in Steel, ed., *Correspondence*, pp. 177–80.

55. John Walker to Mother Jones, July 19, 1917; Jones to Walker (n.d.); Jones to Walker, August 25, 1918; Walker to Jones, August 29, 1918; Mother Jones to Terence Powderly, June 19, 1919, all in Steel, ed., *Correspondence*, pp. 177–82, 193.

56. Mother Jones, speech in Peoria, Illinois, April 6, 1919, in Steel, ed., *Speeches and Writings*, pp. 194–99. This was a "Mooney Day" speech, one of three in Peoria on that occasion, all addressing the plight of Tom Mooney; the other speeches, by Duncan MacDonald and T. H. Tippett, were printed, along with Mother Jones's address, in *Mooney Day, Held at Coliseum, Peoria, ILL* (n.p., n.d.), a pamphlet available in Military Intelligence Division Correspondence, 1917–1941, record group 165, box 2864, file 10110-G-4-1, NARA. As early as April 1918, Mother Jones was being watched by the War Department's Military Intelligence Division and, after the war, by J. Edgar Hoover's Bureau of Investigation. Lieutenant Rolin G. Watkins, for example, reported to Washington that Mother Jones spoke at great length in San Francisco on April 16, 1918, regarding Mooney. Her audience was supportive until she condemned the military for shooting down working men and their families. Watkins recommended that federal or local authorities pressure her to stop making speeches; see record group 165, box 2718, file 10110-76, and Name Index to Correspondence, 1917–1941, M1194, reel 110, "Jones, Mother," NARA.

57. On labor and society during the war, see Conner, *National War Labor Board*; John F. McClymer, *War and Welfare: Social Engineering in America, 1890–1925* (Westport, Conn.: Greenwood Press, 1980); Robert D. Cuff, *The War Industries Board: Business-Government Relations during World War I* (Baltimore: Johns Hopkins University Press, 1973); and David Kennedy, *Over Here: The First World War and American Society* (New York: Oxford University Press, 1980).

58. Montgomery, *Fall of the House of Labor*, pp. 392–95; Painter, *Standing at Armageddon*, pp. 334–38; Mother Jones to Ed Nockles, January 14, 1919, intercepted by military censor, Washington, January 24, 1919, in Federal Bureau of Investigation Case Files, record group 65, M1085, roll 708, file 291337, NARA. While some operatives called Mother Jones a dangerous radical, others dismissed her as innocuous. In Cabin Creek, for example, Special Agent A. E. Hayes of the Bureau of Investigation reported that her speeches "are of the union organizing type rather than of the Bolsheviki tendency," and Agent Ward Thompson wrote of her address in Rockford, Illinois, "The speech of Mother Jones was not radical in any way, in fact it might be considered a patriotic address." Her support for the war gave her considerable cover. See FBI Investigative Case Files, 1908–1922, record group 65, M1085, reel 801, file 364074, July 28, 1919, and reel 376, file 32351, July 30, 1919, NARA.

59. Mother Jones to Terence Powderly, June 19, 1919, in Steel, ed., *Correspondence*, p. 193; William B. Wilson to Attorney General A. Mitchell Palmer, July 10, 1919, A. Mitchell Palmer to Superintendent of Prisons, and response by Acting Superintendent Dickerson, July 10, 1919, and A. Mitchell Palmer to Mother Jones, July 11, 1919, all in Justice Department, Attorney General's Office, record group 60, file 203233, NARA; Frank W. Snyder, "A Seething, Burning Hellish Hole: The Sissonville Road Prison Camp," *West Virginia Federationist*, July 3, 1919, p. 1.

60. William Serrin, *Homestead: The Glory and Tragedy of an American Steel Town* (New York: Vintage, 1992), pp. 3–95; David Brody, *Steelworkers in America: The Nonunion Era* (Cambridge, Mass.: Harvard University Press, 1960), pp. 1–79; Arthur G. Burgoyne, *Homestead: A Complete History of the Struggle, July, 1892* (Pittsburgh, Pa.: University of Pittsburgh Press, 1979); Painter, *Standing at Armageddon*, pp. 110–14.

61. Serrin, *Homestead*, pp. 96–145; David Brody, *Labor in Crisis: The Steel Strike of 1919* (Philadelphia: J. B. Lippincott, 1965), pp. 13–28. Also see Cliff Brown, *Racial Conflict and Violence in the Labor Market: Roots of the 1919 Steel Strike* (New York: Garland, 1998); Mary Heaton Vorse, *Men and Steel* (New York: Boni and Liveright, 1920); William Z. Foster, *The Great Steel Strike and Its Lessons* (New York: Da Capo Press, 1971).

62. Brody, *Labor in Crisis*, pp. 34–43. On the difficulties of organizing during this era, see David Brody, *Workers' Control in America: Studies in the History of Work, Technology, and Labor Struggles* (Cambridge, U.K.: Cambridge University Press, 1979), pp. 91–112.

63. Brody, *Labor in Crisis*, pp. 45–53. That the President's Mediation Commission recommended a new trial for Tom Mooney was evidence of labor's new power.
64. Brody, *Labor in Crisis*, pp. 61–69; Serrin, *Homestead*, pp. 146–60. On Foster, see James R. Barrett, *William Z. Foster and the Tragedy of American Radicalism* (Urbana: University of Illinois Press, 1999).
65. Mother Jones to John Walker, February 5, 1919, in Steel, ed., *Correspondence*, pp. 190–91; Report submitted by Confidential Informant 101, FBI Investigative Case Files, record group 65, M1085, reel 783, file 352037, Pittsburgh, March 2, 1919, pp. 1–3, NARA; Brody, *Labor in Crisis*, pp. 78–87.
66. Brody, *Labor in Crisis*, pp. 89–95.
67. Mother Jones, *Autobiography*, pp. 211–13; Fetherling, *Mother Jones*, pp. 157–58. To make the point that workers must be allowed to blow off steam, she opened with the sort of racist joke common to the era: A captain on a steamship was in a hurry to make port. "He told a darkey to sit on the valve. He did. After a while he said, 'Massa, this thing's getting too hot.' 'Never mind, keep your seat.' After a while the darkey said, 'This getting too hot, sure.' 'No matter, I want to get into port.' The darkey stayed a while longer and said, 'Massa, if you don't let that steam out it will blow hell out of all of us.' What happened? In a few minutes the steam blew the captain and all of them into the Mississippi River." See Mother Jones, speech at UMW convention, Indianapolis, September 16, 1919, in Steel, ed., *Speeches and Writings*, pp. 203–4.
68. Brody, *Labor in Crisis*, pp. 82–83, 108, 112–15.
69. Mary Heaton Vorse, *A Footnote to Folly* (New York: Farrar and Rinehart, 1935), pp. 287–89. On Vorse's life, see Dee Garrison, *Mary Heaton Vorse: The Life of an American Insurgent* (Philadelphia: Temple University Press, 1989). Mother Jones spoke to the UMW about the steel strike in her speeches at its convention, Indianapolis, September 16, 1919, and September 17, 1919, in Steel, ed., *Speeches and Writings*, pp. 203–4, 208–10.
70. Vorse, *Footnote to Folly*, pp. 287–89.
71. Mother Jones, speech, October 22, 1919, in Military Intelligence Division, record group 165, box 3646, file 10634-670-81 and 82, Steel Strike, Chicago, October 22, 1919, NARA; in that same file, also see items 83–87, which allege a massive conspiracy of organizations and individuals, including the IWW, socialists, communists, anarchists, Big Bill Haywood, John Fitzpatrick, and William Z. Foster.
72. "Mother Jones Urges Strikers to Violence," *New York Times*, October 24, 1919, p. 12; *Chicago Tribune*, October 24, 1919, in Foner, ed., *Mother Jones Speaks*, pp. 317–19. Eugene Debs used almost exactly the same words, calling himself a Bolshevist from prison. The *New York Times* report accused Mother Jones of inciting violence yet offered little evidence.
73. Mother Jones, *Autobiography*, pp. 222–24.
74. Ibid., pp. 217–18; Brody, *Labor in Crisis*, pp. 112–78.
75. Mother Jones, *Autobiography*, p. 225; Brody, *Labor in Crisis*, pp. 112–78; Edward

B. Clark, "How General Wood Restored Order in Gary Strike," *Chicago Evening Post*, October 31, 1919, in Military Intelligence Division, record group 165, box 3646, file 10634-670-86, NARA. William Z. Foster, *Great Steel Strike*, pp. 110–39, argued that sheer terror by the police was a very important factor in breaking the strike.

76. On the Red Scare, see Robert K. Murray, *Red Scare: A Study in National Hysteria, 1919–1920* (Minneapolis: University of Minnesota Press, 1955); and William Preston, Jr., *Aliens and Dissenters: Federal Suppression of Radicals, 1903–1933* (Cambridge, Mass.: Harvard University Press, 1963).

77. The story is well told in Painter, *Standing at Armageddon*, pp. 346–64, 376–82.

78. Foster, *Great Steel Strike*, pp. 110–39, 186–90; Brody, *Labor in Crisis*, pp. 128–78, including quote from *The New York Times* on p. 132.

79. Murray, *Red Scare*, esp. chs. 6, 11, 13, 16; Preston, *Aliens and Dissenters*, pp. 88–237; Painter, *Standing at Armageddon*, pp. 346–64.

80. See, for example, Mother Jones, speech, Milwaukee, May 25, 1919, FBI Investigative Case Files, record group 65, M1085, reel 798, file 362780, May 25, 1919, NARA.

81. Foster, *Great Steel Strike*, pp. 146–48. Fannie Sellins's story is told in Stephen Sage Burnett, "Women and Steel: Gender and Labor in the Great Steel Strike of 1919" (master's thesis, University of Missouri, 1995).

82. Foner, ed., *Mother Jones Speaks*, pp. 314–15; Fetherling, *Mother Jones*, p. 158; Vorse, *Men and Steel*, p. 69.

10. The Last Decade

1. Fred Mooney, *Struggle in the Coal Fields: The Autobiography of Fred Mooney* (Morgantown: West Virginia University Library, 1967), pp. 79–85; Edward M. Steel, ed., *The Speeches and Writings of Mother Jones* (Pittsburgh, Pa.: University of Pittsburgh Press, 1988), pp. 232–33; Edward M. Steel, ed., *The Correspondence of Mother Jones* (Pittsburgh, Pa.: University of Pittsburgh Press, 1985), pp. xxxv–xxxvi. For a Mexican view of her trip, see " 'Madre Juanita' on Social Issues," *Excelsior*, January 10, 1921, translated and reprinted in Philip Foner, ed., *Mother Jones Speaks* (New York: Monad Press, 1983), pp. 528–31.

2. Sinclair Snow, *The Pan-American Federation of Labor* (Durham, N.C.: Duke University Press, 1964), p. 112; Dale Fetherling, *Mother Jones: The Miners' Angel* (Carbondale: Southern Illinois University Press, 1974), p. 173; Steel, ed., *Speeches and Writings*, pp. 232–33; Steel, ed., *Correspondence*, pp. xxxv–xxxvi.

3. *New York Times*, January 10, 1921, p. 15; *El Heraldo*, quoted in memo on War Department letterhead, Chief of Staff's office, June 18, 1921, in "Correspondence," Military Intelligence Division, record group 165, box 2292, item 10058-0-92, 1, NARA; Mother Jones, *Autobiography of Mother Jones*, ed. Mary Field

Parton (Chicago: Charles H. Kerr and Company, 1925), p. 239. Mother Jones distinguished between the Russian Revolution and the Soviet government, which she criticized.

4. Mother Jones, speech, Pan-American Federation of Labor meeting, Mexico City, January 13, 1921, in Steel, ed., *Speeches and Writings*, pp. 232–37, originally printed in *Report of the Proceedings of the Third Congress of the Pan-American Federation of Labor*, 1921.

5. Snow, *Pan-American Federation*, pp. 120–50; Fetherling, *Mother Jones*, pp. 175–76; Steel, ed., *Speeches and Writings*, pp. 232–33; Mother Jones to John H. Walker, April 5, 1921, in Steel, ed., *Correspondence*, p. 223.

6. Roberto Haberman to Mother Jones, April 1921, in Steel, ed., *Correspondence*, pp. 225–26.

7. Mother Jones to John Fitzpatrick and Ed Nockles, May 16, 1921, in Steel, ed., *Correspondence*, pp. 226–28.

8. Ibid., pp. 227–28.

9. Mother Jones to John H. Walker, May 27, 1921, June 21, 1921, April 5, 1921, all in Steel, ed., *Correspondence*, pp. 228–30, 232, 223; Foner, ed., *Mother Jones Speaks*, p. 328. Roberto Haberman wrote her, "The so-called 'Communists' are as damnable a lot of whelps as they were when you were down here, but they do not amount to anything, and we don't pay any attention to them, any more than does any worker." See Haberman to Jones, April 1921, in Steel, ed., *Correspondence*, pp. 225–26. On the significance of the conference, see Snow, *Pan-American Federation*, pp. 25–73, 128–50.

10. FBI Investigative Case Files, 1908–1922, record group 65, M1085, reel 581, file 180980, and reel 731, file 311343, NARA; Military Intelligence Division Correspondence, record group 165, box 57, file 10110-1620-19-list, NARA; Mother Jones to Otto Branstetter, April 21, 1920, in Steel, ed., *Correspondence*, p. 200.

11. Mother Jones to John H. Walker, June 18, 1920, July 21, 1920, and December 28, 1920, all in Steel, ed., *Correspondence*, pp. 203, 206, 216.

12. Terence Powderly to Mother Jones, April 9, 1921; Katherine Schmidt to Mother Jones, September 4, 1922; Federated Shopcrafts and Brotherhoods of Texas to Mother Jones, September 6, 1922; Ephraim F. Morgan to Mother Jones, September 6, 1922; Dan W. Stevens to Mother Jones, September 7, 1922; all in Steel, ed., *Correspondence*, pp. 225, 255–56. " 'Mother Jones' Too Ill to Aid Rail Strikers," *New York Times*, September 5, 1922, p. 8; " 'Mother' Jones Recovering," *New York Times*, September 6, 1922, p. 19.

13. Mother Jones, speech at Williamson, West Virginia, June 20, 1920, and speech at Princeton, West Virginia, August 15, 1920, in Steel, ed., *Speeches and Writings*, pp. 211–31. For a fine discussion of the 1920s crackdown on the left, see Lynn Dumenil, *The Modern Temper: American Culture and Society in the 1920s* (New York: Hill and Wang, 1995), pp. 58–71, 201–49.

14. Mother Jones to Ryan Walker, December 12, 1919; Mother Jones to John H. Walker, June 18, 1920; Mother Jones to Theodore Debs, August 18, 1920;

Mother Jones to Woodrow Wilson, December 16, 1920; all in Steel, ed., *Correspondence*, pp. 194, 204, 211, 213–14.

15. David A. Corbin, *Life, Work, and Rebellion in the Coal Fields: The Southern West Virginia Miners, 1880–1922* (Urbana: University of Illinois Press, 1981), pp. 195–205; Steel, ed., *Speeches and Writings*, pp. 211, 238: Maier B. Fox, *United We Stand: The United Mine Workers of America, 1890–1990* (Washington, D.C.: United Mine Workers, 1990), pp. 245–51; Fetherling, *Mother Jones*, pp. 180–83; Ronald Eller, *Miners, Millhands, and Mountaineers: Industrialization of the Appalachian South, 1880–1930* (Knoxville: University of Tennessee Press, 1982), pp. 210–24; Daniel P. Jordan, "The Mingo War: Labor Violence in the Southern West Virginia Coal Fields, 1919–1922," in Gary M. Fink and Merl E. Reed, eds., *Essays in Southern Labor History* (Westport, Conn.: Greenwood Press, 1977), pp. 101–4. Jordan points out that the non-union fields of southern West Virginia produced as much as 10 percent of the nation's bituminous coal by the 1920s. A classic account of the West Virginia situation is found in Winthrop D. Lane, *Civil War in West Virginia* (New York: B. W. Huebsch, Inc., 1921). Southern West Virginia was Hatfield and McCoy country, and American journalists still invoked that blood feud of a generation before to explain events there. Not only was this perspective hopelessly out of date in the 1920s, it was even wrong in the 1890s. Hatfields fought McCoys not out of some rite of violence, some primordial code of honor. Indeed, Hatfields battled Hatfields, McCoys turned on McCoys. Economics more than family background divided West Virginians; violence broke out between those who wished to retain the old locally based economy and others who favored building railroads, logging timber, and selling mineral rights. In other words, the battle for West Virginia remained, as it had been for a long time, primarily economic. See Altina Waller, *Feud: Hatfields, McCoys, and Social Change in Appalachia, 1860–1900* (Chapel Hill: University of North Carolina Press, 1988); Lon Savage, *Thunder in the Mountains: The West Virginia Mine War, 1920–21* (Pittsburgh, Pa.: University of Pittsburgh Press, 1991), p. 26.

16. Corbin, *Life, Work, and Rebellion*, pp. 195–200; Savage, *Thunder in the Mountains*, pp. 13–16; Jordan, "Mingo War," pp. 108–9. According to Jordan, Keeney estimated the number of dead at one hundred as of July 1921. On the heightened expectations of workers in this era, see the 1922 essay by Secretary of Labor James J. Davis, "The Saving and Earning Wage," General Records of the Department of Labor, Chief Clerk's Files, record group 174, box 183, file 167/832, NARA.

17. Savage, *Thunder in the Mountains*, pp. 19–24; Corbin, *Life, Work, and Rebellion*, p. 201; Jordan, "Mingo War," pp. 108–9; Howard B. Lee, *Bloodletting in Appalachia* (Morgantown: West Virginia University Press, 1969), pp. 51–58. John Sayles's outstanding film *Matewan* dramatizes these events.

18. Not long after becoming UMW president, Lewis made his hostility toward women abundantly clear. He adamantly opposed the formation of women's

auxiliaries, arguing that men always did the fighting for the UMW while the women stayed at home. When he learned that Agnes Burns Wieck was a delegate to a joint UMW–Progressive Miners meeting in 1933, Lewis sneered at men who "hide behind women's skirts." His remarks were published, and the *St. Louis Star Times*, May 18, 1933, responded, "Who fights the battle, the real battle, when the dreadful word goes out of a mine disaster far underground? The women who gather around the mine shaft, waiting. . . . And what about the labor struggle itself, the strike? Is it true that always before they have been fought without the aid of women? That should have been told to Mother Jones before she died." From a manuscript, transcribed from various sources, titled "Lewis on Women in 1933—'Behind Women's Skirts,' " in box 15, folder titled "Lewis, John L., 1910–1952," Ed Wieck Collection, WSU. Alice and Ed's son, David Thoreau Wieck, noted Lewis's misogyny—Lewis condemned the tendency of some union men "to shove their women out on the picket line while they remained at home and did the cooking"—and observed that ten thousand women had organized against "King John" in auxiliaries of the Progressive Mine Workers Union. See David Thoreau Wieck, *Woman from Spillertown: A Memoir of Agnes Burns Wieck* (Carbondale: Southern Illinois University Press, 1992), p. 5. Ed Wieck wrote a scathing personal letter to the socialist editor Oscar Ameriger on Lewis. He noted how many former Lewis opponents now supported him, including Ameriger, and he raged against the mistaken notion that Lewis was a different man in the 1930s from the one he had been in decades past. Wieck viewed him as power mad and compared him to the rising fascists Hitler and Mussolini: "No he is the same old Lewis you fought in past years—a glamorous figure, keen, intelligent, quick to grasp opportunities, but ruthless, unscrupulous, dictatorial, with his eye on the road to power for John L. Lewis. A reincarnation of the Medicis or the Borgias—will he flop or succeed? I don't know—but I am sure of his intentions. The thing that is disheartening is the many that are allowing their emotions—the worship of success and boldness to sway their judgement." See box 15, folder titled "Lewis, John L., 1910–1952," Ed Wieck Collection, WSU.

19. Mother Jones, speech at Williamson, Mingo County, June 20, 1920, in Steel, ed., *Speeches and Writings*, pp. 211–23. Jordan, "The Mingo War," p. 120, points out that almost 20 percent of the miners in Mingo and Logan Counties were black, and they were well integrated into the union and the mining communities.

20. "The labor movement will never be wrecked from out side," she wrote John Walker, "the wrecking force will be from within." See Mother Jones to Ryan Walker, December 12, 1919; Mother Jones to John H. Walker, June 18, 1920; Mother Jones to John H. Walker, March 22, 1921; Mother Jones to John H. Walker, July 21, 1920; all in Steel, ed., *Correspondence*, pp. 194–95, 204–5, 222, 206. On Mother Jones's opponents in District 17, see Corbin, *Life, Work, and Rebellion*, p. 232.

21. Special Agent A. E. Hayes, "Radical Activities in Southern West Virginia," October 23, 1920, Federal Bureau of Investigation Files, record group 65, M1085, reel 740, file 318841, NARA; Lee, *Bloodletting*, p. 97.

22. Corbin, *Life, Work, and Rebellion*, pp. 200–8; Savage, *Thunder in the Mountains*, pp. 68–80; Jordan, "Mingo War," pp. 109–10.

23. Fetherling, *Mother Jones*, pp. 184–85; Jordan, "Mingo War," p. 110; Corbin, *Life, Work, and Rebellion*, pp. 217–19; Savage, *Thunder in the Mountains*, pp. 75–80. Of the August 7 meeting in Charleston, Savage, *Thunder in the Mountains*, p. 75, writes, "Mother Jones alone was conciliatory; she urged the miners to calm down; nothing would bring Sid back." But another historian, Michael Meador, "The Red Neck War of 1921: The Miners' March and the Battle of Blair Mountain," in Ken Sullivan, ed., *The Goldenseal Book of the West Virginia Mine Wars* (Charleston, W.Va.: Pictorial Histories Publishing Co., 1991), p. 58, writes, "She reviled the governor and coal companies in the foulest language and called upon the miners to march into Logan and Mingo counties and set up the union by force. . . . Mother Jones called for the miners to lynch Chafin and to establish the union at all costs."

24. Jordan, "Mingo War," p. 110; Fetherling, *Mother Jones*, p. 186; Savage, *Thunder in the Mountains*, pp. 78–79; Corbin, *Life, Work, and Rebellion*, pp. 218, 232 n. 111.

25. *New York Times*, August 25, 1921, p. 15; Corbin, *Life, Work, and Rebellion*, pp. 218–19; Fetherling, *Mother Jones*, p. 186; Jordan, "Mingo War," pp. 110–11; Savage, *Thunder in the Mountains*, pp. 78–80. Lee, *Bloodletting*, p. 97, writes, "At the time [after the false telegram] there was much talk among the miners that Mother Jones had 'sold out to the operators.' But in the summer of 1962, Frank Keeney said to me: 'No, Mother Jones never took money from the operators. At that time she was 91 years old, and age had quenched much of the fighting spirit that characterized her early years.' "

26. The fullest treatment of these events is in Savage, *Thunder in the Mountains*, pp. 81–164.

27. Savage, *Thunder in the Mountains*, pp. 81–164. Corbin, *Life, Work, and Rebellion*, pp. 219–24, estimates the miners' army at fifteen to twenty thousand and argues that they operated as an effective military unit; Jordan, "Mingo War," pp. 111–21, has a fine analysis of why the operators succeeded; Meador, "Red Neck War," pp. 59–62, describes the battle scene vividly, and he estimates the total number of fatalities at between ten and thirty per side.

28. Meador, "Red Neck War," p. 63; Savage, *Thunder in the Mountains*, pp. 165–67; Corbin, *Life, Work, and Rebellion*, pp. 219–24; Jordan, "Mingo War," p. 112; Fetherling, *Mother Jones*, pp. 186–91.

29. Keeney's role is a bit unclear. Corbin sees him as the hero of a near revolution, the young local favorite who knew the men personally and urged them to the barricades. Yet shortly after the march began, Keeney tried to stop it. Bandholz made it clear that UMW officials would be held personally responsible for vio-

lence, and they then worked frantically to call the men back. On the ARU strike, see Nick Salvatore, *Eugene Debs: Citizen and Socialist* (Urbana: University of Illinois Press, 1982), pp. 122–38.

30. Unspoken was the fact that without the persona of Mother Jones, she had no influence at all; as a woman, she could not exercise power like Keeney or Mooney.

31. The return address she gave was Terence Powderly's house in Washington, where she often went when she felt ill and to which she must have retreated after the Harding telegram. See Mother Jones to Ephraim Morgan, August 29, 1921, and Morgan to Jones, August 29, 1921, in Steel, ed., *Correspondence*, pp. 233–34.

32. Mother Jones to William Green, December 27, 1921; Mother Jones to Ephraim Morgan, December 27, 1921; in Steel, ed., *Correspondence*, pp. 237, 239; Fetherling, *Mother Jones*, pp. 190–91.

33. Mother Jones to Ephraim Morgan, December 27, 1921, and Morgan to Jones, April 10, 1923, in Steel, ed., *Correspondence*, pp. 239, 274.

34. Mother Jones to Ephraim Morgan, April 16, 1923, and Jones to Morgan, July 12, 1923, in Steel, ed., *Correspondence*, pp. 275, 285–86. Later she wrote Powderly, "Morgan is a good Christian man, but that gang has given the man a dirty deal." See Mother Jones to Terence Powderly, May 3, 1923, in Steel, ed., *Correspondence*, p. 279.

35. Mother Jones to John H. Walker, December 20, 1922; also see Jones to Walker, June 26, 1922, both in Steel, ed., *Correspondence*, pp. 264, 249–50.

36. Mother Jones to William Green, December 27, 1921, in Steel, ed., *Correspondence*, pp. 236–38, also see pp. 255–61.

37. Quoted in Mother Jones, *Autobiography*, p. 238; " 'Sir, a Woman,' " *Time*, July 16, 1923, p. 6; Judith Elaine Mikeal, "Mother Mary Jones: The Labor Movement's Impious Joan of Arc" (master's thesis, University of North Carolina, 1965), p. 132; Foner, ed., *Mother Jones Speaks*, pp. 360–65. As Foner points out, neither the *Chicago Tribune* nor the *Chicago Daily News* covered her remarks. William Green advised Mother Jones not to attend the conference; see Mother Jones to William Green, May 18, 1923; Green to Jones, May 21, 1923; Jones to Green, May 24, 1923, July 23, 1923; and Green to Jones, July 25, 1923, all in Steel, ed., *Correspondence*, pp. 280–88.

38. See Mother Jones to William Green, December 27, 1921, March 4, 1922; John H. Walker to Mother Jones, December 13, 1923; Jones to Walker, December 14, 1923; Walker to Jones, December 17, 1923; Jones to Walker, December 18, 1923; all in Steel, ed., *Correspondence*, pp. 236, 242, 293–94, 294–95, 295–96, 296–97. Her friends covered her expenses. In 1922, for example, Terence Powderly wrote to Ed Nockles that medical costs for Mother Jones's recent illness came to about one hundred dollars, which Nockles offered to pay. However, Powderly insisted that her living expenses were his responsibility: "My home is hers and as one of the family she don't count when it comes to ex-

pense. Her fidelity to the labor movement is her claim with me and my wife feels the same way about it." See Ed Nockles and John Fitzpatrick to Terence Powderly, September 4, 1922, and Powderly to Nockles, September 20, 1922, in CUA, 7/2.2; Jones to Green, October 2, 1922, and Jones to Walker, March 29, 1922, in Steel, ed., *Correspondence*, pp. 256, 246.

39. Mother Jones, speeches at UMW convention, September 26 and 29, 1921, in Steel, ed., *Speeches and Writings*, pp. 239–50, 251–253; *New York Times*, September 27, 1921, p. 19.

40. For Father Harris's obituary, see Toronto *Globe*, March 6, 1923, p. 1; for his funeral, see Toronto *Globe*, March 9, 1923, pp. 1, 2.

41. Robert J. Scollard, "Reverend William Richard Harris, 1846–1923," *Proceedings of the 41st Canadian Catholic Historical Association Meetings*, June 5–6, 1974, p. 66. Harris was the subject of another article-length biography: Michael Power, "An Introduction to the Life and Work of Dean Harris, 1847–1923," in Mark George McGowan and Brian P. Clarke, eds., *Catholics at the "Gathering Place": Historical Essays on the Archdiocese of Toronto, 1841–1991* (Toronto: Canadian Catholic Historical Association, 1993), pp. 119–36. Note that Scollard and Power disagree on the year of Harris's birth in their titles; like his sister, Harris gave more than one date of birth. The quote is from William Richard Harris, *The Catholic Church in the Niagara Peninsula, 1626–1895* (Toronto: William Briggs, 1895), p. 233.

42. Scollard, "Reverend William Richard Harris," p. 67; Power, "Life and Work of Dean Harris," p. 122; Toronto *Globe*, March 9, 1923, p. 2. It is impossible to say which sister this was since the *Globe* only listed her as Mrs. William Hickey of Chicago, a common name in the Chicago directories. The niece was Frances O'Brien of Toronto. If Mother Jones stayed in contact with these members of her family, no traces remain.

43. Scollard, "Reverend William Richard Harris," pp. 66–76; Power, "Life and Work of Dean Harris," pp. 119–36.

44. *Miners' Magazine*, September 29, 1910, p. 4; Clarence Darrow to Mary Field; Mother Jones to John H. Walker, June 26, 1922; Jones to Walker, December 20, 1922; Mother Jones to Terence Powderly, May 3, 1923, all in Steel, ed., *Correspondence*, pp. 250, 264, 279.

45. The Charles Kerr archives at the Newberry Library in Chicago contain little publication information on *The Autobiography of Mother Jones*, and Mary Field Parton did not discuss the subject. See Mary Field biography, box 38, file 8, and box 58, file 5, Margaret Parton Papers, Special Collections (Collection 36), Inventory, p. 3, University of Oregon. In Cook County Probate Court, Ed Nockles swore that he had known Mother Jones for forty years, and added, "I have talked to her several times in her life and she has repeatedly told me that she has absolutely nobody belonging to her any more. I was secretary for her in writing up her biography." Cook County Probate Court in the Matter of the Estate of Mary Jones, Final Account and Final Report, Docket 319, page 333, no. 178889, Proof of Heirship, filed October 8, 1932.

46. Fred Thompson, "Notes on 'The Most Dangerous Woman in America,' " in Mother Jones, *Autobiography* (1990 ed.), pp. 282–84; Mother Jones to Emma Powderly, June 11, 1923, in Steel, ed., *Correspondence*, p. 284. I assume that Mother Jones finished before the end of the summer because her letters no longer carry a Chicago address after July. Mother Jones's discussion of the *revoltosos* reads very much like her testimony before Congressman William Wilson's committee described above in Chapter 6. There appears to be no original manuscript of the autobiography extant. Parton wrote in her diary for March 9, 1925, "The poor woman who works for me has burned my manuscript. That is the Mother Jones original." In her anger, Parton added, "It may be that 'children are of the kingdom of heaven' but 'morons are of the kingdom of earth.' She is typical. . . . Humanity burning up the precious work of the great martyrs." See box 58, file 5, Parton Papers.

47. "Record of Kerr Publications and Units Sold," p. 80, Charles H. Kerr Company Archives, vol. 39, NL; Thompson, "Notes," pp. 282–85. Kerr's 1929 catalogue quoted a review from the New Orleans *Times-Picayune*: "This profane and lovable old woman, who for over fifty years has fought for the laboring man and his wife and children, is one of the saints of the democracy." See 1929 publications catalogue, p. 5, Kerr Archives.

48. Darrow, introduction to Mother Jones, *Autobiography*, pp. 5–8.

49. There is a growing critical literature on women's autobiography; for a recent compilation from England, see Pauline Polkey, ed., *Women's Lives into Print: The Theory, Practice, and Writing of Feminist Auto/biography* (New York: St. Martin's, 1999). For an excellent essay on African American women, see Deborah Gray White, "Private Lives, Public Personae: A Look at Early Twentieth Century African American Clubwomen," in Nancy Hewitt, Jean O'Barr, and Nancy Rosebaugh, eds., *Talking Gender* (Chapel Hill: University of North Carolina Press, 1996), pp. 106–23.

50. Mother Jones, *Autobiography*, p. 42.

51. Ibid., pp. 11–16.

52. Ibid., pp. 155, 204.

53. Ibid., pp. 157–58, 199.

54. Ibid., pp. 46–48; Mary Field, "She 'Stirreth Up the People,' " *Everybody's Magazine*, April–May 1914, pp. 8–11.

55. Mother Jones, *Autobiography*, pp. 213, 64, 142–43, 225–26.

56. Ibid., pp. 14, 16, 25, 41, 63–64, 151–52, 221, 237.

57. On the lives of working women, see, for example, Joanne Jay Meyerowitz, *Women Adrift: Independent Wage Earners in Chicago, 1880–1930* (Chicago: University of Chicago Press, 1991).

58. Kathryn Kish Sklar, *Florence Kelley and the Nation's Work: The Rise of Women's Political Culture, 1830–1900* (New Haven, Conn.: Yale University Press, 1995); Candace Falk, *Love, Anarchy, and Emma Goldman* (New Brunswick, N.J.: Rutgers University Press, 1990); Rosalyn Fraad Baxandall, *Words on Fire: The Life and Writing of Elizabeth Gurley Flynn* (New Brunswick, N.J.: Rutgers University Press,

1987); Helen C. Camp, *Iron in Her Soul: Elizabeth Gurley Flynn and the American Left* (Pullman: Washington State University Press, 1995); and, for Europe, see Marie Marmo Mullaney, *Revolutionary Women: Gender and the Socialist Revolutionary Role* (New York: Praeger, 1983).

59. For example, she discusses the Moyer, Haywood, and Pettibone trial without mentioning the IWW, then she skips to the Paint and Cabin Creek strikes, ignoring her years with the Socialist Party. Her only comment on the incidents surrounding the Harding telegram was "Once it was my duty to go before the rank and file and expose their leaders who would betray them. And when my boys understood, West Virginia's climate wasn't healthy for them"; see Mother Jones, *Autobiography*, p. 235.

60. Mother Jones, *Autobiography*, pp. 239–42.

61. See, for example, Warren Van Tine, *The Making of the Labor Bureaucrat: Union Leadership in the United States, 1870–1920* (Amherst: University of Massachusetts Press, 1973); David Montgomery, *The Fall of the House of Labor: The Workplace, the State, and American Labor Activism, 1865–1925* (New York: Cambridge University Press, 1987); Irving Bernstein, *The Lean Years: A History of the American Worker, 1920–1933* (Baltimore: Penguin, 1966); Sanford M. Jacoby, *Employing Bureaucracy: Managers, Unions, and the Transformation of Work in American Industry, 1900–1945* (New York: Columbia University Press, 1985); Melvyn Dubofsky and Warren Van Tine, *John L. Lewis: A Biography* (New York: Quadrangle Books, 1977).

62. Mother Jones, *Autobiography*, pp. 195–96, 125.

63. See Leon Trotsky's discussion of the *Autobiography* and Emma Goldman's *Living My Life* in his *Diary in Exile, 1935* (New York: Atheneum, 1963), pp. 151–52.

64. George P. West, "Correspondence: Mother Jones among the Twelve," *The Nation*, July 19, 1922, pp. 70–71.

65. Mother Jones to John H. Walker, February 15, 1926, in Steel, ed., *Correspondence*, pp. 321–22.

66. Business ledgers, vol. 39, p. 80, Kerr Archives, NL; *Book Review Digest* lists no reviews of *Autobiography*; it failed to receive notices in popular journals such as *The Literary Digest*, the *Saturday Review of Literature*, or *Review of Reviews*.

67. Mother Jones to John H. Walker, January 11, 1924, July 30, 1925, September 28, 1926, November 13, 1925, all in Steel, ed., *Correspondence*, pp. 303, 320, 327–28, 329–30; Fetherling, *Mother Jones*, pp. 198–99; Wilfred Carsel, *A History of the Chicago Ladies Garment Workers Union* (Chicago: Normandie House, 1940), pp. 168–70; "Mother Jones Fights for Sacco and Vanzetti," interview at Garfield Hospital, Washington, D.C., unidentified newspaper clipping, August 25, 1927, in Foner, ed., *Mother Jones Speaks*, pp. 531–32. Interestingly, Walker refused to have anything to do with her plan to use proceeds from the *Autobiography* to help free political prisoners. Mother Jones, Walker felt, was naive about her "boys" in prison, many of whom, he argued, were agents provocateurs, or

crazy, or both. Walker also objected to her vilification of John Mitchell. See Walker to Jones, February 22, 1926, in Steel, ed., *Correspondence*, pp. 323–25. Mother Jones was enraged when Mooney declared that only a full pardon was acceptable, and so refused parole in late 1927; Mother Jones to John Fitzpatrick, December 14, 1927, January 11, 1928, in Steel, ed., *Correspondence*, pp. 337–39. In 1927, she condemned the prosecution of the anarchists Nicola Sacco and Bartolomeo Vanzetti.

68. Mother Jones to John H. Walker, February 15, 1926; William Green to Mother Jones, July 18, 1924; Jones to Walker, January 11, 1924, July 30, 1925, January 1925; Walker to Jones, June 14, 1926; all in Steel, ed., *Correspondence*, pp. 321, 315, 303, 320, 318, 326. Green's generosity toward Mother Jones was not always reciprocated. She wrote John H. Walker, "Green is a good fellow, kind hearted and honest to the core, and well meaning but there are a lot of well meaning people in the Insain Asylum." Also see "Coolidge Endorsed by Mother Jones," *New York Times*, September 27, 1924, p. 3; Fetherling, *Mother Jones*, p. 198.

69. Lillie May Burgess, "The Last Years of Mother Jones (Personal Reminiscences)," MS, p. 42, WVaU; Catherine Yarnell to Mother Jones, November 24, 1927, in Steel, ed., *Correspondence*, p. 337; Yarnell to Jones, April 29, 1925, CUA, 7/2.3; "General Release," January 9, 1930, CUA, 7/2.4; Louise Maguire to Mother Jones, January 22, 1928, CUA, 7/2.3; Mother Jones to Emma Powderly, January 22, 1926, CUA, 7/2.3.

70. Mother Jones to Emma Powderly, January 22, 1926, CUA, 7/2.3. Other old friends took her in for short stretches, such as Susana DeWolfe and her brother Samuel Steiner of Alliance, Ohio, who knew Mother Jones from the days when Julius Wayland founded his colony in Ruskin, Tennessee; Mother Jones to John H. Walker, September 28, 1926, and Susana DeWolfe to Mother Jones, March 24, 1927, and September 9, 1927, in Steel, ed., *Correspondence*, pp. 327–28, 332–34; Burgess, "Last Years of Mother Jones," p. 65. Burgess's unpublished biography of Mother Jones is all but useless, based as it is on an uncritical reading of the *Autobiography* and of newspaper sources. However, the hundred-page introduction to the manuscript, a personal reminiscence of Mother Jones's last months in the Burgess home, contains some worthwhile material.

71. Mother Jones to John H. Walker, September 13, 1928, and Walker to Jones, September 18, 1928, in Steel, ed., *Correspondence*, pp. 340–41.

72. On her assets, see "General Release," a legal document signed by Mother Jones and dated January 9, 1930, absolving Emma Powderly of her role as custodian of Mother Jones's assets, CUA, 7/2.4; also see Burgess, "Last Years of Mother Jones," pp. 33–36. There is a discrepancy in Mother Jones's estate. Her probate records from 1933 list only ten shares of Reading company common stock, valued at one hundred dollars—nothing else. Yet the "General Release" she signed relieving Emma Powderly of guardianship at the beginning of 1930

enumerated six thousand dollars' worth of stocks, bonds, and cash. Four months later, a new will drawn up by Hyattsville attorney Hodges Carr mentioned various forms of property, including cash in the Hyattsville Bank, but gave no specific values. The new will named Nockles and Fitzpatrick as her beneficiaries. What happened to the six thousand dollars? According to Burgess, "Last Years of Mother Jones," pp. 33–36, she and her husband wanted nothing from Mother Jones; they were very embarrassed by rumors in town that they were handsomely compensated for taking care of her. Burgess claimed that Mother Jones originally planned to leave the money to an orphanage, then decided that the Church usually took care of such matters. With the Great Depression now a year old, Mother Jones decided to donate her estate to laboring families in need of assistance. But Burgess did not specify how this was to be done, and given the apparent disappearance of the money between late April 1930 and Mother Jones's death six months later, it makes sense that Nockles and Fitzpatrick donated it to an appropriate charity. See Cook County, Illinois, Probate Court, Estate of Mary (also known as Mother) Jones, deceased, docket 319, p. 333, no. 178889, originally filed March 14, 1933.

73. Mother Jones, "Special Request to the Miners of Mt. Olive Illinois," November 12, 1923, filed January 9, 1924, in Miscellaneous Records of Macoupin County, vol. 332, p. 292, reprinted in John Keiser, *The Union Miners Cemetery* (Chicago: Illinois Labor History Society, 1980), pp. 1–30, 31–34, reprinted from *Journal of the Illinois State Historical Society* (Autumn 1969). Adolph Germer claimed that it was while visiting his family near Mount Olive that Mother Jones made her decision; "Oral History Interview of Adolph Germer," interview by Jack W. Skeels, November 22, 1960, pp. 15–18, Adolph Germer Collection, WSU.

74. Too ill to attend the Twenty-seventh Annual Commemoration of the Virden Massacre in Mount Olive, Illinois, in 1925, she repeated her request in an open letter to the arrangements committee, giving her regrets, but declaring, "My heart beats today with devotion to those brave boys as it did the morning they gave up their lives for a holy cause. . . . When I am called I want to take my last sleep with my brave boys in Mt. Olive." See Mother Jones to the Arrangements Committee, Twenty-seventh Annual Commemoration of the Virden Massacre, October 1925, in *Daily Worker*, October 22, 1925, reprinted in Foner, ed., *Mother Jones Speaks*, p. 683; Germer interview, in Adolph Germer Papers, pp. 15–18, WSU; Agnes Burns Wieck Collection, box 2, file 22, Agnes Wieck diary MS, Thursday, October 12, 1924, p. 78, WSU. A fine telling of the Virden Massacre can be found in Keiser, *Union Miners Cemetery*, pp. 1–25. In retrospect, the Battle of Virden marked one of those dubious victories of the American labor movement. The operators claimed that outside agitators (Slavic miners in particular) caused the trouble, that the "better class" of English, Irish, Welsh, and German men resisted them. For their part, the miners were proud of having

built a movement that transcended ethnic lines, proud that men with names from all over Europe stood and died together for their union. But it was black strikebreakers that aroused the miners' hatred. For days before the battle, all blacks near Virden feared for their lives; see Keiser, *Union Miners Cemetery*, pp. 22–26.

75. Keiser, *Union Miners Cemetery*, pp. 1–6.

76. " 'Mother' Jones Urges Hoover Aid Strike," *Washington Times*, 1929, CUA, 7/2.7; "Mother Jones Passes her 99th Birthday," *Labor*, May 4, 1929, and "Mother Jones, 98 Years Old, Intends to Reach Age of 115," *Washington Evening Star*, 1928, both in CUA, 7/2.5; Burgess, "Last Years of Mother Jones," pp. 13–25. Burgess says that Mother Jones took increasing comfort in the church in her final years.

77. Mother Jones to John Fitzpatrick and Ed Nockles, November 14, 1927, in Foner, ed., *Mother Jones Speaks*, p. 691; Burgess, "Last Years of Mother Jones," p. 45; "Mother Jones Alert as She Nears 100," *New York Times*, April 20, 1930.

78. David Rankin Barbee, "Mother Jones Approaches a Century," Baltimore *Sun*, April 27, 1930, Magazine section, pp. 1–2.

79. "Mother Jones 100 Years Old, Fires Broadside at Dry Law," *Washington Herald*, May 2, 1930; "Unemployed Trek to Honor Mother Jones," *Washington Daily News*, May 1, 1930; "Mother Jones 100 Years Old, but Still Vigorous, Profane," *Norfolk Ledger-Dispatch*, May 2, 1930, all in CUA, 7/2.6, 7; Burgess, "Last Years of Mother Jones," pp. 49–58.

80. "Mother Jones at 100 Years Is Still Fiery; Loudly Denounces 'Capitalists' for Talkie," *New York Times*, May 2, 1930, p. 25; "Rockefeller Jr. Felicitates Mother Jones; 'He's a Good Sport,' She Says of Former Foe," *New York Times*, May 4, 1930, p. 1; Fetherling, *Mother Jones*, p. 198; "Mother Jones, 100, Forgives Enemies," *Washington Star*, May 4, 1930, CUA, 7/3.1.

81. "Mother Jones, 100, Wires Greeting to Rockefeller," *New York Times*, July 9, 1930, p. 25; Burgess, "Last Years of Mother Jones," pp. 61, 80, 82; " 'Mother' Jones Aids Fight on John L. Lewis," *New York Times*, September 6, 1930, p. 16. The definitive work on Lewis is Dubofsky and Van Tine, *John L. Lewis*, pp. 67–178.

82. "Mother Jones near Death in Maryland," *New York Times*, September 14, 1930, p. 26; " 'Mother' Jones Growing Weaker," *New York Times*, October 4, 1930, p. 12; "Mother Jones Sinking," *New York Times*, November 23, 1930, p. 27; State of Maryland, Division of Vital Records, Prince George's County, Registration District 245, Certificate of Death for Mary Jones.

83. Fetherling, *Mother Jones*, pp. 206–9; "Funeral by Miners for Mother Jones," *New York Times*, December 2, 1930, p. 30.

84. " 'Mother' Jones Honored," *New York Times*, December 6, 1930, p. 17; "Body of Mother Jones Lies in State," *St. Louis Post-Dispatch*, December 6, 1930. Adolph Germer told the story of how Mother Jones selected Mount Olive for her funeral, and he estimated the crowd to have been at least fifteen thousand peo-

ple; see Adolph Germer to Ralph and Piri Korngold, February 16, 1963, Letters, Korngold Papers, NL.

85. " 'Mother' Jones Honored," p. 17; Keiser, *Union Miners Cemetery*, pp. 31–34; "Mother Jones Is Borne to Grave," *St. Louis Post-Dispatch*, December 8, 1930, p. 3a. Father Maguire's address, "Panegyric to Mother Jones," was reprinted in the *Illinois State Federation of Labor Weekly Newsletter* 16, no. 37 (1930), pp. 1–3. Alexander Howatt, John Walker, and Adolph Germer, now all officials of the renegade United Mine Workers Reorganized, led the way into church.

86. Maguire, "Panegyric," p. 3.

87. "Mother Jones Dies; Led Mine Workers," *New York Times*, December 1, 1930, p. 21; " 'Mother' Jones, Labor Leader, Dies at Age 100," *Chicago Tribune*, pp. 1, 4; *The Nation*, December 10, 1930, p. 637; the *Herald*, *Daily Vindicator*, and *Evening News* are all quoted in "Mother Jones Dies Honored by All Classes of Americans," *Washington Star*, December 11, 1930, in CUA, 7/2.5; *Labor*, December 9, 1930, p. 1. *Labor*, too, failed to mention her socialist beliefs but dwelled on her venerability in the union movement, how workers worshipped her and even Presidents did her bidding.

Epilogue: "Mother Jones Is Not Forgotten"

1. John Keiser, *The Union Miners Cemetery* (Chicago: Illinois Labor History Society, 1980), pp. 34–38.

2. Keiser, *Union Miners Cemetery*, pp. 34–38; George H. Luker to Adolph Germer, October 17, 1940, box 4, folder 6, Adolph Germer Papers, SHSW.

3. It would be another year before Autry began recording songs that made him one of America's most popular "singing cowboys." See Archie Green, *Only a Miner: Studies in Recorded Coal-Mining Songs* (Urbana: University of Illinois Press, 1972), pp. 241–53. Autry attempted to follow in the footsteps of the very successful recording artist of the 1920s Jimmie Rodgers, the "singing cowboy." See Nolan Porterfield, *Jimmie Rodgers: The Life and Times of America's Blue Yodeler* (Urbana: University of Illinois Press, 1979). "The Death of Mother Jones" was re-recorded by New World Records (NW 270, band 6) in 1977.

4. Green, *Only a Miner*, pp. 253–66 (Autry, by the way, claimed that his agent taught him the song); "Sprinkle Coal Dust on My Grave," in *Songs and Ballads of the Bituminous Miners*, ed. George Korson (Washington, D.C.: Library of Congress, 1965), p. 5.

5. Archie Green, *Calf's Head and Union Tale: Labor Yarns at Work and Play* (Urbana: University of Illinois Press, 1996), p. 118. As Green observes, folklore collected around Mother Jones. Activist Helen Valestra Bary went to lunch with her in Los Angeles. Mother Jones insisted on paying. She left a tip for the waiter, but the young man refused it, saying, "Oh no, Mother, not in the family." Interview with Helen Valestra Bary, 1974, pp. 37–39, Oral History Collec-

tion, Bancroft Library, University of California. Thanks to Mary Odem for this source.

6. Interview with Grace Jackson in Anne Lawrence, *On Dark and Bloody Ground: An Oral History of the UMWA in Central Appalachia, 1920–1935* (Charleston, W.Va.: privately printed by The Miners' Voice, 1973), pp. 26–27, in WVaU; interview with Mandy "Grandma" Porter, in Lawrence, *Dark and Bloody Ground,* pp. 135–36; interview with Monia Baumgartner, in Lois McLean, "I'll Teach You Not to Be Afraid," in Ken Sullivan, ed., *The Goldenseal Book of the West Virginia Mine Wars* (Charleston, W.Va.: Pictorial Histories Publishing Co., 1991), p. 42.

7. Green, *Only a Miner,* pp. 266–67. For example, after her death, Mother Jones's name virtually disappeared from the *Readers' Guide to Periodical Literature* and *The New York Times Index.*

8. Keith Dix, "Mother Jones," in *People's Appalachia* 1, no. 3 (June–July 1970), pp. 6–13; Jim Axelrod, *The Thoughts of Mother Jones* (Huntington, W.Va.: Appalachian Movement Press, 1971), pp. 1–10; George Vecsey, "Ideal of Unity Stirs Appalachian Poor," *New York Times,* April 23, 1972, pp. 1, 55. She also received an entry in Edward T. James, ed., *Notable American Women,* vol. 2 (Cambridge, Mass.: Belknap Press of Harvard University Press, 1971), pp. 286–88.

9. For folk songs, see Green, *Only a Miner,* pp. 256–73; "Mother Jones and the Singing Miners' Wives," *Sing Out* 10, no. 1 (April–May 1960), pp. 21–22; Utah Phillips and Rosie Sorrells, "The Charge of Mother Jones," *Long Memory;* Dale Fetherling, *Mother Jones: The Miners' Angel* (Carbondale: Southern Illinois University Press, 1974). *Mother Jones* magazine was still going twenty-four years after its launch. For an example of union newspapers reintroducing their readers to Mother Jones, see "Mother Jones' Hundred Years War against Injustice," *Retail, Wholesale, and Department Store Union Record* 24, no. 6 (June 1977), pp. 8–9. Juvenile literature includes Linda Atkinson, *Mother Jones: The Most Dangerous Woman in America* (New York: Crown, 1978); Irving Werstein, *Labor's Defiant Lady: The Story of Mother Jones* (New York: Crowell, 1969); Jean Bethell and Kathleen Garry-McCord, *Three Cheers for Mother Jones* (New York: Holt, Rinehart, and Winston, 1980); Judith Pinkerton Josephson, *Mother Jones: Fierce Fighter for Workers' Rights* (Minneapolis, Minn.: Lerner Publications, 1997); Penny Coleman, *Mother Jones and the March of the Mill Children* (Brookfield, Conn.: Millbrook Press, 1994); Madelyn Horton, *The Importance of Mother Jones* (San Diego, Calif.: Lucent Books, 1996). Fred Thompson lists several plays in his bibliography for "Notes on 'The Most Dangerous Woman in America,' " in Mother Jones, *Autobiography of Mother Jones,* ed. Mary Field Parton (Chicago: Charles Kerr Company, 1990 ed.), pp. 299–300, but also see Ronnie Gilbert, *On Mother Jones* (Berkeley, Calif.: Conari Press, 1993); Bob Damron and Carole Damron, *Brimstone and Lace,* excerpted in Sullivan, ed., *Goldenseal Book of the Mine Wars,* pp. 11–13; Joe Pollack, " 'The Most Dangerous Woman in America,' " *St. Louis Post-Dispatch,* July 13, 1992, pp. 1, 4. Treatments in women's history in-

clude Judith Nies, *Seven Women: Portraits from the American Radical Tradition* (New York: Viking, 1977), pp. 95–123; Mary Jo Weaver, *New Catholic Women: A Contemporary Challenge to Traditional Religious Authority* (San Francisco: Harper and Row, 1988), pp. 23–25; Karen Kennelly, ed., *American Catholic Women* (New York: Macmillan, 1989), pp. 161–62. For editions of work, see Edward M. Steel, ed., *The Speeches and Writings of Mother Jones* (Pittsburgh, Pa.: University of Pittsburgh Press, 1988); Edward M. Steel, ed., *The Correspondence of Mother Jones* (Pittsburgh, Pa.: University of Pittsburgh Press, 1985); and Philip Foner, ed., *Mother Jones Speaks* (New York: Monad Press, 1983). For a sampling of newspaper stories, see Lois Clements McLean, " 'Foul-Mouthed Bitch' or Labor's 'Joan of Arc,' " Beckley, West Virginia, *Post-Herald*, May 30, 1972, CUA, 7/2, f15; Lee Pnazek, "Labor Leader Jones: An Uncommon Mother," Minneapolis *Star Tribune*, May 13, 1979, section 3, p. 23; Sylvia Ruland, "Mother Jones: The Most Dangerous Woman in America," *Denver Post*, June 7, 1981, pp. 49–53; "Mother Jones, Labor Reformer," *Denver Post*, February 2, 1986, Magazine section, p. 7; John J. Dunphy, " 'Mother Jones' Untiring Fight for Workers' Rights," *St. Louis Post-Dispatch*, July 25, 1997. Leah Beth Ward, "The State of Labor," *Cincinnati Enquirer*, September 4, 1994, Business section, pp. 1, 12, features a picture of Deborah Schneider, a service workers union official, in front of an image of "her idol," Mother Jones.

10. On the Pittston strike, see Denise Giardina, "Solidarity in Appalachia," *The Nation*, July 3, 1989, pp. 12–14; Mike Hudson, "Legend Revived," *Roanoke Times*, November 19, 1989, pp. F1–F5; Dwayne Yancey, "Thunder in the Coalfields," special section of the *Roanoke Times*, April 29, 1990, pp. 1–16. During the same time as the Pittston strike, aluminum workers in Ravenswood, West Virginia, paraded with an eight-foot effigy of Mother Jones; see "How Workers Won at Ravenswood," *Labor Party Press* 5, no. 1 (January 2000), p. 7.

11. "Labor Hall of Fame," *Monthly Labor Review*, November 1992, p. 2; Labor Hall of Fame visitors' guide; Historical Marker Suggestion Form and Governor's Proclamation for Mary Harris Jones, Pennsylvania Historical and Museum Commission, 51-f1, my thanks to Robert Weible for this information; "Celebrating Our Heroes," *Life*, May 5, 1997, pp. 30–45; "Mary Harris 'Mother' Jones," *Irish America*, October–November 1999, p. 42; Steven Greenhouse, "The Most Innovative Figure in Silicon Valley?" *New York Times*, November 14, 1999, p. 26; also see "Mother Jones Meets the Microchip," *Economist*, June 12, 1999, p. 64.

Index

Irish, 53, 160, 288, 301, 303, 322*n55*; in
Canada, 19–31, 312*n43*, 318*n18*; in
Chicago, 43–45; in coal mines, 69,
70, 72, 390*n74*; in Memphis, 34–36,
38
Irish America magazine, 301
Irish Parliament, 14
iron molders, unionization of, 37–39
Iron Molders' International Journal, 37–
38, 318*n19*
Irons, Martin, 167, 285
ironworkers, 162
Italians, 70, 101, 202, 204, 209, 238,
253, 318*n18*

Jackson, Grace, 299
Jackson, John J., 95–100, 331*n21*,
332*n26*
James, Danny, 132
James, William, 124
Japanese, 194, 357*n59*
Jefferson, Thomas, 159, 217, 255, 264
Jews, 158, 357*n59*; in garment trades,
162, 238
Jones, George (husband), 33, 36–39,
41, 54, 119, 195, 196, 318*nn15, 17,
18*, 319*n24*
Jones, Mary Harris: arrest and imprisonment of, 187–93, 210–12; autobiography of, *see Autobiography of Mother
Jones, The*; birth of, 7, 9; during
Chicago fire, 44–45; childhood of,
12–14, 19, 20, 22–24, 28–29; child
labor opposed by, 124–41; children
born to, 38; and Coxey's Army, 62–
63; creation of Mother Jones persona
by, 57–58, 61–62, 65–69; death of,
292; death of family of, 40–42, 180,
195, 196, 232; declining health of,
260–61, 266–67, 276; defense of arrested labor activists by, 154–56,

240–41; dressmaking business of,
42–44; education of, 23, 29–31; family background of, 9–12, 16, 27; and
Farmer-Labor Party, 276–77; final
years of, 286–92; at founding of
IWW, 150–52; funeral of, 292–94;
garment workers organized by, 238;
and great strike of 1877, 47–49; and
Haymarket affair, 52–53; House Subcommittee testimony of, 213–15; in
Knights of Labor, 45; legacy of, 297–
303; legend of, 117–24, 199–200,
227–29; marriage of, 33, 34; Mexican
Revolution supported by, 155–61;
newspaper interviews with, 194–99;
obituaries for, 294–95; at Pan-
American Federation of Labor conference, 263–66; *Polly Pry* charges
against, 107–12, 144, 220; and Pullman strike, 64; radicalization of, 53–
55; and Red Scare, 259–60; relationship of brother William and, 278–79;
Rockefeller and, 222–25; sadness as
undercurrent in life of, 165–68; and
Socialist Party, 143–44, 146–50, 161–
65, 241–42; steelworkers organized
by, 238, 252, 254–58; streetcar workers organized by, 239–40; as UMW
organizer, 73–76, 79–89, 91–100,
103–7, 112–15, 165, 169, 172–94,
200–5, 207–10, 215–18, 237, 243–
45, 248–50, 268–76; Wilson endorsed by, 240–41; on women's role,
228–35; during World War I, 243–48
Jones, Mrs. Henry B., 58–62
Justice Department, U.S., 210, 260

Kanawha Coal Operators Association,
201
Kansas City Star, The, 63
Kaplan, David, 375*n33*